Nonlinear Time Series Models
in Empirical Finance

Although many of the models commonly used in empirical finance are linear, the nature of financial data suggests that nonlinear models are more appropriate for forecasting and accurately describing returns and volatility. The enormous number of nonlinear time series models appropriate for modelling and forecasting economic time series models makes choosing the best model for a particular application daunting. This classroom-tested advanced undergraduate and graduate textbook – the most up-to-date and accessible guide available – provides a rigorous treatment of recently developed nonlinear models, including regime-switching models and artificial neural networks. The focus is on the potential applicability for describing and forecasting financial asset returns and their associated volatility. The models are analysed in detail and are not treated as 'black boxes' and are illustrated using a wide range of financial data, drawn from sources including the financial markets of Tokyo, London and Frankfurt.

PHILIP HANS FRANSES is based at Erasmus University, Rotterdam. He has published widely in journals, and his books include *Time Series Models for Business and Economic Forecasting* (Cambridge University Press, 1998).

DICK VAN DIJK is based at Erasmus University, Rotterdam. He is the author of several journal articles on econometrics.

Nonlinear Time Series Models in Empirical Finance

Philip Hans Franses

and

Dick van Dijk

CAMBRIDGE
UNIVERSITY PRESS

PUBLISHED BY THE PRESS SYNDICATE OF THE UNIVERSITY OF CAMBRIDGE
The Pitt Building, Trumpington Street, Cambridge, United Kingdom

CAMBRIDGE UNIVERSITY PRESS
The Edinburgh Building, Cambridge CB2 2RU, UK
40 West 20th Street, New York, NY 10011-4211, USA
477 Williamstown Road, Port Melbourne, VIC 3207, Australia
Ruiz de Alarcón 13, 28014 Madrid, Spain
Dock House, The Waterfront, Cape Town 8001, South Africa

http://www.cambridge.org

First published 2000
Reprinted 2002

Printed in the United Kingdom at the University Press, Cambridge

Typeface Times 10/12pt.   System LaTeX

A catalogue record for this book is available from the British Library

Library of Congress Cataloguing in Publication data
Franses, Philip Hans, 1963–
Nonlinear time series models in empirical finance/Philip Hans Franses, Dick van Dijk.
    p. cm.
Includes bibliographical references and index.
ISBN 0 521 77041 6   ISBN 0 521 77965 0 (pbk.)
1. Finance–Mathematical models. 2. Time-series analysis. I. Dijk, Dick van. II. Title.

HG106 .F73 2000   332′.01′5118–dc21   99-088504

ISBN 0521 77041 6 hardback
ISBN 0521 77965 0 paperback

To our parents

Bas and Jessie
and
Gerrit and Justa

Contents

List of figures	*page*	ix
List of tables		xi
Preface		xv

1 Introduction — 1
1.1 Introduction and outline of the book — 1
1.2 Typical features of financial time series — 5

2 Some concepts in time series analysis — 20
2.1 Preliminaries — 20
2.2 Empirical specification strategy — 27
2.3 Forecasting returns with linear models — 44
2.4 Unit roots and seasonality — 51
2.5 Aberrant observations — 61

3 Regime-switching models for returns — 69
3.1 Representation — 71
3.2 Estimation — 83
3.3 Testing for regime-switching nonlinearity — 100
3.4 Diagnostic checking — 108
3.5 Forecasting — 117
3.6 Impulse response functions — 125
3.7 On multivariate regime-switching models — 132

4 Regime-switching models for volatility — 135
4.1 Representation — 136
4.2 Testing for GARCH — 157
4.3 Estimation — 170

4.4	Diagnostic checking	182
4.5	Forecasting	187
4.6	Impulse response functions	197
4.7	On multivariate GARCH models	200
5	**Artificial neural networks for returns**	206
5.1	Representation	207
5.2	Estimation	215
5.3	Model evaluation and model selection	222
5.4	Forecasting	234
5.5	ANNs and other regime-switching models	237
5.6	Testing for nonlinearity using ANNs	245
6	**Conclusions**	251
	Bibliography	254
	Author index	272
	Subject index	277

Figures

1.1	Stock indexes – levels and returns	*page* 7
1.2	Exchange rates – levels and returns	8
1.3	Distributions of stock index returns	11
1.4	Distributions of exchange rate returns	12
1.5	Scatterplot of daily returns on the Amsterdam stock index	14
1.6	Scatterplot of daily returns on the Frankfurt stock index	15
1.7	Scatterplot of daily returns on the London stock index	16
1.8	Scatterplot of daily returns on the British pound	17
1.9	Scatterplot of daily returns on the Canadian dollar	18
1.10	Scatterplot of daily returns on the Dutch guilder	19
2.1	Autocorrelations of stock index returns	31
2.2	Autocorrelations of exchange rate returns	32
2.3	Additive and innovative outliers in an AR(1) model	63
2.4	Weight functions for robust estimation	67
3.1	Logistic functions	72
3.2	Realizations from a SETAR model	73
3.3	Scatterplots for realizations from a SETAR model	74
3.4	Sequences of LR-statistics for realizations from a SETAR model	86
3.5	Absolute weekly returns on the Frankfurt stock index and regime probabilities in a Markov-Switching model	97
3.6	Weekly returns on the Dutch guilder exchange rate and weights from robust estimation of a SETAR model	99
3.7	Transition function in a STAR model for returns on the Dutch guilder exchange rate	109
3.8	Transition function in a STAR model for absolute returns on the Tokyo stock index	111
3.9	Conditional distributions for a SETAR model	123
3.10	Generalized impulse responses in a STAR model for returns on the Dutch guilder exchange rate	131

3.11 Generalized impulse responses in a STAR model for returns
     on the Dutch guilder exchange rate   131
4.1 News impact curves for nonlinear GARCH models   150
4.2 News impact curve for the ANST-GARCH model   154
4.3 Conditional standard deviation in nonlinear GARCH models
     for returns on the Tokyo stock index   176
4.4 Conditional standard deviation in GARCH(1,1) models for
     weekly stock index and exchange rate returns   179
5.1 Skeleton of an ANN   209
5.2 Structure of the hidden layer in an ANN   211
5.3 Architecture of the single hidden layer feedforward ANN   213
5.4 ANN and additive outliers   215
5.5 ANN and innovative outliers   216
5.6 ANN and level shifts   217
5.7 Output of hidden units in an ANN for returns on the Japanese
     yen exchange rate   224
5.8 Skeleton of an ANN for returns on the Japanese yen exchange
     rate   225
5.9 Output of hidden units in an ANN for absolute returns on
     the Frankfurt stock index   227
5.10 Skeleton of an ANN for absolute returns on the Frankfurt
     stock index   228
5.11 Moving averages for returns on the Japanese yen exchange
     rate   229
5.12 Output–input derivatives in an ANN for returns on the
     Japanese yen exchange rate   233
5.13 Output–input derivatives in an ANN for absolute returns on
     the Frankfurt stock index   233
5.14 Impulse responses in an ANN for absolute returns on the
     Frankfurt stock index   238

Tables

1.1 Summary statistics for stock returns   *page* 9

1.2 Summary statistics for exchange rate returns   10

1.3 Correlation between squared returns at day t and returns at day $t - 1$ 18

2.1 Average ranks of linear models to forecast stock returns according to MSPE, 1991–1997   46

2.2 Average ranks of linear models to forecast stock returns according to MAPE, 1991–1997   47

2.3 Average ranks of linear models to forecast stock returns according to MedSPE, 1991–1997   48

2.4 Forecast comparison of linear models with random walk – stock returns, squared prediction errors, 1991–1997   49

2.5 Forecast comparison of linear models with random walk – stock returns, absolute prediction errors, 1991–1997   50

2.6 Performance of linear models in forecasting sign of stock returns, 1991–1997   52

2.7 Daily means and variances of stock index returns   59

2.8 Periodic autocorrelations of stock returns   61

3.1 AIC for AR(p) models estimated on simulated SETAR series   78

3.2 AIC values for SETAR models for weekly returns on the Dutch guilder exchange rate   88

3.3 SETAR estimates for weekly percentage returns on the Dutch guilder exchange rate   89

3.4 Parameter estimates for a MSW model for weekly absolute returns on the Frankfurt stock index   96

3.5 p-values for HCC test of linearity against a SETAR alternative for weekly returns on the Dutch guilder exchange rate   106

3.6 p-values of LM-type test for STAR nonlinearity for weekly returns on the Dutch guilder exchange rate   107

3.7   Parameter estimates for a STAR model for weekly returns
      on the Dutch guilder exchange rate   108
3.8   *p*-values of LM-type test for STAR nonlinearity for weekly
      absolute returns on the Tokyo stock index   110
3.9   Parameter estimates for a STAR model for weekly absolute
      returns on the Tokyo stock index   110
3.10 Diagnostic tests of a STAR model estimated for weekly
      returns on the Dutch guilder exchange rate   115
3.11 Diagnostic tests of a STAR model estimated for absolute
      weekly returns on the Tokyo stock index   116
3.12 Forecast evaluation of a STAR model for weekly returns on
      the Dutch guilder exchange rate   126
3.13 Forecast evaluation of a STAR model for weekly returns on
      the Dutch guilder exchange rate, 1990–1997   127
4.1   Testing for ARCH in weekly stock index returns   158
4.2   Testing for ARCH in weekly exchange rate returns   159
4.3   Testing for asymmetric ARCH effects in weekly stock index
      and exchange rate returns   161
4.4   Testing for nonlinear ARCH in weekly stock index returns   163
4.5   Testing for nonlinear ARCH in weekly exchange rate returns   164
4.6   Testing for ARCH and QARCH in simulated SETAR series   165
4.7   Rejection frequencies of standard and robust tests for
      (nonlinear) ARCH in the presence of outliers   167
4.8   Properties of standard and robust tests for ARCH in the
      presence of patchy outliers   169
4.9   Estimates of nonlinear GARCH(1,1) models for weekly
      returns on the Tokyo stock index   175
4.10 Estimates of GARCH(1,1) models for weekly stock index
      and exchange rate returns   177
4.11 Percentiles of the distribution of the outlier detection statistic
      in GARCH(1,1) models   182
4.12 Estimates of GARCH(1,1) models for weekly returns on the
      Amsterdam and New York stock indexes, before and after
      outlier correction   183
4.13 Diagnostic tests for estimated GARCH models for weekly
      stock index and exchange rate returns   187
4.14 Forecast evaluation of nonlinear GARCH models for weekly
      returns on the Tokyo stock index, as compared to the GARCH
      (1,1) model   197
4.15 Forecast evaluation of nonlinear GARCH models for weekly
      returns on the Tokyo stock index   198

4.16 Testing for common ARCH effects in weekly stock index
       and exchange rate returns   205
5.1   Performance of ANNs when series are generated from an
       AR(2) model contaminated with AOs   218
5.2   Performance of ANNs when series are generated from an
       AR(2) model contaminated with IOs   219
5.3   Performance of ANNs applied to weekly returns on the
       Japanese yen exchange rate   223
5.4   Performance of ANNs applied to absolute weekly returns on
       the Frankfurt stock index   226
5.5   Performance of ANNs with technical trading rule applied to
       weekly returns on Japanese yen   231
5.6   Performance of ANNs when series are generated from a
       SETAR model   242
5.7   Performance of ANNs when series are generated from a
       Markov-Switching model   243
5.8   Performance of ANNs when series are generated from a
       bilinear model   244
5.9   Performance of ANNs when series are generated from a
       GARCH(1,1) model   245
5.10 Testing for nonlinearity in weekly stock index and exchange
       rate returns with ANN-based tests   248
5.11 Testing for nonlinearity in weekly absolute stock index and
       exchange rate returns with ANN-based tests   249

Preface

A casual glance at the relevant literature suggests that the amount of nonlinear time series models that can be potentially useful for modelling and forecasting economic time series is enormous. Practitioners facing this plethora of models may have difficulty choosing the model that is most appropriate for their particular application, as very few systematic accounts of the pros and cons of the different models are available. In this book we provide an in-depth treatment of several recently developed models, such as regime-switching models and artificial neural networks. We narrow our focus to examining their potential applicability for describing and forecasting financial asset returns and their associated volatilities. The models are presented in substantial detail and are not treated as 'black boxes'. All models are illustrated on data concerning stock markets and exchange rates.

Our book can be used as a textbook for (advanced) undergraduate and graduate students. In fact, this book emerges from our own lecture notes prepared for courses given at the Econometric Institute, Rotterdam and the Tinbergen Institute graduate school. It must be stressed, though, that students must have had a solid training in mathematics and econometrics and should be familiar with at least the basics of time series analysis. We do review some major concepts in time series analysis in the relevant chapters, but this can hardly be viewed as a complete introduction to the field. We further believe that our book is most useful for academics and practitioners who are confronted with an overwhelmingly large literature and who want to have a first introduction to the area.

We thank the Econometric Institute at the Erasmus University Rotterdam and the Tinbergen Institute (Rotterdam branch) for providing a stimulating research and teaching environment. We strongly believe that 'learning by doing' (that is, learning how to write this book by teaching on the subject first) helped to shape the quality of this book. We thank all our co-authors on joint papers, elements of which are used in this book. We would specifically like to mention André Lucas, whose econometrics skills are very impressive. Also, we thank Ashwin Rattan at Cambridge University Press for his support.

Finally, we hope that the reader enjoys reading this book as much as we enjoyed writing it.

Rotterdam, August 1999

1   Introduction

This book deals with the empirical analysis of financial time series with an explicit focus on, first, describing the data in order to obtain insights into their dynamic patterns and, second, out-of-sample forecasting. We restrict attention to modelling and forecasting the conditional mean and the conditional variance of such series – or, in other words, the return and risk of financial assets. As documented in detail below, financial time series display typical nonlinear characteristics. Important examples of those features are the occasional presence of (sequences of) aberrant observations and the plausible existence of regimes within which returns and volatility display different dynamic behaviour. We therefore choose to consider only nonlinear models in substantial detail, in contrast to Mills (1999), where linear models are also considered. Financial theory does not provide many motivations for nonlinear models, but we believe that the data themselves are quite informative. Through an extensive forecasting experiment (for a range of daily and weekly data on stock markets and exchange rates) in chapter 2, we also demonstrate that linear time series models simply do not yield reliable forecasts. Of course, this does not automatically imply that nonlinear time series models might, but it is worth a try. As there is a host of possible nonlinear time series models, we review only what we believe are currently the most relevant ones and the ones we think are most likely to persist as practical descriptive and forecasting devices.

1.1   Introduction and outline of the book

Forecasting future returns on assets such as stocks and currencies' exchange rates is of obvious interest in empirical finance. For example, if one were able to forecast tomorrow's return on the Dow Jones index with some degree of precision, one could use this information in an investment decision today. Of course, we are seldom able to generate a very accurate prediction for asset returns, but hopefully we can perhaps at least forecast, for example, the sign of tomorrow's return.

1

The trade-off between return and risk plays a prominent role in many financial theories and models, such as Modern Portfolio theory and option pricing. Given that volatility is often regarded as a measure of this risk, one is interested not only in obtaining accurate forecasts of returns on financial assets, but also in forecasts of the associated volatility. Much recent evidence shows that volatility of financial assets is not constant, but rather that relatively volatile periods alternate with more tranquil ones. Thus, there may be opportunities to obtain forecasts of this time-varying risk.

Many models that are commonly used in empirical finance to describe returns and volatility are linear. There are, however, several indications that nonlinear models may be more appropriate (see section 1.2 for details). In this book, we therefore focus on the construction of nonlinear time series models that can be useful for describing and forecasting returns and volatility. While doing this, we do not aim to treat those models as 'black boxes'. On the contrary, we provide ample details of representation and inference issues. Naturally, we will compare the descriptive models and their implied forecasts with those of linear models, in order to illustrate their potential relevance.

We focus on forecasting out-of-sample returns and volatility as such and abstain from incorporating such forecasts in investment strategies. We usually take (functions of) past returns as explanatory variables for current returns and volatility. With some degree of market efficiency, one may expect that most information is included in recent returns. Hence, we do not consider the possibility of explaining returns by variables that measure aspects of the underlying assets – such as, for example, specific news events and key indicators of economic activity. Another reason for restricting the analysis to univariate models is that we focus mainly on short-term forecasting – that is, not more than a few days or weeks ahead. Explanatory variables such as dividend yields, term structure variables and macroeconomic variables have been found mainly useful for predicting stock returns at longer horizons, ranging from one quarter to several years (see Kaul, 1996, for an overview of the relevant literature).

Numerous reasons may be evinced for the interest in nonlinear models. For example, in empirical finance it is by now well understood that financial time series data display *asymmetric behaviour*. An example of this behaviour is that large negative returns appear more frequently than large positive returns. Indeed, the stock market crash on Monday 19 October 1987 concerned a return of about -23 per cent on the S&P 500 index, while for most stock markets we rarely observe positive returns of even 10 per cent or higher. Another example is that large negative returns are often a prelude to a period of substantial volatility, while large positive returns are less so. Needless to say, such asymmetries should be incorporated in a time series model used for description and out-of-sample forecasting, otherwise one may obtain forecasts that are always too low or too high. We will call such time series models, which allow for an explicit description of asymmetries, *nonlinear time series models*.

An important debate in empirical finance concerns the question whether large negative returns, such as the 1987 stock market crash, are events that are atypical or naturally implied by an underlying process, which the nonlinear time series model should capture. It is well known that neglected *atypical events* can blur inference in linear time series models and can thus be the culprit of rather inaccurate forecasts. As nonlinear time series models are typically designed to accommodate features of the data that cannot be captured by linear models, one can expect that neglecting such atypical observations will have even more impact on out-of-sample forecasts. Therefore, in this book we pay quite considerable attention to take care of such observations while constructing nonlinear models.

Most descriptive and forecasting models in this book concern univariate financial time series – that is, we construct separate models for, for example, the Dow Jones and the FTSE index, ignoring the potential links between these two important stock markets. A multivariate model for the returns or volatilities of two or more stock markets jointly while allowing for asymmetries is a possible next step once univariate models have been considered. In specific sections in relevant chapters, we will give some attention to multivariate nonlinear models. It must be stressed, though, that the theory of multivariate nonlinear time series models has not yet been fully developed, and so we limit our discussion to only a few specific models.

This book is divided into six chapters. The current chapter and chapter 2 offer a first glance at some typical features of many financial time series and deal with some elementary concepts in time series analysis, respectively. Chapter 2 reviews only the key concepts needed for further reading, and the reader should consult textbooks on time series analysis, such as Hamilton (1994), Fuller (1996), Brockwell and Davis (1997) and Franses (1998), among others, for more detailed treatments. The concepts in chapter 2 can be viewed as the essential tools necessary for understanding the material in subsequent chapters. Readers who already are acquainted with most of the standard tools of time series analysis can skip this chapter and proceed directly to chapter 3.

Many economic time series display one or more of the following five features: a trend, seasonality, atypical observations, clusters of outliers and nonlinearity (see Franses, 1998). In this book, we focus on the last three features, while considering financial time series. The purpose of section 1.2 is to describe some of the characteristic features of financial time series, which strongly suggest the necessity for considering nonlinear time series models instead of linear models. In particular, we show that (1) large returns (in absolute terms) occur more frequently than one might expect under the assumption that the data are normally distributed (which often goes hand-in-hand with the use of linear models and which often is assumed in financial theory), (2) such large absolute returns tend to appear in clusters (indicating the possible presence of time-varying risk or volatility), (3) large negative returns appear more often than large positive ones in stock markets, while it may be the other way around for exchange rates, and (4) volatile periods are often preceded by large negative returns. The empirical analysis relies only on simple statistical techniques, and aims merely at highlighting which features of financial time series suggest the potential usefulness of, and should be incorporated in, a nonlinear time series model. For returns, features (1) and (3) suggest the usefulness of models that have different regimes (see also Granger, 1992). Those models will be analysed in detail in chapter 3 (and to some extent also in chapter 5). Features (2) and (4) suggest the relevance of models that allow for a description of time-varying volatility, with possibly different impact of positive and negative past returns. These models are the subject of chapter 4. A final feature of returns, which will be discussed at length in section 2.3, is that linear time series models do not appear to yield accurate out-of-sample forecasts, thus providing a more pragmatic argument for entertaining nonlinear models.

As running examples throughout this book, we consider daily indexes for eight major stock markets (including those of New York, Tokyo, London and Frankfurt), and eight daily exchange rates *vis-à-vis* the US dollar (including the Deutschmark and the British pound). We do not use all data to illustrate all models and methods, and often we take only a few series for selected applications. For convenience, we will analyse mainly the daily data in temporally aggregated form – that is, we mainly consider weekly data. In our experience, however, similar models can be useful for data sampled at other frequencies. As a courtesy to the reader who wishes to experiment with specific models, all data used in this book can be downloaded from ⟨http://www.few.eur.nl/few/people/franses⟩.

Chapter 3 focuses on nonlinear models for returns that impose a regime-switching structure. We review models with two or more regimes, models where the regimes switch abruptly and where they do not and models in which the switches between the different regimes are determined by specific functions of past returns or by an unobserved process. We pay attention to the impact of atypical events, and we show how these events can be incorporated in the model or in the estimation method, using a selective set of returns to illustrate the various models. In the last section of chapter 3 (3.7), we touch upon the issue of multivariate nonlinear models. The main conclusion from the empirical results in chapter 3 is that nonlinear models for returns may sometimes outperform linear models (in terms of within-sample fit and out-of-sample forecasting).

In chapter 4, we discuss models for volatility. We limit attention to those models that consider some form of autoregressive conditional heteroscedasticity (ARCH), although we briefly discuss the alternative class of stochastic volatility models as well. The focus is on the basic ARCH model (which itself can be viewed as a nonlinear time series model) as was proposed in Engle (1982), and on testing, estimation, forecasting and the persistence of shocks. Again, we pay substantial attention to the impact of atypical events on estimated volatility. We also discuss extensions of the class of ARCH models in order to capture the asymmetries described in section 1.2. Generally, such extensions amount to modifying the standard ARCH model to allow for regime-switching effects in the persistence of past returns on future volatility.

Chapter 5 deals with models that allow the data to determine if there are different regimes that need different descriptive measures, while the number of regimes is also indicated by the data themselves. These flexible models are called 'artificial neural network models'. In contrast to the prevalent strategy in the empirical finance literature (which may lead people to believe that these models are merely a passing fad), we decide, so to say, to 'open up the black box' and to explicitly demonstrate how and why these models can be useful in practice. Indeed, the empirical applications in this chapter suggest that neural networks can be quite useful for out-of-sample forecasting and for recognizing a variety of patterns in the data. We discuss estimation and model selection issues, and we pay attention to how such neural networks handle atypical observations.

Finally, chapter 6 contains a brief summary and some thoughts and suggestions for further research.

All computations in this book have been performed using GAUSS, version 3.2.35. The code of many of the programs that have been used can be downloaded from ⟨http://www.few.eur.nl/few/people/franses⟩.

In the remainder of this chapter we will turn our focus to some typical features of financial time series which suggest the potential relevance of nonlinear time series models.

1.2   Typical features of financial time series

Empirical research has brought forth a considerable number of stylized facts of high-frequency financial time series. The purpose of this section is to describe some of these characteristic features. In particular, we show that returns on financial assets display erratic behaviour, in the sense that large outlying observations occur with rather high-frequency, that large negative returns occur more often than large positive ones, that these large returns tend to occur in clusters and that periods of high volatility are often preceded by large negative returns. Using simple and easy-to-compute statistical and graphical techniques, we illustrate these properties for a number of stock index and exchange rate returns, sampled at daily and weekly frequencies. The data are described in more detail below. Throughout this section we emphasize that the above-mentioned stylized facts seem to imply the necessity of considering nonlinear models to describe the observed patterns in such financial time series adequately and to render sensible out-of-sample forecasts. In chapter 2, we will show more rigorously that linear models appear not to be useful for out-of-sample forecasting of returns on financial assets.

Finally, it should be remarked that the maintained hypothesis for high-frequency financial time series is that (logarithmic) prices of financial assets display random walk-type behaviour (see Campbell, Lo and MacKinlay, 1997). Put differently, when linear models are used, asset prices are assumed to conform to a martingale – that is, the expected value of (the logarithm of) tomorrow's price P_{t+1}, given all relevant information up to and including today, denoted as Ω_t, should equal today's value, possibly up to a deterministic growth component which is denoted as μ, or,

$$\mathrm{E}[\ln P_{t+1}|\Omega_t] = \ln P_t + \mu, \tag{1.1}$$

where $\mathrm{E}[\cdot]$ denotes the mathematical expectation operator and ln denotes the natural logarithmic transformation. In section 2.3 we will examine if (1.1) also gives the best forecasts when compared with other linear models.

The data

The data that we use to illustrate the typical features of financial time series consist of eight indexes of major stock markets and eight exchange rates *vis-à-vis* the US dollar. To be more precise, we employ the indexes of the stock markets in Amsterdam (EOE), Frankfurt (DAX), Hong Kong (Hang Seng), London (FTSE100), New York, (S&P 500), Paris (CAC40), Singapore (Singapore All Shares) and Tokyo (Nikkei). The exchange rates are the Australian dollar, British pound, Canadian dollar, German Deutschmark, Dutch guilder, French franc, Japanese yen and Swiss franc, all expressed as a number of units of the foreign currency per US dollar. The sample period for the stock indexes runs from 6 January 1986 until 31 December 1997, whereas for the exchange rates the sample covers the period from 2 January 1980 until 31 December 1997. The original series are sampled at daily frequency. The sample periods correspond with 3,127 and 4,521 observations for the stock market indexes and exchange rates, respectively. We often analyse the series on a weekly basis, in which case we use observations recorded on Wednesdays. The stock market data have been obtained from Datastream, whereas the exchange rate data have been obtained from the New York Federal Reserve.

Figures 1.1 and 1.2 offer a first look at the data by showing a selection of the original price series P_t and the corresponding logarithmic returns measured in percentage terms, denoted y_t and computed as

$$y_t = 100 \cdot (p_t - p_{t-1}), \tag{1.2}$$

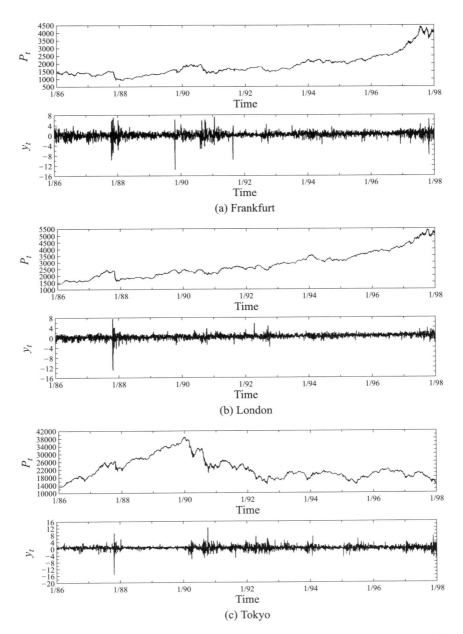

Figure 1.1   Daily observations on the level (upper panel) and returns (lower panel) of (a) the Frankfurt, (b) the London and (c) the Tokyo stock indexes, from 6 January 1986 until 31 December 1997

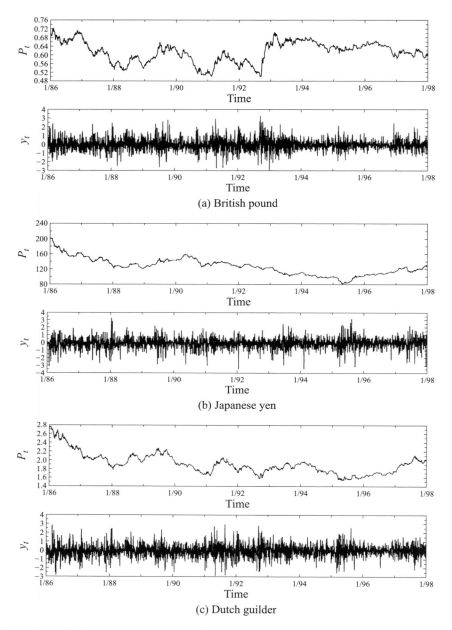

Figure 1.2   Daily observations on the level (upper panel) and returns (lower panel) of (a) the British pound, (b) the Japanese yen and (c) the Dutch guilder exchange rates *vis-à-vis* the US dollar, from 6 January 1986 until 31 December 1997

where $p_t = \ln(P_t)$. Strictly speaking, returns should also take into account dividends, but for daily data one often uses (1.2). Prices and returns for the Frankfurt, London and Tokyo indexes are shown in figure 1.1, and prices and returns for the British pound, Japanese yen and Dutch guilder exchange rates are shown in figure 1.2 (also for the period 1986–97).

Summary statistics for the stock and exchange rate returns are given in tables 1.1 and 1.2, respectively, for both daily and weekly sampling frequencies. These statistics are used in the discussion of the characteristic features of these series below.

Large returns occur more often than expected

One of the usual assumptions in the (theoretical) finance literature is that the logarithmic returns y_t are normally distributed random variables, with mean μ and variance σ^2, that is,

$$y_t \sim N(\mu, \sigma^2). \tag{1.3}$$

Table 1.1   *Summary statistics for stock returns*

Stock market	Mean	Med	Min	Max	Var	Skew	Kurt
Daily returns							
Amsterdam	0.038	0.029	−12.788	11.179	1.279	−0.693	19.795
Frankfurt	0.035	0.026	−13.710	7.288	1.520	−0.946	15.066
Hong Kong	0.057	0.022	−40.542	17.247	2.867	−5.003	119.241
London	0.041	0.027	−13.029	7.597	0.845	−1.590	27.408
New York	0.049	0.038	−22.833	8.709	0.987	−4.299	99.680
Paris	0.026	0.000	−10.138	8.225	1.437	−0.529	10.560
Singapore	0.019	0.000	−9.403	14.313	1.021	−0.247	28.146
Tokyo	0.005	0.000	−16.135	12.430	1.842	−0.213	14.798
Weekly returns							
Amsterdam	0.190	0.339	−19.962	7.953	5.853	−1.389	11.929
Frankfurt	0.169	0.354	−18.881	8.250	6.989	−1.060	8.093
Hong Kong	0.283	0.556	−34.969	11.046	13.681	−2.190	18.258
London	0.207	0.305	−17.817	9.822	4.617	−1.478	15.548
New York	0.246	0.400	−16.663	6.505	4.251	−1.370	11.257
Paris	0.128	0.272	−20.941	11.594	8.092	−0.995	9.167
Singapore	0.091	0.110	−27.335	10.510	6.986	−2.168	23.509
Tokyo	0.025	0.261	−10.892	12.139	8.305	−0.398	4.897

Notes: Summary statistics for returns on stock market indexes.
The sample period is 6 January 1986 until 31 December 1997, which equals 3,127 (625) daily (weekly) observations.

Table 1.2   *Summary statistics for exchange rate returns*

Currency	Mean	Med	Min	Max	Var	Skew	Kurt
Daily returns							
Australian dollar	0.012	−0.012	−5.074	10.554	0.377	1.893	35.076
British pound	0.006	0.000	−4.589	3.843	0.442	0.058	5.932
Canadian dollar	0.006	0.000	−1.864	1.728	0.076	0.101	6.578
Dutch guilder	−0.000	0.012	−3.985	3.188	0.464	−0.143	4.971
French franc	0.008	0.016	−3.876	5.875	0.457	0.054	6.638
German Dmark	−0.001	0.017	−4.141	3.227	0.475	−0.136	4.921
Japanese yen	−0.016	0.006	−5.630	3.366	0.478	−0.541	6.898
Swiss franc	−0.003	0.020	−4.408	3.300	0.582	−0.188	4.557
Weekly returns							
Australian dollar	0.057	−0.022	−5.526	10.815	1.731	1.454	11.906
British pound	0.033	−0.027	−7.397	8.669	2.385	0.218	6.069
Canadian dollar	0.022	0.016	−2.551	2.300	0.343	0.040	4.093
Dutch guilder	0.007	0.051	−7.673	7.212	2.416	−0.155	4.518
French franc	0.043	0.074	−7.741	6.858	2.383	−0.014	5.006
German Dmark	0.005	0.052	−8.113	7.274	2.483	−0.168	4.545
Japanese yen	−0.064	0.059	−6.546	6.582	2.192	−0.419	4.595
Swiss franc	−0.008	0.105	−7.969	6.636	2.929	−0.314	3.930

Notes: Summary statistics for exchange rate returns.
The sample period is 2 January 1980 until 31 December 1997, which equals 4,521 (939) daily (weekly) observations.

The *kurtosis* of y_t is defined as

$$K_y = E\left[\frac{(y_t - \mu)^4}{\sigma^4}\right]. \tag{1.4}$$

For an observed time series $y_1, \ldots, y_n$, the kurtosis can be estimated consistently by the sample analogue of (1.4),

$$\widehat{K}_y = \frac{1}{n}\sum_{t=1}^{n}\frac{(y_t - \hat{\mu})^4}{\hat{\sigma}^4}, \tag{1.5}$$

where $\hat{\mu} = \frac{1}{n}\sum_{t=1}^{n} y_t$ and $\hat{\sigma}^2 = \frac{1}{n}\sum_{t=1}^{n}(y_t - \hat{\mu})^2$ are the sample mean and variance, respectively. The kurtosis for the normal distribution is equal to 3. One of the features which stands out most prominently from the last columns of tables 1.1 and 1.2 is that the kurtosis of all series is much larger than this normal value, especially for the daily series. This reflects the fact that the tails of the distributions of these series are fatter than the tails of the normal distribution. Put differently, large observations occur (much) more often than one might expect for a normally distributed variable.

This is illustrated further in figures 1.3 and 1.4, which show estimates of the distributions $f(y)$ of the daily returns on the Frankfurt and London stock indexes

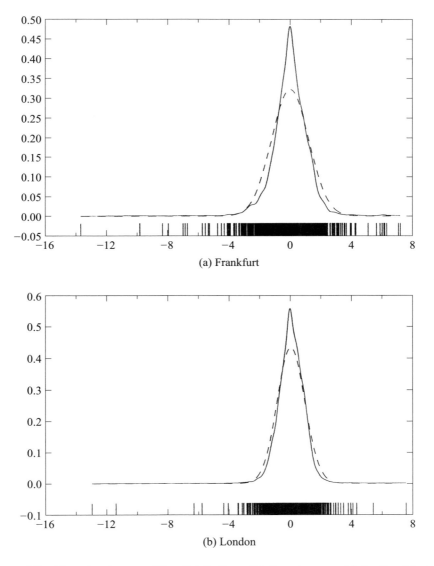

Figure 1.3   Kernel estimates of the distribution of daily returns on (a) the Frankfurt and (b) the London stock indexes (solid line) and normal distribution with same mean and variance (dashed line); each whisker represents one observation

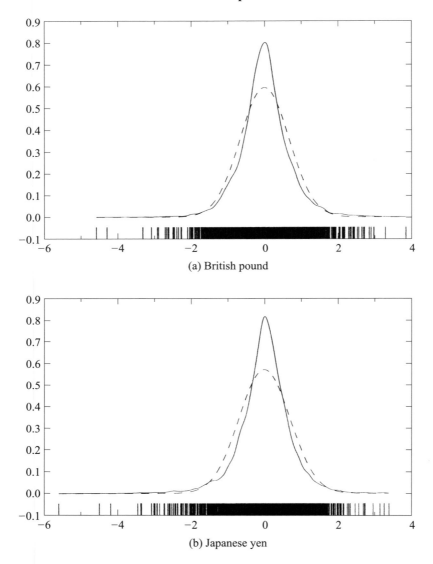

(a) British pound

(b) Japanese yen

Figure 1.4   Kernel estimates of the distribution of daily returns on (a) the British pound and (b) Japanese yen exchange rates *vis-à-vis* the US dollar (solid line) and normal distribution with same mean and variance (dashed line); each whisker represents one observation

and the British pound and Japanese yen exchange rates, respectively. The estimates are obtained with a kernel density estimator,

$$\hat{f}(y) = \frac{1}{nh} \sum_{t=1}^{n} K\left(\frac{y_t - y}{h}\right),$$

where $K(z)$ is a function which satisfies $\int K(z)\,dz = 1$ and h is the so-called bandwidth. Usually $K(z)$ is taken to be a unimodal probability density function; here we use the Gaussian kernel

$$K(z) = \frac{1}{\sqrt{2\pi}} \exp\left(-\frac{1}{2}z^2\right).$$

Following Silverman (1986), we set the bandwidth h according to $h = 0.9 \cdot \min(\hat{\sigma}, \text{iqr}/1.349)n^{-1/5}$, where iqr denotes the sample interquartile range – that is, $\text{iqr} = y_{\lfloor(3n/4)\rfloor} - y_{\lfloor(n/4)\rfloor}$, where $y_{(i)}$ is the ith order statistic of the series $y_t, t = 1, \ldots, n$, and $\lfloor \cdot \rfloor$ denotes the integer part. (See Wand and Jones, 1995, for discussion of this and other kernel estimators, and various methods of bandwidth selection.) In all graphs, a normal distribution with mean and variance obtained from tables 1.1 and 1.2 for the different series has also been drawn for ease of comparison. Each whisker on the horizontal axis represents one observation. Clearly, all distributions are more peaked and have fatter tails than the corresponding normal distributions. Thus, both very small and very large observations occur more often compared to a normally distributed variable with the same first and second moments.

Finally, it is worth noting that the kurtosis of the stock returns is much larger than the kurtosis of the exchange rate returns, at both the daily and weekly sampling frequency. This may reflect the fact that central banks can intervene in the foreign exchange market, while there are virtually no such opportunities in stock markets.

Large stock market returns are often negative
The *skewness* of y_t is defined as

$$\text{SK}_y = \text{E}\left[\frac{(y_t - \mu)^3}{\sigma^3}\right], \tag{1.6}$$

and is a measure of the asymmetry of the distribution of y_t. The skewness for an observed time series $y_1, \ldots, y_n$ can be estimated consistently by the sample analogue of (1.6) as

$$\widehat{\text{SK}}_y = \frac{1}{n} \sum_{t=1}^{n} \frac{(y_t - \hat{\mu})^3}{\hat{\sigma}^3}. \tag{1.7}$$

All symmetric distributions, including the normal distribution, have skewness equal to zero. From table 1.1 it is seen that the stock return series all have negative skewness, which implies that the left tail of the distribution is fatter than the right tail, or that large negative returns tend to occur more often than large positive ones. This is visible in the distributions displayed in figure 1.3 as well, as more whiskers are present in the left tail than in the right tail.

Skewness of the daily exchange rate returns is positive for certain currencies, while it is negative for others. This makes sense, as it is not *a priori* clear why exchange rate returns should have either positive or negative skewness when measured in the way we do here.

Large returns tend to occur in clusters

From figures 1.1 and 1.2 it appears that relatively volatile periods, characterized by large price changes – and, hence, large returns – alternate with more tranquil periods in which prices remain more or less stable and returns are, consequently, small. In other words, large returns seem to occur in clusters. This feature of our time series becomes even more apparent when inspecting scatterplots of the return of day t, denoted y_t, against the return of day $t - 1$. Figures 1.5–1.7 provide such plots for the daily observed Amsterdam, Frankfurt and London stock indexes. Similar scatterplots for daily data on the British

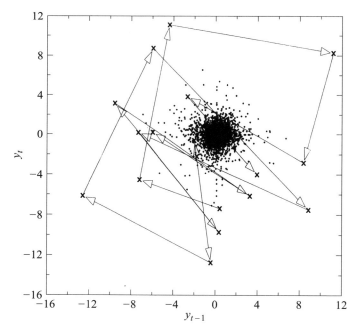

Figure 1.5   Scatterplot of the return on the Amsterdam stock index on day t, y_t, against the return on day $t - 1$

The observations for the three largest negative and the three largest positive values of y_t are connected with the two preceding and the two following observations by means of arrows, pointing in the direction in which the time series evolves; all observations that are starting- and/or end-points of arrows are marked with crosses

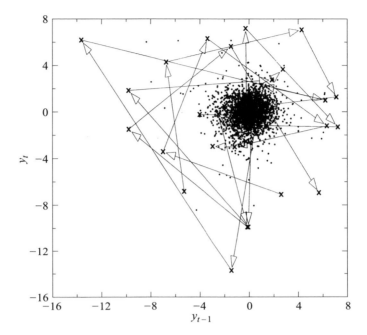

Figure 1.6   Scatterplot of the return on the Frankfurt stock index on day t, y_t, against
the return on day $t - 1$

The observations for the three largest negative and the three largest positive values of y_t are
connected with the two preceding and the two following observations by means of arrows,
pointing in the direction in which the time series evolves; all observations that are starting- and/or
end-points of arrows are marked with crosses

pound, Canadian dollar and Dutch guilder are shown in figures 1.8–1.10. In
these scatterplots, the observations for the three largest negative and the three
largest positive values of y_t are connected with the two preceding and the two
following observations by means of arrows, pointing in the direction in which
the time series evolves. All observations that are starting and/or end-points of
arrows are marked with crosses.

Following the route indicated by the arrows reveals that the return series
frequently travel around the main cloud of observations for an extended period
of time. This holds for stock returns in particular. For example, the arrows in
figure 1.5 really comprise only two stretches of large returns. The first stretch
starts at $(y_{t-1}, y_t) = (-1.90, -2.15)$ which corresponds to 14 and 15 October
1987. On subsequent trading days, the return on the Amsterdam stock index was
equal to -0.58, -12.79 (19 October), -6.10, 8.81, -7.52, 0.22, -9.74, 3.21,
-6.14 and 0.25 per cent on 29 October, which is where the first path ends. The
second one starts with the pair of returns on 6 and 9 November 1987, which are

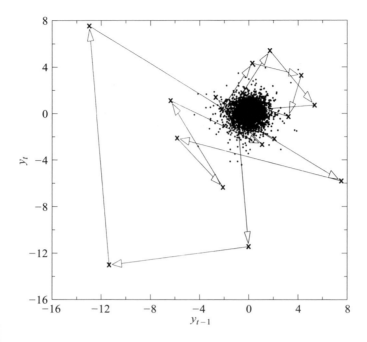

Figure 1.7   Scatterplot of the return on the London stock index on day t, y_t, against the return on day $t - 1$

The observations for the three largest negative and the three largest positive values of y_t are connected with the two preceding and the two following observations by means of arrows, pointing in the direction in which the time series evolves; all observations that are starting- and/or end-points of arrows are marked with crosses

equal to 0.31 and -7.39, respectively, and were followed by returns of -4.52, 11.18, 8.35, -2.79, 3.89 and -3.99 per cent.

From figures 1.8–1.10 it appears that clustering of large returns occurs less frequently for exchange rates. The arrows seem to constitute a three-cycle quite often, where 'three-cycle' refers to the situation where the return series leaves the main cloud of observations owing to a large value of y_t, moves to the next observation (which necessarily is outside of the main cloud as well, as now y_{t-1} is large) and moves back into the main clutter the next day. Evidently, such three-cycles are caused by a single large return. Still, some longer stretches of arrows are present as well.

Large volatility often follows large negative stock market returns
Another property of the stock return series that can be inferred from the scatterplots presented is that periods of large volatility tend to be triggered by a

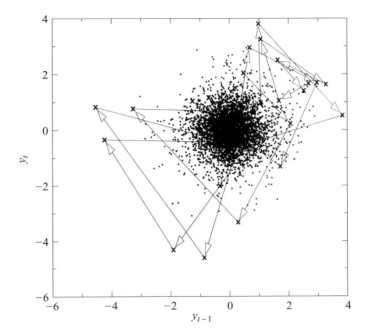

Figure 1.8   Scatterplot of the return on the British pound/US dollar exchange rate on day t, y_t, against the return on day $t-1$

The observations for the three largest negative and the three largest positive values of y_t are connected with the two preceding and the two following observations by means of arrows, pointing in the direction in which the time series evolves; all observations that are starting- and/or end-points of arrows are marked with crosses

large negative return. Further inspection of figures 1.5–1.7 shows that the stock return series almost invariably leave the central cloud in a southern direction – that is, today's return is large and negative. Given that it can take quite some time before the return series calms down and that scatter observations disappear into the main cloud again, it seems justified to state that a volatile period often starts with a large negative return.

The second column of table 1.3 contains estimates of the correlation between the squared return at day t and the return at day $t-1$ for the various stock indexes. The fact that all these correlations are negative also illustrates that large volatility often follows upon a negative return.

For the exchange rate returns this property is much less clear-cut (as it should be, as the return series can be inverted by simply expressing the exchange rate as the number of US dollars per unit of foreign currency). Figures 1.8–1.10 do not reveal any preference of the exchange rate return series to leave the main cloud of observations either to the north or to the south. The estimates of the

Table 1.3   *Correlation between squared returns at day t and returns at day t − 1*

Stock market	Corr(y_t^2, y_{t-1})	Exchange rate	Corr(y_t^2, y_{t-1})
Amsterdam	−0.049	Australian dollar	0.168
Frankfurt	−0.095	British pound	0.074
Hong Kong	−0.081	Canadian dollar	0.041
London	−0.199	Dutch guilder	0.042
New York	−0.108	French franc	0.047
Paris	−0.042	German Dmark	0.041
Singapore	−0.107	Japanese yen	−0.008
Tokyo	−0.130	Swiss franc	0.014

Note: Correlation between squared return at day t and return at day $t − 1$ for stock market indices and exchange rates.

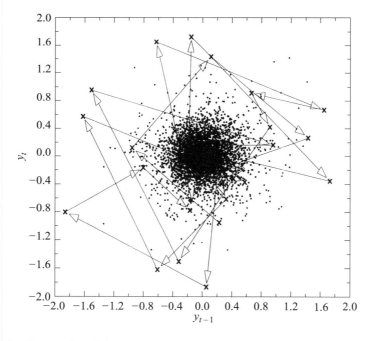

Figure 1.9   Scatterplot of the return on the Canadian dollar/US dollar exchange rate on day t, y_t, against the return on day $t − 1$

The observations for the three largest negative and the three largest positive values of y_t are connected with the two preceding and the two following observations by means of arrows, pointing in the direction in which the time series evolves; all observations that are starting- and/or end-points of arrows are marked with crosses

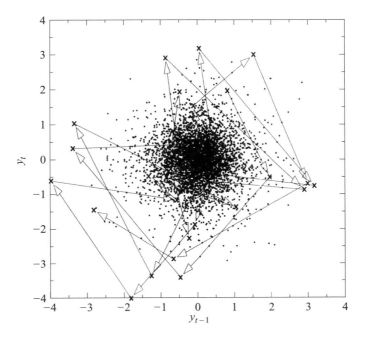

Figure 1.10 Scatterplot of the return on the Dutch guilder exchange rate on day t, y_t, against the return on day $t - 1$

The observations for the three largest negative and the three largest positive values of y_t are connected with the two preceding and the two following observations by means of arrows, pointing in the direction in which the time series evolves; all observations that are starting- and/or end-points of arrows are marked with crosses

correlations between y_t^2 and y_{t-1}, as shown in the final column of table 1.3, are positive for all exchange rate series except the Japanese yen.

To summarize, the typical features of financial time series documented in this first chapter seem to require nonlinear models, simply because linear models would not be able to generate data that have these features. Before we turn to a discussion of nonlinear models for the returns in chapter 3, we first review several important time series analysis tools in chapter 2, which are needed for a better understanding of the material later in the book.

2 Some concepts in time series analysis

In this chapter we discuss several concepts that are useful for the analysis of time series with linear models, while some of them can also fruitfully be applied to nonlinear time series. Examples of these concepts are autocorrelation functions, estimation, diagnostic measures, model selection and forecasting. After introducing the linear time series models which are of interest in section 2.1, we discuss these concepts in section 2.2 in the context of an empirical model specification strategy, to demonstrate how the various elements can be used in practice. In section 2.3 we demonstrate that linear time series models are less useful for out-of-sample forecasting of returns on stock indexes and exchange rates. Subsequent sections elaborate on concepts which are of special interest when dealing with economic time series – such as unit roots, seasonality and aberrant observations, first two being included for the sake of completeness.

As will become clear in later chapters, not all statistical tools which are commonly applied in linear time series analysis are useful in nonlinear time series analysis. However, as one often starts the analysis of empirical time series with linear models even if one is ultimately interested in nonlinear features, we feel that a basic knowledge and understanding of the most important concepts in linear time series analysis are indispensable. This chapter highlights only the main aspects. Readers interested in more detailed or advanced expositions may consult textbooks such as Box and Jenkins (1970); Anderson (1971); Granger and Newbold (1986); Mills (1990); Hamilton (1994); Fuller (1996); Brockwell and Davis (1997); and Franses (1998), among many others. Readers who already are acquainted with most of the standard tools of linear time series analysis can skip this chapter and proceed directly to chapter 3.

2.1 Preliminaries

We denote the univariate time series of interest as y_t, where y_t can be a return on a financial asset. The variable y_t is observed for $t = 1, 2, \ldots, n$, while we assume that initial conditions or pre-sample values $y_0, y_{-1}, \ldots, y_{1-p}$ are available whenever necessary. We denote by Ω_{t-1} the history or *information set* at time $t-1$, which contains all available information that can be exploited for forecasting future values $y_t, y_{t+1}, y_{t+2}, \ldots$ Where Ω_{t-1} does not contain any information that can be used in a linear forecasting model for y_t, the corresponding time series is usually called a *white noise time series*. Throughout we denote such series as ε_t. Usually it is required that ε_t has a constant (unconditional) mean equal to zero and a constant (unconditional) variance as well. Hence, a white noise series ε_t is defined by

$$E[\varepsilon_t] = 0, \tag{2.1}$$

$$E[\varepsilon_t^2] = \sigma^2, \tag{2.2}$$

$$E[\varepsilon_t \varepsilon_s] = 0 \qquad \forall\, s \neq t. \tag{2.3}$$

The condition that all autocovariances of ε_t are equal to zero, as stated in (2.3), is equivalent to the statement that the information set Ω_{t-1} does not contain information to forecast ε_t with linear models. This will be explained in more detail below.

Linear time series models

In general, any time series y_t can be thought of as being the sum of two parts: what can and what cannot be predicted using the knowledge from the past as gathered in Ω_{t-1}. That is, y_t can be decomposed as

$$y_t = E[y_t|\Omega_{t-1}] + v_t, \tag{2.4}$$

where $E[\cdot|\cdot]$ denotes the conditional expectation operator and v_t is called the unpredictable part, with $E[v_t|\Omega_{t-1}] = 0$. In this chapter we assume that v_t satisfies the white noise properties (2.1)–(2.3).

A commonly applied model for the predictable component of y_t assumes that it is a linear combination of p of its lagged values, that is,

$$y_t = \phi_1 y_{t-1} + \phi_2 y_{t-2} + \cdots + \phi_p y_{t-p} + \varepsilon_t, \quad t = 1, \ldots, n, \tag{2.5}$$

where $\phi_1, \ldots, \phi_p$ are unknown parameters. This simple model, which often turns out to be very useful for descriptive and forecasting purposes, is called an *autoregressive model* of order p [AR(p)] or *autoregression* of order p. For many financial returns p is unlikely to be very large (see section 2.3), while for volatility, p can take large values (see chapter 4). Using the *lag operator* L, defined by $L^k y_t = y_{t-k}$ for $k = 0, 1, 2, \ldots$, (2.5) can be written in a more concise form as

$$\phi_p(L)y_t = \varepsilon_t,$$

where

$$\phi_p(L) = 1 - \phi_1 L - \cdots - \phi_p L^p, \tag{2.6}$$

which is called the AR-polynomial in L of order p.

When p in the AR(p) model is large, one may try to approximate the AR-polynomial by a ratio of two polynomials which together involve a smaller number of parameters. The resultant model then is

$$\phi_p(L)y_t = \theta_q(L)\varepsilon_t, \quad t = 1, \ldots, n, \tag{2.7}$$

with

$$\phi_p(L) = 1 - \phi_1 L - \cdots - \phi_p L^p,$$
$$\theta_q(L) = 1 + \theta_1 L + \cdots + \theta_q L^q,$$

where the p in (2.7) is usually much smaller than the p in (2.5). This model is called an *autoregressive moving average model* of order (p, q) [ARMA(p, q)]. The ARMA model class was popularized by Box and Jenkins (1970). We will see in chapter 4 that an ARMA-type model is relevant for modelling volatility.

Sometimes it is convenient to assume that the predictable part of y_t is a linear combination of the q most recent shocks $\varepsilon_{t-1}, \ldots, \varepsilon_{t-q}$. This effectively reduces the ARMA model (2.7) to a *moving average model* of order q [MA(q)], given by

$$y_t = \varepsilon_t + \theta_1 \varepsilon_{t-1} + \cdots + \theta_q \varepsilon_{t-q}, \quad t = 1, \ldots, n. \tag{2.8}$$

Covariance stationarity

A white noise series as defined by (2.1)–(2.3) is a special case of a covariance stationary time series. In general, a given time series y_t is said to be *covariance stationary* if it has constant mean, variance and autocovariances, that is,

$$E[y_t] = \mu \quad \forall\, t = 1, \ldots, n, \tag{2.9}$$

$$E[(y_t - \mu)^2] = \gamma_0 \quad \forall\, t = 1, \ldots, n, \tag{2.10}$$

$$E[(y_t - \mu)(y_{t-k} - \mu)] = \gamma_k \quad \forall\, t = 1, \ldots, n \text{ and } k = 0, 1, 2, \ldots, \tag{2.11}$$

where μ, γ_0 and γ_k are finite-valued numbers.

Whether or not a time series y_t generated by an ARMA(p, q) model is covariance stationary is determined by the autoregressive parameters $\phi_1, \ldots, \phi_p$. For example, consider the first-order autoregression

$$y_t = \phi_0 + \phi_1 y_{t-1} + \varepsilon_t, \tag{2.12}$$

where we have included an intercept ϕ_0 to describe a nonzero mean of y_t. By taking expectations of both sides of (2.12), that is,

$$E[y_t] = \phi_0 + \phi_1 E[y_{t-1}] + E[\varepsilon_t], \tag{2.13}$$

and assuming that y_t is covariance stationary and using (2.9) and (2.1), it follows that

$$\mu = \frac{\phi_0}{1 - \phi_1}. \tag{2.14}$$

Notice that (2.14) makes sense only if $|\phi_1| < 1$. For example, when ϕ_1 exceeds 1 and ϕ_0 is a positive number, (2.14) implies that the mean of y_t is negative, whereas (2.12) says that, on average, y_t is a multiple of its previous value *plus* a positive constant. This apparent contradiction is caused by the fact that in order to derive (2.14) we assumed y_t to be covariance stationary in the first place, which is not the case when $|\phi_1| \geq 1$, as will become clear below.

Another way to understand the relevance of the condition $|\phi_1| < 1$ is to rewrite (2.12) by recursive substitution as

$$y_t = \phi_1^t y_0 + \sum_{i=0}^{t-1} \phi_1^i \phi_0 + \sum_{i=0}^{t-1} \phi_1^i \varepsilon_{t-i}, \tag{2.15}$$

from which it follows that $E[y_t] = \phi_1^t y_0 + \sum_{i=0}^{t-1} \phi_1^i \phi_0$. When $|\phi_1| < 1$, it holds that

$$\sum_{i=0}^{t-1} \phi_1^i = (1 - \phi_1^t)/(1 - \phi_1) < \infty \quad \text{for all } t \geq 0,$$

whereas $\phi_1^t \to 0$ as $t \to \infty$. It then follows that $E[y_t] = \phi_0/(1 - \phi_1)$ for t sufficiently large. On the other hand, when $|\phi_1| \geq 1$, the summation $\sum_{i=0}^{t-1} \phi_1^i$ does not converge when t becomes larger and the above does not hold. For example, in case $\phi_1 = 1$ we obtain $E[y_t] = y_0 + \phi_0 t$, which certainly is not constant.

To derive the variance and autocovariances for the AR(1) model it is convenient to rewrite (2.12) as

$$(y_t - \mu) = \phi_1(y_{t-1} - \mu) + \varepsilon_t, \tag{2.16}$$

with $\mu = \phi_0/(1 - \phi_1)$. Taking expectations of the squares of both sides of (2.16) results in

$$E[(y_t - \mu)^2] = \phi_1^2 E[(y_{t-1} - \mu)^2] + E[\varepsilon_t^2] + 2\phi_1 E[(y_{t-1} - \mu)\varepsilon_t]. \tag{2.17}$$

From (2.15) lagged one period it follows that y_{t-1} can be expressed as a function of the shocks $\varepsilon_{t-1}, \varepsilon_{t-2}, \ldots$ (and the starting value y_0). Combining this with (2.3) it should be clear that y_{t-1} and ε_t are uncorrelated and, hence, the last term on the right-hand side of (2.17) is equal to zero. Under the assumption that y_t is covariance stationary or, equivalently, $|\phi_1| < 1$, we thus have

$$\gamma_0 = \frac{\sigma^2}{1 - \phi_1^2}. \tag{2.18}$$

The first-order autocovariance for an AR(1) time series is

$$\begin{aligned}
\gamma_1 &= E[(y_t - \mu)(y_{t-1} - \mu)] \\
&= \phi_1 E[(y_{t-1} - \mu)(y_{t-1} - \mu)] + E[\varepsilon_t(y_{t-1} - \mu)] \\
&= \phi_1 \gamma_0.
\end{aligned} \tag{2.19}$$

For the AR(1) model it holds more generally that for any $k > 1$

$$E[(y_t - \mu)(y_{t-k} - \mu)] = \phi_1 E[(y_{t-1} - \mu)(y_{t-k} - \mu)], \tag{2.20}$$

and hence that

$$\gamma_k = \phi_1 \gamma_{k-1} \quad \text{for } k = 1, 2, 3, \ldots \tag{2.21}$$

An AR(1) model with $\phi_1 = 1$

In case the parameter ϕ_1 in (2.12) exceeds 1, the time series y_t is explosive, in the sense that y_t diverges to $\pm\infty$. As this is quite unlikely for financial returns or volatility, from now on we do not consider such explosive processes. An interesting case, though, concerns $\phi_1 = 1$. In that case, assuming $\phi_0 = 0$ (without loss of generality), (2.15) can be rewritten as

$$y_t = y_0 + \sum_{i=1}^{t} \varepsilon_i. \tag{2.22}$$

From this expression it follows that $\gamma_{0,t} \equiv E[y_t^2] = t\sigma^2$ and in general $\gamma_{k,t} \equiv E[y_t y_{t-k}] = (t - k)\sigma^2$ for all $k \geq 0$. The additional index t on the γs is used to highlight the fact that the variance and autocovariances are not constant over time but rather increase linearly.

The expression in (2.22) also shows that the effects of all past shocks ε_i, $i = 1, \ldots, t$, on y_t are equally large. Equivalently, the effect of the shock ε_t on y_{t+k} is the same for $k = 0, 1, \ldots$ Therefore, shocks are often called *permanent* in this case. This is to be contrasted with stationary time series y_t. From (2.15) it follows that the effect of ε_t on y_{t+k}, $k \geq 0$ becomes smaller as k increases and eventually dies out as $k \to \infty$. In this case, shocks are called *transitory*. The time series in (2.22) is called a 'random walk'. As noted in chapter 1, the random walk model as a description of the behaviour of asset prices is an important hypothesis in empirical finance (see Campbell, Lo and MacKinlay, 1997, chapter 2).

When shocks are permanent, it is common practice to proceed with an analysis of $\Delta_1 y_t \equiv (1 - L)y_t = y_t - y_{t-1}$ – that is, the differenced series instead of y_t. An extended motivation for this practice is given in section 2.4. When p_t denotes the natural logarithm of an asset price P_t – that is, $p_t = \ln P_t$ – the application of the differencing filter results in $p_t - p_{t-1}$, which approximates the returns when P_t/P_{t-1} is close to 1. When a time series needs to be differenced d times – that is, the filter Δ_1^d has to be applied – one says that it is *integrated* of order d $[I(d)]$. When an ARMA model is considered for $\Delta_1^d y_t$, one says that y_t is described by an *autoregressive integrated moving average model* of order (p, d, q) [ARIMA(p, d, q)].

To provide more insights in the peculiarity of a random walk time series, consider again (2.22). As $E[\varepsilon_t] = 0$, the expected value of y_t is y_0, which is rather odd for a time series that wanders around freely. In fact, this means that the sample mean is not a good estimator for the expected value. Note, however, that one is always able, given a series of observed y_t values, to calculate $\bar{y} = 1/n \sum_{t=1}^{n} y_t$, but for the random walk this sample mean is not a useful statistic.

AR(p) models and stationarity
   The above results generalize to AR(p) models with $p \geq 1$. To see how, consider the *characteristic equation* of the AR(1) and AR(p) models, given by

$$1 - \phi_1 z = 0, \tag{2.23}$$

and

$$1 - \phi_1 z - \cdots - \phi_p z^p = 0, \tag{2.24}$$

respectively. The solution, or root, of (2.23) is $z = \phi_1^{-1}$. Hence, the condition that $|\phi_1|$ is less than 1 for time series y_t generated by an AR(1) model to be stationary is equivalent to the condition that the root of (2.23) is larger than 1.

The condition for covariance stationarity of time series generated by an AR(p) model then simply is that all p solutions of (2.24) are larger than 1 – or, rather, as the solutions can be complex numbers, that they are outside the unit circle (see, for example, Fuller, 1996). Notice that (2.24) can be rewritten as

$$(1 - \alpha_1 z)(1 - \alpha_2 z) \cdots (1 - \alpha_p z) = 0 \qquad (2.25)$$

which shows that the stationarity condition is equivalent to the requirement that all $\alpha_i, i = 1, \ldots, p$, are inside the unit circle. When the largest of the α_is is equal to 1, $z = 1$ is a solution to (2.24). In this case we say that the AR(p) polynomial has a unit root.

MA models and invertibility

One of the properties of MA models is that time series which are generated from such models are always covariance stationary. In fact, from (2.8) it follows directly that E$[y_t] = 0$ and that the variance of y_t equals

$$\gamma_0 = (1 + \theta_1^2 + \theta_2^2 + \cdots + \theta_q^2)\sigma^2. \qquad (2.26)$$

Furthermore, it can simply be derived that

$$\gamma_k = \begin{cases} \sigma^2 \sum_{i=0}^{q-k} \theta_i \theta_{i+k} & \text{for } k = 1, \ldots, q, \\ 0 & \text{for } k > q, \end{cases} \qquad (2.27)$$

with $\theta_0 \equiv 1$.

Another desirable property of time series is that of invertibility. A time series y_t is said to be invertible if it is possible to reconstruct the value of the shock at time t, ε_t, given only the current and past observations $y_t, y_{t-1}, y_{t-2}, \ldots$ Whether or not a time series y_t generated by an ARMA(p, q) model is invertible is determined by the moving average parameters $\theta_1, \ldots, \theta_q$.

The fact that time series generated by AR models are always invertible follows trivially from (2.5), for example. The condition for invertibility of time series generated by the MA(q) model (2.8) is that the q solutions to the characteristic equation

$$1 + \theta_1 z + \cdots + \theta_q z^q = 0, \qquad (2.28)$$

are all outside the unit circle. Notice that this is analogous to the stationarity condition for the AR(p) model. If the invertibility condition is satisfied, the MA model can be expressed alternatively as an AR(∞) model. For example, for the MA(1) model $y_t = \varepsilon_t + \theta_1 \varepsilon_{t-1}$ with $|\theta_1| < 1$

$$\begin{aligned} \varepsilon_t &= \frac{y_t}{(1 + \theta_1 L)} \\ &= y_t - \theta_1 y_{t-1} + \theta_1^2 y_{t-2} - \theta_1^3 y_{t-3} + \cdots, \end{aligned} \qquad (2.29)$$

from which it is easily seen that y_t depends on an infinite number of its own lagged values.

2.2 Empirical specification strategy

In this section we describe a typical specification strategy for linear time series models. In general, the various steps in this strategy also hold for nonlinear models, although at times there are differences in the statistical tools which should be used. We will indicate where the main differences are expected to be found across linear and nonlinear models. The modelling sequence usually involves the following steps:

(1) calculate certain statistics for a time series at hand
(2) compare the values or sizes of these statistics with the theoretical values that would hold true if a certain model is adequate (or a certain null hypothesis holds true)
(3) estimate the parameters in the time series model suggested by the results in step (2)
(4) evaluate the model using diagnostic measures
(5) respecify the model if necessary
(6) use the model for descriptive or forecasting purposes.

The principal advantage of modelling sequentially observed time series data is that specific models imply specific properties of data that are generated by these models. By comparing these properties with the corresponding characteristics of the time series under investigation, one can get an idea of the usefulness of the model for describing the time series. For example, it follows from (2.27) that a moving average model of order 1 implies that only the first order autocovariance for y_t differs from zero. Statistical tests can be used to see if this holds for the estimated autocovariances for an observed time series – and, if yes, one can start off with an MA(1) model in step (3).

If attention is restricted to linear ARIMA models, the main objective of steps (1) and (2) in the specification strategy is to determine the appropriate AR and MA orders p and q. This part of the specification strategy is often called *model identification* (see Box and Jenkins, 1970). Note that this is a different concept than parameter identification, which is often used in simultaneous models and in several nonlinear time series models below. As an example, in the model $y_t = \alpha\phi_1 y_{t-1} + \varepsilon_t$, the parameters α and ϕ_1 are not identified, unless a restriction on one of them is imposed. Identification of an ARIMA model also includes determining the appropriate order of differencing d. This topic is discussed in some detail in section 2.4; here we assume for convenience that d is known to be equal to 0.

The most relevant statistics that may suggest the appropriate orders of a linear ARMA type model are contained in the *autocorrelation function* [ACF] and *partial autocorrelation function* [PACF], which are defined more precisely below. If a time series is most adequately described by an ARMA(p,q) model, it should in theory obey certain (partial) autocorrelation properties. In practice, the orders p and q are of course unknown and have to be estimated from the data. It is hoped that this can be achieved by comparing the values of the estimated (P)ACF [E(P)ACF] with the theoretical values as implied by ARMA(p,q) models for different p and q. If a reasonable match between the estimated and theoretical correlations is found for certain ARMA orders, one can select this model and proceed with estimation of the parameters in step (3). It should be stressed here, though, that only for simple models are the ACF and PACF easy to interpret. When the models become more complicated – say, an ARMA model of order (4,3) – one needs considerable skill and experience to deduce the correct orders of this model based on estimated autocorrelation functions only. On the other hand, for many financial returns, memory in the data is expected not to be very long, and the estimated autocorrelation functions may prove useful.

The ACF of a time series y_t is defined by

$$\rho_k = \gamma_k/\gamma_0, \quad k = 1, 2, 3, \ldots, \tag{2.30}$$

where γ_k is the kth order autocovariance of y_t defined in (2.11).

Given (2.3), it is clear that for a white noise series, $\rho_k = 0$ for all $k \neq 0$. In section 2.1 it was shown that for the stationary AR(1) model (2.12) with $|\phi_1| < 1$ it holds that $\gamma_k = \phi_1 \gamma_{k-1}$ for $k = 1, 2, 3, \ldots$ Hence, the theoretical first-order autocorrelation ρ_1 for an AR(1) model equals

$$\rho_1 = \gamma_1/\gamma_0 = \phi_1, \tag{2.31}$$

and, in general,

$$\rho_k = \phi_1 \rho_{k-1} = \phi_1^k \quad \text{for } k = 1, 2, 3, \ldots, \tag{2.32}$$

with $\rho_0 = 1$. Hence, the ACF of an AR(1) model starts at $\rho_1 = \phi_1$ and then decays geometrically towards zero.

As an aside, it is useful to note here that for an AR(1) model with $\phi_1 = 1$, it follows from the analysis just below (2.22) that the kth order autocorrelation at time t is equal to

$$\rho_{k,t} = \frac{t - k}{t}, \tag{2.33}$$

for $k = 1, 2, \ldots$ Obviously, as the autocovariances are varying over time, the autocorrelations are as well. The main point to take from (2.33) is that if we erroneously assume that the autocorrelations $\rho_{k,t}$ are constant and estimate common ρ_ks for $k = 1, 2, \ldots$ at time n using the observations $y_1, \ldots, y_n$, we are most likely to observe that all values of $\hat{\rho}_k$ are very close to 1, provided that the sample size n is large enough.

The ACF is useful for identification of the order of a pure MA model. From (2.27) it follows that for the MA(q) model the autocorrelations at lags $q + i$, with $i = 1, 2, \ldots$ are equal to zero. For mixed ARMA models, the theoretical ACF already becomes quite involved for fairly small values of the orders p and q. The pattern can also become difficult to distinguish from patterns of pure AR models or of ARMA models with different values of p and q. Hence, in practice, one usually takes a casual glance at the estimated autocorrelation function. If there is clear-cut evidence that an MA model can be useful, one proceeds with estimating its parameters – that is, with step (3). Otherwise, one starts off with an ARMA model with small values of p and q, and uses diagnostic measures in step (4) to see if the model is in need of modification. For linear time series models this would mean that, for example, p or q are increased to $p + 1$ or $q + 1$, respectively.

The kth order partial autocorrelation can be interpreted as the correlation between y_t and y_{t-k} after accounting for the correlation which is caused by intermediate observations $y_{t-1}, \ldots, y_{t-k+1}$. For example, where a time series is generated by an AR(1) model (2.12), the normal correlation between y_t and y_{t-2} is equal to ρ_1^2. However, this correlation is caused entirely by the fact that both y_t and y_{t-2} are correlated with y_{t-1}. After removing this common component from both y_t and y_{t-2}, the remaining or partial correlation is zero. An intuitive way to see this is to notice that there is no need to add the regressor y_{t-2} to an AR(1) model, and where one does so, the corresponding parameter should equal 0. In general, the regressors $y_{t-(p+i)}, i = 1, 2, \ldots$ are redundant variables if the series is really generated by an AR(p) model. Hence, for such a series, the partial autocorrelations of orders $k > p$ are equal to zero. For invertible MA(q) models, on the other hand, there is no clear cut-off point but, rather, the partial autocorrelations slowly decay towards zero. This can be understood from (2.29), which demonstrates that an invertible MA(q) model has an equivalent AR(∞) representation. The same holds for mixed ARMA(p,q) processes with both p and q greater than zero. In sum, the PACF is most useful to identify the order of a pure AR model.

In practice, the correlation and partial correlation functions have to be estimated from the observed time series. The kth order autocorrelation can be estimated by means of the sample covariances as

$$\hat{\rho}_k = \frac{\frac{1}{n}\sum_{t=k+1}^{n}(y_t - \bar{y})(y_{t-k} - \bar{y})}{\frac{1}{n}\sum_{t=1}^{n}(y_t - \bar{y})^2}, \tag{2.34}$$

where $\bar{y}$ is the sample mean of y_t, $t = 1, \ldots, n$. An easy way to obtain estimates of the partial autocorrelations is by estimating AR(k) models

$$y_t - \bar{y} = \psi_1^{(k)}(y_{t-1} - \bar{y}) + \cdots + \psi_k^{(k)}(y_{t-k} - \bar{y}) + v_t, \qquad (2.35)$$

for increasing orders $k = 1, 2, \ldots$ The kth order partial autocorrelation is given by the last coefficient in the estimated AR(k) model, $\hat{\psi}_k^{(k)}$.

In figures 2.1 and 2.2 we give the first 50 autocorrelations for the log prices, daily returns, absolute returns and squared returns of the Frankfurt and Tokyo stock indexes and the British pound and Dutch guilder exchange rate series, respectively. Clearly, the log asset prices have autocorrelations close to unity at all selected lags and, hence, they seem to mimic the correlation properties of a random walk process as given in (2.33). It is seen that the autocorrelations of the return series are very small, even at low lags. Given that the asymptotic variance of the autocorrelation estimates is roughly equal to $1/\sqrt{n}$, the appropriate (two-sided) 5 per cent critical value for evaluating these estimates is equal to 0.035 ($= 1.96/\sqrt{3,127}$) for the stock returns and 0.029 ($= 1.96/\sqrt{4,521}$) for the exchange rate returns. By contrast, for the absolute and squared returns, the autocorrelations start off at a moderate level (the first-order autocorrelation generally ranges between 0.2 and 0.3 for the stock returns and 0.1 and 0.2 for the exchange rate returns) but remain (significantly) positive for a substantial number of lags. In addition, the autocorrelation in the absolute returns is generally somewhat higher than the autocorrelation in the squared returns, especially for the stock market indices. This illustrates what has become known as the 'Taylor property' (see Taylor, 1986, pp. 52–5) – that is, when calculating the autocorrelations for the series $|y_t|^\delta$ for various values of δ, one almost invariably finds that the autocorrelations are largest for $\delta = 1$.

The autocorrelations and partial autocorrelations as discussed above are measures of linear association and predictability. Their usefulness in a specification procedure for nonlinear models is very limited. For example, one may derive the autocorrelation function of a nonlinear time series model like

$$y_t = \phi_1 y_{t-1} + \beta_1 \varepsilon_{t-1} y_{t-1} + \varepsilon_t, \qquad (2.36)$$

which is a so-called *bilinear time series model* (see Granger and Andersen, 1978). However, even for this simple example, it already becomes quite difficult to use (see Li, 1984). Moreover, it is not difficult to construct nonlinear time series models for which all autocorrelations are equal to zero. An example is the bilinear model

$$y_t = \beta_2 \varepsilon_{t-1} y_{t-2} + \varepsilon_t. \qquad (2.37)$$

When only the autocorrelation properties of time series generated by this model are considered, one might conclude that the series is white noise – and, hence,

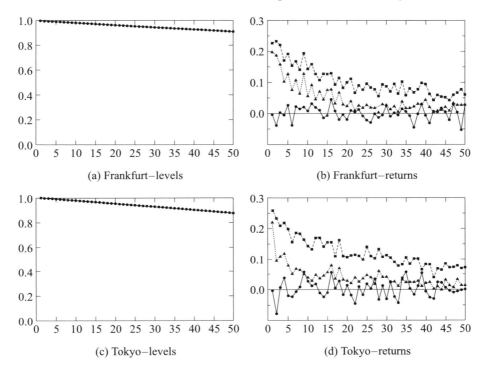

(a) Frankfurt–levels

(b) Frankfurt–returns

(c) Tokyo–levels

(d) Tokyo–returns

Figure 2.1   First 50 autocorrelations of (a), (b) daily Frankfurt and (c), (d) Tokyo stock market indexes
Figures (a) and (c) show autocorrelations of the log prices; figures (b) and (d) show autocorrelations of returns (solid line with circles), absolute returns (dashed line with squares) and squared returns (dotted line with triangles)

not linearly forecastable. Of course, the series is forecastable using a nonlinear model. An alternative strategy is to start off with a linear time series model, based on a rough guess using linear autocorrelation functions, and then, in a next step, to use diagnostic tests which have power against the alternative model of interest. In the bilinear model (2.36), for example, one might first estimate an AR(1) model for y_t – that is, $y_t = \kappa y_{t-1} + u_t$ – and then investigate if the regressor $u_{t-1}y_{t-1}$ adds significantly to the fit. Before we return to this strategy in subsequent chapters, we first outline the other elements in the specification procedure for linear models.

Estimation
The parameters in the AR(p) model

$$y_t = \phi_0 + \phi_1 y_{t-1} + \phi_2 y_{t-2} + \cdots + \phi_p y_{t-p} + \varepsilon_t, \qquad (2.38)$$

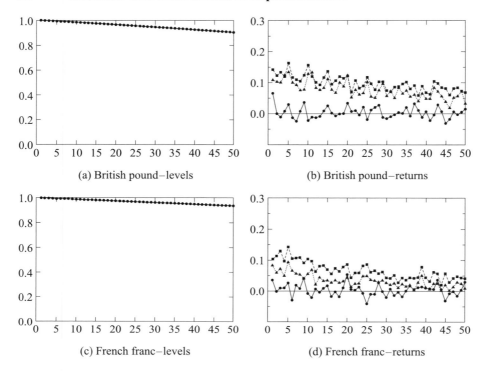

Figure 2.2   First 50 autocorrelations of (a), (b) daily British pound and (c), (d) French franc exchange rates *vis-à-vis* the US dollar

Figures (a) and (c) show autocorrelations of the log exchange rates; figures (b) and (d) show autocorrelations of returns (solid line with circles), absolute returns (dashed line with squares) and squared returns (dotted line with triangles)

can be estimated by Ordinary Least Squares (OLS). It can be shown that under relatively weak assumptions about the properties of the innovations ε_t (much weaker than the white noise assumptions (2.1)–(2.3) which we use here), the OLS estimates of the parameters are consistent and asymptotically normal, and that standard t-statistics can be used to investigate the significance of ϕ_1 to ϕ_p (see Box and Jenkins, 1970). The mean μ of y_t can be estimated from $\hat{\mu} = \hat{\phi}_0/(1 - \hat{\phi}_1 - \hat{\phi}_2 - \cdots - \hat{\phi}_p)$. Using the parameter estimates, the residual series $\hat{\varepsilon}_t$ can be constructed.

Several methods for estimating the parameters of (AR)MA models have been developed (see Box, Jenkins and Reinsel, 1994; Brockwell and Davis, 1997, for examples of maximum likelihood and least squares methods). The fact that there is no unanimously preferred estimation method is mainly caused by the fact that the lagged ε_t variables in the MA part are unobserved, and their realizations have to be estimated jointly with the parameters. The proposed estimation procedures mainly differ in the way they estimate these unobserved shocks. A method often applied is an iterative least squares method. To provide intuition for this procedure, consider the ARMA(1,1) model when it is written as

$$(1 + \theta_1 L)^{-1} y_t = \phi_1 (1 + \theta_1 L)^{-1} y_{t-1} + \varepsilon_t. \qquad (2.39)$$

Denoting $z_t = (1 + \theta_1 L)^{-1} y_t$, (2.39) implies that we can define (assuming $y_0 = 0$ and n to be odd)

$$z_1 = y_1,$$
$$z_2 = y_2 - \theta_1 y_1,$$
$$z_3 = y_3 - \theta_1 y_2 + \theta_1^2 y_1,$$
$$\vdots$$
$$z_n = y_n - \theta_1 y_{n-1} + \cdots + \theta_1^{n-1} y_1.$$

For a given value of θ_1, one can generate observations z_t, and apply OLS to (2.39) written in terms of z_t – that is, $z_t = \phi_1 z_{t-1} + \varepsilon_t$ – to obtain an estimate $\hat{\phi}_1$ of the AR parameter. This results in a residual series $\hat{\varepsilon}_t$ which, when setting $\hat{\varepsilon}_1 = 0$, can be used to obtain a new estimate for the MA parameter θ by considering the regression $\hat{\varepsilon}_t - (y_t - \hat{\phi}_1 y_{t-1}) = \theta_1 \hat{\varepsilon}_{t-1}$. This new estimate of θ_1 can be used to construct a new z_t series, which can be used to obtain a new estimate of the AR parameter, and so on. These steps should be iterated until convergence – that is, until the estimates of the parameters ϕ_1 and θ_1 do not change any more.

Diagnostic testing for residual autocorrelation

Testing the adequacy of an estimated ARMA model in step (4) of the suggested specification strategy usually involves several elements. It is quite common to start with examining whether the residual series $\hat{\varepsilon}_t$ is approximately white noise, by testing whether its autocovariances – or autocorrelations – are equal to zero (see (2.3)). If this turns out not to be the case, there is a need to modify the model by increasing the value of p and/or q. There are three commonly applied methods to test for *residual autocorrelation*, all of which can also be considered (or modified) for nonlinear time series models. The first method is to look at individual elements of the sample ACF of the residuals, given by

$$r_k(\hat{\varepsilon}) = \frac{\sum_{t=k+1}^{n} \hat{\varepsilon}_t \hat{\varepsilon}_{t-k}}{\sum_{t=1}^{n} \hat{\varepsilon}_t^2}, \qquad (2.40)$$

for $k = 1, 2, 3, \ldots$ Box and Jenkins (1970) show that, given model adequacy, the population equivalents of $r_k(\hat{\varepsilon})$ are asymptotically uncorrelated and have variances approximately equal to n^{-1}. Assuming normality, one may use the interval $(-1.96/\sqrt{n}, 1.96/\sqrt{n})$ to examine if certain residual autocorrelations are different from zero at the 5 per cent significance level.

A second method amounts to testing for the joint significance of the first m residual autocorrelations. The test-statistic developed by Ljung and Box (1978), given by

$$\text{LB}(m) = n(n+2) \sum_{k=1}^{m} (n-k)^{-1} r_k^2(\hat{\varepsilon}), \tag{2.41}$$

can be used for this purpose. Under the null hypothesis of no residual autocorrelation at lags 1 to m in the residuals from an ARMA(p, q) model, the LB test has an asymptotic $\chi^2(m - p - q)$ distribution, provided that m/n is small and m is moderately large. Simulation studies have shown that this LB test may not have much power (see, for example, Hall and McAleer, 1989). Despite this unfortunate property, the test is often used because of its ease of computation.

The third method follows the Lagrange Multiplier (LM) principle (see, for example, Godfrey, 1979). To test an AR(p) model against an AR$(p + r)$ or an ARMA(p, r) model, we consider the auxiliary regression

$$\hat{\varepsilon}_t = \alpha_1 y_{t-1} + \cdots + \alpha_p y_{t-p} + \beta_1 \hat{\varepsilon}_{t-1} + \cdots + \beta_r \hat{\varepsilon}_{t-r} + v_t, \tag{2.42}$$

where $\hat{\varepsilon}_t$ are the residuals of the AR(p) model with $\hat{\varepsilon}_t = 0$ for $t \leq 0$. The LM test-statistic which tests the significance of the parameters $\beta_1, \ldots, \beta_r$ is calculated as nR^2, where R^2 is the (uncentred) coefficient of determination from (2.42). Under the null hypothesis that the AR(p) is an adequate model – or, equivalently, $\beta_1 = \cdots = \beta_r = 0$ – this LM test has an asymptotic $\chi^2(r)$ distribution. Usually, one considers the F-version of this LM test as it has better size and power properties in small samples.

In case of ARMA(p, q) models, one cannot add the regressor $\hat{\varepsilon}_{t-q}$ to the model as it is already included in the model. For the MA(1) model, for example, one should then create new variables like

$$y_t^* = y_t + \hat{\theta}_1 y_{t-1}^* \quad \text{with } y_0^* = 0,$$
$$\hat{\varepsilon}_t^* = \hat{\varepsilon}_t + \hat{\theta}_1 \hat{\varepsilon}_{t-1}^* \quad \text{with } \hat{\varepsilon}_0^* = 0,$$

and consider the auxiliary regression

$$\hat{\varepsilon}_t = \hat{\alpha}_1 \hat{\varepsilon}_{t-1}^* + \beta_1 y_{t-1}^* + \cdots + \beta_r y_{t-r}^* + v_t, \tag{2.43}$$

to test against an MA$(1 + r)$ or an ARMA$(r, 1)$ model.

Several nonlinear time series models contain linear components, and then the above three methods may still be useful as a rough-and-ready first check.

In case one is interested to see if, for example, the variable $y_{t-1}\varepsilon_{t-1}$ should be added, one should however preferably use the LM principle, as it leads to specifically designed tests.

Diagnostic testing for homoscedasticity of the residuals

Another property of the residuals which should be tested concerns the constancy of their variance. If this is indeed the case, the residuals are said to be homoscedastic, while if the variance changes they are called heteroscedastic.

Neglecting heteroscedasticity of the residuals has potentially quite severe consequences. For example, even though the OLS estimates of the ARMA parameters are still consistent and asymptotically normal distributed, their variance–covariance matrix is no longer the usual one. Hence, ordinary t-statistics cannot be used to assess the significance of individual regressors in the model. Furthermore, other diagnostic tests, such as tests for nonlinearity (some of which will be discussed in chapter 3), are affected by heteroscedasticity as well, in the sense that their usual asymptotic distributions no longer apply. In particular, neglected heteroscedasticity can easily suggest spurious nonlinearity in the conditional mean. Davidson and MacKinnon (1985) and Wooldridge (1990, 1991) discuss general principles for constructing heteroscedasticity-consistent test statistics. Finally, confidence intervals for forecasts, which are discussed in detail below, can no longer be computed in the usual manner.

Several statistics for testing the null hypothesis of constant residual variance can be applied. Which test is used depends partly on whether or not one has a specific alternative in mind – and, if so, which alternative. For example, suppose the alternative of interest is a change in the unconditional variance at a certain point in the sample, that is,

$$\sigma_t^2 = \begin{cases} \sigma_1^2 & \text{for } t \leq \tau, \\ \sigma_2^2 & \text{for } t > \tau, \end{cases} \tag{2.44}$$

for certain $1 < \tau < n$, where σ_t^2 is the variance of the shock at time t. A test against this alternative can be computed by comparing the variance of the residuals before and after the hypothesized change point τ. Another alternative of interest might be to assume that the variance of ε_t depends on a regressor x_t – for example, $\sigma_t^2 = \alpha_0 + \alpha_1 x_t^2$. In this case, the null hypothesis of constant variance can be tested by testing $\alpha_1 = 0$.

Of course, it happens much more often that an obvious alternative to homoscedasticity is not available – in such cases a general test against an unspecified alternative can be applied. The test-statistic developed by McLeod and Li (1983) is commonly used for this purpose. This statistic is in fact computed in exactly the same way as the LB test (2.41), except that it tests for autocorrelation in the *squared* residuals. The test-statistic is given by

$$\text{McL}(m) = n(n+2) \sum_{k=1}^{m} (n-k)^{-1} r_k^2(\hat{\varepsilon}^2).$$

(2.45)

When applied to the residuals from an ARMA(p,q) model, the McL test has an asymptotic $\chi^2(m-p-q)$ distribution, again provided that m/n is small and m is moderately large.

It was noted above that in the presence of heteroscedasticity the variance–covariance matrix of the asymptotic normal distribution of the OLS estimates of the ARMA parameters is no longer the usual OLS one. As shown by White (1980), however, the OLS estimates can be used to compute standard errors which are robust against unspecified heteroscedasticity (see also Hsieh, 1983). As heteroscedasticity plays quite a prominent role in financial data, we elaborate on this issue in some more detail.

Consider the AR(1) model without an intercept,

$$y_t = \phi_1 y_{t-1} + \varepsilon_t, \quad t = 1, 2, \ldots, n.$$

(2.46)

The OLS estimate of the AR parameter ϕ_1 is equal to

$$\begin{aligned}
\hat{\phi}_1 &= \left[\sum_{t=1}^{n} y_{t-1}^2 \right]^{-1} \left[\sum_{t=1}^{n} y_{t-1} y_t \right] \\
&= \left[\sum_{t=1}^{n} y_{t-1}^2 \right]^{-1} \left[\sum_{t=1}^{n} y_{t-1} (\phi_1 y_{t-1} + \varepsilon_t) \right] \\
&= \phi_1 + \left[\sum_{t=1}^{n} y_{t-1}^2 \right]^{-1} \left[\sum_{t=1}^{n} y_{t-1} \varepsilon_t \right],
\end{aligned}$$

(2.47)

from which it follows that

$$\sqrt{n}(\hat{\phi}_1 - \phi_1) = \left[\frac{1}{n} \sum_{t=1}^{n} y_{t-1}^2 \right]^{-1} \left[\frac{1}{\sqrt{n}} \sum_{t=1}^{n} y_{t-1} \varepsilon_t \right].$$

(2.48)

If the shocks ε_t are homoscedastic with $E[\varepsilon_t^2] = \sigma^2$ for all t, $\frac{1}{n} \sum_{t=1}^{n} y_{t-1}^2$ is equal to $\hat{\gamma}_0$, the estimate of the variance of y_t. Furthermore, it can be shown that $\frac{1}{\sqrt{n}} \sum_{t=1}^{n} y_{t-1} \varepsilon_t$ converges to a normally distributed random variable with mean zero and variance equal to $E[y_{t-1}^2 \varepsilon_t^2] = E[y_{t-1}^2] \cdot E[\varepsilon_t^2] = \gamma_0 \sigma^2$. It then follows that $\sqrt{n}(\hat{\phi}_1 - \phi_1)$ is asymptotically normal with mean zero and variance $\sigma^2 \gamma_0^{-1}$. Hence, in finite samples, the standard error of $\hat{\phi}_1$ can be estimated as the square root of

$$\left[\frac{1}{n} \sum_{t=1}^{n} \hat{\varepsilon}_t^2 \right] \left[\sum_{t=1}^{n} y_{t-1}^2 \right]^{-1}.$$

If, on the other hand, the shocks ε_t are heteroscedastic with $E[\varepsilon_t^2] = \sigma_t^2$, it is not clear what is estimated by $\frac{1}{n} \sum_{t=1}^{n} y_{t-1}^2$, while in general it is also the case that $E[y_{t-1}^2 \varepsilon_t^2] \neq E[y_{t-1}^2] \cdot E[\varepsilon_t^2]$. Fortunately, it still holds that $\frac{1}{\sqrt{n}} \sum_{t=1}^{n} y_{t-1} \varepsilon_t$ converges to a normally distributed random variable with mean zero and variance now given by the limit of $\frac{1}{n} \sum_{t=1}^{n} y_{t-1}^2 \varepsilon_t^2$. Assuming that $\frac{1}{n} \sum_{t=1}^{n} y_{t-1}^2$ also converges to some nonzero number ζ, it then follows that $\sqrt{n}(\hat{\phi}_1 - \phi_1)$ is asymptotically normal with mean zero and variance given by the limit of the square of the right-hand side of (2.48). Hence, in finite samples, the heteroscedasticity-consistent [HCC] standard error of $\hat{\phi}_1$ can be estimated as the square root of

$$\left[\sum_{t=1}^{n} y_{t-1}^2 \right]^{-1} \left[\sum_{t=1}^{n} \hat{\varepsilon}_t^2 y_{t-1}^2 \right] \left[\sum_{t=1}^{n} y_{t-1}^2 \right]^{-1}. \tag{2.49}$$

In general, for an AR(p) model, the HCC variance–covariance matrix of the OLS estimates of the AR parameters $\phi = (\phi_1, \ldots, \phi_p)'$ is computed as

$$V(\hat{\phi}) = \left[\sum_{t=1}^{n} x_{t-1} x_{t-1}' \right]^{-1} \left[\sum_{t=1}^{n} \hat{\varepsilon}_t^2 x_{t-1} x_{t-1}' \right] \left[\sum_{t=1}^{n} x_{t-1} x_{t-1}' \right]^{-1}, \tag{2.50}$$

where $x_{t-1} = (y_{t-1}, \ldots, y_{t-p})'$. The HCC standard errors for $\hat{\phi}_1, \ldots, \hat{\phi}_p$ can be obtained as the square roots of the diagonal elements of $V(\hat{\phi})$.

Diagnostic testing for normality of the residuals
A usual assumption for the series ε_t is that its realizations are independent and identically distributed according to a normal distribution with mean 0 and common variance σ^2. The notation for this assumption is $\varepsilon_t \sim \text{NID}(0, \sigma^2)$. Notice that this assumption adds Gaussianity to (2.1)–(2.3). Given this assumption, we can use standard tools to evaluate the parameter estimates and their t-ratios. Importantly, and relevant for the material in this book, if we erroneously consider a linear time series model while a nonlinear model would have been more appropriate, the estimated residuals from the linear model often are not NID. Hence, it can be relevant to test the assumption of NID. For this purpose, we typically use a $\chi^2(2)$ normality test which consists of a component for the skewness and for the kurtosis.

Defining the jth moment of the estimated residuals as

$$\hat{m}_j = \frac{1}{n} \sum_{t=1}^{n} \hat{\varepsilon}_t{}^j, \qquad (2.51)$$

the skewness of $\hat{\varepsilon}_t$ can be calculated as

$$\widehat{SK}_{\hat{\varepsilon}} = \frac{\hat{m}_3}{\sqrt{\hat{m}_2^3}}, \qquad (2.52)$$

and the kurtosis as

$$\widehat{K}_{\hat{\varepsilon}} = \frac{\hat{m}_4}{\hat{m}_2^2}. \qquad (2.53)$$

As noted already in section 1.2, the normal distribution has skewness equal to 0 and kurtosis equal to 3. Under the null hypothesis of normality (and no autocorrelation in $\hat{\varepsilon}_t$), the standardized skewness $\sqrt{n/6} \cdot \widehat{SK}_{\hat{\varepsilon}}$ and kurtosis $\sqrt{n/24} \cdot (\widehat{K}_{\hat{\varepsilon}} - 3)$, are independent and have an asymptotic $N(0, 1)$ distribution (see Lomnicki, 1961). A joint test for normality is then given by

$$\text{norm} = \frac{n}{6} \widehat{SK}_{\hat{\varepsilon}}^2 + \frac{n}{24} (\widehat{K}_{\hat{\varepsilon}} - 3)^2, \qquad (2.54)$$

which has an asymptotic $\chi^2(2)$ distribution. Rejection of normality may indicate that there are outlying observations, that the error process is not homoscedastic, and/or that the data should better be described by a nonlinear time series model.

Model selection by evaluating in-sample fit

In case one has two or more linear (or nonlinear) time series models that pass relevant diagnostic tests, one may want to investigate which model yields the best in-sample fit. Unfortunately, the R^2 measure is not useful for linear time series models (see Nelson, 1976; Harvey, 1989), as it is only a function of the parameter values. For example, the R^2 of an AR(1) model simply equals ϕ_1^2.

More appropriate model selection criteria are the information criteria put forward by Akaike (1974) and Schwarz (1978) (which equals that proposed by Rissanen, 1978, who uses a different derivation). These criteria compare the in-sample fit, which is measured by the residual variance, against the number of estimated parameters. Let k denote the total number of parameters in the ARMA model – that is, $k = p + q + 1$. The Akaike Information Criterion (AIC) is computed as

$$\text{AIC}(k) = n \ln \hat{\sigma}^2 + 2k, \qquad (2.55)$$

where $\hat{\sigma}^2 = 1/n \sum_{t=1}^{n} \hat{\varepsilon}_t^2$, with $\hat{\varepsilon}_t$ the residuals from the ARMA model. The values of p and q that minimize AIC(k) are selected as the appropriate orders for the ARMA model. The minimization is done by varying p and q such that $k \in \{1, \ldots, \bar{k}\}$ for a certain upper bound $\bar{k}$ on the total number of parameters, which needs to be set in advance. The same rule applies to the Schwarz criterion (BIC) (originating from Bayesian arguments), which is computed as

$$\text{BIC}(k) = n \ln \hat{\sigma}^2 + k \ln n. \tag{2.56}$$

Because $\ln n > 2$ for $n > 8$, the BIC penalizes additional parameters more heavily than the AIC. Therefore, the model order selected by the BIC is likely to be smaller than that selected by the AIC. The improvement in fit caused by increasing the AR and/or MA orders needs to be quite substantial for the BIC to favour a more elaborate model. In practice, one often finds that the BIC prefers very parsimonious models, containing only few parameters. This has implications for the use of these criteria in evaluating nonlinear time series models, where sometimes quite a large number of parameters is needed to obtain only a slightly improved fit (see, for example, chapter 5).

Out-of-sample forecasting

The other main purpose of specifying a statistical model for a time series y_t, besides describing certain of its features, is to forecast future values. Let $\hat{y}_{t+h|t}$ denote a forecast of y_{t+h} made at time t, which has an associated forecast error or prediction error $e_{t+h|t}$,

$$e_{t+h|t} = y_{t+h} - \hat{y}_{t+h|t}. \tag{2.57}$$

Obviously, many different forecasts $\hat{y}_{t+h|t}$ could be used to obtain an estimate of the future value y_{t+h}. Analogous to the estimation of a time series model, where the parameters are chosen such that the residual variance is minimized, in forecasting it is often considered desirable to choose the forecast $\hat{y}_{t+h|t}$ which minimizes the squared prediction error (SPE)

$$\text{SPE}(h) \equiv \mathrm{E}[e_{t+h|t}^2] = \mathrm{E}[(y_{t+h} - \hat{y}_{t+h|t})^2]. \tag{2.58}$$

It turns out that the forecast that minimizes (2.58) is the conditional expectation of y_{t+h} at time t, that is,

$$\hat{y}_{t+h|t} = \mathrm{E}[y_{t+h}|\Omega_t] \tag{2.59}$$

(see Box and Jenkins, 1970).

To illustrate the principles of forecasting from linear ARMA models, consider first the MA(q) model

$$y_t = \sum_{i=0}^{q} \theta_i \varepsilon_{t-i}, \tag{2.60}$$

with $\theta_0 \equiv 1$. Using (2.59) and the white noise properties of ε_t, it follows that the optimal forecast ('optimal' in the squared prediction error sense) is given by

$$\hat{y}_{t+h|t} = \begin{cases} \sum_{i=h}^{q} \theta_i \varepsilon_{t+h-i} & \text{for } h = 1, \ldots, q, \\ 0 & \text{for } h > q, \end{cases} \tag{2.61}$$

whereas the corresponding forecast error follows from combining (2.60) and (2.61) as

$$e_{t+h|t} = \begin{cases} \sum_{i=0}^{h-1} \theta_i \varepsilon_{t+h-i} & \text{for } h = 1, \ldots, q, \\ \sum_{i=0}^{q} \theta_i \varepsilon_{t+h-i} & \text{for } h > q, \end{cases} \tag{2.62}$$

which can be simplified to $\varepsilon_{t+h|t} = \sum_{i=0}^{h-1} \theta_i \varepsilon_{t+h-i}$ by defining $\theta_i \equiv 0$ for $h > q$. Notice that we assume θ_i known, and hence we do not explicitly introduce additional uncertainty in (2.62) by considering $\hat{\theta}_i$ instead of θ_i. Clements and Hendry (1998) give a taxonomy of forecast errors and discuss the relative importance of the different sources of forecast uncertainty in linear time series models. Given the assumptions on ε_t it follows that

$$E[e_{t+h|t}] = 0, \tag{2.63}$$

and for the squared prediction error

$$E[e_{t+h|t}^2] = \sigma^2 \sum_{i=0}^{h-1} \theta_i^2. \tag{2.64}$$

Assuming normality, a 95 per cent forecasting interval for y_{t+h} is bounded by

$$\hat{y}_{t+h|t} - 1.96 \cdot \text{RSPE}(h) \quad \text{and} \quad \hat{y}_{t+h|t} + 1.96 \cdot \text{RSPE}(h),$$

where RSPE(h) denotes the square root of SPE(h).

Forecasting from AR models (or ARMA models in general) proceeds in a similar way. In fact, forecasts for different forecast horizons h can be obtained quite conveniently by using a recursive relationship. For example, for the AR(2) model

$$y_t = \phi_1 y_{t-1} + \phi_2 y_{t-2} + \varepsilon_t, \tag{2.65}$$

the 1-step-ahead forecast at time t is

$$\hat{y}_{t+1|t} = \phi_1 y_t + \phi_2 y_{t-1}, \tag{2.66}$$

again assuming knowledge of the values of the parameters ϕ_1 and ϕ_2. The 2-steps-ahead forecast can be derived as follows

$$
\begin{aligned}
\hat{y}_{t+2|t} &= \mathrm{E}[y_{t+2}|\Omega_t] \\
&= \phi_1 \mathrm{E}[y_{t+1}|\Omega_t] + \phi_2 y_t \\
&= \phi_1 \hat{y}_{t+1|t} + \phi_2 y_t \\
&= \phi_1(\phi_1 y_t + \phi_2 y_{t-1}) + \phi_2 y_t.
\end{aligned}
\tag{2.67}
$$

The third line of (2.67) shows the relation between the 1- and 2-steps-ahead forecasts at time t. It is not difficult to show that in general it holds that

$$
\hat{y}_{t+h|t} = \phi_1 \hat{y}_{t+h-1|t} + \phi_2 \hat{y}_{t+h-2|t},
\tag{2.68}
$$

with $\hat{y}_{t+i|t} = y_{t+i}$ for $i \leq 0$. Obviously, this recursive relationship can be used to compute multiple-steps-ahead forecasts quite easily.

To obtain expressions for the forecast error and squared prediction errors for forecasts made from ARMA(p, q) models, it is convenient to rewrite the particular model of interest as an MA(∞) model – that is, $y_t = \phi_p(L)^{-1}\theta_q(L)\varepsilon_t$ or

$$
y_t = \varepsilon_t + \eta_1\varepsilon_{t-1} + \eta_2\varepsilon_{t-2} + \eta_3\varepsilon_{t-3} + \cdots,
\tag{2.69}
$$

from which it follows that the h-step-ahead prediction error is given by

$$
e_{t+h|t} = \varepsilon_{t+h} + \eta_1\varepsilon_{t+h-1} + \cdots + \eta_{h-1}\varepsilon_{t+1},
\tag{2.70}
$$

whereas the squared prediction error becomes

$$
\mathrm{SPE}(h) = \sigma^2 \sum_{i=0}^{h-1} \eta_i^2,
\tag{2.71}
$$

with $\eta_0 \equiv 1$. For the AR(2) model, for example, it is easy to verify that $\eta_1 = \phi_1$ and $\eta_2 = \phi_1^2 + \phi_2$.

As we will demonstrate in chapter 3, for most nonlinear time series models the expressions for forecast error variances become much more complicated or even intractable analytically. In that case, we need to rely on simulation techniques to construct confidence intervals for the forecasts $\hat{y}_{t+h|t}$.

Model selection by comparing forecasts

Additional to (or instead of) selecting a model based on measures of the in-sample fit, one may also want to compare the forecasting performance of two or more alternative models. Usually one then retains m observations to evaluate h-steps-ahead forecasts generated from models fitted to the first n observations. To simplify the exposition, the various forecast evaluation criteria which are discussed below are formulated in terms of 1-step-ahead forecasts. It should be remarked in advance that they can also be applied for h-steps-ahead forecasts with $h > 1$.

A simple check on the quality of forecasts which are obtained from a model concerns the percentage of the m observations that is in the 95 per cent forecast confidence intervals. A formal test for this procedure is given in Christoffersen (1998). Additionally, a binomial test can be used to examine if the forecast errors are about equally often positive or negative.

Other criteria are the mean squared prediction error (MSPE)

$$\text{MSPE} = \frac{1}{m} \sum_{j=1}^{m} (\hat{y}_{n+j|n+j-1} - y_{n+j})^2, \tag{2.72}$$

and the mean absolute prediction error (MAPE)

$$\text{MAPE} = \frac{1}{m} \sum_{j=1}^{m} |\hat{y}_{n+j|n+j-1} - y_{n+j}|. \tag{2.73}$$

Also, because returns display rather erratic behaviour and may take sudden exceptional values, as was demonstrated in chapter 1, it sometimes makes more sense to consider the median SPE (MedSPE) and median APE (MedAPE).

If one wants to decide whether the SPEs or APEs of two alternative models A and B are significantly different, a simple procedure is to use the so-called 'loss differential'

$$d_j = e^k_{n+j|n+j-1,A} - e^k_{n+j|n+j-1,B}, \quad j = 1, 2, \ldots, m,$$

with $e_{n+j|n+j-1,A}$ and $e_{n+j|n+j-1,B}$ the forecast errors at time $n + j$ made by the forecasts from models A and B, respectively, and k equal to 2 and 1 if the goal is to compare the SPEs and APEs, respectively. One possibility to test the null hypothesis that there is no qualitative difference between the forecasts from the two models is to use the sign test statistic S, defined by

$$S = \frac{2}{\sqrt{m}} \sum_{j=1}^{m} \left(I[d_j > 0] - \frac{1}{2} \right) \overset{a}{\sim} N(0, 1). \tag{2.74}$$

Simulation results in Diebold and Mariano (1995) indicate that the S test is very useful in practice. For small values of m, one needs to use exact critical values because then the asymptotic $N(0, 1)$ distribution does not hold.

The statistic S compares only the relative magnitude of the prediction errors of models A and B. Diebold and Mariano (1995) also develop a statistic which compares the absolute magnitudes by testing whether the average loss differential $\bar{d} = \frac{1}{m}\sum_{j=1}^{m} d_j$ is significantly different from zero. The relevant test-statistic is given by

$$DM = \frac{\bar{d}}{\sqrt{\omega}} \overset{a}{\sim} N(0, 1),\tag{2.75}$$

where ω is the asymptotic variance of the average difference $\bar{d}$. Diebold and Mariano (1995) suggest estimating ω by an unweighted sum of the autocovariances of d_j, denoted $\hat{\gamma}_i(d)$, as

$$\hat{\omega} = \sum_{i=-(h-1)}^{h-1} \hat{\gamma}_i(d),\tag{2.76}$$

where h is the forecast horizon for which the prediction errors are compared. The reason for using this estimate of ω can be understood intuitively by noting that (2.70) implies that h-step-ahead forecast errors are serially correlated up to order $h - 1$. Notice that where $h = 1$, it follows from (2.76) that $\hat{\omega}$ is simply the variance of d_j, $\hat{\gamma}_0(d)$.

Out-of-sample forecasts can also be evaluated by comparing the sign of the forecasts $\hat{y}_{n+j|n+j-1}$, after subtracting the mean if this is nonzero, with the true withheld observations y_{n+j} for $j = 1, 2, \ldots, m$. This can be particularly relevant for asset returns as investors may be more interested in accurate forecasts of the direction in which, for example, the stock market is moving than in the exact magnitude of the change. For this purpose, consider the so-called success ratio (SR)

$$SR = \frac{1}{m}\sum_{j=1}^{m} I_j[y_{n+j} \cdot \hat{y}_{n+j|n+j-1} > 0].\tag{2.77}$$

Notice that SR is simply the fraction of the m forecasts $\hat{y}_{n+j|n+j-1}$ that have the same sign as the realizations y_{n+j} – or, put differently, the fraction of times the sign of y_{n+j} is predicted correctly. To evaluate the performance of the out-of-sample forecasts on this criterion, we test whether the value of SR differs significantly from the success ratio that would be obtained where y_{n+j} and $\hat{y}_{n+j|n+j-1}$ are independent. A test for this hypothesis is proposed in Pesaran and Timmermann (1992). Define

$$P = \frac{1}{m}\sum_{j=1}^{m} I_j[y_{n+j} > 0],$$

and

$$\hat{P} = \frac{1}{m} \sum_{j=1}^{m} I_j[\hat{y}_{n+j|n+j-1} > 0].$$

The success rate in case of independence (SRI) of y_{n+j} and $\hat{y}_{n+j|n+j-1}$ can be computed as

$$SRI = P\hat{P} + (1 - P)(1 - \hat{P}), \tag{2.78}$$

which has variance given by

$$\text{var}(SRI) = \frac{1}{m}[(2\hat{P} - 1)^2 P(1 - P)+$$
$$(2P - 1)^2 \hat{P}(1 - \hat{P}) + \frac{4}{m} P\hat{P}(1 - P)(1 - \hat{P})]. \tag{2.79}$$

The variance of the success ratio SR in (2.77) is equal to

$$\text{var}(SR) = \frac{1}{m} SRI(1 - SRI). \tag{2.80}$$

The so-called Directional Accuracy (DA) test of Pesaran and Timmermann (1992) is now calculated as

$$DA = \frac{(SR - SRI)}{\sqrt{\text{var}(SR) - \text{var}(SRI)}} \stackrel{a}{\sim} N(0, 1), \tag{2.81}$$

where the asymptotic standard normal distribution is obtained under the null hypothesis that y_{n+j} and $\hat{y}_{n+j|n+j-1}$ are independently distributed.

2.3   Forecasting returns with linear models

The lack of autocorrelation in stock and exchange rate returns in figures 2.1 and 2.2 suggests that *linear* association between consecutive observations is not large. Hence, linear time series models can be expected not to be very useful for forecasting returns. In this section we illustrate that this indeed is the case by performing an out-of-sample forecasting experiment for our daily return series.

In all experiments, the random walk with drift model is the benchmark that is used to evaluate the forecasting performance of more elaborate linear models. We investigate the out-of-sample forecasting performance of three alternative autoregressive models. In the first model the AR order p is specified according to the AIC given in (2.55). The preference of the BIC (2.56) for more parsimonious models is illustrated by the fact that when it is applied to the stock index and foreign exchange returns, it always opts for $p = 0$. As the AR model collapses to the random walk model in this case, this is not considered any further here. The second and third models have the AR order fixed at 5 and 10, respectively. The rationale for considering those specific lag orders is that they correspond to one and two weeks of daily observations, respectively. Furthermore, we consider models with a single intercept and models with daily intercepts. These daily intercepts are included as there is evidence that returns may display a seasonal pattern within a week (see, for example, French, 1980). The forecasts from the latter models are compared with a random walk model with a drift that is allowed to vary over the days of the week.

We examine both short- and long(er)-term forecasting performance, by focusing on return forecasts 1, 5 and 10 days ahead. The initial estimation sample is taken to be the first five years of data, from 1 January 1986 until 12 December 1990 – thus leaving 7 years of data for out-of-sample forecasting. The parameters in the models are re-estimated each day as we move forward in time. We make use of both expanding and moving samples. That is, in case of the expanding sample, the models are estimated using the entire history from January 1986, while in case of the moving sample, only the last 5 years of data are used. Besides re-estimating the model each time a new observation is added, we also allow the order selected by the AIC to vary on a day-to-day basis.

The forecasting performance of the different models is evaluated using a number of different criteria discussed in the previous section. First, we compute the MSPE, the MAPE and the MedSPE for the various models. Second, we directly compare the forecasts of the more elaborate models with the random walk forecasts by means of the *DM*-statistic given in (2.75). Third, we evaluate the ability of the various models to forecast the sign of the returns by computing the *DA*-statistic given in (2.81). All statistics are computed on a year-to-year basis, to see whether the forecastability of returns changes over time.

As the results for the stock index and exchange rate series and for the moving and expanding samples are qualitatively similar, we present only results for the forecasts of stock returns based on an expanding estimation sample. Tables 2.1–2.3 contain information on the relative magnitudes of the MSPE, MAPE and MedSPE of the different models for the expanding sample method, at forecast horizons $h = 1, 5$ and 10 days. To be precise, the tables list the mean rank of the models (taken over the 8 stock index series), where the rank of a model is equal to 1 if it attains the lowest value for the relevant criterion, 2 if it attains the second lowest value, and so on.

It is evident from these tables that the more elaborate linear models do not improve upon the random walk forecasts. On the contrary, the random walk forecasts attain the lowest mean rank in general, suggesting that the AR models

Table 2.1   *Average ranks of linear models to forecast stock returns according to MSPE, 1991–1997*

	Models with single intercept				Models with daily intercepts			
Year	RW	AIC	AR(5)	AR(10)	RW	AIC	AR(5)	AR(10)
h = 1								
1991	1.13	3.25	2.31	3.31	1.13	3.13	2.06	3.69
1992	2.00	3.06	2.06	2.88	1.75	2.88	1.69	3.69
1993	2.50	2.38	2.44	2.69	2.50	2.38	2.69	2.44
1994	1.50	2.75	2.06	3.69	1.75	2.75	1.94	3.56
1995	1.75	2.25	2.94	3.06	1.63	2.63	2.56	3.19
1996	1.81	2.94	2.31	2.94	1.69	3.06	2.31	2.94
1997	1.88	2.88	2.31	2.94	1.88	2.94	2.19	3.00
All	1.79	2.79	2.35	3.07	1.76	2.82	2.21	3.21
h = 5								
1991	1.63	3.25	1.94	3.19	1.50	3.00	1.94	3.56
1992	1.75	3.44	2.06	2.75	1.63	2.88	1.94	3.56
1993	2.13	2.38	2.69	2.81	2.38	2.25	2.69	2.69
1994	1.50	2.63	2.19	3.69	1.75	2.63	1.94	3.69
1995	1.75	2.13	2.94	3.19	2.00	2.38	2.56	3.06
1996	1.69	2.69	2.44	3.19	1.56	2.94	2.19	3.31
1997	1.88	2.75	2.56	2.81	1.75	2.81	2.31	3.13
All	1.76	2.75	2.40	3.09	1.79	2.70	2.22	3.29
h = 10								
1991	2.88	2.38	2.44	2.31	2.50	3.00	2.56	1.94
1992	2.25	2.44	2.81	2.50	2.00	2.63	2.81	2.56
1993	2.50	2.50	2.81	2.19	2.75	2.38	2.31	2.56
1994	2.63	2.00	2.44	2.94	2.50	1.88	2.56	3.06
1995	2.50	2.38	2.31	2.81	2.50	2.75	2.06	2.69
1996	1.94	2.81	2.06	3.19	2.19	2.81	1.94	3.06
1997	2.88	2.88	1.81	2.44	2.75	2.44	2.44	2.38
All	2.51	2.48	2.38	2.63	2.46	2.55	2.38	2.61

Notes: Average ranks of linear models used to forecast stock market returns *h* days ahead based on an expanding sample, according to the MSPE criterion (2.72).
RW denotes the random walk with drift, AIC denotes an AR(p) model with the order p selected by the AIC criterion.

do even worse. Note that this holds for both the models with and without daily intercepts. As the forecast horizon increases, the performance of the models becomes comparable, in the sense that the mean ranks are much closer to the mean rank of the random walk forecasts.

Table 2.2   *Average ranks of linear models to forecast stock returns according to MAPE, 1991–1997*

Year	Models with single intercept				Models with daily intercepts			
	RW	AIC	AR(5)	AR(10)	RW	AIC	AR(5)	AR(10)
$h = 1$								
1991	1.00	3.00	2.31	3.69	1.25	2.88	2.19	3.69
1992	1.25	3.19	2.44	3.13	1.63	2.50	2.56	3.31
1993	2.25	2.75	2.19	2.81	2.25	2.50	2.44	2.81
1994	1.25	3.13	2.19	3.44	1.13	2.75	2.19	3.94
1995	1.13	2.88	2.69	3.31	1.38	2.75	3.06	2.81
1996	1.19	3.19	2.69	2.94	1.94	3.06	2.31	2.69
1997	2.25	2.75	2.19	2.81	2.13	2.94	2.19	2.75
All	1.47	2.98	2.38	3.16	1.67	2.77	2.42	3.14
$h = 5$								
1991	1.13	3.25	1.94	3.69	1.13	3.13	2.06	3.69
1992	1.13	3.19	2.56	3.13	1.63	2.38	2.69	3.31
1993	2.38	2.50	2.19	2.94	2.50	2.63	2.19	2.69
1994	1.50	3.00	2.06	3.44	1.63	2.63	1.81	3.94
1995	1.50	2.75	2.44	3.31	2.13	2.75	2.31	2.81
1996	1.69	2.94	2.19	3.19	1.94	2.94	2.31	2.81
1997	2.00	2.75	2.19	3.06	1.75	2.56	2.44	3.25
All	1.62	2.91	2.22	3.25	1.81	2.71	2.26	3.21
$h = 10$								
1991	2.75	2.25	2.44	2.56	3.00	2.63	2.81	1.56
1992	2.00	2.56	2.31	3.13	2.25	2.38	2.81	2.56
1993	2.75	2.63	2.44	2.19	2.88	2.63	2.44	2.06
1994	2.38	1.88	2.56	3.19	2.25	2.00	2.44	3.31
1995	2.38	2.63	2.19	2.81	2.00	3.00	2.56	2.44
1996	2.56	2.56	2.19	2.69	2.19	2.94	2.06	2.81
1997	2.63	2.50	1.69	3.19	2.13	2.56	2.44	2.88
All	2.49	2.43	2.26	2.82	2.38	2.59	2.51	2.52

Notes: Average ranks of linear models used to forecast stock market returns h days ahead based on an expanding sample, according to the MAPE criterion (2.73).
RW denotes the random walk with drift, AIC denotes an AR(p) model with the order p selected by the AIC criterion.

To test whether the random walk forecasts are significantly different from the forecasts from the linear models, we compute the *DM*-statistic (2.75). Tables 2.4 and 2.5 report the outcomes of this pairwise model comparison, based on the squared and absolute prediction errors, respectively. The various entries indicate

Table 2.3   *Average ranks of linear models to forecast stock returns according to MedSPE, 1991–1997*

Year	Models with single intercept				Models with daily intercepts			
	RW	AIC	AR(5)	AR(10)	RW	AIC	AR(5)	AR(10)
$h = 1$								
1991	2.00	2.81	2.19	3.00	1.38	2.88	2.94	2.81
1992	2.00	2.75	2.81	2.44	1.88	2.88	2.69	2.56
1993	1.63	2.69	2.56	3.13	1.50	3.38	2.44	2.69
1994	1.75	2.75	2.44	3.06	2.13	2.50	2.44	2.94
1995	1.63	2.88	2.69	2.81	2.13	2.63	2.81	2.44
1996	2.19	2.56	2.81	2.44	2.06	2.94	2.31	2.69
1997	2.38	2.38	2.69	2.56	2.75	2.50	2.44	2.31
All	1.94	2.69	2.60	2.78	1.97	2.81	2.58	2.63
$h = 5$								
1991	2.13	3.00	1.69	3.19	1.88	3.13	1.56	3.44
1992	2.38	2.63	2.56	2.44	2.13	2.50	2.94	2.44
1993	2.00	2.38	3.31	2.31	2.13	2.25	2.44	3.19
1994	2.25	2.38	2.56	2.81	1.88	2.88	2.44	2.81
1995	1.63	3.25	2.44	2.69	2.25	2.38	2.81	2.56
1996	2.44	2.44	1.94	3.19	2.44	2.81	1.69	3.06
1997	3.00	2.50	2.19	2.31	2.63	2.38	2.69	2.31
All	2.26	2.65	2.38	2.71	2.19	2.62	2.37	2.83
$h = 10$								
1991	2.50	2.88	2.19	2.44	3.00	2.50	2.31	2.19
1992	2.75	2.25	2.56	2.44	2.25	2.63	2.81	2.31
1993	3.50	1.50	2.19	2.81	2.38	1.63	2.69	3.31
1994	2.75	2.25	2.44	2.56	2.63	2.50	2.56	2.31
1995	1.75	3.00	2.19	3.06	2.31	2.81	2.44	2.44
1996	2.44	2.56	1.94	3.06	2.44	2.44	2.56	2.56
1997	2.25	2.75	2.44	2.56	2.13	2.50	2.56	2.81
All	2.56	2.46	2.28	2.71	2.45	2.43	2.56	2.56

Notes: Average ranks of linear models used to forecast stock market returns h days ahead based on an expanding sample, according to the MedSPE criterion.
RW denotes the random walk with drift, AIC denotes an AR(p) model with the order p selected by the AIC criterion.

the number of series in a particular year (or summed over all 7 years in rows headed 'All') for which the random walk forecasts are better than the forecasts from the linear model and vice versa, at the 5 per cent significance level. As can be seen, the forecasts from the different models are not significantly different

Table 2.4   *Forecast comparison of linear models with random walk – stock returns, squared prediction errors, 1991–1997*

Year	Models with single intercept			Models with daily intercepts		
	AIC	AR(5)	AR(10)	AIC	AR(5)	AR(10)
$h = 1$						
1991	0/0	0/0	0/0	2/0	1/0	2/0
1992	1/0	0/0	0/0	0/0	0/0	0/0
1993	1/1	1/2	1/1	1/1	0/1	1/1
1994	2/0	2/0	3/0	2/0	2/0	3/0
1995	1/0	1/0	1/0	1/0	1/0	1/0
1996	1/0	0/0	1/0	1/0	0/0	1/0
1997	0/0	1/0	0/0	0/0	1/0	0/0
All	6/1	5/2	6/1	7/1	5/1	8/1
$h = 5$						
1991	1/0	1/0	0/0	2/0	0/0	1/0
1992	1/0	0/0	1/0	1/0	0/0	1/0
1993	1/0	0/0	1/1	1/0	0/0	1/1
1994	3/0	1/0	3/0	2/0	1/0	3/0
1995	1/0	2/0	2/0	1/1	2/0	2/1
1996	1/0	1/0	0/0	1/0	1/0	0/0
1997	1/0	2/0	0/0	1/0	1/0	1/0
All	9/0	7/0	7/1	9/1	5/0	9/2
$h = 10$						
1991	1/0	0/0	0/0	1/0	0/0	0/0
1992	1/0	0/0	1/1	0/0	0/0	1/1
1993	0/0	0/0	0/0	0/0	0/0	0/0
1994	0/1	0/0	2/0	0/1	1/0	1/0
1995	0/0	0/0	0/0	0/0	0/0	0/0
1996	0/0	0/0	0/0	0/0	0/0	0/0
1997	2/1	0/1	2/0	2/1	1/1	2/0
All	4/2	0/1	5/1	3/2	2/1	4/1

Notes: Comparison of forecast performance of linear models with random walk forecast of daily stock market returns h days ahead based on an expanding sample. The comparison is based on the *DM*-statistic (2.75), using squared prediction errors.

The figure preceding (following) the slash denotes the number of series for which the random walk (linear model) forecasts outperform the linear model (random walk) forecasts at the 5 per cent significance level.

AIC denotes an AR(p) model with the order p selected by the AIC criterion.

Table 2.5   *Forecast comparison of linear models with random walk – stock returns, absolute prediction errors, 1991–1997*

Year	Models with single intercept			Models with daily intercepts		
	AIC	AR(5)	AR(10)	AIC	AR(5)	AR(10)
h = 1						
1991	1/0	2/0	1/0	2/0	2/0	2/0
1992	3/0	1/0	2/0	3/0	1/0	3/0
1993	1/0	1/0	1/0	2/0	1/0	2/0
1994	3/0	2/0	5/0	2/0	3/0	4/0
1995	4/0	3/0	4/0	2/0	3/0	4/0
1996	1/0	1/0	1/0	0/0	1/0	1/0
1997	0/0	0/0	0/0	0/0	0/0	0/0
All	13/0	10/0	14/0	11/0	11/0	16/0
h = 5						
1991	1/0	1/1	1/0	2/0	0/1	1/0
1992	0/0	0/0	0/0	0/0	1/0	0/0
1993	2/0	0/0	3/0	2/0	0/0	2/0
1994	4/0	2/0	3/0	2/0	0/0	3/0
1995	2/0	3/0	3/0	1/0	3/0	1/1
1996	1/0	0/0	1/0	1/0	0/0	1/0
1997	0/0	0/0	0/0	0/0	0/0	0/0
All	10/0	6/1	11/0	8/0	4/1	8/1
h = 10						
1991	0/0	0/0	0/0	0/1	0/0	0/0
1992	1/0	1/0	2/1	0/0	1/0	1/1
1993	0/0	0/0	0/0	0/1	0/2	0/1
1994	1/1	0/0	2/1	0/1	0/0	0/1
1995	1/0	1/1	1/0	1/0	1/1	0/0
1996	0/0	1/0	0/0	0/0	1/0	0/0
1997	2/1	0/1	1/0	1/1	0/1	1/0
All	5/2	3/2	6/2	2/4	3/4	2/3

Notes: Comparison of forecast performance of linear models with random walk forecast of daily stock market returns *h* days ahead based on an expanding sample. The comparison is based on the *DM*-statistic (2.75), using absolute prediction errors.

The figure preceding (following) the slash denotes the number of series for which the random walk (linear model) forecasts outperform the linear model (random walk) forecasts at the 5 per cent significance level.

AIC denotes an AR(p) model with the order p selected by the AIC criterion.

from each other – although the random walk model seems to do particularly well in 1994.

Finally, we examine the ability of the models to forecast the sign of the stock returns, relative to the mean, by computing the *DA*-statistic (2.81). The results are shown in table 2.6. Here each entry indicates the number of series for which the model predicts the sign significantly worse/better than a completely random forecast of the sign of the return. Note that no statistics for the random walk are given. The reason for this is that forecasts from the random walk model are all equal to the estimated drift. Hence, the difference between the forecasts and their mean is always exactly equal to zero or, in other words, the sign of the forecast relative to its mean is undetermined and the *DA*-statistic cannot be computed.

In sum, we can conclude that generally linear models do not yield useful out-of-sample forecasts. Before we turn our focus on nonlinear models, we conclude this chapter with a discussion of various other features of economic and financial time series, some of which are useful for later chapters.

2.4 Unit roots and seasonality

The discussion in section 2.1 shows that the values of the autoregressive parameters in ARMA models determine whether or not time series generated from such a model are covariance stationary or not. Consider again the AR(p) model

$$y_t = \phi_1 y_{t-1} + \phi_2 y_{t-2} + \cdots + \phi_p y_{t-p} + \varepsilon_t, \tag{2.82}$$

or $\phi_p(L)y_t = \varepsilon_t$, with $\phi_p(L) = 1 - \phi_1 L - \cdots - \phi_p L^p$. Recall that the AR($p$) model is nonstationary if its characteristic equation has a solution equal to unity – or, put differently, a unit root. The presence of a unit root causes the autocorrelations to be varying over time (see (2.33)) and, hence, invalidates their use for specification of the appropriate AR order. Another consequence of nonstationarity of a linear time series is that the effect of shocks on the time series are permanent (see (2.22)).

Notice that in case of a unit root the AR polynomial $\phi_p(L)$ can be factorized as

$$\phi_p(L) = \phi_{p-1}^*(L)(1 - L), \tag{2.83}$$

where $\phi_{p-1}^*(L)$ is a lag-polynomial of order $p - 1$ which has all roots outside the unit circle. It then follows that if we apply the $(1 - L)$ filter to y_t to obtain $w_t = (1 - L)y_t$, this new variable is described by a (covariance) stationary AR($p - 1$) model. Of course, in practice the correct order p is unknown, which complicates matters slightly. The usual practice is to check if the AR polynomial in a model for y_t contains the component $(1 - L)$ – and, if so, use the variable

Table 2.6 *Performance of linear models in forecasting sign of stock returns, 1991–1997*

Year	Models with single intercept			Models with daily intercepts			
	AIC	AR(5)	AR(10)	RW	AIC	AR(5)	AR(10)
$h = 1$								
1991	1/0	2/0	0/0	1/0	1/0	1/0	2/0
1992	0/0	0/0	0/0	0/0	1/0	1/0	1/0
1993	1/0	0/0	0/1	1/0	0/0	0/0	0/0
1994	0/0	0/0	1/0	0/0	0/0	1/0	0/0
1995	1/0	1/0	1/0	0/0	1/0	0/0	0/0
1996	1/0	0/0	0/0	1/0	0/0	0/0	0/0
1997	0/0	0/0	0/0	0/0	0/0	1/0	0/1
All	4/0	3/0	2/0	3/0	3/0	4/0	3/1
$h = 5$								
1991	1/0	2/0	0/0	0/0	1/0	0/0	2/0
1992	0/0	0/0	0/0	0/0	0/0	0/0	0/0
1993	1/0	2/0	1/0	1/0	1/0	1/0	0/0
1994	4/0	1/0	1/0	1/0	1/0	1/0	1/0
1995	2/0	1/0	1/0	0/0	0/0	0/0	0/0
1996	2/0	3/0	1/0	2/0	1/0	2/0	0/0
1997	1/0	1/0	0/0	0/0	1/0	0/0	1/0
All	11/0	10/0	4/0	4/0	5/0	4/0	4/0
$h = 10$								
1991	2/0	5/0	0/0	0/0	0/0	1/0	1/0
1992	2/0	5/0	4/0	0/0	0/0	0/0	0/0
1993	3/0	7/0	1/0	1/0	1/0	1/0	0/0
1994	4/0	8/0	2/0	0/0	1/0	1/0	0/0
1995	4/0	8/0	1/0	0/0	1/0	1/0	0/0
1996	4/0	8/0	1/0	2/0	2/0	2/0	1/0
1997	4/0	7/0	1/0	0/0	1/0	0/0	0/0
All	23/0	48/0	10/0	3/0	6/0	6/0	2/0

Notes: Performance of linear models in forecasting the sign of stock market returns h days ahead based on an expanding sample. The evaluation is based on the *DA*-statistic (2.81).

The figure preceding (following) the slash denotes the number of series for which the no-change (linear model) forecasts outperform the linear model (no-change) forecasts at the 5 per cent significance level.

AIC denotes an AR(p) model with the order p selected by the AIC criterion. Further details concerning the methodology are given in section 2.3.

w_t in a next round of model identification. In this section we provide some details on testing for the presence of unit roots or permanent (or persistent) shocks. There is of course much more to say about this issue, and the interested reader should consult, for example, Banerjee *et al.* (1993); Hatanaka (1996); and Boswijk (2001), among many others.

Deterministic terms

An important consequence of a unit root in the AR(p) polynomial is that the regressors for the nonzero mean and trend appear differently in models with and without unit roots. This can be illustrated for the simple AR(1) model, where we now consider y_t in deviation from a mean and trend, that is,

$$y_t - \mu - \delta t = \phi_1 (y_{t-1} - \mu - \delta(t-1)) + \varepsilon_t, \quad t = 1, \ldots, n. \quad (2.84)$$

This can be written as

$$y_t = \mu^* + \delta^* t + \phi_1 y_{t-1} + \varepsilon_t, \quad (2.85)$$

where $\mu^* = (1 - \phi_1)\mu + \phi_1 \delta$ and $\delta^* = (1 - \phi_1)\delta$. Defining $z_t = y_t - \mu - \delta t$, we can solve (2.85) as

$$z_t = (\phi_1)^t z_0 + \sum_{i=1}^{t} (\phi_1)^{t-i} \varepsilon_i,$$

where z_0 denotes a starting value as usual.

When $|\phi_1| < 1$, the shocks to z_t (and hence to y_t after correction for a mean and trend) are transitory, in the sense that the effect of ε_t on z_{t+k} dies out when k increases without bound. Writing (2.85) as $\Delta_1 z_t = (\phi_1 - 1)z_{t-1} + \varepsilon_t$, positive values of z_{t-1} will lead to a decrease in z_t, and negative values lead to an increase. As positive and negative values of z_t correspond with y_t being larger or smaller than its (trending) mean $\mu + \delta t$, y_t displays so-called *mean- (or trend-)reverting behaviour*. As a deterministic trend variable t is included in (2.85), the time series y_t is said to be *trend-stationary* (TS).

When $\phi_1 = 1$, (2.85) becomes

$$y_t = \delta + y_{t-1} + \varepsilon_t, \quad (2.86)$$

where the trend variable is seen to have disappeared. This model concerns a random walk with drift δ. Recursive substitution results in

$$y_t = y_0 + \delta t + \sum_{i=1}^{t} \varepsilon_i. \quad (2.87)$$

The partial sum time series $S_t = \sum_{i=1}^{t} \varepsilon_i$ is called the *stochastic trend*.

When ε_t in (2.84) is replaced by $\eta_t = [\phi_{p-1}(L)]^{-1}\varepsilon_t$, where $\phi_{p-1}(L)$ does not contain the component $(1 - L)$, one has an $AR(p)$ model with a stochastic trend. Hence, when an $AR(p)$ polynomial can be decomposed as $\phi_{p-1}(L)(1 - L)$, the time series y_t has a stochastic trend. A time series with a stochastic trend can be made stationary by applying the differencing filter Δ_1. Therefore, in this case the time series y_t is called *difference-stationary* (DS).

As noted before, a time series y_t that requires the first-differencing filter Δ_1 to remove the stochastic trend also is called a time series that is integrated of order 1 $(I(1))$. An $I(2)$ time series needs the Δ_1 filter twice to become stationary. Intuitively, a time series with a growth rate that fluctuates as a random walk is an $I(2)$ series. The impact of past shocks can be demonstrated by recursive substitution of lagged y_t in $\Delta_1^2 y_t = \delta + \varepsilon_t$ as

$$y_t = y_0 + z_0 t + \delta t(t + 1)/2 + \sum_{i=1}^{t}\sum_{j=1}^{i}\varepsilon_j, \qquad (2.88)$$

where y_0 and z_0 are values that depend on pre-sample observations. This result shows that when δ is positive, an $I(2)$ time series displays explosive growth because of the $t(t + 1)/2$ component. Haldrup (1998) gives a comprehensive survey of the analysis of $I(2)$ time series.

Testing for unit roots

If $z = 1$ is a solution to the characteristic equation of the $AR(p)$ model, it holds that

$$\phi_p(1) = 1 - \phi_1 - \phi_2 - \cdots - \phi_p = 0. \qquad (2.89)$$

This shows that for an $AR(p)$ time series with a unit root, the sum of the AR parameters equals 1. To test the empirical validity of the relevant parameter restriction, it is useful to decompose the $AR(p)$ polynomial $\phi_p(L)$ as

$$\phi_p(L) = (1 - \phi_1 - \phi_2 - \cdots - \phi_p)L^i + \phi_{p-1}^*(L)(1 - L), \qquad (2.90)$$

which holds for any $i \in \{1, 2, \ldots, p\}$. Setting $i = 1$, an $AR(2)$ polynomial, for example, can be written as

$$1 - \phi_1 L - \phi_2 L^2 = (1 - \phi_1 - \phi_2)L + (1 + \phi_2 L)(1 - L). \qquad (2.91)$$

Hence ϕ_0^* and ϕ_1^* in (2.90) are 1 and $-\phi_2$, respectively. Replacing $\phi_2(L)$ by the right-hand side of (2.91), the $AR(2)$ model can thus be written as

$$\phi_{p-1}^*(L)\Delta_1 y_t = (\phi_1 + \phi_2 - 1)y_{t-1} + \varepsilon_t, \qquad (2.92)$$

with $\phi_{p-1}^*(L) = (1 - \phi_1^* L)$. When $\phi_1 + \phi_2 - 1$ equals zero, (2.92) becomes an $AR(1)$ model for $\Delta_1 y_t$.

Based on (2.90), Dickey and Fuller (1979) propose to test for a unit root by testing the statistical relevance of y_{t-1} in the auxiliary regression

$$\Delta_1 y_t = \rho y_{t-1} + \alpha_1^* \Delta_1 y_{t-1} + \cdots + \alpha_{p-1}^* \Delta_1 y_{t-(p-1)} + \varepsilon_t, \quad (2.93)$$

where $\alpha_i^* = -\phi_i^*$. The null hypothesis is $\rho = 0$ and the relevant alternative is $\rho < 0$, resulting in a one-sided test-statistic. The t-test-statistic for ρ $[t(\hat{\rho})]$ commonly is referred to as the Augmented Dickey–Fuller (ADF) test-statistic. Phillips (1987) derives the nonstandard asymptotic distribution of the ADF statistic. The distribution is nonstandard because under the null hypothesis of a unit root, the y_t series is nonstationary and standard limit theory does not apply. The critical values for $t(\hat{\rho})$ have to be obtained through Monte Carlo simulation (see, for example, Fuller, 1996, for a tabulation of the appropriate critical values).

Hall (1994) shows that when the order p in the AR(p) model for y_t is selected through sequential t-tests on the α_{p-1}^* to α_1^* parameters in the so-called ADF regression (2.93), the same critical values can be used (see also Ng and Perron, 1995). Furthermore, Said and Dickey (1984) argue that the same is true if data which are generated from an ARMA model are approximated by an AR model, provided that the AR order $p - 1$ in (2.93) is set at a high enough value. Obviously, for such an ARMA model, the MA component should not be approximately similar to the AR component because that would lead to (near-) cancellation of polynomials and hence to great difficulties to test for a unit root in the AR polynomial (see Schwert, 1989). Finally, Dickey and Pantula (1987) show that critical values for $t(\hat{\rho})$ can be used for testing for two unit roots, provided that one replaces y_t for $\Delta_1 y_t$ in (2.93). An excellent survey on unit root testing is given in Phillips and Xiao (1998).

Comparing (2.86) with (2.85), we see that the parameter μ for the mean is not identified under the null hypothesis of a unit root, but that it is identified only under the alternative hypothesis. In general, it appears best to include a mean and linear trend in the ADF regression, to make the test independent of nuisance parameters. The ADF regression then becomes

$$\Delta_1 y_t = \mu^{**} + \delta^{**} t + \rho y_{t-1} + \alpha_1^* \Delta_1 y_{t-1} + \cdots + \alpha_{p-1}^* \Delta_1 y_{t-(p-1)} + \varepsilon_t.$$
$$(2.94)$$

Under the unit root hypothesis, ρ and δ^{**} are both equal to zero. Dickey and Fuller (1981) develop a joint F-test for the hypothesis $\rho = \delta^{**} = 0$, and in the case of no trends, for $\rho = \mu^{**} = 0$. A common practical procedure, however, is to test $\rho = 0$ in (2.94) and to consider critical values depending on the type of deterministic regressors included.

Testing for stationarity

A test for the null hypothesis of stationarity (with the unit root hypothesis as the alternative) is developed in Kwiatkowski *et al.* (KPSS). It focuses on the estimated partial sum series

$$\hat{S}_t = \sum_{i=1}^{t} \hat{e}_i, \tag{2.95}$$

where the relevant $\hat{e}_t$ are obtained from an auxiliary regression like

$$y_t = \hat{\tau} + \hat{\delta} t + \hat{e}_t. \tag{2.96}$$

The test-statistic of interest is

$$\eta = \frac{1}{n^2 s^2(l)} \sum_{t=1}^{n} \hat{S}_t^2, \tag{2.97}$$

where the scaling factor $s^2(l)$ is the so-called *long-run variance* of $\hat{e}_t$. Phillips (1987) and Phillips and Perron (1988) propose to estimate this quantity by

$$\hat{s}^2(l) = \frac{1}{n} \sum_{t=1}^{n} \hat{e}_t^2 + \frac{2}{n} \sum_{j=1}^{l} w(j,l) \sum_{t=j+1}^{n} \hat{e}_t \hat{e}_{t-j}, \tag{2.98}$$

where the weights $w(j,l)$ can be set equal to

$$w(j,l) = 1 - j/(l+1), \tag{2.99}$$

following Newey and West (1987), although one can also use other weights. The value of l is usually set at $l = n^{1/2}$ (see Newey and West, 1994).

The test-statistic for the null hypothesis of stationarity is

$$\hat{\eta} = \frac{1}{n^2 \hat{s}^2(l)} \sum_{t=1}^{n} \hat{S}_t^2. \tag{2.100}$$

The asymptotic distribution of this test-statistic is derived in Kwiatkowski *et al.* (1992).

Impulse response function

The two methods for analysing the stationarity properties of time series outlined in this section so far assume that the data can best be described by a linear time series model. For some specific nonlinear models, parameter restrictions have been derived that correspond with persistence of the shocks. We will discuss a few examples in chapter 3. However, for many other nonlinear models, such expressions do not exist. Simulation techniques should then be useful to investigate the persistence of shocks. This persistence is usually measured through the impulse response function (IRF).

Consider again the AR(p) model

$$y_t = \phi_1 y_{t-1} + \phi_2 y_{t-2} + \cdots + \phi_p y_{t-p} + \varepsilon_t \quad t = 1, \ldots, n. \quad (2.101)$$

Using recursive substitution we obtain a generalization of (2.15) in which the current observation y_t is expressed in terms of the starting values $y_0, \ldots, y_{1-p}$, and the current and past shocks $\varepsilon_t, \ldots, \varepsilon_1$, as

$$y_t = \sum_{i=1}^{p} \phi_i^t y_{1-i} + \sum_{i=0}^{t-1} c_i \varepsilon_{t-i}, \quad (2.102)$$

where the sequence $c_1, \ldots, c_{t-1}$ is defined from the recursion

$$c_i = \sum_{j-1}^{\min(i,p)} \phi_j c_{i-j} \quad \text{for } i = 1, 2, \ldots, \quad (2.103)$$

with $c_0 \equiv 1$. Note that the coefficient c_k defines the effect of the shock ε_{t-k} on the current observation y_t – or, equivalently, the effect of the current shock ε_t on the future observation y_{t+k}, provided that all intermediate shocks are held constant. The sequence $\{c_k, k = 0, 1, \ldots\}$ is called the impulse response function. An alternative definition of the IRF, due to Sims (1980), is

$$IRF(k, \delta) = \mathrm{E}[y_{t+k} | \varepsilon_t = \delta, \varepsilon_{t+1} = \cdots = \varepsilon_{t+k} = 0]$$
$$- \mathrm{E}[y_{t+k} | \varepsilon_t = 0, \varepsilon_{t+1} = \cdots = \varepsilon_{t+k} = 0], \quad (2.104)$$

which measures the effect of a shock δ occurring at time t relative to the situation where no shock occurs at time t, while setting the shocks in intermediate periods $t+1, \ldots, t+k$ equal to zero. In linear models, the impulse response (2.104) is in fact independent of the intermediate shocks $\varepsilon_{t+1}, \ldots, \varepsilon_{t+k}$ and of the history or past $y_{t-1}, y_{t-2}, \ldots$, up to the moment when the shock of interest occurs, and linear in the size of the shock δ. To make the latter more precise, it is straightforward to see from (2.102) that IRF$(k, \delta) = c_k \delta$. The time series y_t is said to have transient shocks if the effect of the shock ε_t on future observations dies out eventually – or, more formally, if $\lim_{k \to \infty} c_k = 0$. In the AR($p$) model, this is the case if and only if the characteristic equation $1 - \phi_1 z - \cdots - \phi_p z^p = 0$ does not contain a unit root – that is, if the process is stationary. This can most easily be understood by comparing (2.15) and (2.22) for the AR(1) case. If the impulse responses do not die out, the process has permanent or persistent shocks, and we may define $\lim_{k \to \infty} c_k$ as the degree of persistence, provided the limit exists, of course. In subsequent chapters, we will often rely on (modifications of) the IRF to measure the persistence of shocks for nonlinear models.

Fractional integration

The concept of fractional integration (FI) within the context of ARIMA models was independently put forward by Granger and Joyeux (1980) and Hosking (1981). A fractionally integrated model appears useful to describe a time series with very long cycles for which it is difficult to estimate its mean. Typically, the application of such a model concerns inflation rates and returns on exchange rates and their volatility, see Cheung (1993); Hassler and Wolters (1995); Baillie, Bollerslev and Mikkelsen (1996); and Bos, Franses and Ooms (1999), among others.

The basic fractionally integrated time series model is defined as

$$(1 - L)^d y_t = \varepsilon_t, \quad 0 < \delta < 1, \tag{2.105}$$

where the differencing operator $(1 - L)^d$ can be expanded as

$$(1 - L)^d = 1 - dL - \frac{d(1 - d)}{2} L^2 - \frac{d(1 - d)(2 - d)}{6} L^3$$
$$- \cdots - \frac{d(1 - d)(2 - d) \cdots ((j - 1) - d)}{j!} L^j - \cdots, \tag{2.106}$$

which becomes 1 for $d = 0$ and $(1 - L)$ for $d = 1$. When $0 < d < 0.5$, the time series is said to be long-memory, and when $0.5 < d < 1$, it is nonstationary. Clearly, (2.106) shows that a fractionally integrated time series model compares with an AR(∞) model. The reason why this model is called 'long-memory' is that the autocovariances of fractionally integrated time series decay towards zero at a much slower rate than the autocovariances of stationary AR time series with $d = 0$. Estimation routines for general ARFIMA models, which include additional AR and MA parts in (2.105) are proposed in Sowell (1992) and Beran (1995).

Seasonality

Next to a trend, a second quite dominant source of variation in many economic time series is seasonality. This applies mainly to macroeconomic time series and to data in marketing, but many financial returns series also display some form of seasonal variation, as we will indicate below. Here we briefly outline two commonly considered models for seasonal data. The first assumes that seasonal variation appears in the lag structure. For example, for daily data this means that y_{t-5} may be a relevant variable. The second model assumes seasonal variation in the ARMA parameters. The resultant models are usually called 'periodic models'.

A seasonally observed time series y_t, $t = 1, 2, \ldots, n$, is observed during S seasons in a specific time interval, where S may take such values as 12, 52 or 5. For macroeconomic data, this interval usually concerns a year, while for financial returns, one may think of minutes in a day, or days in a week. The data may have a nonzero mean μ_s for $s = 1, 2, \ldots, S$. Furthermore, $D_{s,t}$, $s = 1, 2, \ldots, S$ denote seasonal dummy variables, where $D_{s,t}$ takes a value of 1 in season s and a value of 0 in other seasons.

Consider again the AR(p) model for y_t

$$y_t = \phi_{0,1} D_{1,t} + \cdots + \phi_{0,S} D_{S,t} + \phi_1 y_{t-1} + \cdots + \phi_p y_{t-p} + \varepsilon_t, \quad (2.107)$$

where the intercept $\phi_{0,S}$ is allowed to vary to allow the mean to vary across different seasons. Note that $\mu_s = \phi_{0,s}/(1 - \phi_1 - \cdots - \phi_p)$. If seasonal variation is approximately deterministic, one will find that the estimated means $\hat{\mu}_s \neq \hat{\mu}$, where $\hat{\mu}$ is the estimated mean from an AR(p) model with a single intercept. Consider for example the evidence in table 2.7, where we observe that returns and volatility of the stock index series tend to be higher on Mondays compared to other days of the week.

Table 2.7   *Daily means and variances of stock index returns*

Stock market	Monday	Tuesday	Wednesday	Thursday	Friday	St. err.
Daily means						
Amsterdam	−0.061	0.089	0.145	0.009	0.010	0.045
Frankfurt	−0.056	0.017	0.125	0.040	0.048	0.049
Hong Kong	−0.142	0.109	0.217	−0.041	0.142	0.068
London	−0.083	0.076	0.095	0.038	0.079	0.037
New York	−0.029	0.105	0.087	−0.005	0.027	0.040
Paris	−0.174	0.088	0.087	0.087	0.041	0.051
Singapore	−0.089	0.034	0.063	0.032	0.056	0.040
Tokyo	−0.160	0.032	0.070	0.103	−0.020	0.054
Daily variances						
Amsterdam	2.013	1.087	1.313	1.082	0.875	0.218
Frankfurt	2.387	1.524	1.347	1.178	1.147	0.225
Hong Kong	5.895	2.214	2.312	2.177	1.651	1.232
London	1.030	0.943	0.730	0.732	0.768	0.172
New York	1.787	0.815	0.666	0.774	0.881	0.391
Paris	2.004	1.213	1.374	1.413	1.127	0.186
Singapore	1.852	0.841	0.785	0.856	0.751	0.213
Tokyo	2.286	1.994	1.780	1.487	1.617	0.273

Notes: Daily means of stock market returns (upper panel) and squared residuals from regression of returns on daily dummies (lower panel).

The sample period is 6 January 1986 until 31 December 1997, which equals 3,127 observations.

Loosely speaking, if seasonal variation appears in the lags, (2.107) contains y_{t-S}, y_{t-2S}, and so on. If the AR parameters in (2.107) are such that the differencing filter Δ_S is required to transform y_t to stationarity, a time series is said to be seasonally integrated. Writing $\Delta_S = (1 - L^S)$ and solving the equation

$$(1 - z^S) = 0 \tag{2.108}$$

or

$$\exp(Si\phi) = 1,$$

for z or ϕ, demonstrates that the solutions to (2.108) are equal to 1 and $\cos(2\pi k/S) + i\sin(2\pi k/S)$ for $k = 1, 2, \ldots, S - 1$. This amounts to S different solutions, which all lie on the unit circle. The first solution 1 is called the nonseasonal unit root and the $S - 1$ other solutions are called seasonal unit roots (see Hylleberg *et al.*, 1990). When a time series has seasonal unit roots, shocks change the seasonal pattern permanently. There are several tests for seasonal unit roots, but empirical evidence obtained so far (see Osborn, 1990; Clare, Psaradakis and Thomas, 1995) indicates that seasonal unit roots are quite unlikely for stock index and exchange rate returns (and their volatility).

An alternative seasonal model is a *periodic autoregression* (PAR) (see Franses, 1996, for extensive discussion). It extends a nonperiodic AR(p) model by allowing the autoregressive parameters $\phi_1, \ldots, \phi_p$ to vary with the seasons. In other words, the PAR model assumes that the observations in each of the seasons can be described by a different model. Such a property may be useful as sometimes one may expect economic agents to have different memory in different seasons. Hence, correlations between daily returns and volatility can also display day-of-the-week effects. For example, it is well documented that returns on Mondays are positively correlated with those on the preceding Fridays, while returns on Tuesdays are negatively correlated with those on Mondays (see Boudoukh, Richardson and Whitelaw, 1994, among others). It is precisely in such situations that PAR models may be useful. Applications of PAR models to stock index returns can be found in Bessembinder and Hertzel (1993) and Abraham and Ikenberry (1994). Bollerslev and Ghysels (1996) discuss PAR models for volatility, while Franses and Paap (2000) explore a combination of periodic models for both returns and volatilities.

To illustrate, table 2.8 contains daily first-order autocorrelations for the returns and squared returns of our stock index series. It appears that the day-of-the-week effects in the autocorrelations for the returns themselves are largely an American phenomenon, in the sense that only for the S&P 500 series it is evident that indeed returns on Mondays are positively correlated with those on the preceding Fridays, while returns on Tuesdays are negatively correlated with

Table 2.8 *Periodic autocorrelations of stock returns*

Stock market	Monday	Tuesday	Wednesday	Thursday	Friday
Daily returns					
Amsterdam	0.002	0.002	−0.027	−0.003	0.006
Frankfurt	0.018	−0.021	−0.013	−0.003	0.006
Hong Kong	0.033	−0.045	−0.028	0.026	−0.008
London	0.026	0.063	−0.035	−0.015	0.023
New York	0.047	−0.085	0.026	−0.004	0.013
Paris	0.018	0.004	−0.009	−0.016	0.022
Singapore	0.071	−0.001	0.004	0.037	0.044
Tokyo	0.028	−0.024	−0.023	−0.002	0.011
Daily squared returns					
Amsterdam	0.004	0.134	0.078	0.412	0.010
Frankfurt	0.004	0.240	0.093	0.097	0.008
Hong Kong	0.001	0.245	0.227	0.109	0.012
London	0.002	0.413	0.637	0.198	0.013
New York	0.116	0.765	0.093	0.059	0.002
Paris	0.016	0.044	0.015	0.156	0.013
Singapore	0.033	0.100	0.061	0.028	0.092
Tokyo	0.015	0.018	0.439	0.050	0.032

Notes: Daily first-order autocorrelations of stock market returns (upper panel) and squared residuals from regression of returns on daily dummies (lower panel).
The sample period is 6 January 1986 until 31 December 1997, which equals 3,127 observations.

those on Mondays. For the squared returns, on the other hand, the autocorrelations vary quite dramatically during the week for all series.

In principle, the nonlinear models discussed in the following chapters can be extended to allow for various forms of seasonality. Although examples of such models exist in the literature, there still is much further research to do on how one should incorporate seasonality in nonlinear time series models. We will therefore abstain from a detailed discussion on this matter and, consequently, consider mainly weekly data for the forthcoming nonlinear models.

2.5 Aberrant observations

As has become clear in chapter 1, quite a number of observations on financial time series may be viewed as aberrant. A recurring question often concerns whether an aberrant observation somehow belongs to the time series, in the sense that it is part of the data-generating process (DGP), or that it should be viewed as a measurement error. Aberrant data may also appear in clusters. For example, returns may sometimes show periods of structurally different volatility (owing to exogenous events), and one may examine if this corresponds to the DGP or not. This is particularly relevant for the models to be discussed in chapter 4, as they assume that temporary periods of high or low volatility are part of the process. Hence, when modelling linear or nonlinear data, it is important to study the presence of aberrant observations and their effects on modelling and forecasting. In this section, we therefore review the time series representations of the so-called *additive outlier* (AO), *innovative outlier* (IO) and *level shift* (LS).

An additive outlier can be viewed as an observation which is the genuine data point plus or minus some value. This latter value can be nonzero because of a recording error or by misinterpreting sudden news flashes, which in turn can cause returns on stock markets to take unexpectedly large absolute values. In other words, in the case of an AO, the data point is aberrant because of a cause outside the intrinsic economic environment that generates the time series data. Given a time series y_t, it is clear that additive outliers cannot be predicted using the historical information set Ω_{t-1}.

An additive outlier can be described by

$$y_t = x_t + \omega I[t = \tau], \quad t = 1, \ldots, n, \tag{2.109}$$

where $I[t = \tau]$ is an indicator variable, taking a value of 1 when $t = \tau$ and a value of zero otherwise. The time series x_t is the uncontaminated but unobserved time series, while y_t is the observed variable. The size of the outlier is denoted by ω. Notice that, in practice, the value of τ may be unknown.

Suppose that we observe a time series y_t as defined by (2.109) and want to describe this series by an AR(1) model. To get a quick impression of the correlation between y_t and y_{t-1} and hence, the value of the autoregressive parameter ϕ_1 that is to be expected, we might make a scatterplot of y_t versus y_{t-1}. In such a plot, the AO shows up as two irregular data points, corresponding to the observation pairs $(y_\tau, y_{\tau-1})$ and $(y_{\tau+1}, y_\tau)$. An example is shown in panels (a) and (c) of figure 2.3, where the time series x_t is generated according to an AR(1) model $x_t = \phi_1 x_{t-1} + \varepsilon_t$, with $\phi_1 = 0.7$ and $\varepsilon_t \sim \text{NID}(0, \sigma^2)$, $\sigma = 0.1$. A single AO of size $\omega = 5\sigma$ occurs at $t = \tau = 50$. When we apply OLS to estimate the parameters in an AR(1) model for y_t, neglecting this AO, the observation $(y_{\tau+1}, y_\tau)$ will have a downward-biasing effect on $\hat{\phi}_1$ (see Lucas, 1996). Also, AOs yield large values of skewness and kurtosis because the two observations at time τ and $\tau + 1$ cannot be properly predicted by the model. Finally, the estimated standard error for the $\hat{\phi}_1$ parameter will increase with increasing ω.

A second important type of outlier is the innovative outlier, where the outlier now occurs in the noise process. An ARMA(p, q) model including an IO at

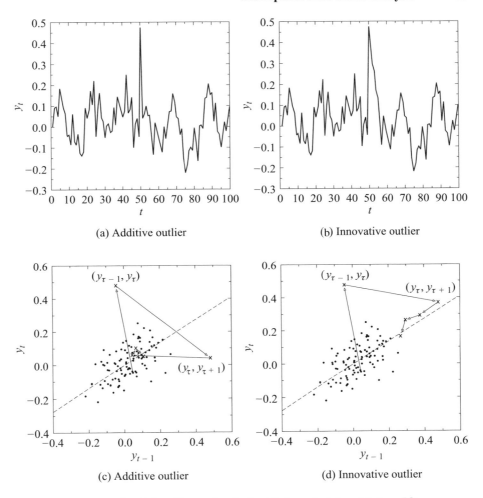

Figure 2.3   Example of the effects of a single AO (panels (a) and (c)) or IO (panels (b) and (d))

The series x_t is generated according to an AR(1) model $x_t = \phi_1 x_{t-1} + \varepsilon_t$, with $\phi_1 = 0.7$ and $\varepsilon_t \sim \text{NID}(0, \sigma^2)$, $\sigma = 0.1$; a single outlier of size 5σ occurs at $t = \tau = 50$; the dashed line in panels (c) and (d) indicates the AR(1) regression line, $y_t = \phi_1 y_{t-1}$

time τ is

$$y_t = x_t + \omega \frac{\theta_q(L)}{\phi_p(L)} I[t = \tau], \qquad (2.110)$$

where $\phi_p(L)x_t = \theta_q(L)\varepsilon_t$. An alternative representation is

$$\phi_p(L)y_t = \theta_q(L)(\varepsilon_t + \omega I[t = \tau]), \qquad (2.111)$$

which clearly shows that an IO is an atypical observation in the noise process. For illustration, consider the AR(1) model with an IO at time τ, that is

$$y_t = \phi_1 y_{t-1} + \varepsilon_t + \omega I[t = \tau]. \tag{2.112}$$

This expression shows that for most observations the predicted value of y_t is $\phi_1 y_{t-1}$. In case the IO is neglected, the optimal 1-step-ahead forecast of y_τ is $\hat{y}_{\tau|\tau-1} = \phi_1 y_{\tau-1}$, and the associated forecast error equals $e_{\tau|\tau-1} = \varepsilon_\tau + \omega$. This forecast error does not have expectation equal to zero – and, hence, the predictor for y_τ is biased. However, in contrast to the AO model, the predictor for the next observation $y_{\tau+1}$ has no bias. In a scatterplot of y_t versus y_{t-1}, one would observe only the single aberrant combination $(y_\tau, y_{\tau-1})$, while all other combinations lie close to the regression line. As this combination lies above the bulk of the data, the OLS estimate $\hat{\phi}_1$ may show little bias. Panels (b) and (d) of figure 2.3 show an example, where the series y_t is generated according to (2.112) with $\phi_1 = 0.7$ and and $\varepsilon_t \sim \text{NID}(0, \sigma^2)$, $\sigma = 0.1$. A single IO of size $\omega = 5\sigma$ occurs at $t = \tau = 50$. When an IO is neglected for an AR(1) series, one will have only a single extraordinarily large estimated residual, owing to the fact that $\hat{\phi}_1 y_{\tau-1}$ is a biased predictor for y_τ.

When ϕ_1 in (2.112) equals 1, it is clear that an IO at time τ can result in a permanent change in the level of a time series. An alternative description of such a level shift in case of an AR(p) model, which does not require that $\phi_1 = 1$, is given by the model including a level shift

$$\phi_p(L)y_t = \phi_0 + \omega I[t \geq \tau] + \varepsilon_t, \tag{2.113}$$

where the mean of y_t shifts from $\phi_0/(1 - \phi_1 - \cdots - \phi_p)$ in the first part of the sample to $(\phi_0 + \omega)/(1 - \phi_1 - \cdots - \phi_p)$ in the second part.

There are several methods to test for the presence of additive outliers, innovative outliers and level shifts. A first set of methods consider a search over all possible dates τ for the presence of some type of aberrant data (see, for example, Tsay, 1988; Chen and Liu, 1993). These techniques can be viewed as diagnostic checks for model adequacy. Notice that because of this searching, which leads to sequences of decision rules based on, for example, the 5 per cent significance level, the test-statistics may not be distributed as χ^2 or standard normal.

A second method to guard against the influence of aberrant observations is to use robust estimation methods (see Huber, 1981; Hampel *et al.*, 1986, for general introductions to such robust estimation methods). Denby and Martin (1979), Bustos and Yohai (1986) and, more recently, Lucas (1996) discuss how these methods can be used to estimate the parameters in linear time series models. Here we illustrate the intuition behind a particular form of such estimation techniques, the Generalized M (GM) estimator, in the context of the AR(1) model

$$y_t = \phi_1 y_{t-1} + \varepsilon_t, \quad t = 1, \ldots, n. \tag{2.114}$$

A GM estimator of the autoregressive parameter ϕ_1 in (2.114) can be defined as the solution to the first-order condition

$$\sum_{t=1}^{n} (y_t - \phi_1 y_{t-1}) y_{t-1} \cdot w_r(r_t) = 0, \tag{2.115}$$

where r_t denotes the standardized residual, $r_t \equiv (y_t - \phi_1 y_{t-1})/(\sigma_\varepsilon w_y(y_{t-1}))$, with σ_ε a measure of scale of the residuals $\varepsilon_t \equiv y_t - \phi_1 y_{t-1}$ and $w_z(\cdot)$ a weight function that is bounded between 0 and 1. From (2.115) it can be seen that the GM estimator is a type of weighted least squares estimator, with the weight for the tth observation given by the value of $w_r(\cdot)$. As mentioned above, an AO at $t = \tau$ shows up as an aberrant value of y_τ and/or $(y_{\tau+1} - \phi_1 y_\tau)/\sigma_\varepsilon$, whereas the latter can also be caused by an AO at time $\tau + 1$ of course. The functions $w_y(\cdot)$ and $w_r(\cdot)$ should be chosen such that the $\tau + 1$st observation receives a relatively small weight if either the regressor y_τ or the standardized residual $(y_{\tau+1} - \phi_1 y_\tau)/\sigma_\varepsilon$ becomes large, such that the outlier does not influence the estimates of ϕ_1 and σ_ε.

The weight function $w_r(r_t)$ usually is specified in terms of a function $\psi(r_t)$ as $w_r(r_t) = \psi(r_t)/r_t$ for $r_t \neq 0$ and $w_r(0) = 1$. Common choices for the $\psi(\cdot)$ function are the Huber and Tukey bisquare functions. The Huber ψ function is given by

$$\psi(r_t) = \begin{cases} -c & \text{if } r_t \leq -c, \\ r_t & \text{if } -c < r_t \leq c, \\ c & \text{if } r_t > c, \end{cases} \tag{2.116}$$

or $\psi(r) = \text{med}(-c, c, r)$, where med denotes the median and $c > 0$. The tuning constant c determines the robustness and efficiency of the resulting estimator. Because these properties are decreasing and increasing functions of c, respectively, the tuning constant should be chosen such that the two are balanced. Usually c is taken equal to 1.345 to produce an estimator that has an efficiency of 95 per cent compared to the OLS estimator if ε_t is normally distributed. The weights $w_r(r_t)$ implied by the Huber function have the attractive property that $w_r(r_t) = 1$ if $-c \leq r_t < c$. Only observations for which the standardized residual is outside this region receive less weight. A disadvantage is that these weights decline to zero only very slowly. Subjective judgement is thus required to decide whether a weight is small or not.

The Tukey bisquare function is given by

$$\psi(r_t) = \begin{cases} r_t(1 - (r_t/c)^2)^2 & \text{if } |r_t| \leq c, \\ 0 & \text{if } |r_t| > c. \end{cases} \tag{2.117}$$

The tuning constant c again determines the robustness and the efficiency of the resultant estimator. Usually c is set equal to 4.685, again to achieve 95 per cent efficiency for normally distributed ε_t. The Tukey function might be considered as the mirror image of the Huber function, in the sense that downweighting occurs for all nonzero values of r_t, but the resulting weights decline to 0 quite rapidly.

A third possibility is the polynomial ψ function as proposed in Lucas, van Dijk and Kloek (1996), given by

$$\psi(r_t) = \begin{cases} r_t & \text{if } |r_t| \leq c_1, \\ \text{sgn}(r_t)g(|r_t|) & \text{if } c_1 < |r_t| \leq c_2, \\ 0 & \text{if } |r_t| > c_2, \end{cases} \tag{2.118}$$

or more compactly,

$$\psi(r_t) = r_t I[|r_t| \leq c_1] + I[|r_t| > c_1]I[|r_t| \leq c_2]\text{sgn}(r_t)g(|r_t|), \tag{2.119}$$

where c_1 and c_2 are tuning constants, sgn is the signum function and $g(|r_t|)$ is a fifth-order polynomial such that $\psi(r_t)$ is twice continuously differentiable. This ψ function combines the attractive properties of the Huber and Tukey ψ functions. Observations receive a weight $w_r(r_t) = \psi(r_t)/r_t$ equal to 1 if their standardized residuals are within $(-c_1, c_1)$ and a weight equal to zero if the residuals are larger than c_2 in absolute value. The polynomial $g(|r_t|)$ is such that partial weighting occurs in between. The tuning constants c_1 and c_2 are taken to be the square roots of the 0.99 and 0.999 quantiles of the $\chi^2(1)$ distribution – that is, $c_1 = 2.576$ and $c_2 = 3.291$.

The weights implied by the three ψ functions discussed above are shown in figure 2.4, which clearly demonstrates the differences and similarities between the different functions.

The weight function $w_x(\cdot)$ for the regressor is commonly specified as

$$w_x(y_{t-1}) = \psi(d(y_{t-1})^\alpha)/d(y_{t-1})^\alpha, \tag{2.120}$$

where $\psi(\cdot)$ is again given by (2.118), $d(y_{t-1})$ is the Mahalanobis distance of y_{t-1} – that is, $d(y_{t-1}) = |y_{t-1} - m_y|/\sigma_y$, with m_y and σ_y measures of location and scale of y_{t-1}, respectively. These measures can be estimated robustly by the median $m_y = \text{med}(y_{t-1})$ and the median absolute deviation (MAD) $\sigma_y = 1.483 \cdot \text{med}|y_{t-1} - m_y|$, respectively. The constant 1.483 is used to make

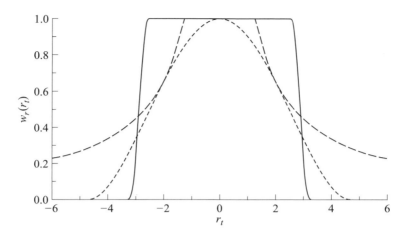

Figure 2.4   Weight functions $w_r(r_t)$ as implied by the polynomial ψ function given in (2.118), with $c_1 = 2.576$ and $c_2 = 3.291$ (solid line), the Huber function given in (2.116) with $c = 1.345$ (long dashed line) and the Tukey function given in (2.117) with $c = 4.685$ (short dashed line)

the MAD a consistent estimator of the standard deviation where y_t is normally distributed. Finally, following Simpson, Ruppert and Carroll (1992), the constant α in (2.120) usually is set equal to 2 to obtain robustness of standard errors.

Notice that the weights $w_r(\cdot)$ depend on the unknown parameter ϕ_1 and therefore are not fixed *a priori* but are determined endogenously. Consequently, the first-order condition (2.115) is nonlinear in ϕ_1 and σ_ε, and estimation of these parameters requires an iterative procedure. In fact, interpreting $w_r(\cdot)$ as a function of $(\phi_1, \sigma_\varepsilon)$, $w_r(\phi_1, \sigma_\varepsilon)$, and denoting the estimates of ϕ_1 and σ_ε at the nth iteration by $\hat{\phi}_1^{(n)}$ and $\hat{\sigma}_\varepsilon^{(n)}$, respectively, it follows from (2.115) that $\hat{\phi}_1^{(n+1)}$ might be computed as the weighted least squares estimate

$$\hat{\phi}_1^{(n+1)} = \frac{\sum_{t=1}^{n} w_r(\hat{\phi}_1^{(n)}, \hat{\sigma}_\varepsilon^{(n)}) y_{t-1} y_t}{\sum_{t=1}^{n} w_r(\hat{\phi}_1^{(n)}, \hat{\sigma}_\varepsilon^{(n)}) y_{t-1}^2}, \tag{2.121}$$

where the estimate of σ_ε can be updated at each iteration using a robust estimator of scale, such as the median absolute deviation (MAD) given by $\sigma_\varepsilon = 1.483 \cdot \text{med}|\varepsilon_t - \text{med}(\varepsilon_t)|$. Following the estimation, the weights $w_r(\cdot)$ assigned to the observations in the GM procedure can be used to detect aberrant data points.

When a time series seems to have many aberrant data, it is possible that a univariate linear time series model such as an ARMA model does not yield a good description of the data. In fact, approximating a nonlinear time series model with a linear model may result in many large residuals. Also, outliers may reflect the fact that a multivariate time series model or an AR model with exogenous variables may have been more appropriate.

In the following chapters we will pay considerable attention to the interplay between outliers, nonlinearity and temporarily volatile periods. Nonlinear models often assume the presence of two or more regimes. When a regime concerns only a few observations, one can be tempted to consider these as outliers. However, it may well be that this regime concerns the most important observations one would want to forecast. On the other hand, one would not want a few genuine outliers to suggest more volatility or a separate regime. Hence, when specifying and estimating the nonlinear models in subsequent chapters, one should somehow take the potential presence of outliers into consideration.

3 Regime-switching models for returns

In this chapter we turn to one of the main subjects of this book, nonlinear models for returns. The problem one immediately faces when considering the use of nonlinear time series models is the vast, if not unlimited, number of possible models. Sometimes economic theory is helpful in choosing a particular model, but more often it is not. Nonlinearity in stock prices and exchange rates has often been detected by various statistical tests, (see Hinich and Patterson, 1985; Scheinkmann and LeBaron, 1989; Hsieh, 1989, 1991; Crato and de Lima, 1994; Brooks, 1996, among others). However, only few attempts have been made to subsequently model the nonlinearity explicitly. In this book we restrict ourselves to models that have a clear interpretation and are plausible from an economic perspective. For previous and more general surveys on nonlinear time series models, the interested reader is referred to Tong (1990) and Granger and Teräsvirta (1993).

A natural approach to modelling economic time series with nonlinear models seems to be to define different *states of the world* or *regimes*, and to allow for the possibility that the dynamic behaviour of economic variables depends on the regime that occurs at any given point in time (see Priestley, 1980, 1988). By 'state-dependent dynamic behaviour' of a time series it is meant that certain properties of the time series, such as its mean, variance and/or autocorrelation, are different in different regimes. An example of such *state-dependent* or *regime-switching* behaviour was encountered in section 2.4, where it was shown that the means and autocorrelations of returns and squared returns on stock market indexes vary during the week. Hence, we can say that each day of the week constitutes a different regime. The interpretation of these seasonal effects as regime-switching behaviour might seem somewhat odd, for in this case the regime process is *deterministic*, in the sense that the regime that occurs at any given in point in time is known with certainty in advance. In contrast, in this chapter we focus on situations in which the regime process is *stochastic*.

The following examples illustrate that stochastic regime-switching is relevant for financial time series. First, LeBaron (1992) shows that the autocorrelations of stock returns are related to the level of volatility of these returns. In particular, autocorrelations tend to be larger during periods of low volatility and smaller during periods of high volatility. The periods of low and high volatility can be interpreted as distinct regimes – or, put differently, the level of volatility can be regarded as the regime-determining process. Of course, the level of volatility in the future is *not* known with certainty. The best one can do is to make a sensible forecast of this level and, hence, of the regime that will occur in the future. As another example, Kräger and Kugler (1993) argue that exchange rates might show regime-switching behaviour, in particular under a system of managed floating such as occurred in the 1980s when it was attempted to stabilize the exchange rate of the US dollar. Intuitively, monetary authorities may intervene in the foreign exchange market as a reaction to large depreciations or appreciations of a currency, which lead to different behaviour for moderate and large changes of the exchange rate. Similar behaviour may be observed for an exchange rate which is constrained to lie within a prescribed band or target zone, as was the case in the Exchange Rate Mechanism (ERM) in Europe (see Chappell *et al.,* 1996). In this case, the level of the exchange rate rather than the change in the exchange rate determines the regimes.

In recent years several time series models have been proposed which formalize the idea of the existence of different regimes generated by a stochastic process. In this chapter we discuss (some of) these models and explore their usefulness for modelling (absolute) returns of financial assets. Nonlinear models for volatility will be discussed in chapter 4. We restrict our attention to models that assume that in each of the regimes the dynamic behaviour of the time series can be described adequately by a linear AR model. In other words, the time series is modelled with an AR model, where the autoregressive parameters are allowed to depend on the regime or state. Generalizations of the MA model to a regime-switching context have also been considered (see Wecker, 1981; de Gooijer, 1998), but we abstain from discussing these models here.

The available regime-switching models differ in the way the regime evolves over time. Roughly speaking, two main classes of models can be distinguished. The models in the first class assume that the regimes can be characterized (or determined) by an observable variable. Consequently, the regimes that have occurred in the past and present are known with certainty (although they have to be found by statistical techniques, of course). The models in the second class assume that the regime cannot actually be observed but is determined by an underlying unobservable stochastic process. This implies that one can never be certain that a particular regime has occurred at a particular point in time, but can only assign probabilities to the occurrence of the different regimes.

In the following sections, we discuss representations of the different regime-switching models, interpretation of the model parameters, estimation, testing for the presence of regime-switching effects, evaluation of estimated regime-switching models, out-of-sample forecasting, measures of the persistence of shocks and the effects of outliers on inference in regime-switching models. As in chapter 2, we emphasize how these different elements can be used in an empirical specification strategy.

3.1   Representation

In this section we introduce the two classes of regime-switching models and discuss their basic properties. To simplify the exposition, we initially focus attention on models which involve only two regimes. Some remarks on extending the models to allow for multiple regimes are made below.

3.1.1   Regimes determined by observable variables

The most prominent member of the first class of models, which assume that the regime that occurs at time t can be determined by an observable variable q_t, is the *Threshold Autoregressive* (TAR) model, initially proposed by Tong (1978) and Tong and Lim (1980), and discussed extensively in Tong (1990). The TAR model assumes that the regime is determined by the value of q_t relative to a *threshold value*, which we denote as c. A special case arises when the *threshold variable* q_t is taken to be a lagged value of the time series itself – that is, $q_t = y_{t-d}$ for a certain integer $d > 0$. As in this case the regime is determined by the time series itself, the resulting model is called a Self-Exciting TAR (SETAR) model.

For example, where $d = 1$ and an AR(1) model is assumed in both regimes, a 2-regime SETAR model is given by

$$y_t = \begin{cases} \phi_{0,1} + \phi_{1,1}\, y_{t-1} + \varepsilon_t & \text{if } y_{t-1} \leq c, \\ \phi_{0,2} + \phi_{1,2}\, y_{t-1} + \varepsilon_t & \text{if } y_{t-1} > c, \end{cases} \tag{3.1}$$

where for the moment the ε_t are assumed to be an i.i.d. white noise sequence conditional upon the history of the time series, which is denoted $\Omega_{t-1} = \{y_{t-1}, y_{t-2}, \ldots, y_{1-(p-1)}, y_{1-p}\}$ as before – that is, $E[\varepsilon_t|\Omega_{t-1}] = 0$ and $E[\varepsilon_t^2|\Omega_{t-1}] = \sigma^2$. An alternative way to write the SETAR model (3.1) is

$$\begin{aligned} y_t = {} & (\phi_{0,1} + \phi_{1,1}\, y_{t-1})(1 - I[y_{t-1} > c]) \\ & + (\phi_{0,2} + \phi_{1,2}\, y_{t-1})I[y_{t-1} > c] + \varepsilon_t, \end{aligned} \tag{3.2}$$

where $I[A]$ is an indicator function with $I[A] = 1$ if the event A occurs and $I[A] = 0$ otherwise.

The SETAR model assumes that the border between the two regimes is given by a specific value of the threshold variable y_{t-1}. A more gradual transition between the different regimes can be obtained by replacing the indicator function $I[y_{t-1} > c]$ in (3.2) by a continuous function $G(y_{t-1}; \gamma, c)$, which changes smoothly from 0 to 1 as y_{t-1} increases. The resultant model is called a Smooth Transition AR (STAR) model and is given by

$$y_t = (\phi_{0,1} + \phi_{1,1} y_{t-1})(1 - G(y_{t-1}; \gamma, c))$$
$$+ (\phi_{0,2} + \phi_{1,2} y_{t-1})G(y_{t-1}; \gamma, c) + \varepsilon_t \qquad (3.3)$$

(see Teräsvirta, 1994, among others). A popular choice for the so-called *transition function* $G(y_{t-1}; \gamma, c)$ is the logistic function

$$G(y_{t-1}; \gamma, c) = \frac{1}{1 + \exp(-\gamma[y_{t-1} - c])}, \qquad (3.4)$$

and the resultant model is then called a Logistic STAR (LSTAR) model. The parameter c in (3.4) can be interpreted as the *threshold* between the two regimes corresponding to $G(y_{t-1}; \gamma, c) = 0$ and $G(y_{t-1}; \gamma, c) = 1$, in the sense that the logistic function changes monotonically from 0 to 1 as y_{t-1} increases, while $G(c; \gamma, c) = 0.5$. The parameter γ determines the *smoothness* of the change in the value of the logistic function, and thus the transition from one regime to the other.

Figure 3.1 shows some examples of the logistic function for various different values of the smoothness parameter γ. From this graph it is seen that as γ becomes very large, the change of $G(y_{t-1}; \gamma, c)$ from 0 to 1 becomes almost

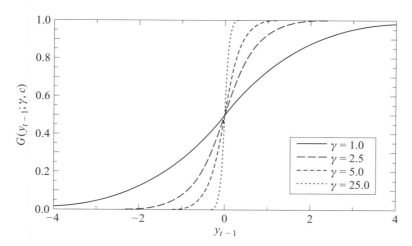

Figure 3.1   Examples of the logistic function $G(y_{t-1}; \gamma, c)$ as given in (3.4) for various values of the smoothness parameter γ and threshold $c = 0$

instantaneous at $y_{t-1} = c$ and, consequently, the logistic function $G(y_{t-1}; \gamma, c)$ approaches the indicator function $I[y_{t-1} > c]$. Hence the SETAR model (3.2) can be approximated arbitrarily well by the LSTAR model (3.3) with (3.4). When $\gamma \to 0$, the logistic function becomes equal to a constant (equal to 0.5) and when $\gamma = 0$, the STAR model reduces to a linear model.

The idea of smooth transition between regimes dates back to Bacon and Watts (1971). It was introduced into the nonlinear time series literature by Chan and Tong (1986) and popularized by Granger and Teräsvirta (1993) and Teräsvirta (1994). A comprehensive review of the STAR model, and extensions that allow for exogenous variables as regressors as well, is given in Teräsvirta (1998).

To see that the SETAR and STAR models are indeed capable of capturing regime-switching behaviour, notice that in the SETAR model (3.1), the first-order autocorrelation of y_t is either $\phi_{1,1}$ or $\phi_{1,2}$, depending on whether $y_{t-1} \le c$ or $y_{t-1} > c$, respectively. In the STAR model (3.3), the first-order autocorrelation changes gradually from $\phi_{1,1}$ to $\phi_{1,2}$ as y_{t-1} increases. In fact, quite a large variety of dynamic patterns can be generated by a simple model such as the SETAR model in (3.1) by choosing the parameters appropriately. To give some impression of the possibilities, figure 3.2 shows four realizations

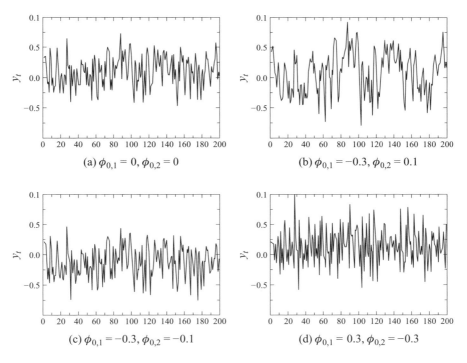

Figure 3.2   Four series generated from the SETAR model (3.1), with $\phi_{1,1} = -0.5$, $\phi_{1,2} = 0.5$, $c = 0$ and $\varepsilon_t \sim \text{NID}(0, 0.25^2)$

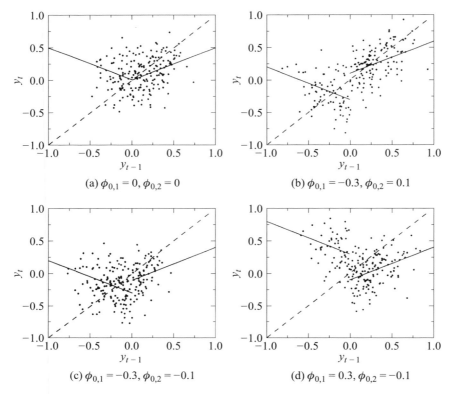

Figure 3.3   Scatterplots of four series generated from the SETAR model (3.1), with $\phi_{1,1} = -0.5$, $\phi_{1,2} = 0.5$, $c = 0$ and $\varepsilon_t \sim \text{NID}(0, 0.25^2)$. The solid lines are the skeletons of the model, the dashed line is the 45-degree line

of $n = 200$ observations from (3.1) with $\phi_{1,1} = -0.5$, $\phi_{1,2} = 0.5$, $c = 0$ and $\varepsilon_t \sim \text{NID}(0, 0.25^2)$. All series are started with $y_0 = 0$, while the same values for the shocks ε_t, $t = 1, \ldots, n$, are used to generate subsequent observations. The intercepts $\phi_{0,1}$ and $\phi_{0,2}$ are varied to generate different behaviour. Figure 3.3 shows the corresponding scatterplots of y_t versus y_{t-1}.

Before we discuss the properties of the various time series that are shown in these figures, we must first introduce some terminology associated with non-linear time series models in general. In the scatterplots in figure 3.3, the deterministic part of the model $F(y_{t-1}) \equiv (\phi_{0,1} + \phi_{1,1} y_{t-1})(1 - I[y_{t-1} > c]) + (\phi_{0,2} + \phi_{1,2} y_{t-1})I[y_{t-1} > c]$ is also shown. Notice that $F(y_{t-1})$ is in fact the conditional expectation of y_t at time $t - 1$. This deterministic and predictable part of the model is commonly referred to as the *skeleton* of the model, a concept introduced by Chan and Tong (1985).

The model is said to have an *equilibrium* at y^* if y^* is a *fixed point* of the skeleton – that is, if $y^* = F(y^*)$. The equilibrium is called *stable* if the time series converges to y^* where the noise ε_t is turned off, which simply means that all ε_t are set equal to zero. A (stationary) linear time series always has a unique and stable equilibrium y^* which is equal to its mean. As will be seen shortly, a nonlinear time series can have a single (stable or unstable) equilibrium, multiple equilibria or no equilibrium at all. Furthermore, even if the equilibrium is unique and stable, it is not necessarily equal to the mean of the time series. As noted above, the equilibria, if any exist, can be found by determining the fixed points of the skeleton $F(\cdot)$ – that is, by solving $y^* = F(y^*)$. If the skeleton only depends on the first-order lag y_{t-1}, as in the examples considered here, an alternative way to find the equilibria is to look for intersection points of the skeleton with the 45-degree line in the scatterplot of y_t versus y_{t-1}. A stable equilibrium is also called an *attractor*, which stems from the fact that in the absence of shocks the time series is attracted by the stable equilibrium. Given that a nonlinear time series can have any number of stable equilibria, it follows that it can also have several attractors. That is, y^* is the attractor for $\bar{y}$ if $y_t = \bar{y}$ and

$$y_{t+h} \to y^* \quad \text{as } h \to \infty \qquad \text{if } \varepsilon_{t+j} = 0 \quad \text{for all } j > 0.$$

A different way to express this is to say that $\bar{y}$ is in the *domain of attraction* of y^*. As will be seen below, a stable equilibrium is not the only possible form of attractor of a nonlinear time series.

Panel (a) of figure 3.3 shows the scatterplot of the series generated from (3.1) with both intercepts equal to 0, which implies that the means of the AR models in the two regimes are equal to 0. In this case, the equilibrium is unique and stable and also equal to 0. However, the mean of the time series y_t is not equal to 0. This can be understood by noting that, because $\phi_{1,1}$ is negative, the series has a tendency to leave the lower regime $y_{t-1} < 0$ quite rapidly. In fact, in the absence of a shock ε_t (or if $\varepsilon_t = 0$) the series reverts to the upper regime immediately, as $E[y_t|y_{t-1}] = \phi_{1,1} y_{t-1} > 0$ if $y_{t-1} < 0$. As $\phi_{1,2}$ is positive, the series is expected to remain in the upper regime (although it will be pulled towards the threshold $c = 0$ because $\phi_{1,2} < 1$). This suggests that y_t will be positive on average and, hence, the mean of y_t will be larger than 0.

The skeleton in panel (b) of figure 3.3 has two points of intersection with the 45-degree line. This is an example of a model with multiple equilibria, at $y_1^* = -0.2$ and $y_2^* = 0.2$, which can easily be checked using (3.1). Both equilibria are stable. An intuitive way to see this is to note that the intercepts are such that the mean of the AR model in the lower regime $y_{t-1} \leq 0$ is within the lower regime, while the mean of the AR model in the upper regime $y_{t-1} > 0$ is within the upper regime. Consequently, in the absence of exogenous shocks the time series has no tendency to move to the other regime, but rather will converge to the mean of the AR model in the particular regime. Put differently, the domains of attraction of y_1^* (y_2^*) are negative (positive) values of the time series, $\bar{y} < 0$ ($\bar{y} > 0$).

Panel (c) of figure 3.3 again shows an example of a model with a unique and stable equilibrium $y^* = -0.2$. Notice that the mean of the AR model in the upper regime in this case is negative (the fact that it is exactly equal to -0.2 is not crucial). Hence, if the series starts in the upper regime, it is attracted by the lower regime. As the mean of the AR model in the lower regime is also negative, this mean is the attractor of the model.

Finally, the intercepts of the model in panel (d) of figure 3.3 are set such that the model has no equilibrium, which can be seen by observing that there are no points y^* such that $y^* = F(y^*)$ – or, equivalently, that the skeleton has no intersection points with the 45-degree line in each of the regimes. Also note that the means of the AR models in the two regimes are both in the other regime. Intuitively, this suggests that the series has no point at which 'it could come to rest'. If it is in the upper regime it is pulled towards the lower regime and vice versa. Still, the model does have an attractor. In fact, the model contains a so-called *limit cycle*. A k-period limit cycle is defined as a set of points $y_1^*, \ldots, y_k^*$, such that $y_j^* = F(y_{j-1}^*)$ for $j = 2, \ldots, k$, and $y_1^* = F(y_k^*)$. That is, if the time series started in one of the points y_j^*, $j = 1, \ldots, k$, and no shocks occurred, the series would cycle among the k-points $y_1^*, \ldots, y_k^*$. In the example shown in panel (d) of figure 3.3, the limit cycle consists of three points, $y_1^* = 0.06667$, $y_2^* = -0.06667$ and $y_3^* = 0.33333$. It can also be shown that the limit cycle is the attractor, in the sense that the series would converge to the cycle if the noise were turned off.

This last example demonstrates that nonlinear models can contain *endogenous dynamics*, which means to say that even in the absence of shocks y_t fluctuates. This is in contrast with linear time series, for which the fluctuations are caused entirely by the exogenous shocks ε_t. The debate whether observed dynamics in time series are endogenous or exogenous has a long history, also in the financial time series literature (see, for example, Brock, Hsieh and LeBaron, 1991; Hsieh, 1991; Creedy and Martin, 1994). A more recent application of endogenous dynamics in finance can be found in Brock and Hommes (1998). A general discussion of nonlinear time series models, endogenous dynamics and the related concept of chaos is given in Tong (1995).

As a final remark, notice that the four models in the example above differ only in the values taken by the intercepts in the two regimes, $\phi_{0,1}$ and $\phi_{0,2}$, whereas the autoregressive parameters $\phi_{1,1}$ and $\phi_{1,2}$ are kept the same. The fact that the four models nevertheless generate series with quite different behaviour illustrates the important role that is played by intercepts in nonlinear time series models.

Higher-order models

Although the SETAR and STAR models with an AR(1) model in both regimes can already generate a large variety of dynamic patterns, in practice one may want to allow for higher-order AR models in the different regimes. For example, in the two-regime case, the AR orders might be set to p_1 and p_2 in the lower and upper regimes, respectively. In this case, the SETAR model becomes

$$y_t = \begin{cases} \phi_{0,1} + \phi_{1,1}\, y_{t-1} + \cdots + \phi_{p_1,1}\, y_{t-p_1} + \varepsilon_t & \text{if } y_{t-1} \le c, \\ \phi_{0,2} + \phi_{1,2}\, y_{t-1} + \cdots + \phi_{p_2,2}\, y_{t-p_2} + \varepsilon_t & \text{if } y_{t-1} > c, \end{cases}$$
$$(3.5)$$

whereas the equivalent STAR model is given by

$$y_t = (\phi_{0,1} + \phi_{1,1}\, y_{t-1} + \cdots + \phi_{p_1,1}\, y_{t-p_1})(1 - G(y_{t-1}; \gamma, c))$$
$$+ (\phi_{0,2} + \phi_{1,2}\, y_{t-1} + \cdots + \phi_{p_2,2}\, y_{t-p_2})G(y_{t-1}; \gamma, c) + \varepsilon_t.$$
$$(3.6)$$

In higher-order models, it may also be relevant to consider the possibility that y_{t-d} with $d > 1$ is the threshold or transition variable. For such higher-order models, it can be quite difficult to establish the existence of equilibria, attractors and/or limit cycles analytically. A pragmatic way to investigate the properties of the skeleton of a higher-order model is to use what might be called *deterministic simulation*. That is, given starting values $y_0, \ldots, y_{1-p}$, with $p = \max(p_1, p_2)$, one computes the values taken by $y_1, y_2, \ldots$, while setting all $\varepsilon_t, t = 1, 2, \ldots$ equal to zero. Doing this for many different starting values gives an impression about the characteristics of the (skeleton of the) model (see Teräsvitra and Anderson, 1992; Peel and Speight, 1996 for applications of this procedure).

Identification of lag orders

An important question concerns determining the appropriate orders p_1 and p_2 in the general 2-regime models (3.5) and (3.6). One of the approaches that is commonly applied, especially in case of STAR models, is to start by specifying a linear AR(p) model for y_t and to assume that the order p, which is based on the (partial) autocorrelations of y_t or an information criterion such as AIC or BIC, is the appropriate order in both regimes of the nonlinear model. This procedure is quite hazardous, in the sense that it can easily happen that the lag order that is obtained in this way is inappropriate. For example, as remarked in chapter 2 for a bilinear model, nonlinear time series may have zero autocorrelations at all lags. In such a case it is very likely that the selected lag order based upon inspection of the estimated autocorrelation function is too low. On the other hand, relatively simple nonlinear time series models may give rise to rather complicated autocorrelation structures, which can be captured only by an AR(p) model with p very large. For example, Granger and Teräsvitra (1999) discuss the so-called sign model,

$$y_t = \text{sign}(y_{t-1}) + \varepsilon_t, \tag{3.7}$$

where $\text{sign}(x) = 1$ if x is positive and -1 if x is negative. It is shown that time series from this model have long-memory properties.

As another example, table 3.1 contains the values for the AIC as given in (2.55) for AR(p) models estimated for the simulated series shown in figure 3.2. For the first three series, the AIC selects the correct value of $p = 1$. For the last series, however, the AIC is minimized at $p = 4$. Hence, the AR order would be overestimated in this last case.

An alternative procedure is to choose the lag orders p_1 and p_2 in (3.5) or (3.6) directly based upon an information criterion. Sin and White (1996) demonstrate that such a procedure is consistent, in the sense that the correct lag orders will be selected with probability one asymptotically. An obvious drawback of this approach is that the SETAR or STAR model has to be estimated for all possible combinations of p_1 and p_2.

In section 2.2 it was argued that, especially in the case of BIC, the improvement in fit from a more elaborate model needs to be considerable to compensate for the penalty incurred for including additional parameters in the model. This seems to be a problem in nonlinear modelling in particular. For example, in applications of regime-switching models it often happens that the large majority of observations is in one of the regimes. In such cases, the improvement in fit compared to a linear model is probably quite modest and not large enough for the nonlinear model to be selected by an information criterion. However, it seems fair to take into account the fact that the parameters in the additional regime(s) are needed for relatively few observations. This can be achieved by not penalizing the inclusion of the additional parameters for the whole

Table 3.1 *AIC for AR(p) models estimated on simulated SETAR series*

Intercepts					p			
$\phi_{0,1}$	$\phi_{0,2}$	0	1	2	3	4	5	6
0	0	−2.652	−2.705	−2.695	−2.685	−2.701	−2.695	−2.684
−0.3	0.1	−2.037	−2.453	−2.443	−2.432	−2.428	−2.431	−2.436
−0.3	−0.1	−2.604	−2.619	−2.609	−2.600	−2.616	−2.607	−2.596
0.3	−0.1	−2.373	−2.423	−2.413	−2.409	−2.450	−2.440	−2.431

Note: Values of AIC for AR(p) models estimated on four series of length $n = 200$ generated from the SETAR model (3.1), with $\phi_{1,1} = -0.5$, $\phi_{1,2} = 0.5$, $c = 0$ and $\varepsilon_t \sim \text{NID}(0, 0.25^2)$.

sample size but only for the number of observations for which these parameters are functional. Tong (1990, p. 379) defines an alternative AIC for a 2-regime SETAR model as the sum of the AICs for the AR models in the two regimes, that is,

$$AIC(p_1, p_2) = n_1 \ln \hat{\sigma}_1^2 + n_2 \ln \hat{\sigma}_2^2 + 2(p_1 + 1) + 2(p_2 + 1), \quad (3.8)$$

where n_j, $j = 1, 2$, is the number of observations in the jth regime, and $\hat{\sigma}_j^2$, $j = 1, 2$, is the variance of the residuals in the jth regime. Even though the ε_t may have the same variance across regimes, the estimates $\hat{\sigma}_1^2$ and $\hat{\sigma}_2^2$ can differ. The BIC for a SETAR model can be defined analogously as

$$BIC(p_1, p_2) = n_1 \ln \hat{\sigma}_1^2 + n_2 \ln \hat{\sigma}_2^2 + (p_1 + 1) \ln n_1 + (p_2 + 1) \ln n_2.$$
$$(3.9)$$

For given upper bounds p_1^* and p_2^* on p_1 and p_2, respectively, the selected lag orders in the two regimes are those for which the information criterion is minimized. Especially the BIC (3.9) demonstrates that the number of observations in each of the regimes is taken into account when computing the information criterion.

Stationarity

Little is known about the conditions under which SETAR and STAR models generate time series that are stationary. Such conditions have been established only for the first-order model (3.1). As shown by Chan and Tong (1985), a sufficient condition for stationarity of (3.1) is $\max(|\phi_{1,1}|, |\phi_{1,2}|) < 1$, which is equivalent to the requirement that the AR(1) models in the two regimes are stationary. Chan *et al.* (1985) show that stationarity of the first-order model actually holds under less restrictive conditions. In particular, the SETAR model (3.1) is stationary if and only if one of the following conditions is satisfied:

(1) $\phi_{1,1} < 1, \phi_{1,2} < 1, \phi_{1,1}\phi_{1,2} < 1$;
(2) $\phi_{1,1} = 1, \phi_{1,2} < 1, \phi_{0,1} > 0$;
(3) $\phi_{1,1} < 1, \phi_{1,2} = 1, \phi_{0,2} < 0$;
(4) $\phi_{1,1} = 1, \phi_{1,2} = 1, \phi_{0,2} < 0 < \phi_{0,1}$;
(5) $\phi_{1,1}\phi_{1,2} = 1, \phi_{1,1} < 0, \phi_{0,2} + \phi_{1,2}\phi_{0,1} > 0$.

Condition (1) corresponds with the sufficient condition of Chan and Tong (1985), although it should be noted that (1) allows one of the AR parameters to become smaller than -1. Conditions (2)–(4) show that the AR model in one or even both regimes may contain a unit root. In such cases, the time series is locally nonstationary. The conditions on the intercepts $\phi_{0,1}$ and $\phi_{0,2}$ are such that the time series has a tendency to revert to the stationary regime and, hence, the time series is globally stationary. Testing for unit roots in SETAR models is discussed in Caner and Hansen (1997), Enders and Granger (1998) and Berben and van Dijk (1999). A rough-and-ready check for stationarity of nonlinear time series models in general is to determine whether or not the skeleton is stable. Intuitively, if the skeleton is such that the series tends to explode for certain starting values, the series is nonstationary. This can be established by simulation.

Even less is known about the stationary distributions of SETAR and STAR time series. Anděl (1989) discusses some analytic results for a special case of the first-order SETAR model (3.1), in which $\phi_{0,1} = \phi_{0,2} = c = 0$, $\phi_{1,1} = -\phi_{1,2}$ and $\phi_{1,1} \in (0, 1)$. In general, one has to resort to numerical procedures to evaluate the stationary distribution of y_t. Some of the methods that can be applied are discussed in Moeanaddin and Tong (1990) and Tong (1990, section 4.2).

Multiple regimes

Sometimes it is of interest to allow for more than two regimes. The SETAR and STAR models can be extended in a relatively straightforward way to allow for this. It is useful to distinguish two cases, depending on whether the regimes are characterized by a single variable or by a combination of several variables.

In the first case, where the prevailing regime is determined by a single variable, an m-regime SETAR model can be obtained by defining a set of $m + 1$ thresholds $c_0, c_1, \ldots, c_m$, such that $-\infty = c_0 < c_1 < \cdots < c_{k-1} < c_m = \infty$. The m-regime equivalent of (3.1) then is given by

$$y_t = \phi_{0,j} + \phi_{1,j} y_{t-1} + \varepsilon_t \quad \text{if } c_{j-1} < y_{t-1} \leq c_j, \tag{3.10}$$

for $j = 1, \ldots, m$. An application of this model can be found in Kräger and Kugler (1993).

For the STAR model, a similar procedure can be followed. First note that (3.3) can be rewritten as

$$y_t = \phi_1' x_t + (\phi_2 - \phi_1)' x_t G(y_{t-1}; \gamma, c) + \varepsilon_t, \tag{3.11}$$

where $x_t = (1, y_{t-1})'$ and $\phi_j = (\phi_{0,j}, \phi_{1,j})'$ for $j = 1, 2$. By using the subset $c_1, \ldots, c_{m-1}$ of the thresholds defined above for the SETAR model, and an additional set of smoothness parameters $\gamma_1, \ldots, \gamma_{m-1}$, a STAR model with m regimes can be defined as

$$y_t = \phi_1' x_t + (\phi_2 - \phi_1)' x_t G_1(y_{t-1}) + (\phi_3 - \phi_2)' x_t G_2(y_{t-1})$$
$$+ \cdots + (\phi_m - \phi_{m-1})' x_t G_{m-1}(y_{t-1}) + \varepsilon_t, \tag{3.12}$$

where the $G_j(y_{t-1}) \equiv G_j(y_{t-1}; \gamma_j, c_j)$, $j = 1, \ldots, m - 1$, are logistic functions as in (3.4) with smoothness parameter γ_j and threshold c_j.

As an example of the case where the regime is determined by more than one variable, suppose that the behaviour of the time series y_t not only depends on the value of y_{t-1} relative to some threshold c_1, but also upon the value of y_{t-2} relative to another threshold c_2. This gives rise to *four* regimes in total, as demonstrated by the SETAR model

$$y_t = \begin{cases} \phi_{0,1} + \phi_{1,1}y_{t-1} + \varepsilon_t & \text{if } y_{t-1} \leq c_1 \text{ and } y_{t-2} \leq c_2, \\ \phi_{0,2} + \phi_{1,2}y_{t-1} + \varepsilon_t & \text{if } y_{t-1} \leq c_1 \text{ and } y_{t-2} > c_2, \\ \phi_{0,3} + \phi_{1,3}y_{t-1} + \varepsilon_t & \text{if } y_{t-1} > c_1 \text{ and } y_{t-2} \leq c_2, \\ \phi_{0,4} + \phi_{1,4}y_{t-1} + \varepsilon_t & \text{if } y_{t-1} > c_1 \text{ and } y_{t-2} > c_2. \end{cases} \tag{3.13}$$

The model in (3.13) is referred to as a Nested TAR (NeTAR) model by Astatkie, Watts and Watt (1997). This name stems from the fact that the time series can be thought of as being described by a 2-regime SETAR model with regimes defined by y_{t-1}, and within each of those regimes by a 2-regime SETAR model with regimes defined by y_{t-2}, or vice versa.

Finally, van Dijk and Franses (1999) propose the corresponding multiple regime STAR model. Its representation is

$$y_t = [\phi'_1 x_t (1 - G_1(y_{t-1})) + \phi'_2 x_t G_1(y_{t-1})][1 - G_2(y_{t-2})]$$
$$+ [\phi'_3 x_t (1 - G_1(y_{t-1})) + \phi'_4 x_t G_1(y_{t-1})]G_2(y_{t-2}) + \varepsilon_t, \tag{3.14}$$

which illustrates the interpretation of nested models perhaps more clearly.

3.1.2 Regimes determined by unobservable variables

The second class of regime-switching models assumes that the regime that occurs at time t cannot be observed, as it is determined by an unobservable process, which we denote as s_t. In case of only two regimes, s_t can simply be assumed to take on the values 1 and 2, such that the model with an AR(1) model in both regimes is given by

$$y_t = \begin{cases} \phi_{0,1} + \phi_{1,1}y_{t-1} + \varepsilon_t & \text{if } s_t = 1, \\ \phi_{0,2} + \phi_{1,2}y_{t-1} + \varepsilon_t & \text{if } s_t = 2, \end{cases} \tag{3.15}$$

or, using an obvious shorthand notation,

$$y_t = \phi_{0,s_t} + \phi_{1,s_t}y_{t-1} + \varepsilon_t. \tag{3.16}$$

To complete the model, the properties of the process s_t need to be specified. The most popular model in this class, which was advocated by Hamilton (1989), is the Markov-Switching (MSW) model, in which the process s_t is assumed to be a first-order Markov-process. This implies that the current regime s_t only depends on the regime one period ago, s_{t-1}. Hence, the model is completed by defining the transition probabilities of moving from one state to the other,

$$P(s_t = 1|s_{t-1} = 1) = p_{11},$$
$$P(s_t = 2|s_{t-1} = 1) = p_{12},$$
$$P(s_t = 1|s_{t-1} = 2) = p_{21},$$
$$P(s_t = 2|s_{t-1} = 2) = p_{22}.$$

Thus, p_{ij} is equal to the probability that the Markov chain moves from state i at time $t-1$ to state j at time t – or, put differently, the probability that regime i at time $t-1$ is followed by regime j at time t. Obviously, for the p_{ij}s to define proper probabilities, they should be nonnegative, while it should also hold that $p_{11} + p_{12} = 1$ and $p_{21} + p_{22} = 1$. Also of interest in the MSW models are the *unconditional* probabilities that the process is in each of the regimes – that is, $P(s_t = i)$ for $i = 1, 2$. Using the theory of ergodic Markov chains it is straightforward to show that for the two-state MSW model these unconditional probabilities are given by

$$P(s_t = 1) = \frac{1 - p_{22}}{2 - p_{11} - p_{22}}, \tag{3.17}$$

$$P(s_t = 2) = \frac{1 - p_{11}}{2 - p_{11} - p_{22}}, \tag{3.18}$$

see Hamilton (1994, pp. 681–3) for an explicit derivation of this result. Stationarity conditions for the 2-regime MSW model are discussed in Holst *et al.* (1994).

Multiple regimes

An MSW model with m regimes is obtained by allowing the unobservable Markov chain s_t to take on any one of $m > 2$ different values, each determining a particular regime. That is, the model becomes

$$y_t = \phi_{0,j} + \phi_{1,j} y_{t-1} + \varepsilon_t, \quad \text{if } s_t = j, \tag{3.19}$$

for $j = 1, \ldots, m$, with transition probabilities

$$p_{ij} \equiv P(s_t = j|s_{t-1} = i), \quad i, j = 1, \ldots, m, \tag{3.20}$$

which satisfy $p_{ij} \geq 0$ for $i, j = 1, \ldots, m$ and $\sum_{j=1}^{m} p_{ij} = 1$ for all $i = 1, \ldots, m$. See Boldin (1996) for an application.

Empirical specification procedure

Granger (1993) strongly recommends employing a specific-to-general procedure when considering the use of nonlinear time series models to describe the features of a particular variable. An empirical specification procedure for SETAR, STAR and MSW models that follows this approach consists of the following steps:

(1) specify an appropriate linear AR model of order p $[AR(p)]$ for the time series under investigation

(2) test the null hypothesis of linearity against the alternative of SETAR-, STAR- and/or MSW-type nonlinearity; for the SETAR and STAR models, this step also consists of selecting the appropriate variable that determines the regimes

(3) estimate the parameters in the selected model

(4) evaluate the model using diagnostic tests

(5) modify the model if necessary

(6) use the model for descriptive or forecasting purposes.

Steps (2)–(6) in this specification procedure are discussed in detail in the following sections. It turns out that tests against SETAR- and MSW-type nonlinearity, which are to be used in step (2), require the input of estimates of the parameters in these models. Hence, in the next section we first discuss parameter estimation, and turn to testing for nonlinearity in section 3.3.

Finally, in step (2) one may also compute several portmanteau tests for nonlinearity, such as the BDS test of Brock *et al.* (1996), the bispectrum tests of Hinich (1982) and Ashley, Patterson and Hinich (1986) or the neural network test which is to be discussed in section 5.6, as a diagnostic check to test the adequacy of the specified linear model. A limitation of portmanteau tests is, though, that they provide (almost) no information concerning the appropriate alternative – that is, if linearity is rejected it is not clear in which direction to proceed or which nonlinear model to consider.

3.2   Estimation

The discussion of estimating the parameters in the different regime-switching models in this section is necessarily rather brief and describes only the general ideas of the estimation methods. For more elaborate discussions we refer to Tong (1990) and Hansen (1997, 2000) for the SETAR model, to Teräsvirta (1994, 1998) for the STAR model and to Hamilton (1990, 1993, 1994) for the MSW model. For notational convenience, we discuss the estimation problem for 2-regime models with equal AR orders in the two regimes – that is, $p_1 = p_2 = p$.

3.2.1 Estimation of SETAR models

The parameters of interest in the 2-regime SETAR model (3.5) – that is, $\phi_{i,j}, i = 0, \ldots, p, j = 1, 2, c$ and σ^2 – can conveniently be estimated by sequential conditional least squares. Under the additional assumption that the ε_ts are normally distributed, the resulting estimates are equivalent to maximum likelihood estimates.

To see why least squares is the appropriate estimation method, rewrite (3.5) as

$$y_t = (\phi_{0,1} + \phi_{1,1} y_{t-1} + \cdots + \phi_{p,1} y_{t-p}) I[y_{t-1} \leq c]$$
$$+ (\phi_{0,2} + \phi_{1,2} y_{t-1} + \cdots + \phi_{p,2} y_{t-p}) I[y_{t-1} > c] + \varepsilon_t, \tag{3.21}$$

or more compactly as

$$y_t = \phi_1' x_t I[y_{t-1} \leq c] + \phi_2' x_t I[y_{t-1} > c] + \varepsilon_t, \tag{3.22}$$

where $\phi_j = (\phi_{0,j}, \phi_{1,j}, \ldots, \phi_{p,j})', j = 1, 2$, and $x_t = (1, y_{t-1}, \ldots, y_{t-p})'$. Note that where the threshold c is fixed, the model is linear in the remaining parameters. Estimates of $\phi = (\phi_1', \phi_2')'$ are then easily obtained by OLS as

$$\hat{\phi}(c) = \left(\sum_{t=1}^{n} x_t(c) x_t(c)' \right)^{-1} \left(\sum_{t=1}^{n} x_t(c) y_t \right), \tag{3.23}$$

where $x_t(c) = (x_t' I[y_{t-1} \leq c], x_t' I[y_{t-1} > c])'$ and the notation $\hat{\phi}(c)$ is used to indicate that the estimate of ϕ is conditional upon c. The corresponding residuals are denoted $\hat{\varepsilon}_t(c) = y_t - \hat{\phi}(c)' x_t(c)$ with variance $\hat{\sigma}^2(c) = \frac{1}{n} \sum_{t=1}^{n} \hat{\varepsilon}_t(c)^2$. The least squares estimate of c can be obtained by minimizing this residual variance, that is

$$\hat{c} = \underset{c \in C}{\text{argmin}}\ \hat{\sigma}^2(c), \tag{3.24}$$

where C denotes the set of all allowable threshold values. The final estimates of the autoregressive parameters are given by $\hat{\phi} = \hat{\phi}(\hat{c})$, while the residual variance is estimated as $\hat{\sigma}^2 = \hat{\sigma}^2(\hat{c})$.

The set of allowable threshold values C in (3.24) should be such that each regime contains enough observations for the estimator defined above to produce reliable estimates of the autoregressive parameters. A popular choice for C is to require that each regime contains at least a (pre-specified) fraction π_0 of the observations, that is,

$$C = \{c \mid y_{([\pi_0(n-1)])} \leq c \leq y_{([(1-\pi_0)(n-1)])}\}, \tag{3.25}$$

where $y_{(0)}, \ldots, y_{(n-1)}$ denote the order statistics of the threshold variable y_{t-1}, $y_{(0)} \leq \cdots \leq y_{(n-1)}$, and $[\cdot]$ denotes integer part. A safe choice for π_0 appears to be 0.15.

The minimization problem (3.24) can be solved by means of direct search. It suffices to compute the residual variance $\hat{\sigma}^2(c)$ only for threshold values equal to the order statistics of y_{t-1} – that is, for $c = y_{(i)}$ for each i such that $y_{(i)} \in C$. This follows from the observation that the value of $\hat{\sigma}^2(c)$ does not change as c is varied between two consecutive order statistics, as no observations move from one regime to the other in this case.

Chan (1993) demonstrates that the LS estimator of the threshold $\hat{c}$ is consistent at rate n and asymptotically independent of the other parameter estimates. Chan (1993) also shows that the asymptotic distribution of $\hat{c}$ depends upon many nuisance parameters, for instance the true regression parameters ϕ. Using an alternative approach, Hansen (1997) derives a limiting distribution for $\hat{c}$ that is free of nuisance parameters apart from a scale parameter. The estimates of the autoregressive parameters are consistent at the usual rate of $\sqrt{n}$ and asymptotically normal.

Confidence intervals

The asymptotic distribution of the threshold estimate is available in closed-form, so in principle it could be used to construct confidence intervals for c. However, this requires estimation of the scale parameter in the distribution, which appears to be quite cumbersome. Hansen (1997) therefore recommends an alternative approach, which is based on inverting the likelihood ratio test-statistic to test the hypothesis that the threshold is equal to some specific value c_0, given by

$$LR(c_0) = n\left(\frac{\hat{\sigma}^2(c_0) - \hat{\sigma}^2(\hat{c})}{\hat{\sigma}^2(\hat{c})}\right). \tag{3.26}$$

Notice that $LR(\hat{c}) = 0$. The $100 \cdot \alpha\%$ confidence interval for the threshold is given by the set $\widehat{C}_\alpha$ consisting of those values of c for which the null hypothesis is not rejected at significance level α. That is,

$$\widehat{C}_\alpha = \{c : LR(c) \le z(\alpha)\}, \tag{3.27}$$

where $z(\alpha)$ is the $100 \cdot \alpha$ percentile of the asymptotic distribution of the LR-statistic. These percentiles are given in Hansen (1997, table 1) for various values of α. The set $\widehat{C}_\alpha$ provides a valid confidence region as the probability that the true threshold value is contained in $\widehat{C}_\alpha$ approaches α as the sample size n becomes large. An easy graphical method to obtain the region $\widehat{C}_\alpha$ is to plot the LR-statistic (3.26) against c and draw a horizontal line at $z(\alpha)$. All points for which the value of the statistic is below the line are included in $\widehat{C}_\alpha$.

To see how this works in practice, SETAR models with $p_1 = p_2 = 1$ are estimated for the series shown in panels (b) and (c) of figure 3.2. Figure 3.4 shows the sequences of LR-statistics for these examples. As can be seen, for the

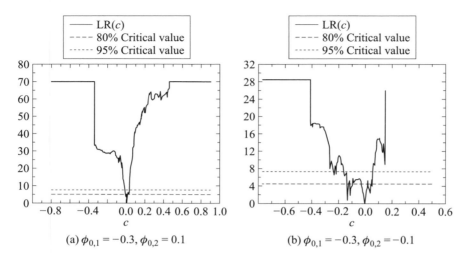

(a) $\phi_{0,1} = -0.3$, $\phi_{0,2} = 0.1$ (b) $\phi_{0,1} = -0.3$, $\phi_{0,2} = -0.1$

Figure 3.4   Sequences of LR-statistics for two series generated from the SETAR model (3.1), with $\phi_{1,1} = -0.5$, $\phi_{1,2} = 0.5$, $c = 0$ and $\varepsilon_t \sim \text{NID}(0, 0.25^2)$ The 95 per cent confidence region for the threshold is given by the values c such that $LR(c)$ is below the 95 per cent critical value

first series the threshold estimate is quite precise, in the sense that the 95 per cent confidence interval is fairly small. For the second series, on the other hand, the threshold estimate is rather imprecise, judged from the wide confidence region.

The estimates of the autoregressive parameters ϕ_1 and ϕ_2 are asymptotically normal distributed. Hence, one might proceed as usual and construct an asymptotic 95 per cent confidence interval for $\phi_{1,2}$, for example, as $(\hat{\phi}_{1,2} - 1.96\hat{\sigma}_{\phi_{1,2}}, \hat{\phi}_{1,2} + 1.96\hat{\sigma}_{\phi_{1,2}})$, where $\hat{\sigma}_{\phi_{1,2}}$ is the estimated standard error of $\phi_{1,2}$. Hansen (1997) shows that the confidence intervals that are obtained in this way do not yield good finite sample approximations. He therefore recommends an alternative procedure, in which a 95 per cent confidence interval for ϕ_1 and ϕ_2 is computed for each value of c in the set $\widehat{C}_\alpha$, and the union of these intervals is taken as the confidence interval for ϕ_1 and ϕ_2. Some simulation evidence suggests that $\alpha = 0.8$ is a reasonable confidence level for the set $\widehat{C}_\alpha$ in this case.

To illustrate the differences that can result from the two approaches, consider again the SETAR models that are estimated for the series shown in panels (b) and (c) of figure 3.2. For the series in panel (b), the confidence region $\widehat{C}_{0.8}$ for the threshold is rather tight (see figure 3.4). Hence it might be expected that the two confidence intervals for the autoregressive parameters are roughly the same, which indeed turns out to be the case. The point estimate and asymptotic standard error of $\phi_{1,2}$ are equal to 0.54 and 0.12, respectively. The confidence interval based on the asymptotic normal distribution thus would be $(0.31, 0.79)$.

This is very similar to the confidence interval based on the region $\widehat{C}_{0.8}$, which is $(0.28, 0.81)$. For the second series, the point estimate of $\phi_{1,2}$ is equal to 0.49, with asymptotic standard error 0.27. Hence, the usual confidence interval for this parameter would be $(-0.05, 1.03)$. The alternative approach based on the set $\widehat{C}_{0.8}$, on the other hand, renders the much wider confidence interval $(-0.17, 1.29)$. This large difference is caused by the fact that the threshold c is estimated rather imprecisely and, therefore, the region $\widehat{C}_{0.8}$ is rather wide. In fact, as shown in figure 3.4, the region $\widehat{C}_{0.8}$ is disjoint. One segment is centred around the point estimate of the threshold, which is equal to 0.01, while there is another segment for threshold values in the range $(-0.12, -0.08)$.

Choosing the threshold variable

So far, we have implicitly assumed that the threshold variable q_t, which defines the regime that occurs at any given point in time, is known (and equal to y_{t-1}). In practice, the appropriate threshold variable is of course unknown and an important question is how it can be determined. In the context of SETAR models we might restrict attention to lagged endogenous variables y_{t-d} for positive integers d as candidate threshold variables. It turns out that in this case d can be estimated along with the other parameters in the model, by performing the above calculations for various choices of d (say, $d \in \{1, \ldots, d^*\}$ for some upper bound d^*), and estimate d as the value that minimizes the residual variance.

An alternative way to interpret this procedure is that effectively the grid search in (3.24) is augmented with a search over d – that is, the minimization problem becomes

$$(\hat{c}, \hat{d}) = \operatorname*{argmin}_{c \in C, d \in D} \hat{\sigma}^2(c, d), \qquad (3.28)$$

where $D = \{1, \ldots, d^*\}$ and the notation $\hat{\sigma}^2(c, d)$ is used to indicate that the estimate of the residual variance now depends on d as well as on c. As the parameter space for d is discrete, the least squares estimate $\hat{d}$ is super-consistent and d can be treated as known when computing confidence intervals for the remaining parameters, for example.

If one wants to allow for an exogenous threshold variable q_t, a similar procedure can be followed. In that case, the SETAR model is estimated with different candidate threshold variables, and the variable that renders the best fit is selected as the most appropriate one. See Chen (1995) for alternative methods of selecting the threshold variable.

Notice that there is a loop in the part of the specification procedure of SETAR models discussed so far. Recall that to determine the appropriate orders of the AR models in the two regimes with, for example, the AIC in (3.8), the threshold variable was assumed known, while to determine the appropriate threshold variable using a grid search as outlined above, the AR orders are assumed known. One way to break this loop is to include the search for the appropriate threshold variable in the minimization of the information criterion – that is, minimize the AIC over p_1, p_2 and d as suggested by Tong (1990, p. 379). Of course, this increases the computational burden considerably, as now $p_1^* \cdot p_2^* \cdot d^*$ different models have to be estimated.

Example 3.1: Dutch guilder   We apply the part of the SETAR specification procedure outlined so far to weekly returns on the exchange rate of the Dutch guilder *vis-à-vis* the US dollar. We use the sample January 1980–December 1989 to specify the model, and hold back the remaining observations for out-of-sample forecasting later in this chapter.

We start by determining the appropriate threshold variable and lag orders in the SETAR model, using the AIC in (3.8). In addition to lagged returns y_{t-d}, we also consider a measure of volatility as candidate threshold variable (cf. LeBaron, 1992). To be precise, we use the variable $v_{t,j}$, which is defined as the average absolute returns over the last j weeks, that is,

$$v_{t,j} = \frac{1}{j} \sum_{i=0}^{j-1} |y_{t-i}|. \tag{3.29}$$

We consider $v_{t-1,j}$ with $j = 1, \ldots, 4$ as possible threshold variables. Lagged returns y_{t-d} are considered for $d = 1, \ldots, d^*$ with $d^* = 4$. In the minimization of the AIC, we consider only models in which the AR orders in the two regimes are equal, and not larger than $p^* = 5$. The results are shown in table 3.2.

Table 3.2   *AIC values for SETAR models for weekly returns on the Dutch guilder exchange rate*

Threshold variable	p					
	0	1	2	3	4	5
y_{t-1}	370.88	371.83	370.28	347.32	341.51	413.40
y_{t-2}	393.41	408.90	404.47	408.32	415.40	408.49
y_{t-3}	402.38	399.76	400.72	403.39	401.50	404.42
y_{t-4}	385.64	402.03	393.58	407.26	403.30	398.38
$v_{t-1,1}$	354.37	354.74	358.25	361.12	361.97	363.23
$v_{t-1,2}$	363.00	378.34	378.89	351.46	348.11	336.38
$v_{t-1,3}$	337.09	349.91	349.15	331.76	333.48	330.70
$v_{t-1,4}$	332.75	327.38	328.03	347.79	351.52	324.62

Note: Values of AIC for SETAR models estimated on weekly returns on the Dutch guilder exchange rate *vis-à-vis* the US dollar.

Table 3.3   *SETAR estimates for weekly percentage returns on the Dutch guilder exchange rate*

| | | Confidence intervals | | | |
| | | Asymptotic | | LR-statistic | |
Variable	Estimate	Low	High	Low	High
$v_{t-1,4} \leq \hat{c}$ (380 obs.)					
Constant	0.034	−0.089	0.157	−0.093	0.210
y_{t-1}	0.245	0.063	0.427	−0.017	0.614
y_{t-2}	0.172	0.011	0.333	−0.047	0.581
$v_{t-1,4} > \hat{c}$ (131 obs.)					
Constant	0.266	−0.071	0.603	−0.149	0.692
y_{t-1}	−0.116	−0.300	0.068	−0.288	0.082
y_{t-2}	0.051	−0.110	0.212	−0.096	0.223
Threshold	1.151	—		0.534	1.532

Notes: Estimates of SETAR model for weekly returns on the Dutch guilder exchange rate *vis-à-vis* the US dollar.

The columns headed 'Asymptotic' and 'LR-statistic' contain limits of the confidence intervals based on the asymptotic normal distribution and on the confidence set for the threshold estimate $\widehat{C}_{0.8}$, respectively.

Minimization of the AIC suggests that the average absolute return over the previous four weeks, $v_{t-1,4}$, is the appropriate threshold variable, with an AR order $p = 5$. Note, however, that the values of the AIC for $p = 1$ and $p = 2$ (and $v_{t-1,4}$ as threshold variable) are quite close to the minimum. For convenience, we proceed with estimating a SETAR model with $p = 2$. Estimates of the parameters of the model are given in table 3.3. Heteroscedasticity-consistent standard errors and the limits of the confidence intervals based on the set $\widehat{C}_{0.8}$ are reported as well.

It appears that the AR parameters in the high volatility regime, $v_{t-1,4} > \hat{c}$ are insignificant as well – even when the confidence interval is based on the asymptotic normal distribution. This corresponds with the findings of Kräger and Kugler (1993), who estimate 3-regime models with y_{t-1} as threshold variable. For four out of their five exchange rates, they find that the return is best described as a white noise series in the outer regimes, where y_{t-1} is large in absolute value (and thus volatility is high), and by means of a stationary AR model in the middle regime, where y_{t-1} (and thus volatility) is moderate.

3.2.2   Estimation of STAR models

Estimation of the parameters in the STAR model (3.6) is a relatively straightforward application of nonlinear least squares (NLS) – that is, the parameters $\theta = (\phi_1', \phi_2', \gamma, c)'$ can be estimated as

$$\hat{\theta} = \underset{\theta}{\operatorname{argmin}}\, Q_n(\theta) = \underset{\theta}{\operatorname{argmin}} \sum_{t=1}^{n} [y_t - F(x_t; \theta)]^2, \tag{3.30}$$

where $F(x_t; \theta)$ is the skeleton of the model, that is,

$$F(x_t; \theta) \equiv \phi_1' x_t (1 - G(y_{t-1}; \gamma, c)) + \phi_2' x_t G(y_{t-1}; \gamma, c).$$

Under the additional assumption that the errors ε_t are normally distributed, NLS is equivalent to maximum likelihood. Otherwise, the NLS estimates can be interpreted as quasi-maximum likelihood estimates. Under certain regularity conditions (which are discussed in White and Domowitz, 1984; Gallant, 1987; Pötscher and Prucha, 1997, among others), the NLS estimates are consistent and asymptotically normal, that is,

$$\sqrt{T}(\hat{\theta} - \theta_0) \rightarrow N(0, C), \tag{3.31}$$

where θ_0 denotes the true parameter values. The asymptotic covariance-matrix C of $\hat{\theta}$ can be estimated consistently as $\widehat{A}_n^{-1} \widehat{B}_n \widehat{A}_n^{-1}$, where $\widehat{A}_n$ is the Hessian evaluated at $\hat{\theta}$

$$\begin{aligned}\widehat{A}_n &= -\frac{1}{n} \sum_{t=1}^{n} \nabla^2 q_t(\hat{\theta}) \\ &= \frac{1}{n} \sum_{t=1}^{n} (\nabla F(x_t; \hat{\theta}) \nabla F(x_t; \hat{\theta})' - \nabla^2 F(x_t; \hat{\theta}) \hat{\varepsilon}_t),\end{aligned} \tag{3.32}$$

with $q_t(\hat{\theta}) = [y_t - F(x_t; \hat{\theta})]^2$, $\nabla F(x_t; \hat{\theta}) = \partial F(x_t; \hat{\theta})/\partial \theta$, and $\widehat{B}_n$ is the outer product of the gradient

$$\widehat{B}_n = \frac{1}{n} \sum_{t=1}^{n} \nabla q_t(\hat{\theta}) \nabla q_t(\hat{\theta})' = \frac{1}{n} \sum_{t=1}^{n} \hat{\varepsilon}_t^2 \nabla F(x_t; \hat{\theta}) \nabla F(x_t; \hat{\theta})'. \tag{3.33}$$

The estimation can be performed using any conventional nonlinear optimization procedure (see Quandt, 1983; Hamilton, 1994, section 5.7; Hendry, 1995, appendix A5, for surveys). Issues that deserve particular attention are the choice of starting values for the optimization algorithm, concentrating the sum of squares function and the estimate of the smoothness parameter γ in the transition function.

Starting values

Obviously, the burden put on the optimization algorithm can be alleviated by using good starting values. Note that for fixed values of the parameters in the transition function, γ and c, the STAR model is linear in the autoregressive parameters ϕ_1 and ϕ_2, similar to the SETAR model. Thus, conditional upon γ and c, estimates of $\phi = (\phi_1', \phi_2')'$ can be obtained by OLS as

$$\hat{\phi}(\gamma, c) = \left(\sum_{t=1}^{n} x_t(\gamma, c) x_t(\gamma, c)' \right)^{-1} \left(\sum_{t=1}^{n} x_t(\gamma, c) y_t \right), \tag{3.34}$$

where $x_t(\gamma, c) = (x_t'(1 - G(y_{t-1}; \gamma, c)), x_t' G(y_{t-1}; \gamma, c))'$ and the notation $\phi(\gamma, c)$ is used to indicate that the estimate of ϕ is conditional upon γ and c. The corresponding residuals can be computed as $\hat{\varepsilon}_t = y_t - \hat{\phi}(\gamma, c)' x_t(\gamma, c)$ with associated variance $\hat{\sigma}^2(\gamma, c) = n^{-1} \sum_{t=1}^{n} \hat{\varepsilon}_t^2(\gamma, c)$. A convenient method to obtain sensible starting values for the nonlinear optimization algorithm then is to perform a two-dimensional grid search over γ and c and select those parameter estimates which render the smallest estimate for the residual variance $\hat{\sigma}^2(\gamma, c)$.

Concentrating the sum of squares function

As suggested by Leybourne, Newbold and Vougas (1998), another way to simplify the estimation problem is to concentrate the sum of squares function. Owing to the fact that the STAR model is linear in the autoregressive parameters for given values of γ and c, the sum of squares function $Q_n(\theta)$ can be concentrated with respect to ϕ_1 and ϕ_2 as

$$Q_n(\gamma, c) = \sum_{t=1}^{n} (y_t - \phi(\gamma, c)' x_t(\gamma, c))^2. \tag{3.35}$$

This reduces the dimensionality of the NLS estimation problem considerably, as the sum of squares function as given in (3.35) needs to be minimized with respect to the two parameters γ and c only.

The estimate of γ

It turns out to be notoriously difficult to obtain a precise estimate of the smoothness parameter γ. One reason for this is that for large values of γ, the shape of the logistic function (3.4) changes only little. Hence, to obtain an accurate estimate of γ one needs many observations in the immediate neighbourhood of the threshold c. As this is typically not the case, the estimate of γ is rather imprecise in general and often appears to be insignificant when judged by its t-statistic. This estimation problem is discussed in a more general context in Bates and Watts (1988, p. 87). The main point to be taken is that insignificance of the estimate of γ should not be interpreted as evidence against the presence of STAR-type nonlinearity. This should be assessed by means of different diagnostics, some of which are discussed below.

3.2.3 Estimation of the Markov-Switching model

The parameters in the MSW model can be estimated using maximum likelihood techniques. However, owing to the fact that the Markov-process s_t is not observed, the estimation problem is highly nonstandard. The aim of the estimation procedure in fact is not only to obtain estimates of the parameters in the autoregressive models in the different regimes and the probabilities of transition from one regime to the other, but also to obtain an estimate of the state that occurs at each point of the sample – or, more precisely, the probabilities with which each state occurs at each point in time.

Consider the 2-regime MSW model with an AR(p) specification in both regimes,

$$
y_t = \begin{cases} \phi_{0,1} + \phi_{1,1} y_{t-1} + \cdots + \phi_{p,1} y_{t-p} + \varepsilon_t & \text{if } s_t = 1, \\ \phi_{0,2} + \phi_{1,2} y_{t-1} + \cdots + \phi_{p,2} y_{t-p} + \varepsilon_t & \text{if } s_t = 2, \end{cases} \tag{3.36}
$$

or in shorthand notation,

$$
y_t = \phi_{0,s_t} + \phi_{1,s_t} y_{t-1} + \cdots + \phi_{p,s_t} y_{t-p} + \varepsilon_t. \tag{3.37}
$$

Under the additional assumption that the ε_t in (3.36) are normally distributed (conditional upon the history Ω_{t-1}), the density of y_t conditional on the regime s_t and the history Ω_{t-1} is a normal distribution with mean $\phi_{0,s_t} + \phi_{1,s_t} y_{t-1} + \cdots + \phi_{p,s_t} y_{t-p}$ and variance σ^2,

$$
f(y_t | s_t = j, \Omega_{t-1}; \theta) = \frac{1}{\sqrt{2\pi}\sigma} \exp\left\{ \frac{-(y_t - \phi'_j x_t)^2}{2\sigma^2} \right\}, \tag{3.38}
$$

where again $x_t = (1, y_{t-1}, \ldots, y_{t-p})'$, $\phi_j = (\phi_{0,j}, \phi_{1,j}, \ldots, \phi_{p,j})'$ for $j = 1, 2$, and θ is a vector that contains all parameters in the model, $\theta = (\phi'_1, \phi'_2, p_{11}, p_{22}, \sigma^2)'$. Notice that the parameters p_{11} and p_{22} completely define all transition probabilities because, for example, $p_{12} = 1 - p_{11}$. Given that the state s_t is unobserved, the conditional log likelihood for the tth observation $l_t(\theta)$ is given by the log of the density of y_t conditional only upon the history Ω_{t-1} – that is, $l_t(\theta) = \ln f(y_t|\Omega_{t-1};\theta)$. The density $f(y_t|\Omega_{t-1};\theta)$ can be obtained from the joint density of y_t and s_t as follows,

$$f(y_t|\Omega_{t-1};\theta) = f(y_t, s_t = 1|\Omega_{t-1};\theta) + f(y_t, s_t = 2|\Omega_{t-1};\theta)$$

$$= \sum_{j=1}^{2} f(y_t|s_t = j, \Omega_{t-1};\theta) \cdot P(s_t = j|\Omega_{t-1};\theta),$$

(3.39)

where the second equality follows directly from the basic law of conditional probability, which states that the joint probability of two events A and B, $P(A \text{ and } B)$, is equal to $P(A|B)P(B)$.

In order to be able to compute the density (3.39), we obviously need to quantify the conditional probabilities of being in either regime given the history of the process, $P(s_t = j|\Omega_{t-1};\theta)$. In fact, it turns out that in order to develop the maximum likelihood estimates of the parameters in the model, three different estimates of the probabilities of each of the regimes occurring at time t are needed: estimates of the probability that the process is in regime j at time t given all observations up to time $t-1$, given all observations up to and including time t and given all observations in the entire sample. These estimates usually are called, respectively, the *forecast, inference* and *smoothed inference* of the regime probabilities.

Intuitively, if the regime that occurs at time $t-1$ were known and included in the information set Ω_{t-1}, the optimal *forecasts* of the regime probabilities are simply equal to the transition probabilities of the Markov-process s_t. More formally,

$$\hat{\xi}_{t|t-1} = P \cdot \xi_{t-1},$$

(3.40)

where $\hat{\xi}_{t|t-1}$ denotes the 2×1 vector containing the conditional probabilities of interest – that is, $\hat{\xi}_{t|t-1} = (P(s_t = 1|\Omega_{t-1};\theta), P(s_t = 2|\Omega_{t-1};\theta))'$, $\xi_{t-1} = (1, 0)'$ if $s_{t-1} = 1$ and $\xi_{t-1} = (0, 1)'$ if $s_{t-1} = 2$, and P is the matrix containing the transition probabilities,

$$P = \begin{pmatrix} p_{11} & 1 - p_{22} \\ 1 - p_{11} & p_{22} \end{pmatrix}.$$

(3.41)

In practice the regime at time $t-1$ is unknown, as it is unobservable. The best one can do is to replace ξ_{t-1} in (3.40) by an estimate of the probabilities of each regime occurring at time $t-1$ conditional upon all information up to and including the observation at $t-1$ itself. Denote the 2×1 vector containing the optimal *inference* concerning the regime probabilities as $\hat{\xi}_{t-1|t-1}$. Given a starting value $\hat{\xi}_{1|0}$ and values of the parameters contained in θ, one can compute the optimal forecast and inference for the conditional regime probabilities by iterating on the pair of equations

$$\hat{\xi}_{t|t} = \frac{\hat{\xi}_{t|t-1} \odot f_t}{\mathbf{1}'(\hat{\xi}_{t|t-1} \odot f_t)} \tag{3.42}$$

$$\hat{\xi}_{t+1|t} = P \cdot \hat{\xi}_{t|t}, \tag{3.43}$$

for $t = 1, \ldots, n$, where f_t denotes the vector containing the conditional densities (3.38) for the two regimes, $\mathbf{1}$ is a 2×1 vector of ones and the symbol $\odot$ indicates element-by-element multiplication. The necessary starting values $\hat{\xi}_{1|0}$ can either be taken to be a fixed vector of constants which sum to unity, or can be included as separate parameters that need to be estimated. See Hamilton (1994, p. 693) for an intuitive explanation of why this algorithm works.

Finally, let $\hat{\xi}_{t|n}$ denote the vector which contains the *smoothed inference* on the regime probabilities – that is, estimates of the probability that regime j occurs at time t given all available observations, $P(s_t = j|\Omega_n; \theta)$. Kim (1993) develops an algorithm to obtain these regime probabilities from the conditional probabilities $\hat{\xi}_{t|t}$ and $\hat{\xi}_{t+1|t}$ given by (3.42) and (3.43). The smoothed inference on the regime probabilities at time t is computed as

$$\hat{\xi}_{t|n} = \hat{\xi}_{t|t} \odot (P'[\hat{\xi}_{t+1|n} \div \hat{\xi}_{t+1|t}]), \tag{3.44}$$

where $\div$ indicates element-by-element division. The algorithm runs backwards through the sample – that is, starting with $\hat{\xi}_{n|n}$ from (3.42) one applies (3.44) for $t = n - 1, n - 2, \ldots, 1$. For more details we refer to Kim (1993).

Returning to (3.42), notice that the denominator of the right-hand-side expression actually is the conditional log likelihood for the observation at time t as given in (3.39), which follows directly from the definitions of $\hat{\xi}_{t|t-1}$ and f_t. As shown in Hamilton (1990), the maximum likelihood estimates of the transition probabilities are given by

$$\hat{p}_{ij} = \frac{\sum_{t=2}^n P(s_t = j, s_{t-1} = i|\Omega_n; \hat{\theta})}{\sum_{t=2}^n P(s_{t-1} = i|\Omega_n; \hat{\theta})}, \tag{3.45}$$

where $\hat{\theta}$ denotes the maximum likelihood estimates of θ. It is also shown in Hamilton (1990) that these satisfy the first-order conditions

$$\sum_{t=1}^n (y_t - \hat{\phi}_j' x_t) x_t P(s_t = j|\Omega_n; \hat{\theta}) = 0, \quad j = 1, 2, \tag{3.46}$$

and

$$\hat{\sigma}^2 = \frac{1}{n} \sum_{t=1}^{n} \sum_{j=1}^{2} (y_t - \hat{\phi}'_j x_t)^2 P(s_t = j | \Omega_n; \hat{\theta}). \tag{3.47}$$

Notice that (3.46) implies that $\hat{\phi}_j$ is the estimate corresponding to a weighted least squares regression of y_t on x_t, with weights given by the square root of the smoothed probability of regime j occurring. Hence, the estimates $\hat{\phi}_j$ can be obtained as

$$\hat{\phi}_j = \left(\sum_{t=1}^{n} x_t(j) x_t(j)' \right)^{-1} \left(\sum_{t=1}^{n} x_t(j) y_t(j) \right), \tag{3.48}$$

where

$$y_t(j) = y_t \sqrt{P(s_t = j | \Omega_n; \hat{\theta})},$$
$$x_t(j) = x_t \sqrt{P(s_t = j | \Omega_n; \hat{\theta})}.$$

Finally, the ML estimate of the residual variance is obtained using (3.47) as the mean of the squared residuals from the two WLS regressions.

Putting all the above elements together suggests the following iterative procedure to estimate the parameters of the MSW model. Given starting values for the parameter vector $\hat{\theta}^{(0)}$, first compute the smoothed regime probabilities using (3.42), (3.43) and (3.44). Next, the smoothed regime probabilities $\hat{\xi}_{t|n}$ are combined with the initial estimates of the transition probabilities $\hat{p}_{ij}^{(0)}$ to obtain new estimates of the transition probabilities $\hat{p}_{ij}^{(1)}$ from (3.45). Finally, (3.48) and (3.47) can be used to obtain a new set of estimates of the autoregressive parameters and the residual variance. Combined with the new estimates of the transition probabilities, this gives a new set of estimates for all parameters in the model, $\hat{\theta}^{(1)}$. Iterating this procedure renders estimates $\hat{\theta}^{(2)}, \hat{\theta}^{(3)}, \ldots$ and this can be continued until convergence occurs – that is, until the estimates in subsequent iterations are the same. This procedure turns out to be an application of the Expectation Maximization (EM) algorithm developed by Dempster, Laird and Rubin (1977). It can be shown that each iteration of this procedure increases the value of the likelihood function, which guarantees that the final estimates are ML estimates.

Example 3.2: Frankfurt stock index   We estimate a 2-regime MSW model with an AR(2) model in both regimes for weekly absolute returns on the

Table 3.4   *Parameter estimates for a MSW model for weekly absolute returns on the Frankfurt stock index*

$\phi_{0,1}$	$\phi_{1,1}$	$\phi_{2,1}$	$\phi_{0,2}$	$\phi_{1,2}$	$\phi_{2,2}$	$p_{1,1}$	$p_{2,2}$
0.909	0.173	0.294	5.860	−0.505	−0.596	0.952	0.754
(0.206)	(0.070)	(0.072)	(0.954)	(0.160)	(0.172)	(0.022)	(0.132)

Frankfurt stock index over the period January 1988–December 1992 (260 observations). Table 3.4 contains the estimates of the autoregressive parameters and the parameters determining the regime transition probabilities, p_{11} and p_{22}. Figure 3.5 shows the filtered and smoothed inference on the regime probabilities $\hat{\xi}_{t|t}$ and $\hat{\xi}_{t|n}$.

Based on the estimated transition probabilities p_{11} and p_{22} it appears that the regime $s_t = 1$ is much more persistent than the regime $s_t = 2$, where this last regime seems to correspond with more volatile periods. The unconditional regime probabilities are computed from (3.17) and (3.18) as $P(s_t = 1) = 0.84$ and $P(s_t = 2) = 0.16$. Indeed, the regime probabilities in figure 3.5 confirm that the regime $s_t = 1$ occurs much more often.

3.2.4   Robust estimation of SETAR models

In section 2.5 it was argued that especially additive outliers (AOs) affect inference in linear time series models, as such aberrant observations lead to biased estimates of the parameters in the model, among other things. It might be expected that AOs have similar effects in nonlinear time series models, although this has not yet been investigated rigorously.

Extending the GM estimation method discussed in section 2.5 to estimate the parameters of a SETAR model turns out to be fairly straightforward (see Chan and Cheung, 1994). Consider for example the 2-regime SETAR model

$$y_t = \begin{cases} \phi_{1,1} y_{t-1} + \varepsilon_t & \text{if } y_{t-1} \leq c, \\ \phi_{1,2} y_{t-1} + \varepsilon_t & \text{if } y_{t-1} > c. \end{cases} \tag{3.49}$$

For fixed threshold c, the autoregressive parameters $\phi_{1,1}$ and $\phi_{1,2}$ can be estimated separately by applying the GM estimator discussed in section 2.5 using

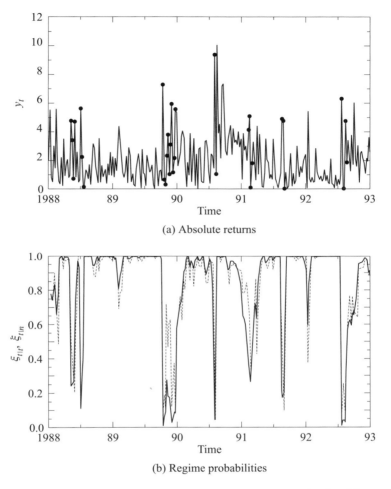

(a) Absolute returns

(b) Regime probabilities

Figure 3.5   The upper graph shows absolute weekly returns on the Frankfurt stock index: observations for which the smoothed probability of being in regime 1 is smaller than 0.5 are marked with a solid circle; the lower graph contains the filtered (dashed line) and smoothed (solid line) probability for the regime $s_t = 1$

the observations in the particular regime only, that is,

$$\hat{\phi}_{1,1}^{(n+1)} = \frac{\sum_{y_{t-1} \leq c} w_r\left(\hat{\phi}_{1,1}^{(n)}, \hat{\sigma}_{\varepsilon,1}^{(n)}\right) y_{t-1} y_t}{\sum_{y_{t-1} \leq c} w_r\left(\hat{\phi}_{1,1}^{(n)}, \hat{\sigma}_{\varepsilon,1}^{(n)}\right) y_{t-1}^2}, \tag{3.50}$$

$$\hat{\phi}_{1,2}^{(n+1)} = \frac{\sum_{y_{t-1} > c} w_r\left(\hat{\phi}_{1,2}^{(n)}, \hat{\sigma}_{\varepsilon,2}^{(n)}\right) y_{t-1} y_t}{\sum_{y_{t-1} > c} w_r\left(\hat{\phi}_{1,2}^{(n)}, \hat{\sigma}_{\varepsilon,2}^{(n)}\right) y_{t-1}^2}, \tag{3.51}$$

where $\sigma_{\varepsilon,j}$, $j = 1, 2$ is the scale of the residuals in each of the regimes. To estimate the threshold c, notice that the GM estimator (2.115) of ϕ_1 in the AR(1) model can be thought of as minimizing the objective function

$$\sum_{t=1}^{n} \rho(y_{t-1}, (y_t - \phi_1 y_{t-1})/\sigma_\varepsilon), \tag{3.52}$$

where $\rho(y_{t-1}, r_t)$ is such that $\partial\rho(y_{t-1}, r_t)/\partial r_t = (y_t - \phi_1 y_{t-1})w_r(r_t)$. Similarly, the GM estimators of parameters in the SETAR model (3.49) can be thought of as minimizing the composite objective function

$$\sum_{y_{t-1} \leq c} \rho(y_{t-1}, (y_t - \phi_{1,1} y_{t-1})/\sigma_\varepsilon)$$
$$+ \sum_{y_{t-1} > c} \rho(y_{t-1}, (y_t - \phi_{1,2} y_{t-1})/\sigma_\varepsilon), \tag{3.53}$$

for fixed c. The threshold itself can be estimated by minimizing (3.53) with respect to c, using a grid search as described in subsection 3.2.1.

To our knowledge, robust estimation methods for STAR and MSW models still have to be developed. The simulation results in van Dijk (1999, chapter 7) show that the usual GM estimators cannot readily be applied.

Example 3.1: Dutch guilder   We apply the robust estimation procedure as outlined above to estimate a SETAR model for weekly returns on the exchange rate of the Dutch guilder *vis-à-vis* the US dollar, over the period January 1980–December 1989. The specification of the model is taken as previously – that is, we use the average absolute returns over the past four weeks $v_{t-1,4}$, as given in (3.29), as the threshold variable and use an AR(p) model with $p = 2$ in both regimes. We use the weight function based on the polynomial ψ-function given in (2.118).

The robust estimation method gives rather different results than the standard method, as reported in table 3.3. Most importantly, the robust estimate of the threshold is equal to $\hat{c} = 0.385$, which is considerably lower than the 'standard' estimate $\hat{c} = 1.151$. Consequently, the lower regime ($v_{t-1,4} < \hat{c}$) now contains only 87 observations, whereas the upper regime contains the remaining 434 observations. The parameters of the AR(2) model in the lower regime are estimated as $\hat{\phi}_{0,1} = -0.059$, $\hat{\phi}_{1,1} = 0.298$, $\hat{\phi}_{2,1} = 0.526$. The corresponding estimates of the AR(2) model in the upper regime are $\hat{\phi}_{0,2} = -0.053$, $\hat{\phi}_{1,2} = 0.012$, $\hat{\phi}_{2,2} = 0.060$.

The upper panel of figure 3.6 shows the weekly returns series, with observations that receive weight less than one in the robust estimation procedure

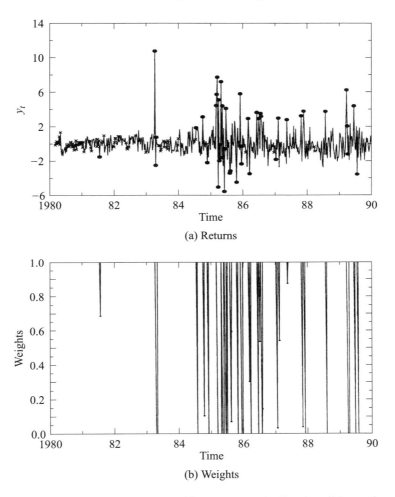

(a) Returns

(b) Weights

Figure 3.6   The upper graph shows weekly returns on the Dutch guilder exchange rate

Observations that receive a weight smaller than 1 in the outlier-robust estimation procedure which is used to estimate a SETAR model, are marked with a solid circle, and observations which are classified as being in the lower regime ($v_{t-1,4} < 0.385$) are marked with a cross; the lower graph contains the actual weights w_t

marked with circles and observations which belong to the lower regime marked with crosses. The actual weights are shown in the lower panel of this figure. It is seen the lower regime is realized mainly during the first few years in the sample period, when volatility appeared to be smaller. Most outliers are found in the second half of the sample with a large concentration in 1985, and are associated with large positive or negative returns.

3.3   Testing for regime-switching nonlinearity

Perhaps the most important question that needs to be answered when considering regime-switching models is whether the additional regime(s) (relative to
the single regime in a linear AR model) add(s) significantly to explaining the
dynamic behaviour of the time series y_t. One possible method of addressing
this question is to compare the in-sample fit of the regime-switching model with
that of a linear model. A natural approach is then to take the linear model as the
null hypothesis and the regime-switching model as the alternative. In the case
of a 2-regime model, the null hypothesis can be expressed as equality of the
autoregressive parameters in the two regimes – that is, $H_0 : \phi_1 = \phi_2$ – which
is tested against the alternative hypothesis $H_1 : \phi_{i,1} \neq \phi_{i,2}$ for at least one
$i \in \{0, \ldots, p\}$.

The statistical tests which take either one of the three regime-switching
models as the alternative all suffer from the problem of so-called *unidentified
nuisance parameters* under the null hypothesis. By this it is meant that the nonlinear model contains certain parameters which are not restricted under the null
hypothesis and which are not present in the linear model. In both the SETAR
and STAR models, the threshold c is such an unidentified nuisance parameter,
whereas in the STAR model, the smoothness parameter γ is one as well. In
the MSW model, the unidentified nuisance parameters are p_{11} and p_{22}, which
define the transition probabilities between the two regimes. The main consequence of the presence of such parameters is that the conventional statistical
theory cannot be applied to obtain the (asymptotic) distribution of the test-
statistics (see Davies, 1977, 1987 and Hansen, 1996, among others). Instead,
the test-statistics tend to have a nonstandard distribution, for which an analytical expression is often not available. This implies that critical values have to be
determined by means of simulation methods.

Although estimation methods for the regime-switching models are readily
available, it still seems a good idea to explore the potential usefulness of these
models before actually attempting to estimate them. It turns out that no such
tests against the SETAR and MSW models are available. Only after estimating a 2-regime model can one assess the relevance of the additional regime
(relative to a linear AR model, which might be thought of as a 1-regime
model). For the STAR model, on the other hand, Lagrange Multiplier (LM)-
statistics are available, which avoid estimating the model under the alternative
hypothesis.

3.3.1   Testing the SETAR model

Testing linearity against the alternative of a SETAR model is discussed
in Chan (1990, 1991), Chan and Tong (1990) and Hansen (1997, 2000). A solution to the above-mentioned identification problem here is to use the estimates

of the SETAR model to define a likelihood ratio or F-statistic which tests the restrictions as given by the null hypothesis, that is

$$F(\hat{c}) = n\left(\frac{\tilde{\sigma}^2 - \hat{\sigma}^2}{\hat{\sigma}^2}\right), \tag{3.54}$$

where $\tilde{\sigma}^2$ is an estimate of the residual variance under the null hypothesis of linearity, $\tilde{\sigma}^2 = \sum_{t=1}^{n} \tilde{\varepsilon}_t^2$ with $\tilde{\varepsilon}_t = y_t - \hat{\phi}' x_t$, and $\hat{\sigma}^2$ is defined just below (3.24). Notice that the statistic (3.54) is a monotonic transformation of $\hat{\sigma}^2$, in the sense that $F(\hat{c})$ always increases when $\hat{\sigma}^2$ decreases, and vice versa. As $\hat{c}$ minimizes the residual variance over the set C of allowable threshold values, $F(\hat{c})$ is equivalent to the supremum over this set C of the pointwise test-statistic $F(c)$,

$$F(\hat{c}) = \sup_{c \in C} F(c), \tag{3.55}$$

where

$$F(c) = n\left(\frac{\tilde{\sigma}^2 - \hat{\sigma}^2(c)}{\hat{\sigma}^2(c)}\right), \tag{3.56}$$

where $\hat{\sigma}^2(c)$ is defined just below (3.34).

The pointwise $F(c)$-statistic can also be computed as nR^2 with R^2 the coefficient of determination of an artificial regression of $\tilde{\varepsilon}_t$ on $x_t I(y_{t-1} \leq c)$ and $x_t I(y_{t-1} > c)$ (or, equivalently, on x_t and $x_t I(y_{t-1} \leq c)$). Hence, $F(c)$ has an asymptotic χ^2 distribution with $p + 1$ degrees of freedom. The test-statistic (3.55) is therefore the supremum of a number of dependent statistics, each of which follows an asymptotic χ^2 distribution. This shows that the distribution of $F(\hat{c})$ itself is nonstandard. Because the exact form of the dependence between the different $F(c)$s is difficult to analyse or characterize, critical values are most easily determined by means of simulation (see Hansen 1997, 2000, for more details).

3.3.2 Testing the STAR model

Testing linearity against the STAR model offers the opportunity to illustrate the problems of unidentified nuisance parameters in a different manner, in the sense that more than one restriction can be used to make the STAR model collapse to a linear AR model. Besides equality of the AR parameters in the two regimes, $H_0 : \phi_1 = \phi_2$, the null hypothesis of linearity can alternatively be expressed as $H_0' : \gamma = 0$. If $\gamma = 0$, the logistic function (3.4) is equal to 0.5 for all values of y_{t-1} and the STAR model reduces to an AR model with parameters $(\phi_1 + \phi_2)/2$. Whichever formulation of the null hypothesis is used, the model contains unidentified parameters. Where H_0 is used to characterize the null hypothesis of linearity, the parameters γ and c in the transition function are the unidentified nuisance parameters. Where H_0' is used, the threshold c and the parameters ϕ_1 and ϕ_2 are. To see the latter, note that under H_0', ϕ_1 and ϕ_2 can take any value as long as their average remains the same.

The approach that has been used in this case to solve the identification problem is slightly different from the one discussed above for the SETAR model. It turns out that in the case of testing against the alternative of a STAR model it is feasible to use a Lagrange Multiplier (LM)-statistic which has an asymptotic χ^2 distribution. The main advantage of the ability to use this statistic is that it is not necessary to estimate the model under the alternative hypothesis.

To demonstrate why the conventional distribution theory is still applicable, we describe the analysis in Luukkonen, Saikkonen and Teräsvirta (1988). Consider again the STAR model as given in (3.6), and rewrite this as

$$y_t = \frac{1}{2}(\phi_1 + \phi_2)'x_t + (\phi_2 - \phi_1)'x_t G^*(y_{t-1}; \gamma, c) + \varepsilon_t, \qquad (3.57)$$

where $G^*(y_{t-1}; \gamma, c) = G(y_{t-1}; \gamma, c) - 1/2$. Notice that under the null hypothesis $\gamma = 0$, $G^*(y_{t-1}, 0, c) = 0$. Luukkonen, Saikkonen and Teräsvirta (1988) suggest approximating the function $G^*(y_{t-1}, \gamma, c)$ with a first-order Taylor approximation around $\gamma = 0$, that is,

$$T_1(y_{t-1}; \gamma, c) \approx G^*(y_{t-1}; 0, c) + \gamma \left. \frac{\partial G^*(y_{t-1}; \gamma, c)}{\partial \gamma} \right|_{\gamma=0}$$

$$= \frac{1}{4}\gamma(y_{t-1} - c), \qquad (3.58)$$

where we have used the fact that $G^*(y_{t-1}; 0, c) = 0$. After substituting $T_1(\cdot)$ for $G_1^*(\cdot)$ in (3.57) and rearranging terms this gives the auxiliary regression model

$$y_t = \beta_{0,0} + \beta_0'\tilde{x}_t + \beta_1'\tilde{x}_t y_{t-1} + \eta_t, \qquad (3.59)$$

where $\tilde{x}_t = (y_{t-1}, \ldots, y_{t-p})'$ and $\beta_j = (\beta_{1,j}, \ldots, \beta_{p,j})'$, $j = 0, 1$. The relationships between the parameters in the auxiliary regression model (3.59) and the parameters in the STAR model (3.57) can be shown to be

$$\beta_{0,0} = (\phi_{0,1} + \phi_{0,2})/2 - \frac{1}{4}\gamma c(\phi_{0,2} - \phi_{0,1}), \qquad (3.60)$$

$$\beta_{1,0} = (\phi_{1,1} + \phi_{1,2})/2 - \frac{1}{4}\gamma(c(\phi_{1,2} - \phi_{1,1}) - (\phi_{0,2} - \phi_{0,1})), \qquad (3.61)$$

$$\beta_{i,0} = (\phi_{i,1} + \phi_{i,2})/2 - \frac{1}{4}\gamma c(\phi_{i,2} - \phi_{i,1}), \quad i = 2, \ldots, p, \qquad (3.62)$$

$$\beta_{i,1} = \frac{1}{4}\gamma c(\phi_{i,2} - \phi_{i,1}), \quad i = 1, \ldots, p. \qquad (3.63)$$

The above equations demonstrate that the restriction $\gamma = 0$ implies $\beta_{i,1} = 0$ for $i = 1, \ldots, p$. Hence testing the null hypothesis $H_0' : \gamma = 0$ in (3.57) is equivalent to testing the null hypothesis $H_0'' : \beta_1 = 0$ in (3.59). This null hypothesis can be tested by a standard variable addition test-statistic in a straightforward manner. Under the null hypothesis of linearity, the test-statistic has a χ^2 distribution with p degrees of freedom asymptotically. As the statistic does not test the original null hypothesis $H_0' : \gamma = 0$ but rather the auxiliary null hypothesis $H_0'' : \beta_1 = 0$, this test is usually referred to as an LM-*type*-statistic.

The test-statistic described above can also be developed from first principles as a genuine LM-statistic (see Granger and Teräsvirta, 1993, pp. 71–2). It can be shown that the statistic is in fact the supremum of the pointwise-statistics for fixed $\phi_2 - \phi_1$ and c and, hence, is similar in spirit to the test-statistic against the SETAR alternative discussed in the previous subsection.

As noted by Luukkonen, Saikkonen and Teräsvirta (1988), the above test-statistic does not have power in situations where only the intercept is different across regimes – that is, when $\phi_{0,1} \neq \phi_{0,2}$ but $\phi_{i,1} = \phi_{i,2}$ for $i = 1, \ldots, p$. This is seen immediately from (3.63) which shows that none of the $\beta_{i,1}$, $i = 1, \ldots, p$ parameters depends on $\phi_{0,2}$ and/or $\phi_{0,1}$. Luukkonen, Saikkonen and Teräsvirta (1988) suggest remedying this deficiency by replacing the transition function $G^*(y_{t-1}; \gamma, c)$ by a third-order Taylor approximation instead, that is,

$$
T_3(y_{t-1}; \gamma, c) \approx \gamma \left. \frac{\partial G^*(y_{t-1}; \gamma, c)}{\partial \gamma} \right|_{\gamma=0}
$$
$$
+ \frac{1}{6} \gamma^3 \left. \frac{\partial^3 G^*(y_{t-1}; \gamma, c)}{\partial \gamma^3} \right|_{\gamma=0}
$$
$$
= \frac{1}{4} \gamma (y_{t-1} - c) + \frac{1}{48} \gamma^3 (y_{t-1} - c)^3, \qquad (3.64)
$$

where we have used the fact the second derivative of $G^*(y_{t-1}; \gamma, c)$ with respect to γ evaluated at $\gamma = 0$ equals zero. Using this approximation yields the auxiliary model

$$
y_t = \beta_{0,0} + \beta_0' \tilde{x}_t + \beta_1' \tilde{x}_t y_{t-1} + \beta_2' \tilde{x}_t y_{t-1}^2 + \beta_3' \tilde{x}_t y_{t-1}^3 + \eta_t, \quad (3.65)
$$

where $\beta_{0,0}$ and the β_j, $j = 1, 2, 3$, again are functions of the parameters ϕ_1, ϕ_2, γ and c. Inspection of the exact relationships demonstrates that the null hypothesis $H_0' : \gamma = 0$ now corresponds to $H_0'' : \beta_1 = \beta_2 = \beta_3 = 0$, which again can be tested by a standard LM-type test. Under the null hypothesis of linearity, the test-statistic has a χ^2 distribution with $3p$ degrees of freedom asymptotically.

In small samples, the usual recommendation is to use F-versions of the LM-test-statistics, as these have better size and power properties. The F-version of the test-statistic based on (3.65) can be computed as follows:

1. estimate the model under the null hypothesis of linearity by regressing y_t on x_t. Compute the residuals $\tilde{\varepsilon}_t$ and the sum of squared residuals $SSR_0 = \sum_{t=1}^{n} \tilde{\varepsilon}_t^2$
2. estimate the auxiliary regression of $\tilde{\varepsilon}_t$ on x_t and $\tilde{x}_t y_{t-1}^j$, $j = 1, 2, 3$, and compute the sum of squared residuals from this regression SSR_1
3. the LM test-statistic can be computed as

$$LM = \frac{(SSR_0 - SSR_1)/3p}{SSR_1/(n - 4p - 1)},\tag{3.66}$$

and is approximately F-distributed with $3p$ and $n - 4p - 1$ degrees of freedom under the null hypothesis.

Choosing the transition variable

Teräsvirta (1994) suggests that the LM-type test (3.66) can also be used to select the appropriate transition variable in the STAR model. The statistic is computed for several candidate transition variables and the one for which the p-value of the test is smallest is selected as the true transition variable. The rationale behind this procedure is that the test should have maximum power if the alternative model is correctly specified – that is, if the correct transition variable is used. Simulation results in Teräsvirta (1994) suggest that this approach works quite well, at least in a univariate setting.

3.3.3 Testing the Markov-Switching model

When assessing the relevance of the MSW model, a natural approach is to use a Likelihood Ratio (LR)-statistic, which tests the null hypothesis of linearity against the alternative of a MSW model – that is, $H_0 : \phi_1 = \phi_2$ is tested by means of the test-statistic

$$LR_{MSW} = \mathcal{L}_{MSW} - \mathcal{L}_{AR},\tag{3.67}$$

where $\mathcal{L}_{MSW}$ and $\mathcal{L}_{AR}$ are the values of the log likelihood functions corresponding to the MSW and AR models, respectively. As noted in the introduction to this section, the parameters p_{11} and p_{22} defining the transition probabilities in the MSW model are unidentified nuisance parameters under the null hypothesis. As shown by Hansen (1992), the LR-statistic (3.67) has a nonstandard distribution which cannot be characterized analytically. Critical values to determine the significance of the test-statistic therefore have to be determined by means of simulation. The basic structure of such a simulation experiment is that one generates a large number of artificial time series y_t^* according to the model that holds under the null hypothesis. Next, one estimates both AR and MSW models for each artificial time series and computes the corresponding LR-statistic LR^*_{MSW} according to (3.67). These test-statistics might be used to obtain an estimate of the complete distribution of the test-statistic under the null hypothesis, or simply to compute the p-value of the LR-statistic for the true time series, which is given by the fraction of artificial samples for which LR^*_{MSW} exceeds the observed LR_{MSW}. Given that the estimation of the MSW model can be rather time-consuming, this procedure demands a considerable amount of computing time.

3.3.4   Outliers and tests for nonlinearity

A consequence of the presence of additive outliers (AOs) is that they affect diagnostic statistics which one might want to use prior to estimating a nonlinear model. van Dijk, Franses and Lucas (1999a) analyse the properties of the tests against STAR nonlinearity discussed in subsection 3.3.2 in the presence of AOs. It is shown that in the case of a linear process with some AOs the tests for STAR nonlinearity tend to reject the correct null hypothesis of linearity too often, even asymptotically. van Dijk, Franses and Lucas (1999a) suggest using outlier-robust estimation techniques, as discussed in section 2.5 to estimate the model under the null hypothesis as a solution to this problem. In addition to rendering better estimates of the model under the null hypothesis, robust estimation procedures allow us to construct test-statistics that are robust to outliers. As shown by van Dijk, Franses and Lucas (1999a), a robust equivalent to test $H_0'' : \beta_1 = \beta_2 = \beta_3 = 0$ in (3.65) is nR^2, using the R^2 from the regression of the weighted residuals $\hat{\psi}(\hat{r}_t) = \hat{w}_r(\hat{r}_t)\hat{r}_t$ on the weighted regressors $\hat{w}_y(x_t) \odot (x_t \ \tilde{x}_t y_{t-1} \ \tilde{x}_t y_{t-1}^2 \ \tilde{x}_t y_{t-1}^3)'$. The weights $\hat{w}_r(\hat{r}_t)$ and $\hat{w}_y(x_t)$ are obtained from GM estimation of the $AR(p)$ model, analogous to (2.121). The resulting LM-type-statistic has an asymptotic χ^2 distribution with $3p$ degrees of freedom. An outlier-robust equivalent of the F-version (3.66) can also be computed straightforwardly.

3.3.5   Heteroscedasticity and tests for nonlinearity

Neglected heteroscedasticity may also lead to spurious rejection of the null hypothesis of linearity. Intuitively, this can be understood from the auxiliary model (3.65), for example. Davidson and MacKinnon (1985) and Wooldridge (1990, 1991) have developed specification tests that can be used in the presence of heteroscedasticity, without the need to specify the form of the heteroscedasticity (which often is unknown). Their procedures may be readily applied to robustify linearity tests (see also Granger and Teräsvirta, 1993, pp. 69–70; Hansen, 1996).

For example, a heteroscedasticity-consistent (HCC) variant of the LM-type test-statistic against STAR based upon (3.65) can be computed as follows:
1. regress y_t on x_t and obtain the residuals $\hat{u}_t$
2. regress the auxiliary regressors $\tilde{x}_t y_{t-1}^j$, $j = 1, 2, 3$, on x_t and compute the residuals $\hat{r}_t$
3. weight the residuals $\hat{r}_t$ from the regression in (2) with the residuals $\hat{u}_t$ obtained in (1) and regress 1 on $\hat{u}_t \hat{r}_t$; the explained sum of squares from this regression is the LM-type-statistic.

Similar procedures can be used to compute HCC tests against the SETAR alternative (see Hansen, 1997; Wong and Li, 1997) and the MSW alternative.

Example 3.1: Dutch guilder   Table 3.5 contains p-values for the heteroscedasticity-robust variant of the test of linearity against a 2-regime SETAR alternative applied to the weekly returns on the Dutch guilder exchange rate. We consider the same threshold variables and autoregressive orders as before. The null hypothesis can be rejected at conventional significance levels for several combinations of p and q_t. The smallest p-values are achieved where the threshold variable is the average volatility during the past four weeks $v_{t-1,4}$ and $p = 1$ and 2. This confirms the choices made in the previous section.

Table 3.6 contains p-values of the LM-type test against STAR nonlinearity, based on an AR(2) model. We give p-values for the standard, outlier-robust and heteroscedasticity-consistent variants to highlight the differences that can occur. For example, where y_{t-d} is considered as the transition variable, one might be inclined to reject the null hypothesis of linearity for $d = 1, 2, 3$, based

Table 3.5   *p-values for HCC test of linearity against a SETAR alternative for weekly returns on the Dutch guilder exchange rate*

Threshold variable	p					
	0	1	2	3	4	5
y_{t-1}	0.698	0.315	0.685	0.696	0.918	0.908
y_{t-2}	0.131	0.201	0.871	0.969	0.933	0.584
y_{t-3}	0.592	0.376	0.706	0.137	0.378	0.430
y_{t-4}	0.060	0.147	0.337	0.373	0.819	0.776
$v_{t-1,1}$	0.301	0.544	0.437	0.224	0.443	0.549
$v_{t-1,2}$	0.330	0.062	0.223	0.049	0.066	0.098
$v_{t-1,3}$	0.571	0.090	0.075	0.059	0.128	0.139
$v_{t-1,4}$	0.090	0.004	0.015	0.027	0.086	0.021

Note: p-values of HCC test of linearity against 2-regime SETAR alternative for weekly returns on the Dutch guilder exchange rate *vis-à-vis* the US dollar.

Table 3.6   *p-values of LM-type test for STAR nonlinearity for*
weekly returns on the Dutch guilder exchange rate

Transition variable	LS	HCC	GM
y_{t-1}	0.079	0.192	0.248
y_{t-2}	0.097	0.253	0.976
y_{t-3}	0.099	0.496	0.601
y_{t-4}	0.293	0.525	0.253
$v_{t-1,1}$	0.313	0.403	0.204
$v_{t-1,2}$	0.075	0.103	0.046
$v_{t-1,3}$	0.008	0.013	0.006
$v_{t-1,4}$	0.002	0.003	0.001

Notes: The LM-type test is based on an AR(2) model.
LS, HCC and GM denote the standard, HCC (Wooldridge method)
and outlier-robust variants of the test, respectively.

on the outcomes of the standard test, given that the *p*-values are smaller than
0.10. The *p*-values for the GM and HCC test, on the other hand, are much
higher, and suggest that the evidence for nonlinearity is spurious, and might be
caused either by the presence of outliers or heteroscedasticity. For other choices
of transition variables, notably for $v_{t-1,4}$, the *p*-values for all variants of the
test are very small. On the basis of the minimum *p*-value rule discussed at the
end of subsection 3.3.2, we select $v_{t-1,4}$ as the appropriate transition variable
in the STAR model (which is not really surprising given the earlier estimation
results for the SETAR model).

After estimating a 2-regime STAR model with an AR(2) model in both
regimes, it turns out that the autoregressive parameters in the regime corresponding to $G(v_{t-1,4}; \gamma, c) = 1$ are not significant, similar to the findings
for the SETAR model reported in table 3.3. Consequently, the model is re-
estimated after deleting those insignificant parameters. The final estimates of
the model are given in table 3.7. Standard errors for the smoothness parameter
γ are not given, for reasons discussed in subsection 3.2.2. The transition function $G(v_{t-1,4}; \hat{\gamma}, \hat{c})$ is graphed in figure 3.7, both over time and against the
transition variable $v_{t-1,4}$. As suggested by the small magnitude of the point
estimate of γ, the transition from one regime to the other is seen to be rather
smooth.

Example 3.3: Tokyo stock index   We also apply the STAR modelling procedure to absolute values of weekly percentage returns on the Tokyo stock index.
The sample period is January 1988–December 1993. It turns out that we can

Table 3.7   *Parameter estimates for a STAR model for weekly returns on the Dutch guilder exchange rate*

Variable	Estimate	LS st. err.	HCC st. err.
Lower regime $(G(v_{t-1,4}; \hat{\gamma}, \hat{c}) = 0)$			
Constant	0.060	0.101	0.091
y_{t-1}	0.287	0.107	0.093
y_{t-2}	0.213	0.100	0.094
Upper regime $(G(v_{t-1,4}; \hat{\gamma}, \hat{c}) = 1)$			
Constant	−0.180	0.131	0.155
$\hat{c}$	1.355	0.152	0.153
$\hat{\gamma}$	4.316		

set $p = 2$ in the AR model that is used as the model under the null hypothesis of linearity. The p-values for the LM-type tests for linearity are given in table 3.8. Comparing these values, we are again tempted to select $v_{t-1,4}$ as the transition variable. The parameter estimates of the resultant model are given in table 3.9. The large value of the estimate of the parameter γ suggests that the transition from one regime to another occurs instantaneously at the estimated threshold $\hat{c}$. This is confirmed by the graphs of the transition function in figure 3.8.

3.4   Diagnostic checking

In this section we discuss several diagnostic tests which can be used to evaluate estimated regime-switching models. First and foremost, one might subject the residuals to a battery of diagnostic tests, comparable to the usual practice in the Box–Jenkins approach in linear time series modelling, as described in section 2.2. It turns out however, that not all the test-statistics that have been developed in the context of ARMA models are applicable to the residuals from nonlinear models as well. The test for normality of the residuals given in (2.54) is an example of a test which remains valid, while the Ljung–Box test-statistic (2.41) is an example of a test which does not (see Eitrheim and Teräsvirta, 1996). The LM approach to testing for serial correlation can still be used, however, as shown by Eitrheim and Teräsvirta (1996) and discussed in some detail below.

3.4.1   Diagnostic tests for SETAR and STAR models

In this subsection we discuss three important diagnostic checks for SETAR and STAR models, developed by Eitrheim and Teräsvirta (1996). Other

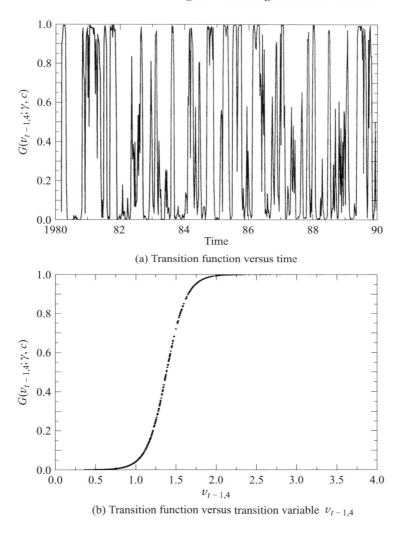

(a) Transition function versus time

(b) Transition function versus transition variable $v_{t-1,4}$

Figure 3.7   Transition function in STAR model for weekly returns on the Dutch guilder exchange rate; each dot in the graph in panel (b) represents an observation

methods for evaluating estimated SETAR models are discussed in Tong (1990, section 5.6).

Testing for serial correlation
Consider the general nonlinear autoregressive model of order p,

$$y_t = F(x_t; \theta) + \varepsilon_t, \tag{3.68}$$

where $x_t = (1, y_{t-1}, \ldots, y_{t-p})'$ as before and the skeleton $F(x_t; \theta)$ is a general nonlinear function of the parameters θ which is at least twice continuously

Table 3.8   *p-values of LM-type test for STAR nonlinearity for weekly absolute returns on the Tokyo stock index*

Transition variable	LS	HCC	GM
y_{t-1}	0.592	0.794	0.256
y_{t-2}	0.001	0.085	0.012
y_{t-3}	0.098	0.184	0.033
y_{t-4}	0.064	0.322	0.000
$v_{t-1,1}$	0.347	0.338	0.549
$v_{t-1,2}$	0.001	0.296	0.043
$v_{t-1,3}$	0.028	0.132	0.074
$v_{t-1,4}$	0.009	0.063	0.000

Notes: The LM-type test is based on an AR(2) model.
LS, HCC and GM denote the standard, HCC (Wooldridge method) and outlier-robust variants of the test, respectively.

Table 3.9   *Parameter estimates for a STAR model for weekly absolute returns on the Tokyo stock index*

Variable	Estimate	LS st. err.	HCC st. err.
Lower regime ($G(v_{t-1,4}; \hat{\gamma}, \hat{c}) = 0$)			
Constant	1.319	0.237	0.163
y_{t-1}	0.145	0.110	0.069
y_{t-2}	−0.033	0.113	0.068
Upper regime ($G(v_{t-1,4}; \hat{\gamma}, \hat{c}) = 1$)			
Constant	2.695	0.459	0.600
y_{t-1}	−0.027	0.071	0.097
y_{t-2}	0.232	0.074	0.109
$\hat{c}$	2.406	0.038	0.020
$\hat{\gamma}$	500.0		

differentiable. An LM test for qth order serial dependence in ε_t can be obtained as nR^2, where R^2 is the coefficient of determination from the regression of $\hat{\varepsilon}_t$ on $\hat{z}_t \equiv \partial F(x_t; \hat{\theta})/\partial\theta$ and q lagged residuals $\hat{\varepsilon}_{t-1}, \ldots, \hat{\varepsilon}_{t-q}$, where hats indicate that the relevant quantities are estimates under the null hypothesis of serial independence of ε_t. The resulting test-statistic is χ^2 distributed with q degrees of freedom asymptotically.

This test-statistic is in fact a generalization of the LM test for serial correlation in an AR(p) model of Breusch and Pagan (1979), which is based

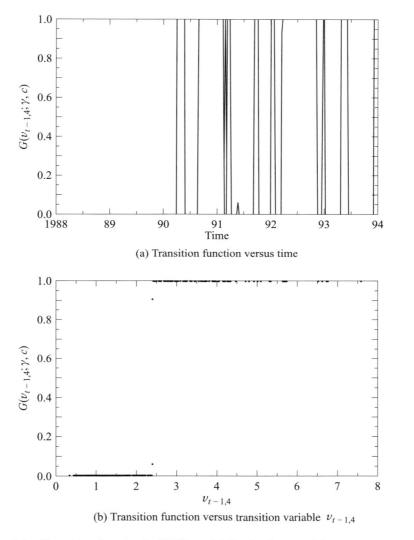

(a) Transition function versus time

(b) Transition function versus transition variable $v_{t-1,4}$

Figure 3.8   Transition function in STAR model for absolute weekly percentage returns on Tokyo stock index; each dot in the graph in panel (b) represents an observation

on the auxiliary regression (2.42). To understand why, note that for a linear AR(p) model (without an intercept) $F(x_t; \theta) = \sum_{i=1}^{p} \phi_i y_{t-i}$ and $\hat{z}_t = \partial F(x_t; \hat{\theta})/\partial \theta = (y_{t-1}, \ldots, y_{t-p})'$. In case of a STAR model, the skeleton is given by $F(x_t; \theta) = \phi_1' x_t (1 - G(y_{t-1}; \gamma, c)) + \phi_2' x_t G(y_{t-1}; \gamma, c)$. Hence, in this case $\theta = (\phi_1, \phi_2, \gamma, c)$ and the relevant partial derivatives $\hat{z}_t = \partial F(x_t; \hat{\theta})/\partial \theta$ can be obtained in a straightforward manner (see Eitrheim and Teräsvirta, 1996, for details).

The nonlinear function $F(x_t; \theta)$ needs to be twice continuously differentiable for the above approach to be valid. The skeleton of the SETAR model does not satisfy this requirement, as it is possibly discontinuous and in no case differentiable at the threshold value (see the examples in figure 3.3). Therefore, the LM-statistic for serial correlation cannot be applied to the residuals from an estimated SETAR model. A possible way to circumvent this problem is to approximate the SETAR model with a STAR model by setting γ equal to some large but finite value. Recall that in this case the logistic function (3.4) effectively becomes a step function which equals 0 for $y_{t-1} < c$ and 1 for $y_{t-1} > c$. Fixing γ at γ_0, say, the remaining parameters in the STAR model can again be estimated by NLS. When computing the test-statistic for residual autocorrelation in this case, the partial derivative of the regression function with respect to γ should be omitted from the auxiliary regression as this parameter is kept fixed.

Testing for remaining nonlinearity

An important question when using nonlinear time series models is whether the proposed model adequately captures all nonlinear features of the time series under investigation. One possible way to examine this is to apply a test for remaining nonlinearity to an estimated model. For the SETAR and STAR models, a natural approach is to specify the alternative hypothesis of remaining nonlinearity as the presence of an additional regime. For example, one might want to test the null hypothesis that a 2-regime model is adequate against the alternative that a third regime is necessary.

It turns out that only for the STAR model an LM test is available which allows us to test this hypothesis without the necessity to estimate the more complicated model. For the SETAR model, testing for remaining nonlinearity necessarily involves estimating the multiple-regime model. In fact, this is analogous to the situation of testing linearity against a 2-regime model, compare the discussion in the introduction to section 3.3.

For the SETAR model, one can essentially apply the methodology described in subsection 3.3.1 to each of the two subsamples defined by the estimated threshold $\hat{c}$ – that is, test linearity against the alternative of a 2-regime SETAR model on the subsamples for which $y_{t-1} \leq \hat{c}$ and $y_{t-1} > \hat{c}$ by using the test-statistic (3.55). Recall that computing the test involves estimating the 2-regime model under the alternative. Hence, it appears that where the statistics indicate the presence of an additional regime, estimates of the 3-regime model are readily available by combining the original estimation results for the 2-regime SETAR model with those for the 2-regime model on the subsample for which linearity is rejected. However, in case the true model is indeed a 3-regime model, it can be shown that while the estimate of the second threshold $\hat{c}_2$, say, is consistent, the estimate of the first threshold $\hat{c}_1 \equiv \hat{c}$ is not. To obtain a consistent estimate of the first threshold as well, it is necessary to perform a so-called 'repartitioning step', in which a 2-regime SETAR model is estimated on the subsample defined by $y_{t-1} \le \hat{c}_2$ if $\hat{c}_1 < \hat{c}_2$ and on the subsample defined by $y_{t-1} > \hat{c}_2$ if $\hat{c}_1 > \hat{c}_2$. See Bai (1997) and Bai and Perron (1998) for an application of this idea in the context of testing for multiple structural breaks in time series.

Eitrheim and Teräsvirta (1996) develop an LM-statistic to test a 2-regime STAR model against the alternative of an additive 3-regime model which can be written as,

$$y_t = \phi_1' x_t + (\phi_2 - \phi_1)' x_t G_1(y_{t-1}; \gamma_1, c_1)$$
$$+ (\phi_3 - \phi_2)' x_t G_2(y_{t-1}; \gamma_2, c_2) + \varepsilon_t, \tag{3.69}$$

where $x_t = (1, \tilde{x}_t')'$, $\tilde{x}_t = (y_{t-1}, \ldots, y_{t-p})'$, where both G_1 and G_2 are given by (3.4) and where we assume $c_1 < c_2$ without loss of generality. The null hypothesis of a 2-regime model can be expressed as $H_0 : \gamma_2 = 0$. This testing problem suffers from similar identification problems as the problem of testing the null hypothesis of linearity against the alternative of a 2-regime STAR model discussed in subsection 3.3.2. The solution here is the same as well. The transition function $G_2(y_{t-1}; \gamma_2, c_2)$ is replaced by a Taylor approximation around the point $\gamma_2 = 0$. In case of a third-order approximation, the resulting auxiliary model is given by

$$y_t = \beta_0' x_t + (\phi_2 - \phi_1)' x_t G_1(y_{t-1}; \gamma_1, c_1)$$
$$+ \beta_1' \tilde{x}_t y_{t-1} + \beta_2' \tilde{x}_t y_{t-1}^2 + \beta_3' \tilde{x}_t y_{t-1}^3 + \eta_t, \tag{3.70}$$

where the β_j, $j = 0, 1, 2, 3$, are functions of the parameters ϕ_1, ϕ_3, γ_2 and c_2. The null hypothesis $H_0 : \gamma_2 = 0$ in (3.69) translates into $H_0' : \beta_1 = \beta_2 = \beta_3 = 0$ in (3.70). The test-statistic can be computed as nR^2 from the auxiliary regression of the residuals obtained from estimating the model under the null hypothesis $\hat{\varepsilon}_t$ on the partial derivates of the regression function with respect to the parameters in the 2-regime model, ϕ_1, ϕ_2, γ_1 and c_1, evaluated under the null hypothesis, and the auxiliary regressors $\tilde{x}_t y_{t-1}^j$, $j = 1, 2, 3$. The resulting test-statistic has an asymptotic χ^2 distribution with $3p$ degrees of freedom. For more details we again refer to Eitrheim and Teräsvirta (1996).

In the above, it has been implicitly assumed that the additional regime is determined by the same variable (y_{t-1} in our case) as the original two regimes. As discussed previously, one might also consider situations where the regimes are determined by several variables – for example, y_{t-1} and y_{t-2}. For the STAR model, the null hypothesis of a 2-regime model can be tested against the alternative of the 4-regime model (3.14) by testing $H_0 : \gamma_2 = 0$. The LM test-statistic derived by van Dijk and Franses (1999) is similar to the LM-type-statistic for testing against a 3-regime alternative discussed above. Starting from the model given in (3.14), the second transition function $G_2(y_{t-2}; \gamma_2, c_2)$ is again replaced by a third-order Taylor approximation to render the auxiliary regression

$$
\begin{aligned}
y_t = {}& \beta_0' x_t + (\phi_2 - \phi_1)' x_t G_1(y_{t-1}; \gamma_1, c_1) \\
& + \beta_1' \tilde{x}_t y_{t-2} + \beta_2' \tilde{x}_t y_{t-2}^2 + \beta_3' \tilde{x}_t y_{t-2}^3 \\
& + \beta_4' \tilde{x}_t G_1(y_{t-1}; \gamma_1, c_1) y_{t-2} + \beta_5' \tilde{x}_t G_1(y_{t-1}; \gamma_1, c_1) y_{t-2}^2 \\
& + \beta_6' \tilde{x}_t G_1(y_{t-1}; \gamma_1, c_1) y_{t-2}^3 + \eta_t.
\end{aligned}
\tag{3.71}
$$

The null hypothesis $H_0 : \gamma_2 = 0$ in (3.14) now becomes into $H_0' : \beta_j = 0$, $j = 1, \ldots, 6$ which can be tested in exactly the same way as outlined before.

Testing parameter constancy

An interesting special case of the multiple-regime model (3.14) arises if the transition variable in the second transition function G_2 is not taken to be y_{t-2} but time t instead. This gives rise to a so-called Time-Varying STAR model, which allows for both nonlinear dynamics of the STAR-type and time-varying parameters. This model is discussed in detail in Lundbergh, Teräsvirta and van Dijk (1999). The point of interest here is that by testing the hypothesis $\gamma_2 = 0$ in this case, one tests for parameter constancy in the 2-regime STAR model (3.6), against the alternative of smoothly changing parameters. Again this test can be adopted to test for parameter constancy in a SETAR model by approximating it with a STAR model with γ_1 fixed at a large value.

Example 3.1: Dutch guilder   To evaluate the estimated STAR model for the weekly returns on the Dutch guilder exchange rate, we apply the diagnostic tests for serial correlation, remaining nonlinearity and parameter constancy. Table 3.10 contains p-values for the various test-statistics. These results suggest that the model is adequate, in the sense that the p-values are such that neither null hypothesis needs to be rejected.

Example 3.3: Tokyo stock index   The estimated STAR model for absolute weekly returns on the Tokyo stock index is evaluated in a similar manner. Table 3.11 contains p-values for the various diagnostic tests. Again the results do not suggest any serious misspecification of the model.

Table 3.10   *Diagnostic tests of a STAR model estimated for weekly returns on the Dutch guilder exchange rate*

Tests for qth-order serial correlation

q	4	8	12
p-value	0.436	0.175	0.169

Tests for parameter constancy

	LM_{C1}	LM_{C2}	LM_{C3}
p-value	0.411	0.436	0.121

Tests for remaining nonlinearity

Tr. var.	LM_{ET}	LM_{VDF}
y_{t-1}	0.299	0.614
y_{t-2}	0.199	0.399
y_{t-3}	0.301	0.475
y_{t-4}	0.646	0.732
$v_{t-1,1}$	0.781	0.169
$v_{t-1,2}$	0.652	0.702
$v_{t-1,3}$	0.596	0.612
$v_{t-1,4}$	0.522	0.371

Notes: LM_{Ci}, $i = 1, 2, 3$, denote the LM-type test for parameter constancy based on an ith-order Taylor approximation of the transition function.
LM_{ET} and LM_{VDF} denote the tests for no remaining nonlinearity based upon (3.70) and (3.71), respectively.

3.4.2   *Diagnostic tests for Markov-Switching models*

Diagnostic checking of estimated Markov-Switching models has been dealt with by Hamilton (1996). He develops tests for residual autocorrelation, heteroscedasticity, misspecification of the Markov-process s_t, and omitted explanatory variables. The tests are LM-type tests, and thus have the attractive property that their computation only requires estimation of the model under the null hypothesis. The tests make heavy use of the score $h_t(\theta)$, which is defined as the derivative of the log of the conditional density (or likelihood) $f(y_t|\Omega_{t-1}; \theta)$, given in (3.39), with respect to the parameter vector θ,

$$h_t(\theta) \equiv \frac{\partial \ln f(y_t|\Omega_{t-1}; \theta)}{\partial \theta}. \tag{3.72}$$

Table 3.11   *Diagnostic tests of a STAR model estimated for absolute weekly returns on the Tokyo stock index*

Tests for qth-order serial correlation

q	4	8	12
p-value	0.382	0.222	0.219

Tests for parameter constancy

	LM_{C1}	LM_{C2}	LM_{C3}
p-value	0.142	0.116	0.159

Tests for remaining nonlinearity

Tr. var.	LM_{ET}	LM_{VDF}
y_{t-1}	0.359	0.209
y_{t-2}	0.017	0.177
y_{t-3}	0.332	0.341
y_{t-4}	0.463	0.822
$v_{t-1,1}$	0.359	0.209
$v_{t-1,2}$	0.128	0.945
$v_{t-1,3}$	0.851	0.852
$v_{t-1,4}$	0.765	0.796

Notes: LM_{Ci}, $i = 1, 2, 3$, denote the LM-type test for parameter constancy based on an ith-order Taylor approximation of the transition function. LM_{ET} and LM_{VDF} denote the tests for no remaining non-linearity based upon (3.70) and (3.71), respectively.

For example, for the 2-regime MSW model in (3.36) it can be shown that

$$\frac{\partial \ln f(y_t|\Omega_{t-1};\theta)}{\partial \phi_j} = \frac{1}{\sigma^2}(y_t - \phi_j'x_t)x_t \cdot P(s_t = j|\Omega_t)$$

$$+ \frac{1}{\sigma^2}\sum_{\tau=2}^{t-1}(y_\tau - \phi_j'x_\tau)x_\tau \cdot (P(s_\tau = j|\Omega_t;\theta)$$

$$- P(s_\tau = j|\Omega_{t-1};\theta)), \tag{3.73}$$

for $j = 1, 2$. Hamilton (1996) describes an algorithm to compute the change in the inference concerning the state the process was in at time τ that is brought about by the addition of y_t, $P(s_\tau = j|\Omega_t;\theta) - P(s_\tau = j|\Omega_{t-1};\theta)$. The remaining elements of the score in (3.73) can be computed directly after estimation of the model. The same holds for the score with respect to the parameters p_{11} and p_{22}, which determine the transition probabilities of the Markov-process s_t

(see Hamilton, 1996, eq. (3.12)). By construction, the score evaluated at the ML estimates $\hat{\theta}$ has sample mean zero, $\sum_{t=1}^{n} h_t(\hat{\theta}) = 0$.

One of the possible uses of the conditional scores is to construct standard errors for the ML estimates of θ. To be precise, standard errors are obtained as the square roots of the diagonal elements of the inverse of the outer product of the scores,

$$\sum_{t=1}^{n} h_t(\hat{\theta}) h_t(\hat{\theta})'. \tag{3.74}$$

Another use of the scores is to construct LM-statistics. For example, suppose we want to test that some variables z_t have been omitted from the 2-regime MSW model – that is, we want to test (3.37) against the alternative

$$y_t = \phi_{0,s_t} + \phi_{1,s_t} y_{t-1} + \cdots + \phi_{p,s_t} y_{t-p} + \delta' z_t + \varepsilon_t. \tag{3.75}$$

The score with respect to δ, evaluated under the null hypothesis $H_0 : \delta = 0$ is equal to

$$\left. \frac{\partial \ln f(y_t|\Omega_{t-1}; \theta)}{\partial \delta} \right|_{\delta=0} = \sum_{j=1}^{2} (y_t - \hat{\phi}_j' x_t) z_t \cdot P(s_t = j|\Omega_n; \hat{\theta}),$$

$$\tag{3.76}$$

where $\hat{\theta}$ are ML estimates of the parameter vector $\theta' = (\phi_1', \phi_2, p_{11}, p_{22}, \delta)$ under the null hypothesis. The LM test-statistic to test H_0 is given by

$$n \left(\frac{1}{n} \sum_{t=1}^{n} h_t(\hat{\theta}) \right)' \left(\frac{1}{n} \sum_{t=1}^{n} h_t(\hat{\theta}) h_t(\hat{\theta})' \right)^{-1} \left(\frac{1}{n} \sum_{t=1}^{n} h_t(\hat{\theta}) \right), \tag{3.77}$$

and has an asymptotic χ^2 distribution with degrees of freedom equal to the number of variables in z_t.

3.5 Forecasting

Nonlinear time series models may be considered for various purposes. Sometimes the main objective is merely obtaining an adequate description of the dynamic patterns that are present in a particular variable. Very often, however, an additional goal is to employ the model for forecasting future values of the time series. Furthermore, out-of-sample forecasting can also be considered as a way to evaluate estimated regime-switching models. In particular, comparison of the forecasts from nonlinear models with those from a benchmark linear model might enable one to determine the added value of the nonlinear features of the model. In this section we discuss several ways to obtain point and interval forecasts from nonlinear models. This is followed by some remarks on how to evaluate forecasts from nonlinear models, and on how to compare forecasts from linear and nonlinear models.

Point forecasts

Computing point forecasts from nonlinear models is considerably more involved than computing forecasts from linear models. Consider the case where y_t is described by the general nonlinear autoregressive model of order 1,

$$y_t = F(y_{t-1}; \theta) + \varepsilon_t, \tag{3.78}$$

for some nonlinear function $F(y_{t-1}; \theta)$. When using a least squares criterion, the optimal point forecasts of future values of the time series are given by their conditional expectations, as discussed in section 2.2. That is, the optimal h-step-ahead forecast of y_{t+h} at time t is given by

$$\hat{y}_{t+h|t} = \mathrm{E}[y_{t+h}|\Omega_t], \tag{3.79}$$

where Ω_t again denotes the history of the time series up to and including the observation at time t. Using (3.78) and the fact that $\mathrm{E}[\varepsilon_{t+1}|\Omega_t] = 0$, the optimal 1-step-ahead forecast is easily obtained as

$$\hat{y}_{t+1|t} = \mathrm{E}[y_{t+1}|\Omega_t] = F(y_t; \theta), \tag{3.80}$$

which is equivalent to the optimal 1-step-ahead forecast where the model $F(y_{t-1}; \theta)$ is linear.

When the forecast horizon is longer than 1 period, things become more complicated, however. For example, the optimal 2-step-ahead forecast follows from (3.79) and (3.78) as

$$\hat{y}_{t+2|t} = \mathrm{E}[y_{t+2}|\Omega_t] = \mathrm{E}[F(y_{t+1}; \theta)|\Omega_t]. \tag{3.81}$$

In general, the *linear* conditional expectation operator E cannot be interchanged with the *nonlinear* operator F, that is

$$\mathrm{E}[F(\cdot)] \neq F(\mathrm{E}[\cdot]).$$

Put differently, the expected value of a nonlinear function is not equal to the function evaluated at the expected value of its argument. Hence,

$$\mathrm{E}[F(y_{t+1}; \theta)|\Omega_t] \neq F(\mathrm{E}[y_{t+1}|\Omega_t]; \theta) = F(\hat{y}_{t+1|t}; \theta). \tag{3.82}$$

Rather, the relation between the 1- and 2-step-ahead forecasts is given by

$$
\begin{aligned}
\hat{y}_{t+2|t} &= \mathrm{E}[F(F(y_t; \theta) + \varepsilon_{t+1}; \theta)|\Omega_t] \\
&= \mathrm{E}[F(\hat{y}_{t+1|t} + \varepsilon_{t+1}; \theta)|\Omega_t].
\end{aligned}
\tag{3.83}
$$

The above demonstrates that a simple recursive relationship between forecasts at different horizons, which could be used to obtain multiple-step-ahead forecasts in an easy fashion analogous to (2.68) for the AR(1) model, does not exist for nonlinear models in general. Of course, a 2-step-ahead forecast might still be constructed as

$$
\hat{y}^{(n)}_{t+2|t} = F(\hat{y}_{t+1|t}; \theta).
\tag{3.84}
$$

Brown and Mariano (1989) show that this 'naïve' approach, which takes its name from the fact that it effectively boils down to setting $\varepsilon_{t+1} = 0$ in (3.83) (or interchanging E and F in (3.81)), renders biased forecasts. Over the years, several methods have been developed to obtain more adequate multiple-step-ahead forecasts, some of which are discussed below.

First, one might attempt to obtain the conditional expectation (3.83) directly by computing

$$
\hat{y}^{(c)}_{t+2|t} = \int_{-\infty}^{\infty} F(\hat{y}_{t+1|t} + \varepsilon; \theta) f(\varepsilon) \, d\varepsilon,
\tag{3.85}
$$

where f denotes the density of ε_t. Brown and Mariano (1989) refer to this forecast as the closed-form forecast – hence the superscript (c). An alternative way to express this integral follows from (3.81) as

$$
\begin{aligned}
\hat{y}^{(c)}_{t+2|t} &= \int_{-\infty}^{\infty} F(y_{t+1}; \theta) g(y_{t+1}|\Omega_t) \, dy_{t+1} \\
&= \int_{-\infty}^{\infty} \mathrm{E}[y_{t+2}|y_{t+1}] g(y_{t+1}|\Omega_t) \, dy_{t+1},
\end{aligned}
\tag{3.86}
$$

where $g(y_{t+1}|\Omega_t)$ is the distribution of y_{t+1} conditional upon Ω_t. This conditional distribution is in fact equal to the distribution $f(\cdot)$ of the shock ε_{t+1} with mean equal to $F(y_t; \theta)$ – that is, $g(y_{t+1}|\Omega_t) = f(y_{t+1} - F(y_t; \theta))$. As an analytic expression for the integral (3.85) (or (3.86)) is not available in general, it needs to be approximated using numerical integration techniques. An additional complication is the fact that the distribution of ε_t is never known with certainty. Usual practice is to assume normality of ε_t.

The closed-form forecast becomes quite tedious to compute for forecasts more than 2 periods ahead. To see why, consider the Chapman–Kolgomorov relation

$$g(y_{t+h}|\Omega_t) = \int_{-\infty}^{\infty} g(y_{t+h}|y_{t+h-1})g(y_{t+h-1}|\Omega_t)\,dy_{t+h-1}, \quad (3.87)$$

where $g(y_{t+h}|y_{t+h-1})$ is the conditional distribution of y_{t+h} conditional upon y_{t+h-1}. By taking conditional expectations on both sides of (3.87) it follows that

$$E[y_{t+h}|\Omega_t] = \int_{-\infty}^{\infty} E[y_{t+h}|y_{t+h-1}]g(y_{t+h-1}|\Omega_t)\,dy_{t+h-1}, \quad (3.88)$$

which can be recognized as a generalization of (3.86). In order to evaluate this integral to obtain the h-step-ahead exact forecast, one needs the conditional distribution $g(y_{t+h-1}|\Omega_t)$. In principle, this distribution can be obtained recursively from (3.87), by observing that $g(y_{t+1}|y_{t+h-1})$ is again equal to the distribution of the shocks ε_{t+1} with its mean shifted to $F(y_{t+h-1};\theta)$. The recursion can be started for $h = 2$ by using the fact that $g(y_{t+1}|\Omega_t) = f(y_{t+1} - F(y_t;\theta))$ as noted above. To obtain the conditional distribution $g(y_{t+h-1}|\Omega_t)$ for $h > 2$ involves repeated numerical integration, which may become rather time-consuming, in particular if a large number of forecasts has to be made.

An alternative is to assume that the $(h-1)$-step-ahead forecast error $e_{t+h-1|t} = y_{t+h-1} - \hat{y}_{t+h-1|t}$ is normally distributed with mean zero and variance σ_{h-1}^2. In that case, $g(y_{t+h-1}|\Omega_t)$ is normal with mean equal to the $(h-1)$-step-ahead forecast $\hat{y}_{t+h-1|t}$ and variance σ_{h-1}^2. This so-called 'normal forecast error' (NFE) method was developed by Pemberton (1987) for general nonlinear autoregressive models, and applied by Al-Qassam and Lane (1989) to exponential autoregressive models (which are closely related to STAR models) and by de Gooijer and de Bruin (1998) to SETAR models. For the 2-regime SETAR model (3.1), h-step-ahead NFE forecasts can be computed from the recursion

$$\begin{aligned}
\hat{y}_{t+h|t}^{(nfe)} &= \Phi(z_{t+h-1|t})(\phi_{0,1} + \phi_{1,1}\hat{y}_{t+h-1|t}) \\
&\quad + \Phi(-z_{t+h-1|t})(\phi_{0,2} + \phi_{1,2}\hat{y}_{t+h-1|t}) \\
&\quad + \phi(z_{t+h-1|t})(\phi_{1,2} - \phi_{1,1})\sigma_{h-1},
\end{aligned} \quad (3.89)$$

where $\Phi(\cdot)$ and $\phi(\cdot)$ are the standard normal distribution and density, respectively, σ_{h-1}^2 is the variance of the $(h-1)$-step-ahead forecast error $e_{t+h-1|t}$ and $z_{t+h-1|t} = (c - \hat{y}_{t+h-1|t})/\sigma_{h-1}$. Observe that (3.89) is essentially a weighted average of the optimal forecasts from the two regimes, with weights equal to the probability of being in the particular regime at time $t + h - 1$ under normality, *plus* an additional correction factor. A similar recursion for the variance of the forecast error, σ_h^2, is also available (see de Gooijer and de Bruin, 1998).

An alternative approach to computing multiple-step-ahead forecasts is to use Monte Carlo or bootstrap methods to approximate the conditional expectation (3.83). The 2-step-ahead Monte Carlo forecast is given by

$$\hat{y}_{t+2|t}^{(mc)} = \frac{1}{k} \sum_{i=1}^{k} F(\hat{y}_{t+1|t} + \varepsilon_i; \theta), \tag{3.90}$$

where k is some large number and the ε_i are drawn from the presumed distribution of ε_{t+1}. The bootstrap forecast is very similar, the only difference being that the residuals from the estimated model, $\hat{\varepsilon}_t, t = 1, \ldots, n$ are used,

$$\hat{y}_{t+2|t}^{(b)} = \frac{1}{k} \sum_{i=1}^{k} F(\hat{y}_{t+1|t} + \hat{\varepsilon}_i; \theta). \tag{3.91}$$

The advantage of the bootstrap over the Monte Carlo method is that no assumptions need to be made about the distribution of ε_{t+1}.

Lin and Granger (1994) and Clements and Smith (1997) compare various methods to obtain multiple-step-ahead forecasts for STAR and SETAR models, respectively. Their main findings are that the Monte Carlo and bootstrap methods compare favourably to the other methods.

An attractive feature of the Markov-Switching model is the relative ease with which analytic expressions for multiple-step-ahead forecasts can be obtained. The essential thing to note is that the forecast of the future value of the time series, y_{t+h}, can be decomposed into a forecast of y_{t+h} conditional upon the regime that will be realized at $t+h$, s_{t+h}, and a forecast of the probabilities with which each of the regimes will occur at $t+h$. For example, the 1-step-ahead forecast for the two-state MSW model given in (3.15) can be written as

$$\hat{y}_{t+1|t} = \mathrm{E}[y_{t+1}|s_{t+1} = 1, \Omega_t] \cdot P(s_{t+1} = 1|\Omega_t; \theta)$$
$$\times \mathrm{E}[y_{t+1}|s_{t+1} = 2, \Omega_t] \cdot P(s_{t+1} = 2|\Omega_t; \theta). \tag{3.92}$$

The forecasts of y_{t+1} conditional upon the regime at $t+1$ follow directly from (3.15) as

$$\mathrm{E}[y_{t+1}|s_{t+1} = j, \Omega_t] = \phi_{0,j} + \phi_{1,j} y_t,$$

whereas $P(s_{t+1} = j|\Omega_t; \theta) j = 1, 2$ are given by the optimal forecasts of the regime probabilities $\hat{\xi}_{t+1|t}$, which can be obtained from (3.42) and (3.43). Multiple-step-ahead forecasts can be computed in a similar way (see Tjøstheim, 1986; Hamilton, 1989, for details).

Interval forecasts

In addition to point forecasts one may also be interested in confidence intervals for these point forecasts. As discussed in section 2.2, for forecasts obtained from linear models, the usual forecast confidence region is taken to be an interval symmetric around the point forecast. This is based upon the fact that the conditional distribution $g(y_{t+h}|\Omega_t)$ of a linear time series is normal (under the assumption of normally distributed innovations) with mean $\hat{y}_{t+h|t}$.

For nonlinear models this is not the case. In fact, the conditional distribution can be asymmetric and even contain multiple modes. Whether a symmetric interval around the mean is the most appropriate forecast confidence region in this case can be questioned. This topic is discussed in detail in Hyndman (1995). He argues that there are three methods to construct a $100(1-\alpha)\%$ forecast region:

1. An interval symmetric around the mean, that is,

$$S_\alpha = (\hat{y}_{t+h|t} - w, \hat{y}_{t+h|t} + w),$$

   where w is such that $P(y_{t+h} \in S_\alpha|\Omega_t) = 1 - \alpha$.
2. The interval between the $\alpha/2$ and $(1 - \alpha/2)$ quantiles of the forecast distribution, denoted $q_{\alpha/2}$ and $q_{1-\alpha/2}$, respectively,

$$Q_\alpha = (q_{\alpha/2}, q_{1-\alpha/2}).$$

3. The highest-density region (HDR), that is

$$HDR_\alpha = \{y_{t+h}|g(y_{t+h}|\Omega_t) \geq g_\alpha\}, \tag{3.93}$$

   where g_α is such that $P(y_{t+h} \in HDR_\alpha|\Omega_t) = 1 - \alpha$.

For symmetric and unimodal distributions, these three regions are identical. For asymmetric or multimodal distributions they are not. Hyndman (1995) argues that the HDR is the most natural choice. The reasons for this claim are that first, HDR_α is the smallest of all possible $100(1-\alpha)\%$ forecast regions and, second, every point inside the HDR has conditional density $g(y_{t+h}|\Omega_t)$ at least as large as every point outside the region. Furthermore, only the HDR will reveal features such as asymmetry or multimodality of the conditional distribution $g(y_{t+h}|\Omega_t)$.

HDRs are straightforward to compute when the Monte Carlo or bootstrap methods described previously are used to compute the point forecast $\hat{y}_{t+h|t}$. Let $y_{t+h|t}^i$, $i = 1, \ldots, k$, denote the ith element used in computing the Monte Carlo forecast (3.90) or bootstrap forecast (3.90) – that is, $y_{t+h|t}^i = F(y_{t+h-1|t} + \varepsilon_i; \theta)$ or $y_{t+h|t}^i = F(y_{t+h-1|t} + \hat{\varepsilon}_i; \theta)$. Note that the $y_{t+h|t}^i$ can be thought of as being realizations drawn from the conditional distribution of interest $g(y_{t+h}|\Omega_t)$. Estimates $g_i \equiv g(y_{t+h|t}^i|\Omega_t)$, $i = 1, \ldots, k$, can then can be obtained by using a standard kernel density estimator, that is

$$g_i = \frac{1}{k} \sum_{j=1}^{k} K\left([y_{t+h|t}^i - y_{t+h|t}^j]/b\right), \tag{3.94}$$

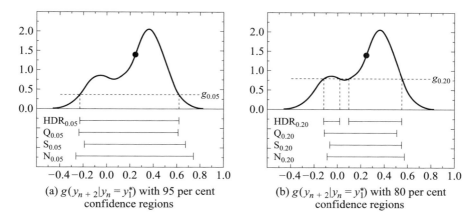

(a) $g(y_{n+2}|y_n = y_1^*)$ with 95 per cent
confidence regions

(b) $g(y_{n+2}|y_n = y_1^*)$ with 80 per cent
confidence regions

Figure 3.9   2-step-ahead conditional distributions for the SETAR model (3.1), with $\phi_{0,1} = 0.3$, $\phi_{1,1} = -0.5$, $\phi_{0,2} = -0.1$, $\phi_{1,2} = 0.5$, $c = 0$ and $\varepsilon_t \sim NID(0, 0.125^2)$, together with confidence regions for the 2-step-ahead forecast

where $K(\cdot)$ is a kernel function such as the Gaussian density and $b > 0$ is the bandwidth. An estimate of g_α in (3.93) is given by $\hat{g}_\alpha = g_{(\lfloor \alpha k \rfloor)}$, where $g_{(i)}$ are the ordered g_i and $\lfloor \cdot \rfloor$ denotes integer part. See Hyndman (1995) for more details and some suggestions about the display of HDRs.

As an example, consider again the SETAR model (3.1), with $\phi_{0,1} = 0.3$, $\phi_{1,1} = -0.5$, $\phi_{0,2} = -0.1$ and $\phi_{1,2} = 0.5$ and $\varepsilon_t \sim N(0, 0.125^2)$. Notice that the variance of ε_t has been reduced compared to previous examples. Naturally, this does not change the properties of the skeleton. Recall that this model has a limit cycle consisting of three points, $y_1^* = 0.06667$, $y_2^* = -0.06667$ and $y_3^* = 0.33333$. The optimal 2-step-ahead forecast given $y_n = y_1^*$ is equal to $E[y_{n+2}|y_n = y_1^*] = 0.238$, which can be obtained using the recursive NFE forecast (3.89), as this is identical to the exact forecast ahead for 2 steps ahead where the errors are normally distributed. The corresponding 2-step-ahead forecast error variance is equal to 0.258^2. The conditional distribution $g(y_{n+2}|y_1^*)$ is given in figure 3.9, and is seen to be bimodal. Intuitively, if $y_n = y_1^*$, it is very likely that y_{n+2} will be close to y_3^* as the time series iterates among the three points of the limit cycle if no shocks occur. This corresponds with the largest mode of the conditional distribution. There is, however, a small probability that the time series will linger around either y_1^* or y_2^*, giving rise to the smaller mode. The optimal point forecast $\hat{y}_{n+2|n}$ is shown as a solid circle.

Below the conditional densities, 95 and 80 per cent confidence regions have been drawn in the left and right panels, respectively. For the 95 per cent confidence regions, the HDR is almost identical to the region $Q_{0.05}$ based on the quantiles of the conditional distribution. The interval symmetric around the point forecast, $S_{0.05}$ is shifted somewhat to the right. Also shown is a region $N_{0.05}$, which is the confidence interval obtained when the conditional distribution is assumed to be normal, and the confidence interval is constructed in the usual manner as $(\hat{y}_{n+2|n} - 1.96\sigma_2, \hat{y}_{n+2|n} + 1.96\sigma_2)$. Clearly, this renders far too wide an interval this case, which has more than 95 per cent coverage. The 80 per cent confidence region shown in the right panel demonstrates that the HDR needs not be a continuous interval, but can consist of several disjoint segments.

Evaluating forecasts

In general, the fact that a particular model describes the features of a time series within the estimation sample better than other models is no guarantee that this model also renders better out-of-sample forecasts. Clements and Hendry (1998) provide an in-depth analysis of forecasting with linear models and discuss various reasons why a model with a superior in-sample fit may nevertheless yield inferior out-of-sample forecasts. The above seems particularly relevant for nonlinear time series models. It is found quite often that, even though a nonlinear model appears to describe certain characteristics of the time series at hand much better than a linear model, the forecasting performance of the linear model is no worse than that of the nonlinear model (see Brooks, 1997, for specific examples in the context of high-frequency financial time series and de Gooijer and Kumar, 1992, for a general review). Many reasons can be brought up why this may be the case (see also Diebold and Nason, 1990). For example, the nonlinearity may be spurious, in the sense that other features of the time series, such as heteroscedasticity, structural breaks or outliers, suggest the presence of nonlinearity (see also subsections 3.3.4 and 3.3.5). Even though one might successfully estimate a nonlinear model for such a series, it is very unlikely that this will result in improved forecasts.

Another cause for poor forecast performance of nonlinear models is that the nonlinearity does not show up during the forecast period. In the case of regime-switching models it might be that only one of the regimes is realized during the entire forecast period. Hence, empirical forecasts do not always allow us to assess the forecasting quality of the nonlinear model completely. A potential solution to this problem of the absence of nonlinearity during the forecast period is to perform a simulation experiment in which one uses an estimated regime-switching model (or a set of models if the goal is to compare their forecasting performance) to generate artificial time series and to perform an out-of-sample forecasting exercise on each of those series. In this controlled environment one can make sure that forecasts in each of the regimes are involved. See Clements and Smith (1998, 1999) for an example of this approach.

The choice of evaluation criteria is also of importance. Even though traditional criteria such as the MSPE are applicable to forecasts from nonlinear models, they may not do justice to the nonlinear model. As noted by Tong (1995), 'how well we can forecast depends on where we are'. In the case of regime-switching models for example, it might very well be that the forecastability of the time series is very different in different regimes. One might therefore evaluate the forecasts for each regime individually to investigate whether the nonlinear model is particularly useful to obtain forecasts in a particular regime or state (see Tiao and Tsay, 1994, and Clements and Smith, 1999). A related point is made by Dacco and Satchell (1999), who demonstrate that even if time series are generated according to a regime-switching process, the MSPE of a linear model for such series can be smaller than the MSPE of the true nonlinear model if there is a possibility of incorrectly predicting which regime the process will be in. Finally, it should be noted that the issue of evaluating forecasts from nonlinear time series models is a topic of much current research, and that at the time of writing no conclusive results have been obtained.

Example 3.1: Dutch guilder   We examine the forecast performance of the STAR model that was estimated for weekly returns on the Dutch guilder exchange rate. Using the bootstrap method (3.91), we compute 1- to 5-step-ahead forecasts from the STAR model for the years 1990–7. Tables 3.12 and 3.13 contain ratios of the MSPE and MedSPE criteria, relative to an AR(2) model which is used as the benchmark linear model. Besides the ratios for all forecasts jointly (rows 'Overall'), table 3.12 also shows ratios for sets of forecast origins which are constructed such that they correspond with the quintiles of the distribution of the transition variable $v_{t-1,4}$. Table 3.13 shows ratios for the individual years in the forecast period.

Based upon the MSPE criterion, there is not much to be gained in terms of out-of-sample forecasting by using the STAR model, as the MSPE ratios in general are larger than 1. The MedSPE ratios suggest that occasionally the nonlinear model renders superior forecasts, especially for 4 and 5 weeks ahead when the transition variable is in the first, second or third quintile.

3.6   Impulse response functions

Another method to evaluate the properties of estimated regime-switching models is to examine the effects of the shocks ε_t on the evolution of the time series y_t. Impulse response functions are a convenient tool to carry out such an analysis.

As discussed in section 2.4, impulse response functions are meant to provide a measure of the response of y_{t+h} to an impulse δ at time t. The impulse response measure that is commonly used in the analysis of linear models is defined as the

Table 3.12 *Forecast evaluation of a STAR model for weekly returns on the Dutch guilder exchange rate*

	Forecast horizon				
Quintile	1	2	3	4	5
MSPE					
Overall	1.032	1.025	1.023	1.009	0.999
1st	1.073	1.034	1.014	1.019	1.006
2nd	1.078	1.048	1.025	0.999	1.024
3rd	1.087	1.077	1.028	0.995	1.000
4th	0.950	0.986	1.016	1.011	0.985
5th	1.018	1.016	1.027	1.015	0.996
MedSPE					
Overall	0.985	1.099	1.056	1.090	1.043
1st	1.053	0.836	1.180	0.880	0.934
2nd	0.981	0.969	1.154	0.910	0.929
3rd	1.079	0.996	1.114	0.961	0.976
4th	0.732	1.084	1.019	1.173	0.927
5th	1.264	1.450	1.134	1.109	1.058

Notes: The entries in the table 3.12 are the ratio of the MSPE and MedSPE values for forecasts of the STAR model in table 3.7 and an AR(2) model for weekly returns on the Dutch guilder exchange rate *vis-à-vis* the US dollar.
Forecasts are made for the period 1 January 1990–31 December 1997.
Quintile refers to the distribution of the transition variable $v_{t-1,4}$.

difference between two realizations of y_{t+h} which start from identical histories of the time series up to time $t - 1$, ω_{t-1}. In one realization, the process is hit by a shock of size δ at time t, while in the other realization no shock occurs at time t. All shocks in intermediate periods between t and $t + h$ are set equal to zero in both realizations. That is, the traditional impulse response function (TIRF) is given by

$$TIRF_y(h, \delta, \omega_{t-1}) = \mathrm{E}[y_{t+h}|\varepsilon_t = \delta, \varepsilon_{t+1} = \cdots = \varepsilon_{t+h} = 0, \omega_{t-1}]$$
$$- \mathrm{E}[y_{t+h}|\varepsilon_t = 0, \varepsilon_{t+1} = \cdots = \varepsilon_{t+h} = 0, \omega_{t-1}],$$
$$(3.95)$$

for $h = 1, 2, 3, \ldots$. The second conditional expectation usually is called the *benchmark profile*.

Table 3.13 *Forecast evaluation of a STAR model for weekly returns on the Dutch guilder exchange rate, 1990–1997*

	Forecast horizon				
Year	1	2	3	4	5
MSPE					
1990	1.099	1.079	1.014	1.000	1.018
1991	1.014	1.006	1.029	1.023	0.993
1992	0.995	0.998	1.040	1.014	0.984
1993	1.074	1.031	1.008	0.988	1.010
1994	1.114	1.084	1.048	1.008	1.039
1995	1.020	1.032	1.018	1.032	0.992
1996	1.054	1.058	1.027	0.964	0.986
1997	1.006	0.961	0.958	0.981	0.989
MedSPE					
1990	1.200	1.218	1.233	1.035	0.894
1991	1.145	1.146	1.008	0.966	0.943
1992	0.825	1.136	0.967	1.023	1.004
1993	0.934	0.804	1.047	1.002	0.966
1994	1.298	1.543	1.239	1.156	1.179
1995	1.405	0.930	1.107	1.138	0.913
1996	1.002	0.831	0.877	0.959	1.046
1997	0.891	1.430	0.956	1.005	1.060

Note: The entries in the table 3.13 are the ratio of the MSFE and MedSFE values for forecasts of the STAR model in table 3.7 and an AR(2) model for weekly returns on the Dutch guilder exchange rate *vis-à-vis* the US dollar computed on a year-to-year basis.

The traditional impulse response function as defined above has some characteristic properties if the model is linear. First, the TIRF is then *symmetric*, in the sense that a shock of $-\delta$ has exactly the opposite effect as a shock of size $+\delta$. Furthermore, it might be called *linear*, as the impulse response is proportional to the size of the shock. Finally, the impulse response is *history-independent* as it does not depend on the particular history ω_{t-1}. For example, in the AR(1) model (2.6), it follows easily that $TIRF_y(h, \delta, \omega_{t-1}) = \phi^h \delta$ which clearly demonstrates the properties of the impulse response function mentioned above.

These properties do not carry over to nonlinear models. In nonlinear models, the impact of a shock depends on the sign and the size of the shock, as well as on the history of the process. Furthermore, if the effect of a shock on the time series $h > 1$ periods ahead is to be analysed, the assumption that no shocks occur in intermediate periods may give rise to misleading inference concerning the propagation mechanism of the model.

To illustrate these points, consider the simple SETAR model

$$y_t = \begin{cases} \phi_{1,1} y_{t-1} + \varepsilon_t & \text{if } y_{t-1} \leq 0, \\ \phi_{1,2} y_{t-1} + \varepsilon_t & \text{if } y_{t-1} > 0. \end{cases} \tag{3.96}$$

The traditional 1-period impulse response in this case is equal to

$$TIRF_y(1, \delta, \omega_{t-1}) = \begin{cases} \phi_{1,1}\delta & \text{if } y_{t-1} + \delta \leq 0 \text{ and } y_{t-1} \leq 0, \\ \phi_{1,1}\delta + \phi_{1,2}(\phi_{1,1} - \phi_{1,2})y_{t-1} & \text{if } y_{t-1} + \delta \leq 0 \text{ and } y_{t-1} > 0, \\ \phi_{1,2}\delta + \phi_{1,1}(\phi_{1,2} - \phi_{1,1})y_{t-1} & \text{if } y_{t-1} + \delta > 0 \text{ and } y_{t-1} \leq 0, \\ \phi_{1,2}\delta & \text{if } y_{t-1} + \delta > 0 \text{ and } y_{t-1} > 0. \end{cases}$$

This simple example makes clear that the impulse response depends on the combined magnitude of the history y_{t-1} and the shock δ (relative to the threshold $c = 0$). Hence, the impulse response is not symmetric, as it might easily happen that $y_{t-1} + \delta > 0$ while $y_{t-1} - \delta \leq 0$, nor is it linear- or history-independent.

To illustrate the consequences of assuming no shocks occurring after time t, assume that $\phi_{1,1} > 0$, $y_{t-1} = 0$ and the shock δ is negative. As no more shocks enter the system, the process remains in the lower regime after time t, and the effect of the shock δ decays geometrically with rate $\phi_{1,1}$. However, in practice, regime switches are quite likely to occur owing to subsequent shocks, which changes the dynamics of the process and hence the persistence of the shock δ. Thus, it might be misleading to consider only the response that occurs when all shocks in intermediate periods are equal to zero.

In fact, for linear models the assumption of zero shocks in intermediate periods can be justified by the Wold representation,

$$y_t = \sum_{i=0}^{\infty} \psi_i \varepsilon_{t-i}, \tag{3.97}$$

which shows that shocks in different periods do not interact. Nonlinear time series models do not have a Wold representation however. They can be rewritten in terms of (past and present) shocks only by means of the Volterra expansion,

$$y_t = \sum_{i=0}^{\infty} \psi_i \varepsilon_{t-i} + \sum_{i=0}^{\infty} \sum_{i=j}^{\infty} \xi_{ij} \varepsilon_{t-i} \varepsilon_{t-j}$$

$$+ \sum_{i=0}^{\infty} \sum_{i=j}^{\infty} \sum_{k=j}^{\infty} \zeta_{ij} \varepsilon_{t-i} \varepsilon_{t-j} \varepsilon_{t-k} + \dots, \tag{3.98}$$

(see Priestley, 1988). This expression shows that the effect of the shock ε_t on y_{t+h} depends on the shocks $\varepsilon_{t+1}, \ldots, \varepsilon_{t+h}$, as well as on past shocks $\varepsilon_{t-1}, \varepsilon_{t-2}, \ldots$ which constitute the history ω_{t-1}.

The Generalized Impulse Response Function (GIRF), introduced by Koop, Pesaran and Potter (1996) provides a natural solution to the problems involved in defining impulse responses in nonlinear models. The GIRF for an arbitrary shock $\varepsilon_t = \delta$ and history ω_{t-1} is defined as

$$GIRF_y(h, \delta, \omega_{t-1}) = E[y_{t+h}|\varepsilon_t = \delta, \omega_{t-1}] - E[y_{t+h}|\omega_{t-1}],$$

(3.99)

for $h = 1, 2, \ldots$. In the GIRF, the expectations of y_{t+h} are conditioned only on the history and/or on the shock. Put differently, the problem of dealing with shocks occurring in intermediate time periods is dealt with by averaging them out. Given this choice, the natural benchmark profile for the impulse response is the expectation of y_{t+h} given only the history of the process as summarized in ω_{t-1} (that is, in the benchmark profile, the current shock is averaged out as well). It is easily seen that for linear models the GIRF in (3.99) is equivalent to the TIRF in (3.95).

The GIRF is a function of δ and ω_{t-1}, which are realizations of the random variables ε_t and Ω_{t-1}. Koop, Pesaran and Potter (1996) stress that, hence, the GIRF as defined in (3.99) is itself a realization of a random variable given by

$$GIRF_y(h, \varepsilon_t, \Omega_{t-1}) = E[y_{t+h}|\varepsilon_t, \Omega_{t-1}] - E[y_{t+h}|\Omega_{t-1}]. \quad (3.100)$$

Using this interpretation of the GIRF as a random variable, various conditional versions of the GIRF can be defined which are of potential interest. For example, one might consider only a particular history ω_{t-1} and treat the GIRF as a random variable in terms of ε_t, that is,

$$GIRF_y(h, \varepsilon_t, \omega_{t-1}) = E[y_{t+h}|\varepsilon_t, \omega_{t-1}] - E[y_{t+h}|\omega_{t-1}]. \quad (3.101)$$

Alternatively, one could reverse the role of the shock and the history by fixing the shock at $\varepsilon_t = \delta$ and considering the GIRF as a random variable in terms of the history Ω_{t-1}. In general, we might compute the GIRF conditional on particular subsets A and B of shocks and histories respectively – that is, $GIRF_y(h, A, B)$. For example, one might condition on all histories in a particular regime and consider only negative shocks.

In particular, the GIRF can be used to assess the significance of asymmetric effects over time. Potter (1994) defines a measure of asymmetric response to a particular shock $\varepsilon_t = \delta$, given a particular history ω_{t-1}, as the sum of the GIRF for this particular shock and the GIRF for the shock of the same magnitude but with opposite sign, that is,

$$ASY_y(h, \delta, \omega_{t-1}) = GIRF_y(h, \delta, \omega_{t-1}) + GIRF_y(h, -\delta, \omega_{t-1}).$$
(3.102)

Alternatively, we could average across all possible histories to obtain

$$ASY_y^*(h, \delta) = \text{E}[GIRF_y(h, \delta, \omega_{t-1})] + \text{E}[GIRF_y(h, -\delta, \omega_{t-1})]$$
$$= \text{E}[y_{t+h}|\varepsilon_t = \delta] + \text{E}[y_{t+h}|\varepsilon_t = -\delta].$$
(3.103)

Koop, Pesaran and Potter (1996) discuss in detail how the GIRF can be used to examine the persistence of shocks (see also Potter, 1995). It is intuitively clear that if a nonlinear model is stationary, the effect of a particular shock on the time series eventually becomes zero for all possible histories of the process. Hence, the distribution of the GIRF as defined in (3.100) collapses to a spike at zero as the horizon goes to infinity. From this it follows that the dispersion of the distribution of the GIRF at finite horizons can be interpreted as a measure of persistence of shocks. Conditional versions of the GIRF are particularly suited to assess the persistence of shocks. For example, we might compare the dispersion of the distributions of GIRFs conditional on positive and negative shocks to determine whether negative shocks are more persistent than positive, or vice versa. A potential problem with this approach is that no unambiguous measure of dispersion exists, although, as noted by Koop, Pesaran and Potter (1996), the notion of second-order stochastic dominance might be useful.

Notice that the second conditional expectation in the right-hand-side of (3.99) is the optimal point forecasts of y_{t+h} at time $t-1$ (cf. (3.79)), while the first conditional expectation can be interpreted as the optimal forecast of y_{t+h} at time t in case $\varepsilon_t = \delta$. Therefore the GIRF can be interpreted as the change in forecast of y_{t+h} at time t relative to time $t-1$, given that a shock δ occurs at time t. This also suggests that if the distribution of the conditional GIRF (3.101) (or other versions of the GIRF) is effectively a spike at zero for certain $h \geq m$, the nonlinear model is not useful for forecasting more than m periods ahead. As for general nonlinear models analytic expressions for these conditional expectations are not available, the Monte Carlo methods discussed in the previous subsection can be used to obtain estimates of the GIRF (3.99) and subsequent conditional versions. Koop, Pesaran and Potter (1996) suggest using the same realizations of the shocks in intermediate time periods for computing the two components of the GIRF, in order to reduce the Monte Carlo error.

Example 3.1: Dutch guilder   Figures 3.10 and 3.11 contain generalized impulse responses for the STAR model estimated for weekly returns on the Dutch guilder exchange rate. These graphs are meant to illustrate the possible use of GIRFs and to give some impression of possible patterns that may arise.

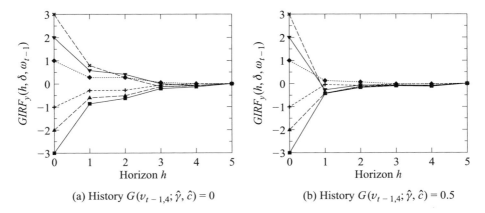

(a) History $G(v_{t-1,4}; \hat{\gamma}, \hat{c}) = 0$ (b) History $G(v_{t-1,4}; \hat{\gamma}, \hat{c}) = 0.5$

Figure 3.10   Generalized impulse responses $GIRF_y(h, \delta, \omega_{t-1})$ for the STAR model estimated for weekly returns on the Dutch guilder exchange rate

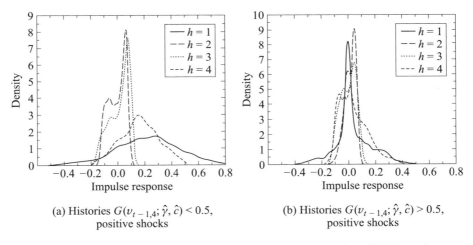

(a) Histories $G(v_{t-1,4}; \hat{\gamma}, \hat{c}) < 0.5$,   (b) Histories $G(v_{t-1,4}; \hat{\gamma}, \hat{c}) > 0.5$,
positive shocks   positive shocks

Figure 3.11   Generalized impulse responses $GIRF_y(h, A, B)$ for a STAR model estimated for weekly returns on Dutch guilder exchange rate

Figure 3.10 contains some shock- and history-specific GIRFs (3.99), for $\delta = \pm 3, \pm 2$ and ± 1, and ω_{t-1} such that the transition function $G(v_{t-1,4}; \hat{\gamma}, \hat{c})$ is equal to 0 (left panel) or equal to 0.5 (right panel). The GIRFs in the left panel resemble traditional impulse responses which may be computed using (3.95). For this history, the past volatility $v_{t-1,4}$ is very low. Even when a large shock δ hits the system, the time series does not move out of the lower regime. Therefore, the effect of the shocks decays roughly as if the model were an AR(2) (which it is in the lower regime). The GIRFs shown in the right panel are different. In particular, the response to large positive shocks is seen to be negative one period after the shocks arrive, followed by a gradual decay towards zero. This response is caused by the fact that for this history, large positive shocks increase the 4-week average volatility such that the time series moves to the upper regime, where it behaves conform a white noise series.

Figure 3.11 contains conditional GIRFs, $GIRF_y(h, A, B)$, where the set A consists of positive shocks, and the set B consists of histories for which the value of the transition function is either smaller or larger than 0.5. The difference between the GIRFs is most pronounced for $h = 1$ and 2. Again this is due to the fact that for the histories for which $G(v_{t-1,4}; \hat{\gamma}, \hat{c}) > 0.5$, a sufficiently large shock increases the volatility such that the series moves to the upper regime, whereas for histories for which $G(v_{t-1,4}; \hat{\gamma}, \hat{c}) < 0.5$ this hardly ever happens. The differences have disappeared for the largest part at horizons larger than 5 periods.

3.7   On multivariate regime-switching models

So far attention has been restricted to univariate models, in which a time series y_t is described in terms of only its own lagged values $y_{t-1}, \ldots, y_{t-p}$ (or possible transformations thereof). Sometimes it may be worthwhile to model several time series jointly, to exploit possible linkages that might exist between them. This might be particularly relevant in the context of empirical finance, where it can be expected that certain characteristics of different assets are related. For example, it is well documented that returns and volatilities of different stock indexes move together over time (Engle and Susmel, 1993), while the same holds for exchange rates (Engle, Ito and Lin, 1990; Baillie and Bollerslev, 1991) and interest rates at different maturities (Hall, Anderson and Granger, 1992). An alternative use of multivariate models is to describe several characteristics of a certain asset, such as returns or volatility and trading volume (Gallant, Rossi and Tauchen, 1992; Hiemstra and Jones, 1994), simultaneously.

In this section we discuss multivariate generalizations of the regime-switching models described earlier in this chapter. For the sake of simplicity we focus on bivariate models only. Generalizations to k-dimensional time series with $k > 2$ are straightforward, at least conceptually. At the outset we should remark that the interest in multivariate nonlinear modelling has started to develop only very recently. Therefore, the relevant statistical theory has by no means been fully developed yet, and still is a topic of much current research.

Let $\mathbf{y}_t = (y_{1t}, y_{2t})'$ be a (2×1) vector time series. A bivariate analogue of the 2-regime SETAR model (3.2) then can be specified as

$$
\begin{aligned}
\mathbf{y}_t = {} & (\boldsymbol{\phi}_{0,1} + \boldsymbol{\phi}_{1,1} \mathbf{y}_{t-1})(1 - I[q_t > c]) \\
& + (\boldsymbol{\phi}_{0,2} + \boldsymbol{\phi}_{1,2} \mathbf{y}_{t-1})I[q_t > c] + \boldsymbol{\varepsilon}_t,
\end{aligned}
\tag{3.104}
$$

where $\boldsymbol{\phi}_{0,j}$, $j = 1, 2$, are (2×1) vectors, $\boldsymbol{\phi}_{1,j}$, $j = 1, 2$, are (2×2) matrices, $\boldsymbol{\varepsilon}_t = (\varepsilon_{1t}, \varepsilon_{2t})'$ is a bivariate white noise process with mean equal to zero and variance-covariance matrix $\boldsymbol{\Sigma}$. The threshold variable q_t can be a lagged value of one the time series contained in $\mathbf{y}_t$ or, for example, a linear combination of the two series. A multivariate LSTAR model can be obtained by replacing the indicator function $I[\cdot]$ by the logistic function given in (3.4) (see Anderson and Vahid, 1998; Weise, 1999, for applications of this model). Similarly, a multivariate MSW model results if the indicator function $I[\cdot]$ is replaced by a Markov-process s_t as defined just below (3.16) (see Krolzig, 1997).

Tsay (1998) describes a specification procedure for multivariate threshold models such as (3.104), based upon the specification procedure for univariate TAR models developed in Tsay (1989). The procedure includes elements such as testing for multivariate threshold nonlinearity and estimation of the parameters in the model.

A particular variant of the TAR model (3.104) which has been popular in financial applications is a 3-regime model, where the time series y_{it}, $i = 1, 2$, behave as unrelated $I(1)$ series in the middle regime and as cointegrated series in the two outer regimes. This so-called threshold error-correction model (TECM) is discussed extensively in Balke and Fomby (1997). The model is applied by Dwyer, Locke and Yu (1996), Martens, Kofman and Vorst (1998) and Tsay (1998) to modelling the relationship between the spot and future prices of the S&P 500 index. These two prices are related to each other by means of a no-arbitrage relationship, and deviations from this relationship should exist for only a very short time. In the presence of transaction costs or other market imperfections, however, small deviations may persist as they cannot be exploited for profitable arbitrage. Taylor *et al.* (2000) use a Smooth Transition ECM (STECM) for the same purpose, while Anderson (1997) and van Dijk and Franses (2000) apply this model to describe the relationship between interest rates with different maturities.

Common nonlinearity

In the case of multiple time series, one has to take into account the possibility that the nonlinearity is caused by common nonlinear components. Following Anderson and Vahid (1998), the time series $\mathbf{y}_t$ is said to contain a common nonlinear component if there exists a linear combination $\boldsymbol{\alpha}'\mathbf{y}_t$ whose conditional expectation is linear in the past of $\mathbf{y}_t$. For example, rewrite model (3.104) as

$$\mathbf{y}_t = \boldsymbol{\phi}_0 + \boldsymbol{\phi}_1 \mathbf{y}_{t-1} + (\boldsymbol{\theta}_0 + \boldsymbol{\theta}_1 \mathbf{y}_{t-1}) I[q_t > c] + \boldsymbol{\varepsilon}_t, \qquad (3.105)$$

where $\boldsymbol{\phi}_i = \boldsymbol{\phi}_{i,1}$, $i = 0, 1$, and $\boldsymbol{\theta}_i = \boldsymbol{\phi}_{i,2} - \boldsymbol{\phi}_{i,1}$, $i = 0, 1$. The existence of a common nonlinear component as defined above then means that there exists a

2×1 vector $\boldsymbol{\alpha}$ such that

$$\boldsymbol{\alpha}'(\boldsymbol{\theta}_0 + \boldsymbol{\theta}_1 y_{t-1}) I[q_t > c] = 0, \tag{3.106}$$

for all y_{t-1} and $q_t > c$. This implies that α is such that

$$\boldsymbol{\alpha}'\boldsymbol{\theta}_0 = 0, \tag{3.107}$$
$$\boldsymbol{\alpha}'\boldsymbol{\theta}_1 = 0. \tag{3.108}$$

Anderson and Vahid (1998) develop test-statistics for the existence of common nonlinearity that are based upon testing restrictions such as (3.107) and (3.108).

Conclusion
    In this chapter we have reviewed several nonlinear time series models, which are potentially useful for modelling and forecasting returns on financial assets. Most attention was given to univariate models, simply because the theory (involving representation, estimation, diagnostics and inference) for multivariate nonlinear models has not yet been fully developed.

4 Regime-switching models for volatility

Uncertainty, or risk, is of paramount importance in financial analysis. For example, the Capital Asset-Pricing Model (CAPM) (Sharpe, 1964; Lintner, 1965; Mossin, 1966; Merton, 1973) postulates a direct relationship between the required return on an asset and its risk, where the latter is determined by the covariance of the returns on the particular asset and some benchmark portfolio. Similarly, the most important determinant of the price of an option is the uncertainty associated with the price of the underlying asset, as measured by its volatility.

One of the most prominent stylized facts of returns on financial assets is that their volatility changes over time. In particular, periods of large movements in prices alternate with periods during which prices hardly change (see section 1.2). This characteristic feature commonly is referred to as *volatility clustering*. Even though the time-varying nature of the volatility of financial assets has long been recognized (see Mandelbrot, 1963a, 1963b, 1967; Fama, 1965), explicit modelling of the properties of the volatility process has been taken up only fairly recently.

In this chapter we discuss (extensions of) the class of (Generalized) Autoregressive Conditional Heteroscedasticity ((G)ARCH) models, introduced by Engle (1982) and Bollerslev (1986). Nowadays, models from the GARCH class are the most popular volatility models among practitioners. GARCH models enjoy such popularity because they are capable of describing not only the feature of volatility clustering, but also certain other characteristics of financial time series, such as their pronounced excess kurtosis or fat-tailedness. Still, the standard GARCH model cannot capture other empirically relevant properties of volatility. For example, since Black (1976), negative shocks or news are believed to affect volatility quite differently than positive shocks of equal size (see also section 1.2). In the standard GARCH model, however, the effect of a shock on volatility depends only on its size. The sign of the shock is irrelevant. Another limitation of the standard GARCH model is that it does not imply that expected returns and volatility are related directly, as is the case in the CAPM.

Over the past few years, quite a few nonlinear variants of the basic GARCH model have been proposed, most of them designed to capture such aspects as the asymmetric effect of positive and negative shocks on volatility, and possible correlation between the return and volatility.

The outline of this chapter is as follows. In section 4.1, we discuss representations of the basic GARCH model and several nonlinear extensions. We emphasize which of the stylized facts of returns on financial assets can and cannot be captured by the various models. Testing for GARCH is the subject of section 4.2. We discuss tests for the standard GARCH model and for its nonlinear variants, and we examine the influence of outliers on the various test-statistics. Estimation of ARCH models is discussed in section 4.3. In section 4.4 various diagnostic checks which can be used to evaluate estimated GARCH models are reviewed. In section 4.5 we focus on out-of-sample forecasting: both the consequences for forecasting the conditional mean in the presence of ARCH, as well as forecasting volatility itself are discussed. Measures of persistence of shocks in GARCH models are discussed in section 4.6; we emphasize the role these various elements play in the empirical specification of ARCH models. The final section of this chapter (section 4.7) contains a brief discussion on multivariate GARCH models.

We should remark that the aim of this chapter is not to provide a complete account of the vast literature on GARCH models, but rather to provide an introduction to this area, with a specific focus on asymmetric GARCH models and the impact of outliers. For topics not covered in this chapter, the interested reader should consult one of the many surveys on GARCH models which have appeared in recent years. Bollerslev, Chou and Kroner (1992) provide a comprehensive overview of empirical applications of GARCH models to financial time series. Bollerslev, Engle and Nelson (1994) focus on the theoretical aspects of GARCH models. Gourieroux (1997) discusses in great detail how GARCH models can be incorporated in financial decision problems such as asset-pricing and portfolio management. Additional reviews of GARCH and related models can be found in Bera and Higgins (1993); Diebold and Lopez (1995); Pagan (1996); Palm (1996); and Shephard (1996).

4.1   Representation

As stated in section 2.1, an observed time series y_t can be written as the sum of a predictable and an unpredictable part,

$$y_t = E[y_t | \Omega_{t-1}] + \varepsilon_t, \tag{4.1}$$

where Ω_{t-1} is the information set consisting of all relevant information up to and including time $t - 1$. In previous chapters we have concentrated on different specifications for the predictable part or conditional mean $E[y_t | \Omega_{t-1}]$, while simply assuming that the unpredictable part or shock ε_t satisfies the white noise properties (2.1)–(2.3). In particular, ε_t was assumed to be both unconditionally and conditionally homoscedastic – that is, $\mathrm{E}[\varepsilon_t^2] = \mathrm{E}[\varepsilon_t^2|\Omega_{t-1}] = \sigma^2$ for all t. Here we relax part of this assumption and allow the *conditional variance* of ε_t to vary over time – that is, $\mathrm{E}[\varepsilon_t^2|\Omega_{t-1}] = h_t$ for some nonnegative function $h_t \equiv h_t(\Omega_{t-1})$. Put differently, ε_t is *conditionally heteroscedastic*. A convenient way to express this in general is

$$\varepsilon_t = z_t \sqrt{h_t}, \tag{4.2}$$

where z_t is independent and identically distributed with zero mean and unit variance. For convenience, we assume that z_t has a standard normal distribution throughout this section. Some remarks on this assumption are made at the end of this section.

From (4.2) and the properties of z_t it follows immediately that the distribution of ε_t conditional upon the history Ω_{t-1} is normal with mean zero and variance h_t. Also note that the *unconditional variance* of ε_t is still assumed to be constant. Using the law of iterated expectations,

$$\sigma^2 \equiv \mathrm{E}[\varepsilon_t^2] = \mathrm{E}[\mathrm{E}[\varepsilon_t^2|\Omega_{t-1}]] = \mathrm{E}[h_t]. \tag{4.3}$$

Hence, we assume that the unconditional expectation of h_t is constant.

To complete the model, we need to specify how the conditional variance of ε_t evolves over time. In this section, we discuss the representation of various linear and nonlinear models for h_t. The properties of the resultant time series ε_t are used to see whether these models can capture (some of) the stylized facts of stock and exchange rate returns.

4.1.1   Linear GARCH models

Engle (1982) introduced the class of AutoRegressive Conditionally heteroscedastic (ARCH) models to capture the volatility clustering of financial time series (even though the first empirical applications did not deal with high-frequency financial data). In the basic ARCH model, the conditional variance of the shock that occurs at time t is a linear function of the squares of past shocks. For example, in the ARCH model of order 1, h_t is specified as

$$h_t = \omega + \alpha_1 \varepsilon_{t-1}^2. \tag{4.4}$$

Obviously, the (conditional) variance h_t needs to be nonnegative. In order to guarantee that this is the case for the ARCH(1) model, the parameters in (4.4) have to satisfy the conditions $\omega > 0$ and $\alpha_1 \geq 0$. Where $\alpha_1 = 0$, the conditional variance is constant and, hence, the series ε_t is conditionally homoscedastic.

To understand why the ARCH model can describe volatility clustering, observe that model (4.2) with (4.4) basically states that the conditional variance of ε_t is an increasing function of the square of the shock that occurred in the previous time period. Therefore, if ε_{t-1} is large (in absolute value), ε_t is expected to be large (in absolute value) as well. In other words, large (small) shocks tend to be followed by large (small) shocks, of either sign.

An alternative way to see the same thing is to note that the ARCH(1) model can be rewritten as an AR(1) model for ε_t^2. Adding ε_t^2 to (4.4) and subtracting h_t from both sides gives

$$\varepsilon_t^2 = \omega + \alpha_1 \varepsilon_{t-1}^2 + v_t, \tag{4.5}$$

where $v_t \equiv \varepsilon_t^2 - h_t = h_t(z_t^2 - 1)$. Notice that $E[v_t|\Omega_{t-1}] = 0$. Using the theory for AR models summarized in chapter 2, it follows that (4.5) is covariance-stationary if $\alpha_1 < 1$. In that case the unconditional mean of ε_t^2, or the unconditional variance of ε_t, can be obtained as

$$\sigma^2 \equiv E[\varepsilon_t^2] = \frac{\omega}{1 - \alpha_1}. \tag{4.6}$$

Furthermore, (4.5) can be rewritten as

$$\begin{aligned}
\varepsilon_t^2 &= (1 - \alpha_1)\frac{\omega}{1 - \alpha_1} + \alpha_1 \varepsilon_{t-1}^2 + v_t \\
&= (1 - \alpha_1)\sigma^2 + \alpha_1 \varepsilon_{t-1}^2 + v_t \\
&= \sigma^2 + \alpha_1(\varepsilon_{t-1}^2 - \sigma^2) + v_t.
\end{aligned} \tag{4.7}$$

Assuming that $0 \leq \alpha_1 < 1$, (4.7) shows that if ε_{t-1}^2 is larger (smaller) than its unconditional expected value σ^2, ε_t^2 is expected to be larger (smaller) than σ^2 as well.

The ARCH model cannot only capture the volatility clustering of financial data, but also their excess kurtosis. From (4.2) it can be seen that the kurtosis of ε_t always exceeds the kurtosis of z_t,

$$E[\varepsilon_t^4] = E[z_t^4]E[h_t^2] \geq E[z_t^4]E[h_t]^2 = E[z_t^4]E[\varepsilon_t^2]^2, \tag{4.8}$$

which follows from Jensen's inequality. As shown by Engle (1982), for the ARCH(1) model with normally distributed z_t the kurtosis of ε_t is equal to

$$K_\varepsilon = \frac{E[\varepsilon_t^4]}{E[\varepsilon_t^2]^2} = \frac{3(1 - \alpha_1^2)}{1 - 3\alpha_1^2}, \tag{4.9}$$

which is finite if $3\alpha_1^2 < 1$. Clearly, K_ε is always larger than the normal value of 3.

Another characteristic of the ARCH(1) model which is worthwhile noting is the implied autocorrelation function for the squared shocks ε_t^2. From the AR(1) representation in (4.5), it follows that the kth order autocorrelation of ε_t^2 is equal to α_1^k. In figures 2.1 and 2.2 it could be seen that the first-order autocorrelation of squared stock and exchange returns generally is quite small, while the subsequent decay is very slow. The small first-order autocorrelation would imply a small value of α_1 in the ARCH(1) model, but this in turn would imply that the autocorrelations would become close to zero quite quickly. Thus it appears that the ARCH(1) model cannot describe the two characteristic features of the empirical autocorrelations of the returns series simultaneously.

To cope with the extended persistence of the empirical autocorrelation function, one may consider generalizations of the ARCH(1) model. One possibility to allow for more persistent autocorrelations is to include additional lagged squared shocks in the conditional variance function. The general ARCH(q) model is given by

$$h_t = \omega + \alpha_1 \varepsilon_{t-1}^2 + \alpha_2 \varepsilon_{t-2}^2 + \cdots + \alpha_q \varepsilon_{t-q}^2. \qquad (4.10)$$

To guarantee nonnegativeness of the conditional variance, it is required that $\omega > 0$ and $\alpha_i \geq 0$ for all $i = 1, \ldots, q$. The ARCH(q) model can be rewritten as an AR(q) model for ε_t^2 in exactly the same fashion as writing (4.4) as (4.5), that is,

$$\varepsilon_t^2 = \omega + \alpha_1 \varepsilon_{t-1}^2 + \alpha_2 \varepsilon_{t-2}^2 + \cdots + \alpha_q \varepsilon_{t-q}^2 + v_t. \qquad (4.11)$$

It follows that the unconditional variance of ε_t is equal to

$$\sigma^2 = \frac{\omega}{1 - \alpha_1 - \cdots - \alpha_q}, \qquad (4.12)$$

while the ARCH(q) model is covariance-stationary if all roots of the lag polynomial $1 - \alpha_1 L - \cdots - \alpha_q L^q$ are outside the unit circle. Milhøj (1985) derives conditions for the existence of unconditional moments of ARCH(q) processes.

To capture the dynamic patterns in conditional volatility adequately by means of an ARCH(q) model, q often needs to be taken quite large. It turns out that it can be quite cumbersome to estimate the parameters in such a model, because of the nonnegativity and stationarity conditions that need to be imposed. To reduce the computational problems, it is common to impose some structure on the parameters in the ARCH(q) model, such as $\alpha_i = \alpha(q+1-i)/(q(q+1)/2)$, $i = 1, \ldots, q$, which implies that the parameters of the lagged squared shocks decline linearly and sum to α (see Engle, 1982, 1983). As an alternative solution, Bollerslev (1986) suggested adding lagged conditional variances to the ARCH model instead. For example, adding h_{t-1} to the ARCH(1) model (4.4) results in the Generalized ARCH (GARCH) model of order (1,1)

$$h_t = \omega + \alpha_1 \varepsilon_{t-1}^2 + \beta_1 h_{t-1}. \tag{4.13}$$

The parameters in this model should satisfy $\omega > 0$, $\alpha_1 > 0$ and $\beta_1 \geq 0$ to guarantee that $h_t \geq 0$, while α_1 must be strictly positive for β_1 to be identified (see also (4.16)).

To see why the lagged conditional variance avoids the necessity of adding many lagged squared residual terms to the model, notice that (4.13) can be rewritten as

$$h_t = \omega + \alpha_1 \varepsilon_{t-1}^2 + \beta_1 (\omega + \alpha_1 \varepsilon_{t-2}^2 + \beta_1 h_{t-2}), \tag{4.14}$$

or, by continuing the recursive substitution, as

$$h_t = \sum_{i=1}^{\infty} \beta_1^i \omega + \alpha_1 \sum_{i=1}^{\infty} \beta_1^{i-1} \varepsilon_{t-i}^2. \tag{4.15}$$

This shows that the GARCH(1,1) model corresponds to an ARCH(∞) model with a particular structure for the parameters of the lagged ε_t^2 terms.

Alternatively, by adding ε_t^2 to both sides of (4.13) and moving h_t to the right-hand side, the GARCH(1,1) model can be rewritten as an ARMA(1,1) model for ε_t^2 as

$$\varepsilon_t^2 = \omega + (\alpha_1 + \beta_1)\varepsilon_{t-1}^2 + v_t - \beta_1 v_{t-1}, \tag{4.16}$$

where again $v_t = \varepsilon_t^2 - h_t$. Using the theory for ARMA models discussed in section 2.1, it follows that the GARCH(1,1) model is covariance-stationary if and only if $\alpha_1 + \beta_1 < 1$. In that case the unconditional mean of ε_t^2 – or, equivalently, the unconditional variance of ε_t – is equal to

$$\sigma^2 = \frac{\omega}{1 - \alpha_1 - \beta_1}. \tag{4.17}$$

The ARMA(1,1) representation in (4.16) also makes clear why α_1 needs to be strictly positive for identification of β_1. If $\alpha_1 = 0$, the AR and MA polynomials both are equal to $1 - \beta_1 L$. Rewriting the ARMA(1,1) model for ε_t^2 as an MA(∞), these polynomials cancel out,

$$\varepsilon_t^2 = \frac{1 - \beta_1 L}{1 - \beta_1 L} v_t = v_t, \tag{4.18}$$

which shows that β_1 then is not identified.

As shown by Bollerslev (1986), the unconditional fourth moment of ε_t is finite if $(\alpha_1 + \beta_1)^2 + 2\alpha_1^2 < 1$. If in addition the z_t are assumed to be normally distributed, the kurtosis of ε_t is given by

$$K_\varepsilon = \frac{3[1 - (\alpha_1 + \beta_1)^2]}{1 - (\alpha_1 + \beta_1)^2 - 2\alpha_1^2}, \tag{4.19}$$

which again is always larger than the normal value of 3. Notice that if $\beta_1 = 0$, (4.19) reduces to (4.9).

The autocorrelations of ε_t^2 are derived in Bollerslev (1988) and are found to be

$$\rho_1 = \alpha_1 + \frac{\alpha_1^2 \beta_1}{1 - 2\alpha_1\beta_1 - \beta_1^2}, \tag{4.20}$$

$$\rho_k = (\alpha_1 + \beta_1)^{k-1} \rho_1 \qquad \text{for } k = 2, 3, \ldots \tag{4.21}$$

Even though the autocorrelations still decline exponentially, the decay factor in this case is $\alpha_1 + \beta_1$. If this sum is close to one, the autocorrelations will decrease only very gradually. When the fourth moment of ε_t is not finite, the autocorrelations of ε_t^2 are time-varying. Of course, one can still compute the sample autocorrelations in this case. As shown by Ding and Granger (1996), if $\alpha_1 + \beta_1 < 1$ and $(\alpha_1 + \beta_1)^2 + 2\alpha_1^2 \geq 1$, such that the GARCH(1,1) model is covariance-stationary but with infinite fourth moment, the autocorrelations of ε_t^2 behave approximately as

$$\rho_1 \approx \alpha_1 + \beta_1/3, \tag{4.22}$$

$$\rho_k \approx (\alpha_1 + \beta_1)^{k-1} \rho_1 \quad \text{for } k = 2, 3, \ldots \tag{4.23}$$

The parameter restriction $(\alpha_1 + \beta_1)^2 + 2\alpha_1^2 = 1$ is equivalent to $1 - 2\alpha_1\beta_1 - \beta_1^2 = 3\alpha_1^2$, from which it follows that (4.22) is identical to (4.20) where this restriction is satisfied. Therefore, the autocorrelations of ε_t^2 can be considered as continuous functions of α_1 and β_1, in the sense that their behaviour does not suddenly change when these parameters take values for which the condition for existence of the fourth moment is no longer satisfied.

The general GARCH(p,q) model is given by

$$h_t = \omega + \sum_{i=1}^{q} \alpha_i \varepsilon_{t-i}^2 + \sum_{i=1}^{p} \beta_i h_{t-i}$$

$$= \omega + \alpha(L)\varepsilon_t^2 + \beta(L)h_t, \tag{4.24}$$

where $\alpha(L) = \alpha_1 L + \cdots + \alpha_q L^q$ and $\beta(L) = \beta_1 L + \cdots + \beta_p L^p$. Assuming that all the roots of $1 - \beta(L)$ are outside the unit circle, the model can be rewritten as an infinite-order ARCH model

$$h_t = \frac{\omega}{1 - \beta(1)} + \frac{\alpha(L)}{1 - \beta(L)} \varepsilon_t^2$$

$$= \frac{\omega}{1 - \beta_1 - \cdots - \beta_p} + \sum_{i=1}^{\infty} \delta_i \varepsilon_{t-i}^2. \tag{4.25}$$

For nonnegativeness of the conditional variance it is required that all δ_i in (4.25) are nonnegative. Nelson and Cao (1992) discuss the conditions this implies for the parameters $\alpha_i, i = 1, \ldots, q$, and $\beta_i, i = 1 \ldots, q$, in the original model (4.24).

Alternatively, the GARCH(p,q) can be interpreted as an ARMA(m,p) model for ε_t^2 given by

$$\varepsilon_t^2 = \omega + \sum_{i=1}^{m} (\alpha_i + \beta_i) \varepsilon_{t-i}^2 - \sum_{i=1}^{p} \beta_i v_{t-i} + v_t, \tag{4.26}$$

where $m = \max(p, q), \alpha_i \equiv 0$ for $i > q$ and $\beta_i \equiv 0$ for $i > p$. It follows that the GARCH(p,q) model is covariance-stationary if all the roots of $1 - \alpha(L) - \beta(L)$ are outside the unit circle.

To determine the appropriate orders p and q in the GARCH(p,q) model, one can use a general-to-specific procedure by starting with a model with p and q set equal to large values, and testing down using likelihood-ratio-type restrictions (see Akgiray, 1989; Cao and Tsay, 1992). Alternatively, one can use modified information criteria, as suggested by Brooks and Burke (1997, 1998).

Even though the general GARCH(p,q) model might be of theoretical interest, the GARCH(1,1) model often appears adequate in practice (see also Bollerslev, Chou and Kroner, 1992). Furthermore, many nonlinear extensions to be discussed below have been considered only for the GARCH(1,1) case.

IGARCH

In applications of the GARCH(1,1) model (4.13) to high-frequency financial time series, it is often found that the estimates of α_1 and β_1 are such that their sum is close or equal to one. Following Engle and Bollerslev (1986), the model that results when $\alpha_1 + \beta_1 = 1$ is commonly referred to as Integrated GARCH (IGARCH). The reason for this is that the restriction $\alpha_1 + \beta_1 = 1$ implies a unit root in the ARMA(1,1) model for ε_t^2 given in (4.16), which then can be written as

$$(1 - L)\varepsilon_t^2 = \omega + v_t - \beta_1 v_{t-1}. \tag{4.27}$$

The analogy with a unit root in an ARMA model for the conditional mean of a time series is however rather subtle. For example, from (4.17) it is seen that the unconditional variance of ε_t is not finite in this case. Therefore, the IGARCH model is not covariance-stationary. However, the IGARCH(1,1) model may still be strictly stationary, as shown by Nelson (1990). This can be illustrated by rewriting (4.13) as

$$
\begin{aligned}
h_t &= \omega + (\alpha_1 z_{t-1}^2 + \beta_1) h_{t-1} \\
&= \omega + (\alpha_1 z_{t-1}^2 + \beta_1)(\omega + (\alpha_1 z_{t-2}^2 + \beta_1) h_{t-2}) \\
&= \omega(1 + (\alpha_1 z_{t-1}^2 + \beta_1)) + (\alpha_1 z_{t-1}^2 + \beta_1)(\alpha_1 z_{t-2}^2 + \beta_1) h_{t-2},
\end{aligned}
$$

and continuing the substitution for h_{t-i}, it follows that

$$
h_t = \omega \left(1 + \sum_{i=1}^{t-1} \prod_{j=1}^{i} (\alpha_1 z_{t-j}^2 + \beta_1) \right) + \prod_{i=1}^{t} (\alpha_1 z_{t-i}^2 + \beta_1) h_0. \qquad (4.28)
$$

As shown by Nelson (1990), a necessary condition for strict stationarity of the GARCH(1,1) model is $E[\ln(\alpha_1 z_{t-i}^2 + \beta_1)] < 0$. If this condition is satisfied, the impact of h_0 disappears asymptotically.

As expected, the autocorrelations of ε_t^2 for an IGARCH model are not defined properly. However, Ding and Granger (1996) show that the approximate autocorrelations are given by

$$
\rho_k = \frac{1}{3}(1 + 2\alpha)(1 + 2\alpha^2)^{-k/2}. \qquad (4.29)
$$

Hence, the autocorrelations still decay exponentially. This is in sharp contrast with the autocorrelations for a random walk model, for which the autocorrelations are approximately equal to 1 (see (2.33)).

FIGARCH

The properties of the conditional variance h_t as implied by the IGARCH model are not very attractive from an empirical point of view. Still, estimates of the parameters of GARCH(1,1) models for high-frequency financial time series invariably yield a sum of α_1 and β_1 close to 1, with α_1 small and β_1 large. This implies that the impact of shocks on the conditional variance diminishes only very slowly. From the ARCH(∞) representation of the GARCH(1,1) model as given in (4.15), the impact of the shock ε_t on h_{t+k} is given by $\alpha_1 \beta_1^{k-1}$. With β_1 close to 1, this impact decays very slowly as k increases. Similarly, the autocorrelations for ε_t^2 given in (4.20) and (4.21) die out very slowly if the sum $\alpha_1 + \beta_1$ is close to 1. However, the decay is still at an exponential rate, which might be too fast to mimic the observed autocorrelation patterns of empirical time series, no matter how small the difference $1 - (\alpha_1 + \beta_1)$ is. For example, Ding, Granger and Engle (1993) suggest that the sample autocorrelations of squared – and, especially, absolute – returns decline only at a hyperbolic rate. This type of behaviour of the autocorrelations can be modelled by means of long-memory or fractionally integrated processes, as discussed in section 2.4.

Baillie, Bollerslev and Mikkelsen (1996) propose the class of Fractionally Integrated GARCH (FIGARCH) models. The basic FIGARCH(1,d,0) model is most easily obtained from (4.27), by simply adding an exponent d to the first-difference operator $(1 - L)$, that is,

$$(1 - L)^d \varepsilon_t^2 = \omega + v_t - \beta_1 v_{t-1}, \tag{4.30}$$

where $0 < d < 1$. Using the definition of $v_t = \varepsilon_t^2 - h_t$, this can be rewritten as an ARCH(∞) process for the conditional variance as

$$
\begin{aligned}
h_t &= \omega/(1 - \beta_1) + (1 - (1 - L)^d/(1 - \beta_1 L))\varepsilon_t^2 \\
&= \omega/(1 - \beta_1) + \lambda(L)\varepsilon_t^2,
\end{aligned} \tag{4.31}
$$

where $\lambda(L) \equiv 1 - (1 - L)^d/(1 - \beta_1 L)$. By using the expansion (2.106) for $(1 - L)^d$, it can be shown that for large k

$$\lambda_k \approx [(1 - \beta_1)\Gamma(d)^{-1}]k^{d-1}, \tag{4.32}$$

where $\Gamma(\cdot)$ is the gamma function. This expression shows that the effect of ε_t on h_{t+k} decays only at a hyperbolic rate as k increases. FIGARCH models are applied to exchange rates by Baillie, Bollerslev and Mikkelsen (1996), while Bollerslev and Mikkelsen (1996) apply the model to stock returns and option prices.

Ding and Granger (1996) argue that the sample autocorrelation functions of squared returns initially decrease faster than exponentially, and that only at higher lags does the decrease become (much) slower. This pattern suggests that volatility may consist of several components, some of which have a strong effect on volatility in the short run but die out quite rapidly, while others may have a small but persistent effect. To formalize this notion, Ding and Granger (1996) put forward the component GARCH model

$$h_t = \gamma h_{1,t} + (1 - \gamma)h_{2,t}, \tag{4.33}$$

$$h_{1,t} = \alpha_1 \varepsilon_{t-1}^2 + (1 - \alpha_1)h_{1,t-1}, \tag{4.34}$$

$$h_{2,t} = \omega + \alpha_2 \varepsilon_{t-1}^2 + \beta_2 h_{2,t-1}. \tag{4.35}$$

In this model, the conditional variance is seen to be a weighted sum of two components, one specified as an IGARCH model and the other as a GARCH model. A similar model is applied by Jones, Lamont and Lumsdaine (1998) to investigate whether shocks that occur on specific days, on which announcements of important macroeconomic figures are made, have different effects on volatility than shocks that occur on other days.

GARCH in mean

Many financial theories postulate a direct relationship between the return and risk of financial assets. For example, in the CAPM the excess return on a risky asset is proportional to its nondiversifiable risk, which is measured by the covariance with the market portfolio. The GARCH in mean (GARCH-M) model introduced by Engle, Lilien and Robins (1987) was explicitly designed to capture such direct relationships between return and possibly time-varying risk (as measured by the conditional variance). This is established by including (a function) of the conditional variance h_t in the model for the conditional mean of the variable of interest y_t, for example,

$$y_t = \phi_0 + \phi_1 y_{t-1} + \cdots + \phi_p y_{t-p} + \delta g(h_t) + \varepsilon_t, \tag{4.36}$$

where $g(h_t)$ is some function of the conditional variance of ε_t, h_t, which is assumed to follow a (possibly nonlinear) GARCH process. In most applications, $g(h_t)$ is taken to be the identity function or square root function – that is, $g(h_t) = h_t$ or $g(h_t) = \sqrt{h_t}$. The additional term $\delta g(h_t)$ in (4.36) is often interpreted as some sort of risk premium. As h_t varies over time, so does this risk premium.

To gain some intuition for the properties of y_t as implied by the GARCH-M model, consider (4.36) with $p = 0$ and $g(h_t) = h_t$ and assume that h_t follows an ARCH(1) process

$$y_t = \delta h_t + \varepsilon_t, \tag{4.37}$$

$$h_t = \omega + \alpha_1 \varepsilon_{t-1}^2. \tag{4.38}$$

Substituting (4.38) in (4.37) and using the fact that $E[\varepsilon_{t-1}^2] = \omega/(1 - \alpha_1)$ (see (4.6)), it follows that the unconditional expectation of y_t is equal to

$$E[y_t] = \delta\omega\left(1 + \frac{\alpha_1}{1 - \alpha_1}\right).$$

Similarly, it can be shown that the unconditional variance of y_t is equal to

$$\sigma_y^2 = \frac{\omega}{1 - \alpha_1} + \frac{(\delta\alpha_1)^2 2\omega^2}{(1 - \alpha_1)^2(1 - 3\alpha_1^2)},$$

which is larger than the unconditional variance of y_t in the absence of the GARCH-M effect, as in that case $\sigma_y^2 = \frac{\omega}{1-\alpha_1}$. Another consequence of the presence of h_t as regressor in the conditional mean equation (4.37) is that y_t is serially correlated. As shown by Hong (1991),

$$\rho_1 = \frac{2\alpha_1^3\delta^2\omega}{2\alpha_1^2\delta^2\omega + (1 - \alpha_1)(1 - 3\alpha_1^2)} \tag{4.39}$$

$$\rho_k = \alpha_1^{k-1}\rho_1 \qquad k = 2, 3, \ldots \tag{4.40}$$

An overview of applications of GARCH-M models to stock returns, interest rates and exchange rates can be found in Bollerslev, Chou and Kroner (1992).

Stochastic volatility

In the GARCH model, the conditional volatility of the observed time series y_t is driven by the same shocks as its conditional mean. Furthermore, conditional upon the history of the time series as summarized in the information set Ω_{t-1}, current volatility h_t is deterministic. An alternative class of volatility models which has received considerable attention assumes that h_t is subject to an additional contemporaneous shock. The basic stochastic volatility (SV) model, introduced by Taylor (1986), is given by

$$\varepsilon_t = z_t \sqrt{h_t}, \tag{4.41}$$

$$\ln(h_t) = \gamma_0 + \gamma_1 \ln(h_{t-1}) + \gamma_2 \eta_t, \tag{4.42}$$

with $z_t \sim \text{NID}(0, 1)$, $\eta_t \sim \text{NID}(0, 1)$, and η_t and z_t uncorrelated. A heuristic interpretation of the SV model is that the shock η_t represents shocks to the intensity of the flow of new information as measured by h_t, whereas the shock z_t represents the contents (large/small, positive/negative) of the news.

To understand the similarities and differences between the GARCH(1,1) and SV models, it is useful to consider the implied moments and correlation properties of ε_t. First note that, if $|\gamma_1| < 1$ in (4.42), $\ln(h_t)$ follows a stationary AR(1) process and $\ln(h_t) \sim N(\mu_h, \sigma_h^2)$ with

$$\mu_h = \text{E}[\ln(h_t)] = \frac{\gamma_0}{1 - \gamma_1}, \tag{4.43}$$

$$\sigma_h^2 = \text{var}[\ln(h_t)] = \frac{\gamma_2^2}{1 - \gamma_1^2}. \tag{4.44}$$

Put differently, h_t has a log-normal distribution. For the series ε_t, this implies that

$$\text{E}[\varepsilon_t^r] = 0 \quad \text{for } r \text{ odd}, \tag{4.45}$$

$$\text{E}[\varepsilon_t^2] = \text{E}[z_t^2 h_t] = \text{E}[z_t^2]\text{E}[h_t] = \exp(\mu_h + \sigma_h^2/2), \tag{4.46}$$

$$\text{E}[\varepsilon_t^4] = \text{E}[z_t^4 h_t^2] = \text{E}[z_t^4]\text{E}[h_t^2] = 3\exp(2\mu_h + 2\sigma_h^2). \tag{4.47}$$

In particular, from (4.46) and (4.47) it follows that

$$K_\varepsilon = \frac{\text{E}[\varepsilon_t^4]}{\text{E}[\varepsilon_t^2]^2} = 3\exp(\sigma_h^2), \tag{4.48}$$

which demonstrates that the SV model implies excess kurtosis in the series ε_t, similar to the GARCH(1,1) model (see (4.19)). A difference, however, is that the GARCH(1,1) model with z_t normally distributed typically cannot capture the excess kurtosis observed in financial time series completely (as will be discussed in more detail below), whereas the SV model can, as $\exp(\sigma_h^2)$ can take any value.

The correlation properties of ε_t^2 can be derived by noting that $E[\varepsilon_t^2 \varepsilon_{t-k}^2] = E[z_t^2 h_t z_{t-k}^2 h_{t-k}] = E[h_t^2 h_{t-k}^2]$. It follows that

$$\rho_k = \frac{\exp(\sigma_h^2 \gamma_1^k) - 1}{3 \exp(\sigma_h^2) - 1} \approx \frac{\exp(\sigma_h^2) - 1}{3 \exp(\sigma_h^2) - 1} \gamma_1^k, \tag{4.49}$$

where the approximation is valid for small values of σ_h^2 and/or large γ_1 (see Taylor, 1986, pp. 74–5). Comparing (4.49) with the autocorrelations of ε_t^2 implied by the GARCH(1,1) model as given in (4.20) and (4.21) shows that in both cases the ACF of ε_t^2 is characterized by exponential decay towards zero. For the GARCH(1,1) model, the sum $\alpha_1 + \beta_1$ determines how fast the autocorrelations decline towards zero, whereas in the SV model this is determined by γ_1. When SV models are applied to high-frequency financial time series, the parameter estimates that are typically found imply that the first-order autocorrelation is small, whereas the subsequent decay is very slow. For example, typical parameter estimates are $\hat{\sigma}_\eta = 0.3$ and $\hat{\gamma}_1 = 0.95$, which according to (4.44) and (4.49) imply $\hat{\rho}_1 \approx 0.21$ and $\hat{\rho}_k \approx 0.95^k \hat{\rho}_1$.

The main difference between the GARCH and SV models is found at the estimation stage. In the GARCH model, the parameters can be estimated by straightforward application of maximum likelihood techniques, as will be discussed in section 4.3. This is owing to the fact that even though the conditional volatility h_t appears to be unobserved, it can be reconstructed using the past shocks $\varepsilon_{t-1}, \varepsilon_{t-2}, \ldots$ (assuming these can be obtained from the observed series $y_{t-1}, y_{t-2}, \ldots,$) and h_0. Technically, h_t is measurable with respect to the information set Ω_{t-1}. As a consequence, the distribution of ε_t conditional upon the history Ω_{t-1} can be obtained directly from the distribution of z_t, and the likelihood function can easily be constructed. By contrast, for the SV model the distribution of $\varepsilon_t | \Omega_{t-1}$ cannot be characterized explicitly, owing to the fact that h_t is not only unobserved, but also cannot be reconstructed from the history of the time series. Therefore, standard maximum likelihood techniques cannot be applied to estimate the parameters in SV models. Several alternative procedures have been examined, such as a (simulation-based) generalized method of moments (Melino and Turnbull, 1990; Duffie and Singleton, 1993), quasi-maximum likelihood via the Kalman filter (Harvey, Ruiz and Shephard, 1994), indirect inference (Gourieroux, Monfort and Renault, 1993), simulation-based maximum likelihood (Danielsson and Richard, 1993; Danielsson, 1994) and Bayesian methods (Jacquier, Polson and Rossi, 1994). As of yet, there is no consensus on the appropriate method(s) of estimation and inference in SV models. For that reason, we do not consider these models any further in this chapter and restrict ourselves to the GARCH class. Surveys of the SV literature can be found in Ghysels, Harvey and Renault (1996) and Shephard (1996).

4.1.2 Nonlinear GARCH models

As shown in section 1.2, for stock returns it appears to be the case that volatile periods often are initiated by a large negative shock, which suggests that positive and negative shocks may have an asymmetric impact on the conditional volatility of subsequent observations. This was recognized by Black (1976), who suggested that a possible explanation for this finding might be the way firms are financed. When the value of (the stock of) a firm falls, the debt-to-equity ratio increases, which in turn leads to an increase in the volatility of the returns on equity. As the debt-to-equity ratio is also known as the 'leverage' of the firm, this phenomenon is commonly referred to as the 'leverage effect'.

The GARCH models discussed above cannot capture such asymmetric effects of positive and negative shocks. As the conditional variance depends only on the square of the shock, positive and negative shocks of the same magnitude have the same effect on the conditional volatility – that is, the sign of the shock is not important. Most nonlinear extensions of the GARCH model which have been developed over the years are designed to allow for different effects of positive and negative shocks or other types of asymmetries. In this section we review several of such nonlinear GARCH models. The models that are discussed below are only a small sample from all the different nonlinear GARCH models which have been proposed. For more complete overviews, the interested reader is referred to Hentschel (1995), among others. We generally concentrate on those models that make use of the idea of regime switching, as discussed in chapter 3 for nonlinear models for the conditional mean.

Most nonlinear GARCH models are motivated by the desire to capture the different effects of positive and negative shocks on conditional volatility or other types of asymmetry. A natural question to ask, then, is whether all these models are indeed different from each other, or whether they are more or less similar. A convenient way to compare different GARCH models is by means of the so-called *news impact curve* (NIC), introduced by Pagan and Schwert (1990) and popularized by Engle and Ng (1993). The NIC measures how new information is incorporated into volatility. To be more precise, the NIC shows the relationship between the current shock or news ε_t and conditional volatility 1 period ahead h_{t+1}, holding constant all other past and current information. In the basic GARCH(1,1) model and nonlinear variants thereof, the only relevant information from the past is the current conditional variance h_t. Thus, the NIC for the GARCH(1,1) model (4.13) is defined as

$$NIC(\varepsilon_t | h_t = h) = \omega + \alpha_1 \varepsilon_t^2 + \beta_1 h = A + \alpha_1 \varepsilon_t^2, \tag{4.50}$$

where $A = \omega + \beta_1 h$. Hence, the NIC is a quadratic function centred on $\varepsilon_t = 0$. As the value of the lagged conditional variance h_t affects only the constant A in (4.50), it only shifts the NIC vertically, but does not change its basic shape. In practice, it is customary to take h_t equal to the unconditional variance σ^2.

Exponential GARCH

The earliest variant of the GARCH model which allows for asymmetric effects is the Exponential GARCH (EGARCH) model, introduced by Nelson (1991). The EGARCH(1,1) model is given by

$$\ln(h_t) = \omega + \alpha_1 z_{t-1} + \gamma_1 (|z_{t-1}| - E(|z_{t-1}|)) + \beta_1 \ln(h_{t-1}). \quad (4.51)$$

As the EGARCH model (4.51) describes the relation between past shocks and the *logarithm* of the conditional variance, no restrictions on the parameters α_1, γ_1 and β_1 have to be imposed to ensure that h_t is nonnegative. Using the properties of z_t, it follows that $g(z_t) \equiv \alpha_1 z_t + \gamma_1 (|z_t| - E(|z_t|))$ has mean zero and is uncorrelated. The function $g(z_t)$ is piecewise linear in z_t, as it can be rewritten as

$$g(z_t) = (\alpha_1 + \gamma_1) z_t I(z_t > 0) + (\alpha_1 - \gamma_1) z_t I(z_t < 0) - \gamma_1 E(|z_t|).$$

Thus, negative shocks have an impact $\alpha_1 - \gamma_1$ on the log of the conditional variance, while for positive shocks the impact is $\alpha_1 + \gamma_1$. This property of the function $g(z_t)$ leads to an asymmetric NIC. In particular, the NIC for the EGARCH(1,1) model (4.51) is given by

$$NIC(\varepsilon_t | h_t = \sigma^2) = \begin{cases} A \exp\left(\dfrac{\alpha_1 + \gamma_1}{\sigma} \varepsilon_t\right) & \text{for } \varepsilon_t > 0, \\[3mm] A \exp\left(\dfrac{\alpha_1 - \gamma_1}{\sigma} \varepsilon_t\right) & \text{for } \varepsilon_t < 0, \end{cases} \quad (4.52)$$

with $A = \sigma^{2\beta_1} \exp(\omega - \gamma_1 \sqrt{2/\pi})$.

Typical NICs for the GARCH(1,1) and EGARCH(1,1) models are shown in panel (a) of figure 4.1. The parameters in the models have been chosen such that the constants A in (4.52) and (4.50) are the same and, hence, the NICs are equal when $\varepsilon_t = 0$. The shape of the NIC of the EGARCH model is typical for parameterizations with $\alpha_1 < 0$, $0 \leq \gamma_1 < 1$ and $\gamma_1 + \beta_1 < 1$. For such parameter configurations, negative shocks have a larger effect on the conditional variance than positive shocks of the same size. For the range of ε_t for which the NIC is plotted in figure 4.1, it also appears that negative shocks in the EGARCH model have a larger effect on the conditional variance than shocks in the GARCH model, while the reverse holds for positive shocks. However, as ε_t increases, the impact on h_t will eventually become larger in the EGARCH model, as the exponential function in (4.52) dominates the quadratic in (4.50) for large ε_t.

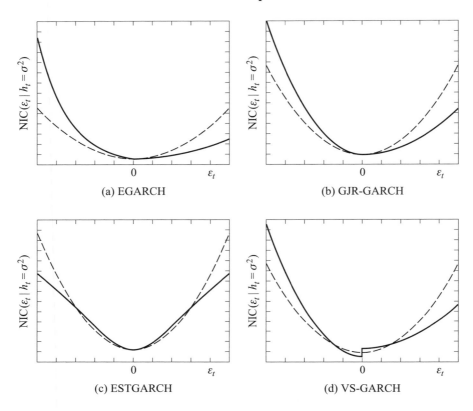

Figure 4.1   Examples of news impact curves for various nonlinear models (solid lines); for comparison, the news impact curve of a GARCH(1,1) model is also shown in each panel (dashed line) (a) The parameters in the EGARCH model (4.51) are such that $\alpha_1 < 0, 0 \leq \gamma_1 < 1$ and $\gamma_1 + \beta_1 < 1$ (b) The parameters in the GJR-GARCH model (4.53) are such that $\alpha_1 > \gamma_1$, while $(\alpha_1 + \gamma_1)/2$ is equal to α_1 in the GARCH(1,1) model (c) The parameters in the ESTGARCH model (4.55) with (4.58) are such that $\alpha_1 > \gamma_1$ and their average is equal to α_1 in the GARCH(1,1) model (d) The parameters in the VS-GARCH model (4.59) are set such that $\alpha_1 > \gamma_1$ and $\omega + \beta_1 h < \zeta + \delta_1 h$, while the averages of all three pairs of parameters in the two regimes are equal to the corresponding parameter in the GARCH(1,1) model

GJR-GARCH

The model introduced by Glosten, Jagannathan and Runkle (1993) offers an alternative method to allow for asymmetric effects of positive and negative shocks on volatility. The model is obtained from the GARCH(1,1) model (4.13) by assuming that the parameter of ε_{t-1}^2 depends on the sign of the shock, that is,

$$h_t = \omega + \alpha_1 \varepsilon_{t-1}^2 (1 - I[\varepsilon_{t-1} > 0]) + \gamma_1 \varepsilon_{t-1}^2 I[\varepsilon_{t-1} > 0] + \beta_1 h_{t-1},$$

$$(4.53)$$

where as usual $I[\cdot]$ is an indicator function. The conditions for nonnegativeness of the conditional variance are $\omega > 0$, $(\alpha_1 + \gamma_1)/2 \geq 0$ and $\beta_1 > 0$. The condition for covariance-stationarity is $(\alpha_1 + \gamma_1)/2 + \beta_1 < 1$. If this condition is satisfied, the unconditional variance of ε_t is $\sigma^2 = \omega/(1 - (\alpha_1 + \gamma_1)/2 - \beta_1)$. The NIC for the GJR-GARCH model follows directly from (4.53) and is equal to

$$NIC(\varepsilon_t | h_t = \sigma^2) = A + \begin{cases} \alpha_1 \varepsilon_t^2 & \text{if } \varepsilon_t < 0, \\ \gamma_1 \varepsilon_t^2 & \text{if } \varepsilon_t > 0, \end{cases} \tag{4.54}$$

where $A = \omega + \beta_1 \sigma^2$. The NIC of the GJR-GARCH model is a quadratic function centred on $\varepsilon_t = 0$, similar to the NIC of the basic GARCH model. However, the slopes of the GJR-GARCH NIC are allowed to be different for positive and negative shocks. Depending on the values of α_1 and γ_1 in (4.53), the NIC (4.54) can be steeper or less steep than the GARCH NIC (4.50). An example of the GJR-GARCH NIC is shown in panel (b) of figure 4.1, where we have set α_1 and γ_1 such that $\alpha_1 > \gamma_1$ while their average is equal to the value of α_1 in the GARCH(1,1) model. In this case, the NIC is steeper than the GARCH NIC for negative news and less steep for positive news. Comparing the NICs of the EGARCH and GJR-GARCH models as shown in panels (a) and (b) of figure 4.1 shows that they are rather similar. Hence, the GJR-GARCH model and the EGARCH model may be considered as alternative models for the same series. It may be difficult to develop criteria that can help to distinguish between the two models.

Smooth Transition GARCH

The GJR-GARCH model (4.53) can be interpreted as a threshold model, as it allows the parameter corresponding to the lagged squared shock to change abruptly from α_1 to γ_1 at $\varepsilon_{t-1} = 0$. Hagerud (1997) and González-Rivera (1998) independently applied the idea of smooth transition, discussed in section 3.1, to allow for a more gradual change of this parameter. The Logistic Smooth Transition GARCH (LSTGARCH) model is given by

$$h_t = \omega + \alpha_1 \varepsilon_{t-1}^2 [1 - F(\varepsilon_{t-1})] + \gamma_1 \varepsilon_{t-1}^2 F(\varepsilon_{t-1}) + \beta_1 h_{t-1}, \tag{4.55}$$

where the function $F(\varepsilon_{t-1})$ is the logistic function

$$F(\varepsilon_{t-1}) = \frac{1}{1 + \exp(-\theta \varepsilon_{t-1})}, \quad \theta > 0. \tag{4.56}$$

As the function $F(\varepsilon_{t-1})$ in (4.56) changes monotonically from 0 to 1 as ε_{t-1} increases, the impact of ε_{t-1}^2 on h_t changes smoothly from α_1 to γ_1. When the parameter θ in (4.56) becomes large, the logistic function approaches a step function which equals 0 for negative ε_{t-1} and 1 for positive ε_{t-1}. In that case, the LSTGARCH model reduces to the GJR-GARCH model (4.53).

The parameter restrictions necessary for h_t to be positive and for the model to be covariance-stationary are the same as for the GJR-GARCH model given above. The NIC for the LSTGARCH model is given by

$$NIC(\varepsilon_t | h_t = \sigma^2) = [A + \alpha_1 \varepsilon_t^2][1 - F(\varepsilon_t)] + \gamma_1 \varepsilon_t^2]F(\varepsilon_t), \qquad (4.57)$$

where $A = \omega + \beta_1 \sigma^2$.

The STGARCH model (4.55) can also be used to describe asymmetric effects of large and small shocks on conditional volatility, by using the exponential function

$$F(\varepsilon_{t-1}) = 1 - \exp(-\theta \varepsilon_{t-1}^2), \quad \theta > 0. \qquad (4.58)$$

The function $F(\varepsilon_{t-1})$ in (4.58) changes from 1 for large negative values of ε_{t-1} to 0 for $\varepsilon_{t-1} = 0$ and increases back again to 1 for large positive values of ε_{t-1}. Thus, the effective parameter of ε_{t-1}^2 in the Exponential STGARCH (ESTGARCH) model given by (4.55) with (4.58) changes from γ_1 to α_1 and back to γ_1 again. Panel (c) of figure 4.1 shows an example of the NIC of the ESTGARCH model.

Volatility-Switching GARCH

The LSTGARCH and GJR-GARCH models assume that the asymmetric behaviour of h_t depends only on the sign of the past shock ε_{t-1}. In applications it is typically found that $\gamma_1 < \alpha_1$, such that a negative shock increases the conditional variance more than a positive shock of the same size. On the other hand, the ESTGARCH model assumes that the asymmetry is caused entirely by the size of the shock. Rabemananjara and Zakoïan (1993) point out that the asymmetric behaviour of h_t may be more complicated and that both the sign and the size of the shock may be important. In particular, they argue that negative shocks increase future conditional volatility more than positive shocks only if the shock is large in absolute value. For small shocks they observe the opposite kind of asymmetry, in that small positive shocks increase the conditional volatility more than small negative shocks.

Fornari and Mele (1996, 1997) discuss a model which allows for such complicated asymmetric behaviour. The model is in fact a generalization of the GJR-GARCH model, and is obtained by allowing all parameters in the conditional variance equation to depend on the sign of the shock ε_{t-1}. The Volatility-Switching GARCH (VS-GARCH) model of order $(1,1)$ is given by

$$h_t = (\omega + \alpha_1 \varepsilon_{t-1}^2 + \beta_1 h_{t-1})(1 - I[\varepsilon_{t-1} > 0])$$
$$+ (\zeta + \gamma_1 \varepsilon_{t-1}^2 + \delta_1 h_{t-1})I[\varepsilon_{t-1} > 0]. \qquad (4.59)$$

Fornari and Mele (1997) show that the unconditional variance of ε_t is equal to $\sigma^2 = [(\omega + \zeta)/2]/[1 - (\alpha_1 + \gamma_1)/2 - (\beta_1 + \delta_1)/2]$. The fourth unconditional moment of ε_t, and hence the kurtosis, implied by (4.59) is typically higher than that of a GARCH(1,1) model with parameters equal to the average of the parameters in the two regimes of the VS-GARCH model (see Fornari and Mele, 1997) for the exact expression.

The NIC for the VS-GARCH model is given by

$$NIC(\varepsilon_t | h_t = h) = \begin{cases} \omega + \alpha_1 \varepsilon_t^2 + \beta_1 h & \text{if } \varepsilon_t < 0, \\ \zeta + \gamma_1 \varepsilon_t^2 + \delta_1 h & \text{if } \varepsilon_t > 0. \end{cases} \tag{4.60}$$

This NIC is seen to be an asymmetric quadratic function centred on $\varepsilon_t = 0$, with possibly different slopes for positive and negative shocks. In this respect, the NIC of the VS-GARCH model is identical to the NIC of the GJR-GARCH model. However, as in general $\omega + \beta_1 h \neq \zeta + \delta_1 h$, the NIC (4.60) can be discontinuous at $\varepsilon_t = 0$. The size of the jump at this point depends on the magnitude of the past conditional volatility $h_t = h$. An example of the NIC (4.60) is shown in panel (d) of figure 4.1. The parameters in the VS-GARCH model (4.59) are set such that $\alpha_1 > \gamma_1$ and $\omega + \beta_1 h < \zeta + \delta_1 h$. For such parameter configurations, small positive shocks have a larger impact on the conditional volatility than small negative shocks, while the reverse holds for large shocks. This demonstrates that the VS-GARCH can describe more complicated asymmetric effects of shocks on conditional volatility than just sign or size effects.

Asymmetric Nonlinear Smooth Transition GARCH

Anderson, Nam and Vahid (1999) modify the VS-GARCH model by allowing the transition from one regime to the other to be smooth. The resulting Asymmetric Nonlinear Smooth Transition GARCH (ANST-GARCH) model is given by

$$h_t = [\omega + \alpha_1 \varepsilon_{t-1}^2 + \beta_1 h_{t-1}][1 - F(\varepsilon_{t-1})]$$
$$+ [\zeta + \gamma_1 \varepsilon_{t-1}^2 + \delta_1 h_{t-1}] F(\varepsilon_{t-1}), \tag{4.61}$$

where $F(\varepsilon_{t-1})$ is the logistic function (4.56). Even though the corresponding NIC,

$$NIC(\varepsilon_t | h_t = h) = [\omega + \alpha_1 \varepsilon_t^2 + \beta_1 h][1 - F(\varepsilon_t)]$$
$$+ [\zeta + \gamma_1 \varepsilon_t^2 + \delta_1 h] F(\varepsilon_t), \tag{4.62}$$

looks similar to the NIC of the VS-GARCH model at first sight, closer inspection of its properties reveals that it is rather different. In particular, the NIC of the ANST-GARCH model is always continuous at $\varepsilon_t = 0$, but it does not necessarily attain its minimum value at this point (which is the case for the NIC of the VS-GARCH model). It might be that the best news, which is defined as the shock that minimizes next period's conditional volatility, is nonzero. The exact size of the shock ε_t that constitutes the best news depends in a nontrivial way on current conditional volatility. Anderson, Nam and Vahid, (1999) demonstrate that the relationship between the best news and h_t is positive when $\delta_1 < \beta_1$. Some examples of NIC for this model are shown in figure 4.2. Evidently, the NIC changes shape as the current conditional volatility changes. As h_t increases, the asymmetry of the NIC becomes more pronounced while the shock ε_t that minimizes next period's volatility becomes increasingly positive.

Quadratic GARCH

Sentana (1995) introduced the Quadratic GARCH (QGARCH) model as another way to cope with asymmetric effects of shocks on volatility. The QGARCH(1,1) model is specified as

$$h_t = \omega + \gamma_1 \varepsilon_{t-1} + \alpha_1 \varepsilon_{t-1}^2 + \beta_1 h_{t-1}. \tag{4.63}$$

The additional term $\gamma_1 \varepsilon_{t-1}$ makes it possible for positive and negative shocks to have different effects on h_t. To see this, note that the model can be rewritten as

$$h_t = \omega + \left(\frac{\gamma_1}{\varepsilon_{t-1}} + \alpha_1 \right) \varepsilon_{t-1}^2 + \beta_1 h_{t-1}, \tag{4.64}$$

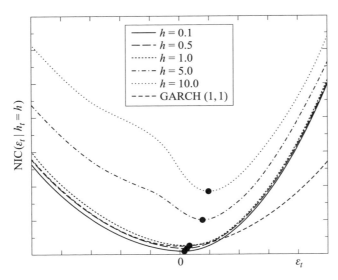

Figure 4.2   Examples of news impact curves for the ANST-GARCH model
The parameters in the model (4.61) are such that $\omega > \zeta$, $\alpha_1 < \gamma_1$ and $\beta_1 > \delta_1$; the location of the best news for each level of past conditional volatility is marked with a solid circle

which shows that the impact of ε_{t-1}^2 on h_t is equal to $\gamma_1/\varepsilon_{t-1} + \alpha_1$. If $\gamma_1 < 0$, the effect of negative shocks on h_t will be larger than the effect of a positive shock of the same size. Notice that in addition the effect depends on the size of the shock.

Alternatively, (4.63) can be expressed as

$$h_t = \omega - \frac{\gamma_1^2}{4\alpha_1} + \alpha_1\left(\varepsilon_{t-1} + \frac{\gamma_1}{2\alpha_1}\right)^2 + \beta_1 h_{t-1} \tag{4.65}$$

(see also Engle and Ng, 1993). This representation shows that in the QGARCH model, the effect of shocks on the conditional variance is symmetric around $\varepsilon_t = -\gamma_1/(2\alpha_1)$.

Apart from the asymmetry, the QGARCH model is very similar to the standard GARCH model. For example, as shown in Sentana (1995), the unconditional variance of ε_t as implied by the QGARCH(1,1) model (4.63) is the same as that implied by the GARCH(1,1) model (4.13) – that is, $\sigma^2 = \omega/(1 - \alpha_1 - \beta_1)$. Furthermore, the condition for covariance-stationarity of the QGARCH(1,1) model and the condition for existence of the unconditional fourth moment are the same as the corresponding conditions in the GARCH(1,1) model. The kurtosis of ε_t is, however, different from (4.19) and depends on the asymmetry parameter γ_1 as follows,

$$\mathrm{K}_\varepsilon = \frac{3[1 - (\alpha_1 + \beta_1)^2 + \gamma_1^2(1 - \alpha_1 - \beta_1)/\omega]}{1 - (\alpha_1 + \beta_1)^2 - 2\alpha_1^2}. \tag{4.66}$$

In particular, (4.66) shows that the kurtosis of the QGARCH model is an increasing function of the absolute value of γ_1. Therefore, for fixed values of the parameters ω, α_1 and β_1, the kurtosis for the QGARCH model is larger than the kurtosis for the corresponding GARCH model, which results if $\gamma_1 = 0$. Finally, from (4.65) it follows that the NIC of the QGARCH model is the same as the NIC of the basic GARCH model, except that it is centred at $-\gamma_1/(2\alpha_1)$.

Markov-Switching GARCH

In the previous specifications, the parameters in the model change according to the sign and/or the size of the lagged shock ε_{t-1}. Therefore, these models can be interpreted as regime-switching models where the regime is determined by an observable variable, similar in spirit to the SETAR and STAR models for the conditional mean discussed in chapter 3.

An obvious alternative is to assume that the regime is determined by an unobservable Markov-process s_t, as in the Markov-Switching model discussed in subsection 3.1.2. A general Markov-Switching GARCH [MSW-GARCH] model is given by

$$h_t = [\omega + \alpha_1 \varepsilon_{t-1}^2 + \beta_1 h_{t-1}]I[s_t = 1]$$
$$+ [\zeta + \gamma_1 \varepsilon_{t-1}^2 + \delta_1 h_{t-1}]I[s_t = 2], \tag{4.67}$$

where s_t is a two-state Markov chain with transition probabilities defined below (3.16). The general form in (4.67) is considered in Klaassen (1999). Various restricted versions are applied in Kim (1993); Cai (1994); Hamilton and Susmel (1994) and Dueker (1997).

Alternative error distributions
So far we have assumed that the innovations z_t in (4.2) are normally distributed, which is equivalent to stating that the conditional distribution of ε_t is normal with mean zero and variance h_t. The *unconditional* distribution of a series ε_t for which the conditional variance follows a GARCH model is nonnormal in this case. In particular, as the kurtosis of ε_t is larger than the normal value of 3, the unconditional distribution has fatter tails than the normal distribution. However, in many applications of the standard GARCH(1,1) model (4.13) to high-frequency financial time series it is found that the unconditional kurtosis of ε_t given in (4.19) is much smaller than the kurtosis of the observed time series. Put differently, the kurtosis of the standardized residuals $\hat{z}_t \equiv \hat{\varepsilon}_t \hat{h}_t^{-1/2}$ is found to be larger than 3. The nonlinear GARCH models discussed above imply a higher kurtosis of ε_t (see, for example, 4.66) for the QGARCH model. Therefore, nonlinear GARCH models might be able to accommodate this deficiency of the standard GARCH model (in addition to the asymmetric response of the conditional variance to positive and negative shocks for which these nonlinear models were originally designed). He and Teräsvirta (1999a, 1999b) derive expressions for the unconditional moments of ε_t (and the autocorrelations of ε_t^2) for various nonlinear GARCH models. In principle, these expressions can be used to select a nonlinear GARCH model which best suits the moment (and correlation) properties of an observed time series, although this has not been thoroughly investigated yet.

An alternative approach which has been followed is to consider alternative distributions for z_t. The unconditional kurtosis of ε_t is an increasing function of the kurtosis of z_t (see Teräsvirta, 1996) and, hence, K_ε can be increased by assuming a leptokurtic distribution for z_t. Following Bollerslev (1987), a popular choice has become the standardized Student-t distribution with η degrees of freedom, that is,

$$f(z_t) = \frac{\Gamma((\eta + 1)/2)}{\sqrt{\pi(\eta - 2)}\Gamma(\eta/2)} \left(1 + \frac{z_t^2}{\eta - 2}\right)^{-(\eta+1)/2}, \tag{4.68}$$

where $\Gamma(\cdot)$ is the Gamma function. The Student-t distribution is symmetric around zero (and thus $E[z_t] = 0$), while it converges to the normal distribution as the number of degrees of freedom η becomes larger. A further characteristic of the Student-t distribution is that only moments up to order η exist. Hence, for $\eta > 4$, the fourth moment of z_t exists and is equal to $3(\eta - 2)/(\eta - 4)$. As this is larger than the normal value of 3, the unconditional kurtosis of ε_t will also be larger than in case z_t followed a normal distribution. The number of degrees of freedom of the Student-t distribution need not be specified in advance. Rather, η can be treated as a parameter and can be estimated along with the other parameters in the model.

4.2   Testing for GARCH

It seems self-evident that a formal test for the presence of conditional heteroscedasticity of ε_t should be part of a specification procedure for GARCH models. In particular, even though it appears obvious from summary statistics and graphs such as those presented in chapter 1 that the conditional volatility of high-frequency financial time series changes over time, one might want to perform such a test prior to actually estimating a GARCH model. In this section we review several tests for linear and nonlinear GARCH models. We also discuss whether these tests are sensitive to various sorts of model misspecification, and elaborate upon the effects of outliers on the test-statistics in some more detail.

4.2.1   Testing for linear GARCH

Engle (1982) developed a test for conditional heteroscedasticity in the context of ARCH models based on the Lagrange Multiplier (LM) principle. The conditional variance h_t in the ARCH(q) model in (4.10) is constant if the parameters corresponding to the lagged squared shocks ε_{t-i}^2, $i = 1, \ldots, q$, are equal to zero. Therefore, the null hypothesis of conditional homoscedasticity can be formulated as $H_0 : \alpha_1 = \ldots = \alpha_q$. The corresponding LM test can be computed as nR^2, where n is the sample size and the R^2 is obtained from a regression of the squared residuals on a constant and q of its lags,

$$\hat{\varepsilon}_t^2 = \omega + \alpha_1 \hat{\varepsilon}_{t-1}^2 + \cdots + \alpha_q \hat{\varepsilon}_{t-q}^2 + u_t, \tag{4.69}$$

where the residuals $\hat{\varepsilon}_t$ are obtained by estimating the model for the conditional mean of the observed time series y_t under the null hypothesis. The LM test-statistic has an asymptotic $\chi^2(q)$ distribution. The test for ARCH can alternatively be interpreted as a test for serial correlation in the squared residuals. In fact, the ARCH test is asymptotically equivalent to the test of McLeod and Li (1983) given in (2.45) (see Granger and Teräsvirta, 1993, pp. 93–4). Lee (1991) shows that the LM test against this GARCH(p, q) alternative is the same as the LM test against the alternative of ARCH(q) errors.

Example 4.1: Testing for ARCH in stock and exchange rate returns We apply the LM test for ARCH(q) to the weekly returns on stock indexes and exchange rates. We calculate the test-statistics for two sample periods of 5 years, from January 1986–December 1990 and January 1991–December 1995. For simplicity, we assume that the conditional mean of the time series can be adequately described by an AR(k) model, where the autoregressive-order k is determined by the AIC. The second–fourth columns of tables 4.1 and 4.2 contain p-values for the LM test for ARCH(q) with $q = 1, 5$ and 10 for the stock and exchange rate returns, respectively.

The results in tables 4.1 and 4.2 show that there is substantial evidence for the presence of ARCH, especially if we allow $q > 1$, which should capture GARCH-type properties. Notice that for the stock returns the p-values for the

Table 4.1   *Testing for ARCH in weekly stock index returns*

Stock market	q	Standard test			Robust test			No. obs. with $w_r(r_t) < 0.05$
		1	5	10	1	5	10	
Sample 1986–90								
Amsterdam		0.000	0.000	0.000	0.125	0.506	0.752	6
Frankfurt		0.020	0.024	0.125	0.359	0.125	0.034	8
Hong Kong		0.006	0.104	0.422	0.004	0.006	0.029	13
London		0.000	0.000	0.000	0.487	0.490	0.563	4
New York		0.000	0.000	0.000	0.832	0.825	0.415	6
Paris		0.277	0.125	0.038	0.070	0.811	0.340	6
Singapore		0.001	0.060	0.330	0.159	0.012	0.036	17
Tokyo		0.000	0.000	0.000	0.003	0.036	0.024	22
Sample 1991–95								
Amsterdam		0.565	0.016	0.199	1.000	0.023	0.311	2
Frankfurt		0.881	0.448	0.606	0.870	0.747	0.854	2
Hong Kong		0.560	0.010	0.004	0.503	0.054	0.176	7
London		0.642	0.922	0.971	0.963	0.093	0.224	2
New York		0.041	0.334	0.052	0.915	0.835	0.284	9
Paris		0.593	0.426	0.456	0.593	0.426	0.456	0
Singapore		0.271	0.026	0.044	0.128	0.015	0.122	2
Tokyo		0.162	0.000	0.000	0.295	0.310	0.083	5

Notes: p-values of the standard and outlier-robust variants of the LM test for ARCH(q) for weekly stock index returns.

The tests are applied to residuals from an AR(k) model, with k determined by the AIC. The last column reports the number of observations (out of 260) which receive a weight less than 0.05 in the robust estimation procedure for the AR(k) model.

Table 4.2   *Testing for ARCH in weekly exchange rate returns*

Currency	q	Standard test			Robust test			No. obs. with $w_r(r_t) < 0.05$
		1	5	10	1	5	10	
Sample 1986–90								
Australian dollar		0.384	0.558	0.664	0.984	0.972	0.438	9
British pound		0.902	0.393	0.516	0.711	0.862	0.941	2
Canadian dollar		0.714	0.000	0.000	0.165	0.606	0.803	5
Dutch guilder		0.790	0.323	0.645	0.326	0.398	0.693	1
French franc		0.494	0.191	0.458	0.213	0.198	0.398	1
German Dmark		0.820	0.325	0.617	0.394	0.373	0.617	1
Japanese yen		0.105	0.257	0.584	0.610	0.948	0.941	3
Swiss franc		0.588	0.190	0.581	0.755	0.342	0.818	0
Sample 1991–95								
Australian dollar		0.184	0.414	0.131	0.198	0.462	0.171	0
British pound		0.000	0.000	0.000	0.425	0.207	0.468	8
Canadian dollar		0.406	0.297	0.401	0.756	0.068	0.283	0
Dutch guilder		0.937	0.018	0.097	0.908	0.571	0.723	6
French franc		0.925	0.001	0.019	0.680	0.841	0.531	5
German Dmark		0.951	0.013	0.084	0.973	0.713	0.644	4
Japanese yen		0.658	0.131	0.061	0.833	0.541	0.976	11
Swiss franc		0.556	0.058	0.184	0.700	0.561	0.517	5

Notes: p-values of the standard and outlier-robust variants of the LM test for ARCH(q) for weekly exchange rate returns.
The tests are applied to residuals from an AR(k) model, with k determined by the AIC. The last column reports the number of observations (out of 260) which receive a weight less than 0.05 in the robust estimation procedure for the AR(k) model.

tests are, in general, much smaller for the first subsample 1986–90. For the exchange rate returns, the evidence for ARCH seems largely confined to the second subsample 1991–95.

4.2.2   *Testing for nonlinear GARCH*

With respect to the specification of nonlinear GARCH models discussed in the previous subsection, there are two possible routes one might follow. First, one can start with specifying and estimating a linear GARCH model and subsequently test the need for asymmetric of other nonlinear components in the model. The test-statistics that are involved in this approach are discussed in detail in section 4.4. Second, one can test the null hypothesis of conditional homoscedasticity directly against the alternative of asymmetric ARCH. In this section we present test-statistics which might be used for this purpose.

Engle and Ng (1993) discuss tests to check whether positive and negative shocks have a different impact on the conditional variance. Let S^-_{t-1} denote a dummy variable which takes the value 1 when $\hat{\varepsilon}_{t-1}$ is negative and 0 otherwise, where $\hat{\varepsilon}_t$ are the residuals from estimating a model for the conditional mean of y_t under the assumption of conditional homoscedasticity. The tests examine whether the squared residual $\hat{\varepsilon}^2_t$ can be predicted by S^-_{t-1}, $S^-_{t-1}\hat{\varepsilon}_{t-1}$, and/or $S^+_{t-1}\hat{\varepsilon}_{t-1}$, where $S^+_{t-1} \equiv 1 - S^-_{t-1}$. The test-statistics are computed as the t-ratio of the parameter ϕ_1 in the regression

$$\hat{\varepsilon}^2_t = \phi_0 + \phi_1 \hat{w}_{t-1} + \xi_t, \tag{4.70}$$

where $\hat{w}_{t-1}$ is one of the three measures of asymmetry defined above and ξ_t the residual.

Where $\hat{w}_t = S^-_{t-1}$ in (4.70), the test is called the Sign Bias (SB) test, as it simply tests whether the magnitude of the square of the current shock ε_t (and, hence, the conditional variance h_t) depends on the sign of the lagged shock ε_{t-1}. In case $\hat{w}_t = S^-_{t-1}\hat{\varepsilon}_{t-1}$ or $\hat{w}_t = S^+_{t-1}\hat{\varepsilon}_{t-1}$, the tests are called the Negative Size Bias (NSB) and Positive Size Bias (PSB) tests, respectively. These tests examine whether the effect of negative or positive shocks on the conditional variance also depends on their size. As the SB-, NSB- and PSB-statistics are t-ratios, they follow a standard normal distribution asymptotically.

The tests can also be conducted jointly, by estimating the regression

$$\hat{\varepsilon}^2_t = \phi_0 + \phi_1 S^-_{t-1} + \phi_2 S^-_{t-1}\hat{\varepsilon}_{t-1} + \phi_3 S^+_{t-1}\hat{\varepsilon}_{t-1} + \xi_t. \tag{4.71}$$

The null hypothesis $H_0 : \phi_1 = \phi_2 = \phi_3 = 0$ can be evaluated by computing n times the R^2 from this regression. The resultant test-statistic has an asymptotic χ^2 distribution with 3 degrees of freedom.

Example 4.2: Testing for Sign and Size Bias in stock and exchange rate returns   We apply the SB, NSB, PSB tests and the general test for asymmetry based on (4.71) to weekly stock and exchange rate returns over the 10-year sample period from January 1986 until December 1995. The tests are computed for the residuals from an AR(k) model, where the order k is determined by minimizing the AIC. The values of the test-statistics along with the corresponding p-values are given in table 4.3. Clearly, there is substantial evidence of asymmetric ARCH effects. Comparing the p-values of the SB test with those of the NSB and PSB tests, for the majority of these series size effects appear to be more important than sign effects.

Table 4.3 *Testing for asymmetric ARCH effects in weekly stock index and exchange rate returns*

Stock market	SB test Test	SB test p-value	NSB test Test	NSB test p-value	PSB test Test	PSB test p-value	General test Test	General test p-value
Amsterdam	1.93	0.027	−22.73	0.000	6.43	0.000	381.78	0.000
Frankfurt	1.65	0.049	−21.15	0.000	6.89	0.000	381.28	0.000
Hong Kong	1.95	0.025	−25.86	0.000	3.15	0.001	375.69	0.000
London	1.18	0.118	−21.34	0.000	7.20	0.000	373.42	0.000
New York	1.94	0.026	−24.44	0.000	4.96	0.000	377.85	0.000
Singapore	1.06	0.145	−25.81	0.000	4.95	0.000	380.05	0.000
Tokyo	1.73	0.042	−16.99	0.000	17.75	0.000	433.18	0.000
Exchange rate								
Australian dollar	−2.87	0.002	−4.12	0.000	49.69	0.000	431.72	0.000
British pound	−2.31	0.010	−4.39	0.000	51.49	0.000	425.98	0.000
Canadian dollar	−2.22	0.013	−10.70	0.000	22.42	0.000	435.07	0.000
Dutch guilder	−0.67	0.250	−9.43	0.000	28.03	0.000	423.55	0.000
French franc	−0.68	0.247	−9.71	0.000	26.42	0.000	418.71	0.000
German Dmark	−0.594	0.278	−9.38	0.000	28.17	0.000	422.17	0.000
Japanese yen	0.80	0.212	−13.90	0.000	20.91	0.000	450.40	0.000
Swiss franc	−0.10	0.462	−12.11	0.000	20.73	0.000	442.13	0.000

Notes: Sign Bias (SB), Negative Size Bias (NSB), Positive Size Bias (PSB) tests and general test for asymmetric volatility effects for weekly stock and exchange rate returns. The sample runs from January 1986 until December 1995. The tests are applied to residuals from an AR(k) model, with k determined by the AIC.

An alternative to the tests of Engle and Ng (1993) are LM tests against various forms of asymmetric ARCH. Sentana (1995) discusses a test of homoscedasticity against the alternative of quadratic ARCH (QARCH). Consider the QARCH(q) model, which can be obtained from (4.63) by setting $\beta_1 = 0$ and adding lagged shocks $\varepsilon_{t-2}, \dots, \varepsilon_{t-q}$ and their squares, that is,

$$
\begin{aligned}
h_t = \omega + \gamma_1 \varepsilon_{t-1} + \gamma_2 \varepsilon_{t-2} + \cdots + \gamma_q \varepsilon_{t-q} \\
+ \alpha_1 \varepsilon_{t-1}^2 + \alpha_2 \varepsilon_{t-2}^2 + \cdots + \alpha_q \varepsilon_{t-q}^2,
\end{aligned}
\tag{4.72}
$$

where $\alpha_1 = \cdots = \alpha_q = \gamma_1 = \cdots = \gamma_q = 0$, h_t is constant. A LM-statistic to test these parameter restrictions can be computed as n times the R^2 from a regression of the squared residuals $\hat{\varepsilon}_t^2$ on $\hat{\varepsilon}_{t-1}, \dots, \hat{\varepsilon}_{t-q}$ and $\hat{\varepsilon}_{t-1}^2, \dots, \hat{\varepsilon}_{t-q}^2$. Asymptotically, the statistic is χ^2 distributed with $2q$ degrees of freedom.

Hagerud (1997) suggests two test-statistics to test constant conditional variance against Smooth Transition ARCH (STARCH). The STARCH(q) model is given by

$$h_t = \omega + \alpha_1 \varepsilon_{t-1}^2 [1 - F(\varepsilon_{t-1})] + \gamma_1 \varepsilon_{t-1}^2 F(\varepsilon_{t-1})$$
$$+ \cdots + \alpha_q \varepsilon_{t-q}^2 [1 - F(\varepsilon_{t-q})] + \gamma_q \varepsilon_{t-q}^2 F(\varepsilon_{t-q}), \qquad (4.73)$$

where $F(\cdot)$ is either the logistic function (4.56) or the exponential function (4.58). The null hypothesis of conditional homoscedasticity can again be specified as $H_0 : \alpha_1 = \cdots = \alpha_q = \gamma_1 = \cdots = \gamma_q = 0$. The testing problem is complicated in this case as the parameter θ in the transition function $F(\cdot)$ is not identified under the null hypothesis. This identification problem is similar to the one discussed in subsection 3.3.2 in case of testing linearity of the conditional mean against STAR-type alternatives. The solution here is also the same – that is, the transition function can be approximated by a low-order Taylor approximation. In case of the Logistic STARCH (LSTARCH) model (4.73) with (4.56), this results in the auxiliary model

$$h_t = \omega + \alpha_1^* \varepsilon_{t-1}^2 + \cdots + \alpha_q^* \varepsilon_{t-q}^2 + \gamma_1^* \varepsilon_{t-1}^3 + \cdots + \gamma_q^* \varepsilon_{t-q}^3. \qquad (4.74)$$

An LM-statistic to test the equivalent null hypothesis $H_0^* : \alpha_1^* = \cdots = \alpha_q^* = \gamma_1^* = \cdots = \gamma_q^* = 0$ can be obtained as n times the R^2 from the regression of $\hat{\varepsilon}_t^2$ on $\hat{\varepsilon}_{t-1}^2, \ldots, \hat{\varepsilon}_{t-q}^2$ and $\hat{\varepsilon}_{t-1}^3, \ldots, \hat{\varepsilon}_{t-q}^3$. Asymptotically, the statistic is χ^2 distributed with $2q$ degrees of freedom. In case of the Exponential STARCH (ESTARCH) model (4.73) with (4.58), the auxiliary model is similar to (4.74) except that ε_{t-i}^4, $i = 1, \ldots, q$, are included instead of ε_{t-i}^3, $i = 1, \ldots, q$. The null hypothesis of constant conditional variance can be tested by n times the R^2 of the auxiliary regression of $\hat{\varepsilon}_t^2$ on $\hat{\varepsilon}_{t-1}^2, \ldots, \hat{\varepsilon}_{t-q}^2$ and $\hat{\varepsilon}_{t-1}^4, \ldots, \hat{\varepsilon}_{t-q}^4$. This statistic also has an asymptotic χ^2 distribution with $2q$ degrees of freedom.

Example 4.3: Testing for nonlinear ARCH in stock and exchange rate returns   We apply the LM tests for QARCH(q), LSTARCH(q) and ESTARCH(q) to the weekly returns on stock indices and exchange rates, using the same strategy as in example 4.1. The left-hand side panels of tables 4.4 and 4.5 contain p-values for the above LM tests with $q = 5$ for the stock and exchange rate returns, respectively. The results in these tables suggest that there is ample evidence of nonlinear ARCH.

Table 4.4   *Testing for nonlinear ARCH in weekly stock index returns*

Stock market	Standard tests			Robust tests		
	LM_Q	LM_L	LM_E	LM_Q	LM_L	LM_E
Sample 1986–90						
Amsterdam	0.000	0.000	0.000	0.509	0.276	0.181
Frankfurt	0.033	0.042	0.000	0.183	0.020	0.291
Hong Kong	0.000	0.000	0.000	0.068	0.063	0.039
London	0.001	0.000	0.000	0.603	0.742	0.908
New York	0.000	0.000	0.000	0.427	0.580	0.778
Paris	0.101	0.136	0.187	0.957	0.858	0.936
Singapore	0.015	0.022	0.000	0.081	0.067	0.026
Tokyo	0.000	0.000	0.002	0.032	0.068	0.107
Sample 1991–5						
Amsterdam	0.064	0.077	0.042	0.088	0.112	0.108
Frankfurt	0.112	0.075	0.492	0.181	0.067	0.446
Hong Kong	0.049	0.005	0.002	0.154	0.144	0.008
London	0.097	0.111	0.720	0.022	0.020	0.127
New York	0.710	0.802	0.336	0.903	0.891	0.960
Paris	0.409	0.312	0.323	0.409	0.312	0.323
Singapore	0.005	0.004	0.008	0.046	0.013	0.101
Tokyo	0.000	0.000	0.000	0.214	0.150	0.123

Notes: p-values of the standard and outlier-robust variants of the LM test for QARCH(q) [LM_Q], LSTARCH(q) [LM_L] and ESTARCH(q) [LM_E] for $q = 5$ applied to weekly stock index returns.
The tests are applied to residuals from an AR(k) model, with k determined by the AIC.

4.2.3   *Testing for ARCH in the presence of misspecification*

The small sample properties of the LM test for linear (G)ARCH have been investigated quite extensively. In particular, it has been found that rejection of the null hypothesis of homoscedasticity might be due to other sorts of model misspecification, such as neglected serial correlation, nonlinearity and omitted variables in the model for the conditional mean. For example, Engle, Hendry and Trumble (1985), Bera, Higgins and Lee (1992) and Sullivan and Giles (1995) show that in the presence of neglected serial correlation, the LM test tends to overreject the null hypothesis. Bera and Higgins (1997) discuss the similarity between ARCH and bilinear processes such as (2.37) and suggest that the two may easily be mistaken. Giles, Giles and Wong (1993) provide simulation evidence on the effects of omitted variables, which demonstrates that this may

Table 4.5   *Testing for nonlinear ARCH in weekly exchange rate returns*

Currency	Standard tests			Robust tests		
	LM_Q	LM_L	LM_E	LM_Q	LM_L	LM_E
Sample 1986–90						
Australian dollar	0.154	0.581	0.514	0.944	0.947	0.997
British pound	0.458	0.202	0.315	0.567	0.752	0.698
Canadian dollar	0.006	0.000	0.001	0.769	0.569	0.303
Dutch guilder	0.563	0.198	0.524	0.545	0.270	0.533
French franc	0.280	0.088	0.374	0.234	0.069	0.504
German Dmark	0.601	0.214	0.549	0.513	0.246	0.475
Japanese yen	0.553	0.535	0.514	0.977	0.978	0.954
Swiss franc	0.454	0.540	0.390	0.715	0.543	0.394
Sample 1991–5						
Australian dollar	0.747	0.841	0.690	0.805	0.741	0.676
British pound	0.000	0.000	0.000	0.223	0.068	0.390
Canadian dollar	0.263	0.035	0.137	0.108	0.070	0.178
Dutch guilder	0.012	0.002	0.001	0.772	0.432	0.494
French franc	0.003	0.000	0.000	0.955	0.881	0.978
German Dmark	0.011	0.002	0.001	0.875	0.705	0.664
Japanese yen	0.198	0.385	0.041	0.697	0.584	0.646
Swiss franc	0.145	0.103	0.116	0.729	0.665	0.284

Notes: p-values of the standard and outlier-robust variants of the LM tests for QARCH(q) [LM_Q], LSTARCH(q) [LM_L] and ESTARCH(q) [LM_E] for $q = 5$ applied to weekly exchange rate returns.
The tests are applied to residuals from an AR(k) model, with k determined by the AIC.

also lead to significant ARCH-statistics. Lumsdaine and Ng (1999) investigate the properties of the LM test for ARCH in the presence of misspecification in the conditional mean model at a general level. They conclude that model misspecification causes the regression residuals $\hat{\varepsilon}_t$ to be serially correlated even if the true errors ε_t are not. Consequently, the squared regression residuals also exhibit spurious correlation and, hence, model misspecification necessarily leads to positive (and never negative) size distortion for the LM test. In the next subsection we elaborate upon the properties of the LM test in the presence of outliers in more detail.

Example 4.4: Properties of the ARCH tests in case of neglected nonlinearity
To illustrate the properties of the LM tests for ARCH, QARCH, LSTARCH and ESTARCH in the presence of misspecification, the following simulation experiment is performed. We generate 5,000 series of length $n = 250$ from

Table 4.6   *Testing for ARCH and QARCH in simulated SETAR series*

Intercepts					
$\phi_{0,1}$	$\phi_{0,2}$	LM_A	LM_Q	LM_L	LM_E
0	0	24.04	23.72	28.82	25.68
−0.3	0.1	67.46	68.24	78.22	65.10
−0.3	−0.1	78.46	90.18	85.92	73.06
0.3	−0.1	9.06	9.96	6.98	22.34

Notes: Rejection frequencies of the null hypothesis of conditional homoscedasticity against ARCH(1) $[LM_A]$, QARCH(1) $[LM_Q]$, LSTARCH(1) $[LM_L]$ and ESTARCH(1) $[LM_E]$, for series of length $n = 250$ generated from the SETAR model (3.1), with $\phi_{1,1} = -0.5$, $\phi_{1,2} = 0.5$, $c = 0$ and $\varepsilon_t \sim \text{NID}(0, 0.25^2)$, based on 5,000 replications.

the SETAR model (3.1), with $\phi_{1,1} = -0.5$, $\phi_{1,2} = 0.5$, $c = 0$ and $\varepsilon_t \sim$ NID$(0, 0.25^2)$. For the intercepts $\phi_{0,1}$ and $\phi_{0,2}$ we take the values that were used to generate the example series discussed in subsection 3.1.1. For each series, we erroneously specify and estimate a linear AR(1) model for the conditional mean, and test the residuals for conditional heteroscedasticity by means of the various LM tests against ARCH with $q = 1$. Table 4.6 contains the rejection frequencies of the null hypothesis using the 5 per cent asymptotic critical value. These frequencies vary substantially, depending on the values of $\phi_{0,1}$ and $\phi_{0,2}$, but in all cases they are above the nominal significance level.

4.2.4   *Testing for ARCH in the presence of outliers*

The adverse effects of outliers on estimates of models for the conditional mean and specification tests for such models have been discussed in chapters 2 and 3, respectively. In the light of these results, it should come as no surprise that outliers, additive outliers in particular, affect the tests for ARCH as well. van Dijk, Franses and Lucas (1999b) show that the behaviour of the LM test for ARCH based on the regression (4.69) in the presence of AOs is very similar to the behaviour of the test for STAR nonlinearity under such circumstances, as discussed in subsection 3.3.4. If the AOs are neglected, the LM test rejects the null hypothesis of conditional homoscedasticity too often when it is in fact true, while the test has difficulty detecting genuine GARCH effects, in the sense that the power of the test is reduced considerably.

An alternative test-statistic which is robust to the presence of AOs can be obtained by employing the robust estimation techniques discussed in section 2.5. For example, where an AR(1) model is entertained for the conditional mean of the series y_t, one can use the standardized residuals r_t defined just below (2.115) and the weights $w_r(r_t)$ to construct the weighted residuals $w_r(r_t)r_t \equiv \psi(r_t)$. A robust equivalent to the LM test for ARCH(q) is obtained as n times the R^2 of a regression of $\psi(r_t)^2$ on a constant and $\psi(r_{t-1})^2, \ldots, \psi(r_{t-q})^2$. Under conventional assumptions, the outlier-robust LM test has a $\chi^2(q)$ distribution asymptotically. A similar procedure can be followed to obtain outlier-robust tests against the alternative of nonlinear ARCH. For example, a robust test against LSTARCH(q) can be computed as n times the R^2 of the auxiliary regression of $\psi(r_t)^2$ on $\psi(r_{t-1})^2, \ldots, \psi(r_{t-q})^2$ and $\psi(r_{t-1})^3, \ldots, \psi(r_{t-q})^3$.

The analysis of van Dijk, Franses and Lucas (1999b) concerns AOs that occur in isolation. Additionally, Franses, van Dijk and Lucas (1998) demonstrate that the effects on the standard LM test can be even more dramatic if outliers appear as consecutive observations. Reassuringly, the outlier-robust test is affected to a much lesser extent by such patches of outliers. Of course, patches of outliers are difficult to distinguish from genuine GARCH effects, as they look very similar upon casual inspection of a graph of a time series. However, combining the outcomes of the standard and robust tests for ARCH can sometimes provide a way to tell the two apart, as illustrated in the example below.

Example 4.5: Properties of the ARCH tests in the presence of neglected outliers   To examine the effects of outliers on the LM tests for ARCH, we conduct the following simulation experiment. We generate artificial time series from an AR(1) model,

$$y_t = \phi_1 y_{t-1} + \varepsilon_t, \quad t = 1, \ldots, n, \tag{4.75}$$

with $\phi_1 = 0.5$. The shocks ε_t are either drawn from a standard normal distribution or defined as $\varepsilon_t = z_t \sqrt{h_t}$, with h_t generated according to a GARCH(1,1) model as in (4.13) and $z_t \sim \text{NID}(0, 1)$. In the GARCH(1,1) model for h_t, we set $\alpha_1 = 0.25$, $\beta_1 = 0.65$ and $\omega = 1 - \alpha_1 - \beta_1$, such that ε_t has unconditional variance equal to 1. The sample size n is set equal to 100, 250 or 500 observations. Next, we add a single outlier of size $\zeta = 0$, 3, 5 or 7 to the observation at the middle of the sample, $y_{n/2}$. For the resultant series, we estimate an AR(1) model and obtain the residuals $\hat{\varepsilon}_t$. Given the AR(1) model for the conditional mean, the AO at $t = n/2$ potentially yields two large consecutive residuals. We compute the standard and outlier-robust test-statistics against qth order ARCH and nonlinear ARCH for $q = 1$ to see whether the tests are affected by these large residuals. Table 4.7 shows the rejection frequencies of the null hypothesis at a nominal significance level of 5 per cent, based on 5,000 replications.

Table 4.7   *Rejection frequencies of standard and robust tests for (nonlinear) ARCH in the presence of outliers*

		Standard tests				Robust tests			
		LM_A	LM_Q	LM_L	LM_E	LM_A	LM_Q	LM_L	LM_E
$\varepsilon_t \sim NID(0, 1)$									
100	0	3.62	3.78	3.62	3.94	4.02	4.14	3.64	4.30
	3	7.84	8.38	10.82	9.82	4.86	4.96	5.42	5.40
	5	20.22	18.90	27.10	22.92	3.96	4.02	4.22	5.02
	7	17.62	16.06	15.98	16.82	3.54	3.96	3.98	4.54
250	0	4.36	4.60	4.86	4.64	4.48	4.68	4.64	4.54
	3	9.46	9.42	13.02	13.70	5.10	5.40	5.30	5.30
	5	35.04	32.06	40.08	43.98	4.86	4.78	4.68	4.88
	7	51.98	45.76	50.48	52.10	4.54	4.86	4.78	4.74
500	0	3.88	4.30	4.38	4.26	4.46	4.32	4.08	3.76
	3	7.42	7.38	10.56	11.94	4.62	4.58	4.44	4.20
	5	37.46	33.62	45.46	57.52	4.54	4.18	3.74	3.92
	7	68.46	62.92	70.04	71.60	4.42	4.28	4.08	3.94
$\varepsilon_t \sim GARCH(1, 1)$									
100	0	43.46	42.64	42.86	46.06	27.96	25.36	26.50	26.68
	3	38.56	36.72	37.20	40.48	27.24	24.76	26.08	26.48
	5	31.66	28.46	29.10	31.18	28.92	26.40	27.24	27.94
	7	19.28	18.02	18.02	19.00	29.64	27.22	28.10	29.06
250	0	83.74	81.24	81.84	85.86	61.96	55.92	57.18	59.14
	3	81.80	78.66	80.22	83.44	61.78	55.46	56.46	58.48
	5	78.82	74.24	74.90	77.06	62.50	56.04	57.54	60.42
	7	70.98	64.74	64.98	66.28	63.28	56.84	58.16	60.88
500	0	98.90	98.18	98.26	99.06	89.20	84.66	84.78	87.20
	3	98.24	97.66	97.86	98.70	88.62	83.80	84.22	86.98
	5	97.20	96.06	96.96	97.46	89.28	85.00	85.44	87.38
	7	95.64	93.90	94.80	95.22	89.50	85.30	85.84	87.82

Notes: Rejection frequencies of the standard and outlier-robust LM statistics for ARCH(1) [LM_A], QARCH(1) [LM_Q], LSTARCH(1) [LM_L] and ESTARCH(1) [LM_E], using the 5 per cent asymptotic critical value.

Time series are generated according to the AR(1) model (4.75) and an AO of magnitude ζ is added to the observation in the middle of the sample.

The empirical power in the lower panel is not adjusted for empirical size.

The results in the upper panel of table 4.7 show that the rejection frequencies under the null hypothesis for the standard tests are much larger than the nominal significance level if the magnitude of the outlier is substantial. The robust tests do not suffer from size distortion at all. The lower panel shows that the power of the robust test where no outliers occur is smaller than the power of the standard test. This illustrates that protection against aberrant observations comes at a cost in terms of a decrease in power where no outliers occur. The rejection frequencies of the non-robust test decrease in the presence of outliers, especially for sample sizes $n = 100$ and 250.

The different effects of isolated outliers and patches of outliers on the LM test for linear ARCH are illustrated by means of a similar simulation experiment. Artificial time series of length $n = 500$ are obtained from (4.75) with $\phi_1 = 0$ and the properties of the shocks ε_t are as specified above. Next, we add either $m = 5$ or 10 isolated outliers, or $m = 1$ or 2 patches of $k = 2, 3$ or 5 outliers at random places in the series. The absolute magnitude of the outliers is set equal to $\zeta = 3, 5$ or 7, while the sign of each outlier is positive or negative with equal probability. The ARCH tests are applied to series from which the mean has been removed, either by estimating it with OLS or the outlier-robust GM estimator. For each replication we record whether we find ARCH with both the standard and robust tests, denoted as (Y,Y), ARCH with the standard test but not with the robust test [(Y,N)], or one of the other combinations [(N,Y) or (N,N)]. The results for this experiment are reported in table 4.8.

From table 4.8, several conclusions emerge. First, the size of both the standard and robust tests, which can be obtained by adding up the entries in the columns headed (Y,Y) and (Y,N) or (Y,Y) and (N,Y), respectively, is hardly affected by the occurrence of isolated outliers. Note that for the standard test this differs from the results in table 4.7. This is due to the fact that in this case the true value of the autoregressive parameter ϕ_1 is assumed to be known (and equal to zero). In contrast to the limited impact of neglecting isolated AOs in white noise series on the standard ARCH test, it is seen that in case of clustering of AOs the standard LM test is affected to a much larger extent. For almost all combinations of m, k and ζ considered here, the test-statistic is severely oversized. In fact, the empirical rejection frequency equals 100 per cent already in case of a single patch of 3 outliers or 2 patches of 2 outliers (of absolute magnitude 5 or 7) out of the 500 observations. In sharp contrast with these findings for the standard test, the empirical size of the robust test is usually close to the nominal 5 per cent significance level.

If isolated outliers occur, the power of the standard test decreases quite dramatically, while the power of the robust test remains high. In the presence of patchy outliers, the power of both the standard and robust tests is very high.

Table 4.8   *Properties of standard and robust tests for ARCH in the presence of patchy outliers*

			$\varepsilon_t \sim$ NID(0, 1)				$\varepsilon_t \sim$ GARCH(1, 1)			
m	k	ζ	(Y,Y)	(Y,N)	(N,Y)	(N,N)	(Y,Y)	(Y,N)	(N,Y)	(N,N)
1	2	3	3.8	25.8	2.6	67.8	90.1	9.7	0.2	0.0
		5	5.6	90.4	0.2	3.8	90.7	9.2	0.1	0.0
		7	5.9	93.8	0.0	0.3	90.7	9.2	0.1	0.0
	3	3	4.9	49.6	2.2	43.3	90.9	9.0	0.0	0.1
		5	6.2	93.1	0.0	0.7	92.1	7.8	0.1	0.0
		7	6.3	93.6	0.0	0.1	92.2	7.7	0.1	0.0
	5	3	5.5	75.4	1.4	17.7	89.3	10.4	0.1	0.2
		5	4.6	95.4	0.0	0.0	91.7	8.1	0.0	0.2
		7	4.9	95.1	0.0	0.0	91.8	8.0	0.0	0.2
2	2	3	3.9	49.3	1.9	44.9	89.6	10.3	0.1	0.0
		5	4.8	95.2	0.0	0.0	91.4	8.6	0.1	0.0
		7	4.8	95.2	0.0	0.0	91.6	8.4	0.0	0.0
	3	3	6.9	76.1	0.7	16.3	88.3	11.7	0.0	0.0
		5	6.1	93.9	0.0	0.0	90.3	9.7	0.0	0.0
		7	6.2	93.8	0.0	0.0	90.2	9.8	0.0	0.0
	5	3	10.3	87.3	0.0	2.4	89.9	10.1	0.0	0.0
		5	5.2	94.8	0.0	0.0	93.0	7.0	0.0	0.0
		7	5.3	94.7	0.0	0.0	93.0	7.0	0.0	0.0
5	1	3	1.4	2.8	4.7	91.1	79.8	9.9	7.9	2.4
		5	0.3	3.3	5.4	91.0	42.3	3.7	47.0	7.0
		7	0.4	4.1	5.3	90.2	17.0	0.9	72.0	10.1
10	1	3	0.9	3.4	4.0	91.7	71.5	7.8	16.9	3.8
		5	0.2	4.9	5.6	89.3	30.2	2.4	60.8	6.6
		7	0.4	6.1	5.2	88.3	13.6	1.2	76.8	8.4

Notes: Rejection frequencies of the standard and robust LM tests against ARCH(1), based on 1,000 replications.

The cells report the number of times that a certain outcome occurs when the test statistics are evaluated at the 5 per cent nominal significance level. For example, (Y,N) means that the standard LM test detects ARCH (Y) while the robust test does not (N).

The series are generated according to an AR(1) process.

m patches of k outliers of absolute magnitude ζ are added at random places in the series.

The above simulation results suggest how the outcomes of the standard and robust ARCH tests can sometimes be helpful to distinguish genuine GARCH effects from outliers. If the robust test finds no ARCH, there probably is no ARCH, and when it finds ARCH, there probably is. Furthermore, the result

(Y,N), meaning finding ARCH with the standard test but not with the robust test, can most likely be seen as evidence against ARCH in favour of a short sequence of extraordinary observations. The opposite result (N,Y), meaning finding ARCH with the robust test but not with the standard test, can be interpreted as evidence of ARCH, possibly contaminated with a few isolated outliers. In both cases it is recommended to have a closer look at the weights from the robust regression and the corresponding observations in the original time series, before carrying on with any subsequent analyses.

Example 4.1/4.3: Testing for (nonlinear) ARCH in stock and exchange rate returns   The sample periods of 5 years for which the LM tests for (nonlinear) ARCH(q) were computed for the weekly returns on stock indices and exchange rates are such that one of the samples is more or less regular, whereas the other clearly contains an unusual event, which might be regarded as an outlier. For the stock index returns, the unusual event is the crash on 19 October 1987, which is part of the first sample from January 1986–December 1990. For the exchange rates, the unusual event is the speculative attack on a number of European currencies in September 1992, which is contained in the second sample running from January 1991 until December 1995. Columns 5–7 of tables 4.1 and 4.2 contain p-values for the outlier-robust variants of the LM test for ARCH(q) with $q = 1, 5$ and 10 for the stock and exchange rate returns, respectively. The same columns of tables 4.4 and 4.5 contain results for the robust test for QARCH(q). The overwhelming evidence for, possibly nonlinear, ARCH found by the standard tests becomes somewhat weaker when we consider the robust tests. In the rightmost columns of tables 4.1 and 4.2, we present the fraction of estimated weights in the robust estimation method that is smaller than 0.05. Apparently, only a few observations may cause the nonrobust tests to reject the null hypothesis of conditional homoscedasticity.

The differences that may occur across robust and nonrobust tests should be interpreted with great care. In particular, the evidence for time variation in the conditional volatility of high-frequency financial time series is so overwhelming that it may seem odd to attribute this entirely to aberrant observations. It is therefore not recommended to discard the GARCH model altogether in case the robust test fails to reject the null hypothesis. It may be better to conclude that AOs are possibly relevant and should be taken into account when estimating the parameters in a GARCH model. Some methods which are potentially useful for this purpose are discussed in subsection 4.3.3.

4.3   Estimation

In this section we discuss estimation of the parameters in GARCH models. General principles are discussed first, followed by some remarks on simplifications which are available in case of linear GARCH models and on estimation in the presence of outliers.

4.3.1   General principles

Consider the general nonlinear autoregressive model of order p,

$$y_t = G(x_t; \xi) + \varepsilon_t, \tag{4.76}$$

where $x_t = (1, y_{t-1}, \ldots, y_{t-p})'$ and the skeleton $G(x_t; \xi)$ is a general nonlinear function of the parameters ξ that is at least twice continuously differentiable. The conditional variance h_t of ε_t is assumed to follow a possibly nonlinear GARCH model with parameters ψ. For example, where a QGARCH(1,1) model (4.63) is specified for h_t, $\psi = (\omega, \alpha_1, \gamma_1, \beta_1)'$. The parameters in the models for the conditional mean and conditional variance are gathered in the vector $\theta \equiv (\xi', \psi')'$. The true parameter values are denoted $\theta_0 = (\xi'_0, \psi'_0)'$. The parameters in θ can conveniently be estimated by maximum likelihood (ML). The conditional log likelihood for the tth observation is equal to

$$l_t(\theta) = \ln f(\varepsilon_t/\sqrt{h_t}) - \ln \sqrt{h_t}, \tag{4.77}$$

where $f(\cdot)$ denotes the density of the i.i.d. shocks z_t. For example, if z_t is assumed to be normally distributed,

$$l_t(\theta) = -\frac{1}{2}\ln 2\pi - \frac{1}{2}\ln h_t - \frac{\varepsilon_t^2}{2h_t}. \tag{4.78}$$

The maximum likelihood estimate (MLE) for θ, which we denote as $\hat{\theta}_{\text{ML}}$, is found by maximizing the log likelihood function for the full sample, which is simply the sum of the conditional log likelihoods as given in (4.77). The MLE solves the first-order condition

$$\sum_{t=1}^{n} \frac{\partial l_t(\theta)}{\partial \theta} = 0. \tag{4.79}$$

The vector of derivatives of the log likelihood with respect to the parameters is usually referred to as the score $s_t(\theta) \equiv \partial l_t(\theta)/\partial\theta$. For the model (4.76) with $\varepsilon_t = z_t\sqrt{h_t}$, the score can be decomposed as $s_t(\theta) = (\partial l_t(\theta)/\partial\xi', \partial l_t(\theta)/\partial\psi')$, where

$$\frac{\partial l_t(\theta)}{\partial\xi} = \frac{\varepsilon_t}{h_t}\frac{\partial G(x_t; \xi)}{\partial\xi} + \frac{1}{2h_t}\left(\frac{\varepsilon_t^2}{h_t} - 1\right)\frac{\partial h_t}{\partial\xi}, \tag{4.80}$$

$$\frac{\partial l_t(\theta)}{\partial\psi} = \frac{1}{2h_t}\left(\frac{\varepsilon_t^2}{h_t} - 1\right)\frac{\partial h_t}{\partial\psi}. \tag{4.81}$$

The second term on the right-hand-side of (4.80) arises because the conditional variance h_t in general depends on ε_{t-1}, and thus on the parameters in the conditional mean for y_t, as $\varepsilon_{t-1} = y_{t-1} - G(x_{t-1}; \xi)$.

As the first-order conditions in (4.79) are nonlinear in the parameters, an iterative optimization procedure has to be used to obtain the MLE $\hat{\theta}_{\mathrm{ML}}$. If the conditional distribution $f(\cdot)$ is correctly specified, the resulting estimates are consistent and asymptotically normal. The asymptotic covariance matrix of $\sqrt{n}(\hat{\theta}_{\mathrm{ML}} - \theta_0)$ is then equal to A_0^{-1}, the inverse of the information matrix evaluated at the true parameter vector θ_0,

$$A_0 = -\frac{1}{n} \sum_{t=1}^{n} \mathrm{E}\left(\frac{\partial^2 l_t(\theta_0)}{\partial \theta \partial \theta'}\right) = \frac{1}{n} \sum_{t=1}^{n} \mathrm{E}(H_t(\theta_0)). \tag{4.82}$$

The negative of the matrix of second-order partial derivatives of the log likelihood with respect to the parameters, $H_t(\theta) \equiv -\partial^2 l_t(\theta)/\partial \theta \partial \theta'$, is called the Hessian. The matrix A_0 can be consistently estimated by its sample analogue

$$A_n(\hat{\theta}_{\mathrm{ML}}) = -\frac{1}{n} \sum_{t=1}^{n} \left(\frac{\partial^2 l_t(\hat{\theta}_{\mathrm{ML}})}{\partial \theta \partial \theta'}\right). \tag{4.83}$$

As argued in section 4.1.2, conditional normality of ε_t is often not a very realistic assumption for high-frequency financial time series, as the resulting model fails to capture the kurtosis in the data. Instead, one sometimes assumes that z_t is drawn from a (standardized) Student-t distribution given in (4.68) or any other distribution. The parameters in the GARCH models can then be estimated by maximizing the log likelihood corresponding with this particular distribution. As one can never be sure that the specified distribution of z_t is the correct one, an alternative approach is to ignore the problem and base the likelihood on the normal distribution as in (4.78). This method usually is referred to as quasi-maximum likelihood estimation (QMLE). In general, the resulting estimates still are consistent and asymptotically normal, provided that the models for the conditional mean and conditional variance are correctly specified. Weiss (1984, 1986) has demonstrated this for ARCH(q) models as in (4.10), while Bollerslev and Wooldridge (1992), Lee and Hansen (1994) and Lumsdaine (1996) have obtained the same result where h_t follows a GARCH(1,1) model as in (4.13), under varying assumptions on the properties of z_t.

Interestingly, consistency and asymptotic normality of the QMLE estimates do not require that the parameters in the GARCH(1,1) model satisfy the covariance-stationarity condition $\alpha_1 + \beta_1 < 1$, but they continue to hold for the IGARCH(1,1) model. This is another difference with unit root models for the conditional mean. Recall from chapter 2 that the properties of the estimates of, for example, autoregressive parameters change dramatically where the model contains a unit root.

As the true distribution of z_t is not assumed to be the same as the normal distribution which is used to construct the likelihood function, the standard errors of the parameters have to be adjusted accordingly. In particular, the asymptotic covariance matrix of $\sqrt{n}(\hat{\theta} - \theta_0)$ is equal to $A_0^{-1} B_0 A_0^{-1}$, where A_0 is the information matrix (4.82) and B_0 is the expected value of the outer product of the gradient matrix,

$$B_0 = \frac{1}{n} \sum_{t=1}^{n} E\left(\frac{\partial l_t(\theta_0)}{\partial \theta} \frac{\partial l_t(\theta_0)}{\partial \theta'}\right) = \frac{1}{n} \sum_{t=1}^{n} E(s_t(\theta_0) s_t(\theta_0)'). \tag{4.84}$$

The asymptotic covariance matrix can be estimated consistently by using the sample analogues for both A_0, as given in (4.83), and B_0, given by

$$B_n(\hat{\theta}_{ML}) = \frac{1}{n} \sum_{t=1}^{n} \left(\frac{\partial l_t(\hat{\theta}_{ML})}{\partial \theta} \frac{\partial l_t(\hat{\theta}_{ML})}{\partial \theta'}\right) = \frac{1}{n} \sum_{t=1}^{n} s_t(\hat{\theta}_{ML}) s_t(\hat{\theta}_{ML})'. \tag{4.85}$$

The finite sample properties of the quasi-maximum likelihood estimates for GARCH(1,1) models are considered in Engle and González-Rivera (1991) and Bollerslev and Wooldridge (1992). It appears that as long as the distribution of z_t is symmetric, QMLE is reasonably accurate and close to the estimates obtained from exact MLE methods, while for skewed distributions this is no longer the case. Lumsdaine (1995) investigates the finite sample properties of the MLE method where the series follow an IGARCH model and she concludes that this method is quite accurate.

The iterative optimization procedures that can be used to estimate the parameters typically require the first- and second-order derivatives of the log likelihood with respect to θ – that is, the score $s_t(\theta)$ and Hessian matrix $H_t(\theta)$ defined above. For example, the iterations in the well known Newton–Raphson method take the form

$$\hat{\theta}^{(m)} = \hat{\theta}^{(m-1)} - \lambda \left(\sum_{t=1}^{n} H_t(\hat{\theta}^{(m-1)})\right)^{-1} \sum_{t=1}^{n} s_t(\hat{\theta}^{(m-1)}), \tag{4.86}$$

where $\hat{\theta}^{(m)}$ is the estimate of the parameter vector obtained in the mth iteration and the scalar λ denotes a step size. In the algorithm of Berndt et al. (1974) (BHHH), which is by far the most popular method to estimate GARCH models, the Hessian $H_t(\hat{\theta}^{(m-1)})$ in (4.86) is replaced by the outer product of the gradient matrix $B_n(\hat{\theta}^{(m-1)})$ obtained from (4.85). It is common to use numerical approximations to these quantities, as the analytical derivatives are fairly complex and contain recursions which are thought to be too cumbersome to compute. However, Fiorentini, Calzolari and Panatoni (1996) show that this is not the case and suggest that it might be advantageous to use analytic derivatives. In general, convergence of the optimization algorithm requires much less iteration, whereas the standard errors of the parameter estimates are far more accurate.

At the outset of this section, it was assumed that the conditional mean function $G(x_t; \xi)$ is at least twice continuously differentiable with respect to the parameters ξ. The STAR and Markov-Switching models discussed in chapter 3 obviously satisfy this requirement. Specification of STAR models for the conditional mean combined with GARCH models for the conditional variance is discussed in detail in Lundbergh and Teräsvirta (1998a). The parameters of such models can be estimated using the (Q)MLE method described above. To estimate the parameters of a model with Markov-Switching in either the conditional mean or variance (or both), the algorithm discussed in section 3.2.3 can be used (see Hamilton and Susmel, 1994, and Dueker, 1997). The SETAR model is not continuous and, hence, the parameters of a SETAR-GARCH models cannot be estimated by the (quasi-)maximum likelihood method outlined above. Li and Li (1996) suggest an alternative estimation procedure for such models, see also Liu, Li and Li (1997).

Example 4.6: Nonlinear GARCH models for Tokyo stock index returns
We estimate several nonlinear variants of the GARCH(1,1) model for weekly returns on the Tokyo stock index (as the relevant tests computed earlier indicate their potential usefulness), for the 10-year sample from January 1986 until December 1995. For convenience, we assume that the conditional mean of the returns is constant and need not be described by a linear or nonlinear model. Parameter estimates for GARCH, GJR-GARCH, QGARCH and VS-GARCH models are given in table 4.9. In the GJR-GARCH model, the estimate of α_1 is larger than the estimate of γ_1, which implies that negative shocks have a larger effect on conditional volatility than positive shocks of the same magnitude. The negative estimate of γ_1 in the QGARCH model implies that the news impact curve (NIC) is shifted to the right, relative to the standard GARCH(1,1) model, implying that positive shocks have smaller impact on the conditional variance than negative shocks. The VS-GARCH model also implies rather different behaviour of h_t following negative and positive shocks. In particular, if the shock in the previous period was negative, the conditional volatility process is explosive (as $\hat{\alpha}_1 + \hat{\beta}_1 > 1$).

The conditional standard deviations as implied by the GARCH(1,1) model and the three nonlinear variants discussed here are shown in figure 4.3. These plots confirm that the main difference between the linear GARCH model and the GJR-GARCH and QGARCH model is the response of conditional volatility to positive shocks. For example, in the second week of August 1992 and the first week of July 1995, the Nikkei index experienced large positive returns of 12.1 per cent and 11.3 per cent, respectively. According to the GARCH model,

Table 4.9 Estimates of nonlinear GARCH(1,1) models for weekly returns on the Tokyo stock index

	ω	α_1	β_1	ζ	γ_1	δ_1	$\bar{l}_t(\hat{\theta}_{ML})$	$SK_{\hat{z}}$	$K_{\hat{z}}$
GARCH	0.313	0.192	0.789				−2.404	−0.64	4.20
	(0.117)	(0.040)	(0.039)						
	[0.134]	[0.040]	[0.038]						
	{0.155}	{0.042}	{0.039}						
GJR-GARCH	0.328	0.231	0.815		0.067		−2.393	−0.50	4.18
	(0.105)	(0.048)	(0.035)		(0.035)				
	[0.133]	[0.052]	[0.038]		[0.035]				
	{0.172}	{0.058}	{0.044}		{0.036}				
QGARCH	0.394	0.158	0.804		−0.296		−2.394	−0.47	4.07
	(0.113)	(0.038)	(0.036)		(0.078)				
	[0.143]	[0.038]	[0.039]		[0.092]				
	{0.184}	{0.038}	{0.044}		{0.110}				
VS-GARCH	0.000	0.214	0.920	0.552	0.062	0.748	−2.390	−0.49	4.52
	(0.328)	(0.045)	(0.076)	(0.290)	(0.035)	(0.061)			
	[0.002]	[0.049]	[0.050]	[0.198]	[0.035]	[0.052]			
	{0.000}	{0.059}	{0.056}	{0.235}	{0.039}	{0.056}			

Notes: The estimation sample runs from January 1986 until December 1995.

Figures in round, straight and curly brackets are standard errors based on the outer product of the gradient matrix $B_n(\hat{\theta}_{ML})$ as given in (4.85), the Hessian matrix $A_n(\hat{\theta}_{ML})$ as given in (4.83) and the robust quasi-maximum likelihood covariance estimator $A_n^{-1}B_nA_n^{-1}$, respectively.

$\bar{l}_t(\hat{\theta}_{ML})$ denotes the mean log likelihood evaluated at the maximum likelihood estimates, $SK_{\hat{z}}$ and $K_{\hat{z}}$ denote the skewness and kurtosis of the standardized residuals $\hat{z}_t = \hat{\varepsilon}_t \hat{h}_t^{-1/2}$, respectively.

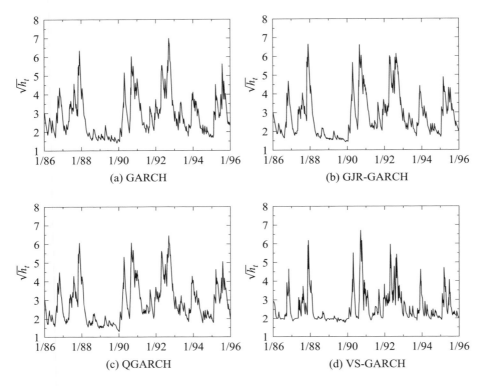

Figure 4.3 Conditional standard deviation for weekly returns on the Tokyo stock index as implied by estimated nonlinear GARCH(1,1) models

the volatility of subsequent returns increases considerably, whereas according to the QGARCH and especially the GJR-GARCH model this was not the case.

4.3.2 *Estimation of linear GARCH models*

As the parameter vector θ consists of the parameters in the models for the conditional mean and variance, the Hessian matrix $H_t(\theta)$ can be partitioned as

$$
H_t(\theta) = \begin{pmatrix} \dfrac{\partial^2 l_t(\theta)}{\partial \xi \partial \xi'} & \dfrac{\partial^2 l_t(\theta)}{\partial \xi \partial \psi'} \\ \dfrac{\partial^2 l_t(\theta)}{\partial \psi \partial \xi'} & \dfrac{\partial^2 l_t(\theta)}{\partial \psi \partial \psi'} \end{pmatrix} = \begin{pmatrix} H_t^{\xi\xi}(\theta) & H_t^{\xi\psi}(\theta) \\ H_t^{\xi\psi}(\theta)' & H_t^{\psi\psi}(\theta) \end{pmatrix}. \quad (4.87)
$$

Where the conditional variance h_t is a symmetric function of ε_t, it can be shown that the expected values of the elements in the block $H_t^{\xi\psi}(\theta)$ are equal to zero (see Engle, 1982). It then follows that the Hessian and, based on (4.82), the information matrix are block-diagonal, which implies that consistent and asymptotically efficient estimates of the parameters ξ and ψ can be obtained separately. In this case, the parameters in the model for the conditional mean can be estimated in a first step by (nonlinear) least squares. In a second step, the parameters in the GARCH model are estimated with maximum likelihood, using the residuals $\hat{\varepsilon}_t$ obtained in the first step. Of the GARCH models discussed in section 4.1, only the basic ARCH and GARCH models and the ESTGARCH model describe the conditional variance as a symmetric function of ε_t. For the other nonlinear GARCH models, the information matrix is not block-diagonal and the parameters in the model for the conditional mean and variance have to be estimated jointly.

Example 4.7: GARCH models for stock index and exchange rate returns
To illustrate the methods discussed in this section, we estimate GARCH(1,1) models for some selected weekly stock index and exchange rate returns. Again we assume that the conditional mean of the series is constant. The parameter estimates that are reported in table 4.10 illustrate the typical findings in empirical applications of the GARCH(1,1) model. For all time series, the estimate of

Table 4.10   *Estimates of GARCH(1,1) models for weekly stock index and exchange rate returns*

Stock index	ω	α_1	β_1	Exchange rate	ω	α_1	β_1
Frankfurt	1.560	0.144	0.635	British pound	0.171	0.071	0.856
	(0.490)	(0.019)	(0.085)		(0.061)	(0.025)	(0.042)
	[0.790]	[0.045]	[0.142]		[0.105]	[0.028]	[0.062]
	{1.742}	{0.118}	{0.330}		{0.191}	{0.037}	{0.105}
New York	0.082	0.099	0.888	French franc	0.367	0.097	0.748
	(0.033)	(0.019)	(0.025)		(0.195)	(0.035)	(0.108)
	[0.054]	[0.038]	[0.041]		[0.174]	[0.037]	[0.093]
	{0.097}	{0.092}	{0.086}		{0.160}	{0.043}	{0.083}
Paris	0.468	0.074	0.852	German Dmark	0.405	0.088	0.754
	(0.315)	(0.039)	(0.080)		(0.239)	(0.039)	(0.122)
	[0.256]	[0.029]	[0.057]		[0.184]	[0.036]	[0.089]
	{0.255}	{0.023}	{0.043}		{0.153}	{0.038}	{0.068}

Estimates of GARCH(1,1) models, $h_t = \omega + \alpha_1 \varepsilon_{t-1}^2 + \beta_1 h_{t-1}$, for weekly stock index and exchange rate returns.

The sample runs from January 1986 until December 1995.

Figures in round, straight and curly brackets are standard errors based on the outer product of the gradient matrix $B_n(\hat{\theta}_{\mathrm{ML}})$ as given in (4.85), the Hessian matrix $A_n(\hat{\theta}_{\mathrm{ML}})$ as given in (4.83) and the robust quasi-maximum likelihood covariance estimator $A_n^{-1} B_n A_n^{-1}$, respectively.

α_1 is fairly small, the estimate of β_1 is large and the sum $\alpha_1 + \beta_1$ is close to unity. The standard errors of the parameter estimates which are given in brackets demonstrate that large differences may exist between the different methods to compute them.

Figure 4.4 shows the conditional standard deviation as implied by the estimated GARCH(1,1) models together with the absolute values of the returns series. One feature which stands out from all graphs is that the models tend to overestimate the conditional volatility during relatively quiet periods. The absolute returns suggest that periods of large changes in the stock indexes and exchange rates are relatively short-lived, and the return to more quiet spells occurs quickly. By contrast, the estimates of the parameters in the GARCH(1,1) model imply that conditional volatility is persistent, in the sense that shocks to the conditional variance die out very slowly. Notice again, though, that the GARCH model describes *unobserved* volatility. It may well be that this latent variable displays strong persistence, but that this does not feed through the returns because of small values of z_t.

4.3.3   Robust estimation of GARCH models

In subsection 4.2.4, it was argued that neglected outliers might easily be mistaken for conditional heteroscedasticity. The evidence for time variation in the conditional volatility of high-frequency financial time series is so overwhelming, though, that it may seem odd to maintain that all of this is caused entirely by one-time exogenous events. However, even if conditional heteroscedasticity is a characteristic of the time series under study, it might still happen that outliers occur (see also Friedman and Laibson, 1989, for a theoretical motivation). Hence, it is of interest to consider statistical methods for inference in GARCH models that are applicable where such aberrant observations are present.

Several approaches to handle outliers in GARCH models have been investigated. Sakata and White (1998) consider outlier-robust estimation for GARCH models, using techniques similar to the ones discussed in subsection 3.2.4. Hotta and Tsay (1998) derive test-statistics to detect outliers in a GARCH model, distinguishing between outliers which do and which do not affect the conditional volatility. Franses and Ghijsels (1999) apply the outlier detection method of Chen and Liu (1993) to GARCH models. For illustrative purposes, the latter method is discussed in more detail below.

Consider the GARCH(1,1) model

$$\varepsilon_t = z_t \sqrt{h_t}, \tag{4.88}$$

$$h_t = \omega + \alpha_1 \varepsilon_{t-1}^2 + \beta_1 h_{t-1}, \tag{4.89}$$

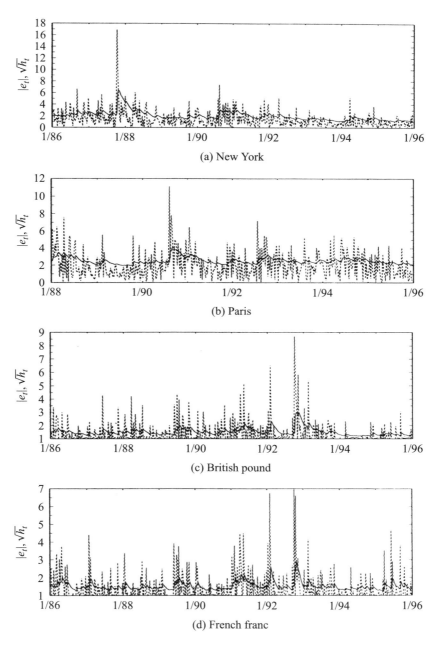

Figure 4.4   Conditional standard deviation for weekly stock index returns as implied by estimated GARCH(1,1) models

where $\omega > 0$, $\alpha_1 > 0$, $\beta_1 > 0$ and $\alpha_1 + \beta_1 < 1$, such that the model is covariance-stationary. For simplicity, we ignore the conditional mean of the observed time series y_t and simply assume that it is equal to 0 – that is, $\varepsilon_t = y_t$. As shown in subsection 4.1.1, the GARCH(1,1) model (4.89) can be rewritten as an ARMA(1,1) model for ε_t^2,

$$\varepsilon_t^2 = \omega + (\alpha_1 + \beta_1)\varepsilon_{t-1}^2 + v_t - \beta_1 v_{t-1}, \tag{4.90}$$

where $v_t = \varepsilon_t^2 - h_t$. Franses and Ghijsels (1999) exploit this analogy of the GARCH model with an ARMA model to adapt the method of Chen and Liu (1993) to detect and correct (additive) outliers in GARCH models. Specifically, suppose that instead of the true series ε_t one observes the series e_t which is defined by

$$e_t^2 = \varepsilon_t^2 + \zeta I[t = \tau], \tag{4.91}$$

where $I[t = \tau]$ is the indicator function defined as $I[t = \tau] = 1$ if $t = \tau$ and zero otherwise, and where ζ is a nonzero constant. Define the lag polynomial $\pi(L)$ as

$$\begin{aligned} \pi(L) &= (1 - \beta_1 L)^{-1}(1 - (\alpha_1 + \beta_1)L) \\ &= \left(1 + \beta_1 L + \beta_1^2 L^2 + \beta_1^3 L^3 + \cdots\right)(1 - (\alpha_1 + \beta_1)L) \\ &= 1 - \alpha_1 L - \alpha_1 \beta_1 L^2 - \alpha_1 \beta_1^2 L^3 - \cdots . \end{aligned} \tag{4.92}$$

The polynomial $\pi(L)$ allows (4.90) to be written as $v_t = -\omega/(1-\beta_1) + \pi(L)\varepsilon_t^2$. Similarly, where the GARCH(1,1) model is applied to the observed series e_t^2, it is straightforward to show that the corresponding residuals v_t are given by

$$\begin{aligned} v_t &= \frac{-\omega}{1 - \beta_1} + \pi(L)e_t^2 \\ &= \frac{-\omega}{1 - \beta_1} + \pi(L)(\varepsilon_t^2 + \zeta I[t = \tau]) \\ &= v_t + \pi(L)\zeta I[t = \tau]. \end{aligned} \tag{4.93}$$

The last line of (4.93) can be interpreted as a regression model for v_t, that is,

$$v_t = \zeta x_t + v_t, \tag{4.94}$$

with

$$\begin{aligned} x_t &= 0 \qquad \text{for } t < \tau, \\ x_\tau &= 1, \\ x_{\tau+k} &= -\pi_k \quad \text{for } k = 1, 2, \ldots. \end{aligned}$$

The magnitude ζ of the outlier at time $t = \tau$ then can be estimated as

$$\hat{\zeta}(\tau) = \left(\sum_{t=\tau}^{n} x_t^2 \right)^{-1} \left(\sum_{t=\tau}^{n} x_t v_t \right). \tag{4.95}$$

For fixed τ, the t-statistic of $\hat{\zeta}(\tau)$, denoted as $t_{\hat{\zeta}(\tau)}$, has an asymptotic standard normal distribution. Hence, one can test for an outlier at time $t = \tau$ by comparing $t_{\hat{\zeta}(\tau)}$ with the normal critical value. In practice, the timing of possible outliers is of course unknown. In that case, an intuitively plausible test-statistic is the maximum of the absolute values of the t-statistic over the entire sample, that is,

$$t_{\max}(\hat{\zeta}) \equiv \max_{1 \leq \tau \leq n} |t_{\hat{\zeta}(\tau)}|. \tag{4.96}$$

The distribution of $t_{\max}(\hat{\zeta})$ is nonstandard. Usually it is compared with a pre-specified critical value C to determine whether an outlier has occurred.

The outlier detection method for GARCH(1,1) models then consists of the following steps.

(1) Estimate a GARCH(1,1) model for the observed series e_t and obtain estimates of the conditional variance $\hat{h}_t$ and $\hat{v}_t \equiv e_t^2 - \hat{h}_t$.

(2) Obtain estimates $\hat{\zeta}(\tau)$ for all possible $\tau = 1, \ldots, n$, using (4.95) and compute the test-statistic $t_{\max}(\hat{\zeta})$ from (4.96). If the value of the test-statistic exceeds the pre-specified critical value C an outlier is detected at the observation for which the t-statistic of $\hat{\zeta}$ is maximized (in absolute value), say $\hat{\tau}$.

(3) Replace $e_{\hat{\tau}}^2$ with $e_{\hat{\tau}}^{*2} \equiv e_{\hat{\tau}}^2 - \hat{\zeta}(\hat{\tau})$ and define the outlier corrected series e_t^* as $e_t^* = e_t$ for $t \neq \hat{\tau}$ and

$$e_{\hat{\tau}}^* = \text{sgn}(e_{\hat{\tau}}) \sqrt{e_{\hat{\tau}}^{*2}}.$$

(4) Return to step (1) to estimate a GARCH(1,1) model for the series e_t^*.

The iterations terminate if the $t_{\max}(\hat{\zeta})$ statistic no longer exceeds the critical value C.

Example 4.8: Outlier detection in GARCH models for stock index returns
We apply the outlier detection method for GARCH(1,1) models to weekly stock index returns using a critical value $C = 10$. This choice for C is based on the outcome of the following simulation experiment. We generate 1,000 series of $n = 250$ and 500 observations from the GARCH(1,1) model (4.88) with (4.89) for various values of α_1 and β_1 and set $\omega = 1 - \alpha_1 - \beta_1$. For each series, we estimate a GARCH(1,1) model and compute the outlier detection statistic $t_{\max}(\hat{\zeta})$ as given in (4.96). In this way we obtain an estimate of the distribution

Table 4.11 *Percentiles of the distribution of the outlier detection statistic in GARCH(1,1) models*

α_1	β_1	$n = 250$				$n = 500$			
		0.80	0.90	0.95	0.99	0.80	0.90	0.95	0.99
0.10	0.50	7.68	8.80	9.67	12.50	8.61	9.96	10.94	14.86
0.10	0.60	7.79	8.84	9.95	12.61	8.70	9.90	11.11	14.99
0.10	0.70	7.94	8.99	10.42	13.27	8.90	10.23	11.35	15.66
0.10	0.80	8.21	9.59	10.59	15.09	9.36	10.73	12.27	16.93
0.20	0.50	8.86	10.54	11.68	16.46	10.35	12.01	15.23	20.65
0.20	0.60	9.11	10.92	12.82	17.91	10.72	12.97	15.45	23.23
0.20	0.70	9.87	11.83	13.96	18.98	11.82	14.29	16.93	25.01

Notes: Percentiles of the distribution of the $t_{max}(\hat{\zeta})$-statistic (4.96) for detection of AOs in the GARCH(1,1) model (4.88) and (4.89), based on 1,000 replications.

of the $t_{max}(\hat{\zeta})$-statistic under the null hypothesis that no outliers are present. Table 4.11 shows some percentiles of this distribution for several values of α_1 and β_1. It is seen that the value of $C = 10$ is reasonably close to the 90th percentile of this distribution for most parameter combinations. Notice that the value $C = 4$, as recommended in Franses and Ghijsels (1999), would imply a much larger nominal size.

Table 4.12 shows estimates of GARCH(1,1) models for weekly returns on the Amsterdam (AEX) and New York (S&P 500) stock indexes over the sample period January 1986–December 1990, before and after applying the outlier-correction method. For both series, two AOs are detected in the weeks ending 21 and 28 October. The outlier-statistic $t_{max}(\hat{\zeta})$ takes the values 14.59 and 22.14 for the AEX returns, with corresponding magnitudes of the AOs $\hat{\zeta} = -12.11$ and -18.74. For the returns on the S&P 500, $t_{max}(\hat{\zeta}) = 29.92$ and 11.52 with outliers of size $\hat{\zeta} = -15.73$ and -9.62, respectively. The parameter estimates in table 4.12 demonstrate that these can be heavily influenced by only very few aberrant observations. Also notice that removing these outliers causes the skewness and kurtosis of the standardized residuals $z_t = \varepsilon_t/\sqrt{h_t}$ to be closer to the normal values of 0 and 3, respectively.

4.4 Diagnostic checking

Just as it is good practice to check the adequacy of a time series model for the conditional mean by computing a number of misspecification tests, such

Table 4.12   *Estimates of GARCH(1,1) models for weekly returns on the Amsterdam and New York stock indexes, before and after outlier correction*

	μ	ω	α_1	β_1	$SK_{\hat{z}}$	$K_{\hat{z}}$
Amsterdam						
Before	0.203	2.220	0.311	0.419	−0.75	5.01
	(0.162)	(0.677)	(0.064)	(0.106)		
After	0.093	0.893	0.110	0.750	−0.56	4.03
	(0.164)	(0.414)	(0.058)	(0.109)		
New York						
Before	0.402	2.248	0.381	0.302	−1.09	5.51
	(0.136)	(0.629)	(0.054)	(0.107)		
After	0.254	0.236	0.052	0.902	−0.62	3.75
	(0.145)	(0.190)	(0.032)	(0.060)		

Notes: Estimates of GARCH(1,1) models for weekly returns on the Amsterdam and New York stock indexes, $y_t = \mu + \varepsilon_t$, with $\varepsilon_t = z_t \sqrt{h_t}$ and $h_t = \omega + \alpha_1 \varepsilon_{t-1}^2 + \beta_1 h_{t-1}$. Models are estimated for the sample January 1986–December 1990.
Standard errors based on the outer product of the gradient are given in parentheses.
The final two columns contain the skewness and kurtosis of the standardized residuals $\hat{z}_t = \hat{\varepsilon}_t \hat{h}_t^{-1/2}$, respectively.

diagnostic checking should also be part of a specification strategy for models for the conditional variance. In this section we discuss tests which might be used for this purpose.

Testing properties of standardized residuals

One of the assumptions which is made in GARCH models is that the innovations $z_t = \varepsilon_t h_t^{-1/2}$ are independent and identically distributed. Hence, if the model is correctly specified, the standardized residuals $\hat{z}_t = \hat{\varepsilon}_t \hat{h}_t^{-1/2}$ should possess the classical properties of well behaved regression errors, such as constant variance, lack of serial correlation, and so on. Standard test-statistics as discussed in section 2.2 can be used to determine whether this is the case or not.

Of particular interest is to test whether the standardized residuals still contain signs of conditional heteroscedasticity. Li and Mak (1994) and Lundbergh and Teräsvirta (1998b) develop statistics which can be used to test for remaining ARCH in the standardized residuals, which are variants of the statistics of McLeod and Li (1983) and Engle (1982), respectively. For example, the LM test for remaining ARCH(m) in $\hat{z}_t$ proposed by Lundbergh and Teräsvirta (1998b) can be computed as nR^2, where R^2 is obtained from the auxiliary regression

$$\hat{z}_t^2 = \phi_0 + \phi_1 \hat{z}_{t-1}^2 + \cdots + \phi_m \hat{z}_{t-m}^2 + \lambda' \hat{x}_t + u_t, \tag{4.97}$$

where the vector $\hat{x}_t$ consists of the partial derivatives of the conditional variance h_t with respect to the parameters in the original GARCH model, evaluated under the null hypothesis – that is, $\hat{x}_t \equiv \hat{h}_t^{-1} \partial \hat{h}_t / \partial \theta$. For example, in the case of a GARCH(1,1) model

$$h_t = \omega + \alpha_1 \varepsilon_{t-1}^2 + \beta_1 h_{t-1}, \tag{4.98}$$

it follows that

$$\frac{\partial h_t}{\partial \theta'} = \left(1, \varepsilon_{t-1}^2, h_{t-1}\right) + \beta_1 \frac{\partial h_{t-1}}{\partial \theta'}. \tag{4.99}$$

As the pre-sample conditional variance h_0 is usually computed as the sample average of the squared residuals, $h_0 = 1/n \sum_{t=1}^{n} \varepsilon_t^2$, h_0 does not depend on θ, and $\partial h_0 / \partial \theta = 0$. This allows (4.99) to be computed recursively. Alternatively, the partial derivatives can be obtained by recursive substitution as

$$\hat{x}_t' = \left(\frac{\sum_{i=1}^{t-1} \hat{\beta}^{i-1}}{\hat{h}_t}, \frac{\sum_{i=1}^{t-1} \hat{\beta}^{i-1} \hat{\varepsilon}_{t-i}^2}{\hat{h}_t}, \frac{\sum_{i=1}^{t-1} \hat{\beta}^{i-1} \hat{h}_{t-i}}{\hat{h}_t} \right). \tag{4.100}$$

The test-statistic based on (4.97), which tests the null hypothesis $H_0 : \phi_1 = \cdots = \phi_m = 0$ is asymptotically χ^2 distributed with m degrees of freedom.

Testing for higher-order GARCH

The statistic discussed above tests for correlation in the squared standardized residuals. This is closely related to the LM-statistics discussed by Bollerslev (1986), which can be used to test a GARCH(p, q) specification against either a GARCH($p + r, q$) or GARCH($p, q + s$) alternative. The test-statistics are given by n times the R^2 from the auxiliary regression (4.97), with the lagged squared standardized residuals $\hat{z}_{t-i}^2$, $i = 1, \ldots, m$ replaced by $\hat{\varepsilon}_{t-q-1}^2, \ldots, \varepsilon_{t-q-r}^2$ or $\hat{h}_{t-p-1}, \ldots, \hat{h}_{t-p-s}$, respectively.

Misspecification tests for linear GARCH models

As discussed in subsection 3.1.2, in specifying a suitable model for the conditional mean of a time series, it is common practice to start with a linear model and consider nonlinear models only if diagnostic checks indicate that the linear model is inadequate. A similar strategy can be pursued when specifying a model for the conditional variance. That is, one may start with specifying and estimating a linear GARCH model and move on to nonlinear variants only if certain misspecification tests suggest that symmetry of the conditional variance function is an untenable assumption.

One possible method to test a linear GARCH specification against nonlinear alternatives is by means of the Sign Bias, Negative Size Bias and Positive Size Bias tests of Engle and Ng (1993), discussed in subsection 4.2.2. In this case, the squared standardized residuals $\hat{z}_t^2$ should be taken as the dependent variable in the regressions that are involved, while the partial derivatives $\hat{x}_t \equiv \hat{h}_t^{-1} \partial \hat{h}_t / \partial \theta$ should be added as regressors. The analogue of (4.70) is given by

$$\hat{z}_t^2 = \phi_0 + \phi_1 \hat{w}_{t-1} + \lambda' \hat{x}_t + \xi_t, \qquad (4.101)$$

where $\hat{w}_{t-1}$ is taken equal to one of the three measures of asymmetry, S_{t-1}^-, $S_{t-1}^- \hat{\varepsilon}_{t-1}$ or $S_{t-1}^+ \hat{\varepsilon}_{t-1}$. Similarly, the analogue of (4.71) is

$$\hat{z}_t^2 = \phi_0 + \phi_1 S_{t-1}^- + \phi_2 S_{t-1}^- \hat{\varepsilon}_{t-1} + \phi_3 S_{t-1}^+ \hat{\varepsilon}_{t-1} + \lambda' \hat{x}_t + \xi_t. \qquad (4.102)$$

Hagerud (1997) examines the ability of the Sign Bias, Negative Size Bias and Positive Size Bias tests to detect various of the asymmetric GARCH effects discussed in subsection 4.1.2 by means of Monte Carlo simulation. In general, the power of the statistics is not very high. Moreover, rejection of the null hypothesis by one or several of the tests does not give much information concerning which nonlinear GARCH model might be the appropriate alternative. It turns out to be difficult to obtain such information on the basis of statistical tests, even if one uses statistics which are designed against a particular alternative model.

Hagerud (1997) develops statistics to test the linear GARCH(1,1) model against the QGARCH(1,1) model given in (4.63) and the LSTGARCH(1,1) model given in (4.55). The test against the QGARCH(1,1) alternative can be computed as nR^2 from the regression of the squared standardized residuals $\hat{z}_t^2$ on the elements of $\hat{x}_t$ given in (4.100) and $\left(\sum_{i=1}^{t-1} \hat{\beta}^{i-1} \hat{\varepsilon}_{t-i} \right) / \hat{h}_t$. This latter quantity is the partial derivative of the conditional variance h_t with respect to the parameter γ_1 in (4.63), evaluated under the null hypothesis $\gamma_1 = 0$. The test-statistic is asymptotically χ^2-distributed with 1 degree of freedom.

If one wants to test the null hypothesis of GARCH(1,1) against the LST-GARCH(1,1) alternative, the same identification problem occurs as encountered when testing homoscedasticity against the LSTARCH alternative, discussed in subsection 4.2.2. The solution is again to replace the logistic function $F(\varepsilon_{t-1})$ in (4.55) with a first-order Taylor approximation, yielding the auxiliary model

$$h_t = \omega^* + \alpha_1^* \varepsilon_{t-1}^2 + \gamma_1^* \varepsilon_{t-1}^3 + \beta_1 h_{t-1}, \qquad (4.103)$$

where ω^*, α_1^* and γ_1^* are functions of the parameters in the original model. The null hypothesis $H_0 : \gamma_1^* = 0$ can now be tested by computing nR^2 from the regression of $\hat{z}_t^2$ on $\hat{x}_t$ as given in (4.100) and $\left(\sum_{i=1}^{t-1} \hat{\beta}^{i-1} \hat{\varepsilon}_{t-i}^3\right)/\hat{h}_t$, which is the partial derivative of h_t with respect to γ_1^* evaluated under $\gamma_1^* = 0$. The resultant test statistic has an asymptotic χ^2 distribution with 1 degree of freedom under the null hypothesis. Even though these test-statistics are derived against an explicit alternative model, it turns out that they also reject the null hypothesis quite often in case of time series generated from other nonlinear GARCH models (see Hagerud, 1997). Hence, these tests cannot be used to distinguish between different forms of nonlinear GARCH, but should instead be interpreted as tests against general asymmetry.

Testing parameter constancy

In empirical applications, GARCH models are frequently estimated for time series which cover a very long period of time, sometimes up to 75 years (see, for example Ding, Granger and Engle, 1993). It is hard to imagine that the properties of a time series over such a long time period can be captured by a model with constant parameters. In fact, it has been argued that the typical estimates of the parameters in the GARCH model, implying very strong persistence of shocks, might be caused by occasional shifts in the parameters (see Lamoureux and Lastrapes, 1990; Franses, 1995, among others). Chu (1995) develops a test for parameter constancy in GARCH models against a single structural break, while Lundbergh and Teräsvirta (1998b) consider testing parameter constancy against the alternative of smoothly changing parameters. In the latter case, constancy of the parameters in a GARCH(1,1) model is tested against the alternative

$$h_t = [\omega + \alpha_1 \varepsilon_{t-1}^2 + \beta_1 h_{t-1}][1 - F(t)] + [\zeta + \gamma_1 \varepsilon_{t-1}^2 + \delta_1 h_{t-1}]F(t),$$
(4.104)

where $F(.)$ is the logistic function given in (4.56). Notice that the model in (4.104) is similar to the ANST-GARCH model given in (4.61). Testing the null hypothesis of parameter constancy, or $H_0 : \omega = \zeta$, $\alpha_1 = \gamma_1$ and $\beta_1 = \delta_1$ is complicated by the fact that the parameter θ in $F(t)$ is not identified under the null hypothesis. Replacing the function $F(t)$ by a first-order Taylor approximation yields the auxiliary model,

$$h_t = \omega^* + \alpha_1^* \varepsilon_{t-1}^2 + \beta_1^* h_{t-1} + \zeta^* t + \gamma_1^* \varepsilon_{t-1}^2 t + \delta_1^* h_{t-1} t.$$ (4.105)

The null hypothesis $H_0 : \zeta^* = \gamma_1^* = \delta_1^* = 0$ can now be tested by an LM-statistic in a straightforward manner. It also is possible to test constancy of individual parameters in a GARCH(1,1) model, assuming that the remaining ones are constant.

Example 4.9: Evaluating estimated GARCH models for stock index and exchange rate returns   Table 4.13 contains p-values of diagnostic tests for the GARCH(1,1) models that are estimated for weekly stock index and exchange rate returns. Especially for the stock index returns, the small p-values indicate that the models suffer from various kinds of misspecification. As most tests also have power against alternatives other than the one for which they are designed, the statistics are not helpful in deciding exactly in which direction one should proceed.

4.5 Forecasting

The presence of time-varying volatility has some pronounced consequences for out-of-sample forecasting. Most of these effects can be understood intuitively.

Table 4.13   *Diagnostic tests for estimated GARCH models for weekly stock index and exchange rate returns*

Test	Stock index			Exchange rate		
	FFT	NY	PRS	BP	FFR	DM
No remaining ARCH ($m = 1$)	0.004	0.145	0.572	0.332	0.055	0.078
Higher-order ARCH ($r = 1$)	0.488	0.068	0.423	0.954	0.032	0.035
Higher-order GARCH ($s = 1$)	0.490	0.068	0.418	0.954	0.032	0.035
Sign Bias	0.183	0.025	0.823	0.562	0.703	0.842
Positive Size Bias	0.067	0.085	0.407	0.158	0.845	0.802
Negative Size Bias	0.042	0.005	0.731	0.050	0.037	0.106
Sign and Size Bias	0.222	0.037	0.800	0.118	0.031	0.067
QGARCH	0.006	0.147	0.002	0.308	0.641	0.171
LSTGARCH	0.001	0.963	0.062	0.633	0.861	0.370
Parameter constancy						
Intercept	0.060	0.022	0.811	0.367	0.809	0.916
ARCH parameter	0.048	0.020	0.552	0.895	0.908	0.932
All parameters	0.065	0.088	0.799	0.338	0.928	0.979
Standardized residuals						
Skewness	−0.680	−1.156	−0.471	0.818	0.338	0.264
Kurtosis	4.881	7.932	3.888	6.312	4.245	4.209
Normality test	0.000	0.000	0.000	0.000	0.000	0.000

Notes: p-values of diagnostic tests for estimated GARCH(1,1) models, $h_t = \omega + \alpha_1 \varepsilon_{t-1}^2 + \beta_1 h_{t-1}$, for weekly stock index and exchange rate returns.
FFT = Frankfurt, NY = New York, PRS = Paris, BP = British pound, FFR = French franc, DM = German Dmark.

First, the optimal h-step-ahead predictor of y_{t+h}, $\hat{y}_{t+h|t}$, is given by the conditional mean, regardless of whether the shocks ε_t are conditionally heteroscedastic or not. The methods discussed in sections 2.3 and 3.5 for forecasting with linear and nonlinear models, respectively, under the assumption of homoscedasticity can still be used in case of heteroscedastic shocks. The analytical expressions for $y_{t+h|t}$ in case of linear models discussed in section 2.3 do not depend on the conditional distribution of y_{t+h}, which implies that the numerical value of $\hat{y}_{t+h|t}$ is the same. For nonlinear models this need not be the case. Second, the conditional variance of the associated h-step-ahead forecast error $e_{t+h|t} = y_{t+h} - \hat{y}_{t+h|t}$ becomes time-varying, which in fact was one of the main motivations for proposing the ARCH model (see Engle, 1982). This makes sense as $e_{t+h|t}$ is a linear combination of the shocks that occur between the forecast origin and the forecast horizon, $\varepsilon_{t+1}, \ldots, \varepsilon_{t+h}$. As the conditional variance of these shocks is time-varying, the conditional variance of any function of these shocks is time-varying as well. Below we discuss these results in detail for the case where the observed time series y_t follows an AR(1) model,

$$y_t = \phi_1 y_{t-1} + \varepsilon_t, \tag{4.106}$$

and the conditional variance of the shocks ε_t is described by a GARCH(1,1) model

$$h_t = \omega + \alpha_1 \varepsilon_{t-1}^2 + \beta_1 h_{t-1}. \tag{4.107}$$

The general case of ARMA(k,l)-GARCH(p,q) models is discussed in Baillie and Bollerslev (1992).

Forecasting the conditional mean in the presence of conditional heteroscedasticity

Let $\hat{y}_{t+h|t}$ denote the h-step-ahead forecast of y_t which minimizes the squared prediction error (SPE)

$$\text{SPE}(h) \equiv \text{E}[e_{t+h|t}^2] = \text{E}[(y_{t+h} - \hat{y}_{t+h|t})^2], \tag{4.108}$$

where $e_{t+h|t}$ is the h-step-ahead forecast error $e_{t+h|t} = y_{t+h} - \hat{y}_{t+h|t}$. Baillie and Bollerslev (1992) show that the forecast that minimizes (4.108) is the same irrespective of whether the shocks ε_t in (4.106) are conditionally homoscedastic or conditionally heteroscedastic. Thus, the optimal h-step-ahead forecast of y_{t+h} is its conditional expectation at time t, that is,

$$\hat{y}_{t+h|t} = \text{E}[y_{t+h}|\Omega_t]. \tag{4.109}$$

For the AR(1) model (4.106) this means that the optimal 1-step-ahead forecast is given by $\hat{y}_{t+1|t} = \phi_1 y_t$. The forecasts for $h > 1$ steps ahead can be obtained from the recursive relationship $\hat{y}_{t+h|t} = \phi_1 \hat{y}_{t+h-1|t}$, or can be computed directly as

$$\hat{y}_{t+h|t} = \phi_1^h y_t. \tag{4.110}$$

For the h-step-ahead prediction error, it follows that

$$
\begin{aligned}
e_{t+h|t} = y_{t+h} - \hat{y}_{t+h|t} &= \phi_1 y_{t+h-1} + \varepsilon_{t+h} - \phi_1^h y_t \\
&= \phi_1^2 y_{t+h-2} + \phi_1 \varepsilon_{t+h-1} + \varepsilon_{t+h} - \phi_1^h y_t \\
&= \dots \\
&= \phi_1^h y_t + \sum_{i=1}^{h} \phi_1^{h-i} \varepsilon_{t+i} - \phi_1^h y_t \\
&= \sum_{i=1}^{h} \phi_1^{h-i} \varepsilon_{t+i}.
\end{aligned}
\tag{4.111}
$$

The *conditional* SPE of $e_{t+h|t}$ is given by

$$
\begin{aligned}
\mathrm{E}[e_{t+h|t}^2 | \Omega_t] &= \mathrm{E}\left[\left(\sum_{i=1}^{h} \phi_1^{h-i} \varepsilon_{t+i} \right)^2 \Big| \Omega_t \right] \\
&= \sum_{i=1}^{h} \phi_1^{2(h-i)} \mathrm{E}[\varepsilon_{t+i}^2 | \Omega_t] \\
&= \sum_{i=1}^{h} \phi_1^{2(h-i)} \mathrm{E}[h_{t+i} | \Omega_t].
\end{aligned}
\tag{4.112}
$$

In the case of homoscedastic errors, the conditional SPE for the optimal h-step-ahead forecast is constant, as $\mathrm{E}[h_{t+i}|\Omega_t]$ is constant and equal to the unconditional variance of ε_t, σ^2. Expression (4.112) shows that in the case of heteroscedastic errors, the conditional SPE is varying over time. To see the relation between the two, rewrite (4.112) as

$$
\mathrm{E}[e_{t+h|t}^2 | \Omega_t] = \sum_{i=1}^{h} \phi_1^{2(h-i)} \sigma^2 + \sum_{i=1}^{h} \phi_1^{2(h-i)} (\mathrm{E}[h_{t+i}|\Omega_t] - \sigma^2).
\tag{4.113}
$$

The first term on the right-hand-side of (4.113) is the conventional SPE for homoscedastic errors. Notice that the second term on the right-hand-side can be both positive and negative, depending on the conditional expectation of future volatility. Hence, the conditional SPE in the case of heteroscedastic errors can be both larger and smaller than in the case of homoscedastic errors.

Recall that in the homoscedastic case, the SPE converges to the unconditional variance of the model as the forecast horizon increases, that is,

$$\lim_{h \to \infty} \mathrm{E}[e^2_{t+h|t}|\Omega_t] = \lim_{h \to \infty} \sum_{i=1}^{h} \phi_1^{2(h-i)}\sigma^2 = \frac{\sigma^2}{1-\phi^2} \equiv \sigma_y^2.$$

(4.114)

Moreover, the convergence is monotonic, in the sense that the h-step-ahead SPE is always smaller than the unconditional variance σ_y^2, while the h-step-ahead SPE is larger than the $(h-1)$-step SPE for all finite horizons h. The convergence of the SPE to the unconditional variance of the time series also holds in the present case of heteroscedastic errors. This follows from the fact that the forecasts of the conditional variance $\mathrm{E}[h_{t+i}|\Omega_t]$ converge to the unconditional variance σ^2 (as will be shown explicitly below). However, the convergence need no longer be monotonic, in the sense that the h-step conditional SPE may be smaller than the $(h-1)$-step conditional SPE. In fact, the conditional SPE may be larger than the unconditional variance of the time series for certain forecast horizons. Intuitively, in periods of large uncertainty, characterized by large values of the conditional variance h_t, it is extremely difficult to forecast the conditional mean of the series y_t accurately. In such cases, the forecast uncertainty may be larger at shorter forecast horizons compared to longer horizons.

The conditional SPE as given in (4.112) might be used to construct prediction intervals. The conditional distribution of the h-step-ahead prediction error $e_{t+h|t}$ is, however, nonnormal and, consequently, the conventional forecasting interval discussed in section 2.3, is not a reliable measure of the true forecast uncertainty. Granger, White and Kamstra (1989) discuss an alternative approach based on quantile estimators (see also Taylor, 1999).

An additional complication in using (4.112) is that conditional expectations of the future conditional variances h_{t+i} at time t are required. How to obtain such forecasts of future volatility is discussed next.

Forecasting the conditional variance

In the case of the GARCH(1,1) model, the conditional expectation of h_{t+s} – or, put differently, the optimal s-step-ahead forecast of the conditional variance – can be computed recursively from

$$\hat{h}_{t+s|t} = \omega + \alpha_1 \hat{\varepsilon}^2_{t+s-1|t} + \beta_1 \hat{h}_{t+s-1|t},$$

(4.115)

where $\hat{\varepsilon}^2_{t+i|t} = \hat{h}_{t+i|t}$ for $i > 0$ by definition, while $\hat{\varepsilon}^2_{t+i|t} = \varepsilon^2_{t+i}$ and $\hat{h}_{t+i|t} = h_{t+i}$ for $i \leq 0$. Alternatively, by recursive substitution in (4.115) we obtain

$$\hat{h}_{t+s|t} = \omega \sum_{i=0}^{s-1} (\alpha_1 + \beta_1)^i + (\alpha_1 + \beta_1)^{s-1} h_{t+1},$$

(4.116)

which allows the s-step-ahead forecast to be computed directly from h_{t+1}. Notice that h_{t+1} is contained in the information set Ω_t, as it can be computed from observations $y_t, y_{t-1}, \ldots$ (given knowledge of the parameters in the model). If the GARCH(1,1) model is covariance-stationary with $\alpha_1 + \beta_1 < 1$, (4.116) can be rewritten as

$$\hat{h}_{t+s|t} = \sigma^2 + (\alpha_1 + \beta_1)^{s-1}(h_{t+1} - \sigma^2), \tag{4.117}$$

where $\sigma^2 = \omega/(1 - \alpha_1 - \beta_1)$ is the unconditional variance of ε_t, which shows that the forecasts for the conditional variance are similar to forecasts from an AR(1) model with mean σ^2 and AR parameter $\alpha_1 + \beta_1$. The right-hand-side of (4.117) follows from the fact that $\sum_{i=1}^{s-1} r^i = (1 - r^{s-1})/(1 - r)$ for all r with $|r| < 1$. Also note that for the IGARCH model with $\alpha_1 + \beta_1 = 1$, (4.116) simplifies to

$$\hat{h}_{t+s|t} = \omega(s - 1) + h_{t+1}, \tag{4.118}$$

which shows that the forecasts for the conditional variance increase linearly as the forecast horizon s increases, provided $\omega > 0$.

To express the uncertainty in the s-step-ahead forecast of the conditional variance, one might consider the associated forecast error $v_{t+s|t} \equiv h_{t+s} - \hat{h}_{t+s|t}$. Subtracting the expression of the s-step-ahead forecast in (4.115) from the definition of the GARCH(1,1) model for h_{t+s}, $h_{t+s} = \omega + \alpha_1 \varepsilon_{t+s-1}^2 + \beta_1 h_{t+s-1}$, we obtain

$$
\begin{aligned}
v_{t+s|t} &\equiv h_{t+s} - \hat{h}_{t+s|t} \\
&= \alpha_1(\varepsilon_{t+s-1}^2 - \hat{\varepsilon}_{t+s-1|t}^2) + \beta_1(h_{t+s-1} - \hat{h}_{t+s-1|t}) \\
&= \alpha_1(\varepsilon_{t+s-1}^2 - h_{t+s-1} + h_{t+s-1} - \hat{h}_{t+s-1|t}^2) \\
&\quad + \beta_1(h_{t+s-1} - \hat{h}_{t+s-1|t}) \\
&= \alpha_1 v_{t+s-1} + (\alpha_1 + \beta_1)v_{t+s-1|t}, \tag{4.119}
\end{aligned}
$$

where we have used the fact that $\hat{\varepsilon}_{t+i|t}^2 = \hat{h}_{t+i|t}$ for $i > 0$ and the definition $v_t \equiv \varepsilon_t^2 - h_t$. By continued recursive substitution, we finally arrive at

$$
\begin{aligned}
v_{t+s|t} &= \alpha_1 v_{t+s-1} + (\alpha_1 + \beta_1)\alpha_1 v_{t+s-2} + \cdots \\
&\quad + (\alpha_1 + \beta_1)^{s-2}\alpha_1 v_{t+1} \\
&= \alpha_1 \sum_{i=1}^{s-1}(\alpha_1 + \beta_1)^{i-1} v_{t+s-i}. \tag{4.120}
\end{aligned}
$$

As the v_ts are serially uncorrelated and can be written as $v_t = h_t(z_t^2 - 1)$, it follows that the conditional SPE of the s-step-ahead forecast $\hat{h}_{t+s|t}$ is given by

$$E[v_{t+s|t}^2|\Omega_t] = (\kappa - 1)\alpha_1^2 \sum_{i=1}^{s-1}(\alpha_1 + \beta_1)^{2(i-1)}E[h_{t+s-i}^2|\Omega_t], \quad (4.121)$$

where κ is the kurtosis of z_t. Baillie and Bollerslev (1992) give expressions for the expectation of h_t^2, the conditional fourth moment of ε_t, which is required to evaluate (4.121). However, even if the value of the conditional SPE is available, it is quite problematic to use it to construct a confidence interval for the s-step-ahead forecast $\hat{h}_{t+s|t}$, because the distribution of h_{t+s} conditional upon Ω_t is highly nonnormal.

Forecasting conditional volatility for nonlinear GARCH models
    In the discussion of out-of-sample forecasting with regime-switching models for the conditional mean in section 3.5, it was argued that one should resort to numerical techniques to obtain multiple-step-ahead forecasts because analytic expressions are impossible to obtain. By contrast, for most nonlinear GARCH models discussed in this chapter, out-of-sample forecasts for the conditional variance can be computed analytically in a straightforward manner. As an example, consider the GJR-GARCH(1,1) model

$$h_t = \omega + \alpha_1\varepsilon_{t-1}^2(1 - I[\varepsilon_{t-1} > 0]) + \gamma_1\varepsilon_{t-1}^2 I[\varepsilon_{t-1} > 0] + \beta_1 h_{t-1}.$$
$$(4.122)$$

Assuming that the distribution of z_t is symmetric around 0, the 2-step-ahead forecast of h_{t+2} is given by

$$\begin{aligned}\hat{h}_{t+2|t} &= E[\omega + \alpha_1\varepsilon_{t+1}^2(1 - I[\varepsilon_{t+1} > 0])\\ &\quad + \gamma_1\varepsilon_{t+1}^2 I[\varepsilon_{t+1} > 0] + \beta_1 h_{t+1}|\Omega_t]\\ &= \omega + ((\alpha_1 + \gamma_1)/2 + \beta_1)h_{t+1},\end{aligned} \quad (4.123)$$

which follows from observing that ε_{t+1}^2 and the indicator function $I[\varepsilon_{t+1} > 0]$ are uncorrelated and $E[I[\varepsilon_{t+1} > 0]] = P(\varepsilon_{t+1} > 0) = 0.5$, and again using $E[\varepsilon_{t+1}^2|\Omega_t] = h_{t+1}$. In general, s-step-ahead forecasts can be computed either recursively as

$$\hat{h}_{t+s|t} = \omega + ((\alpha_1 + \gamma_1)/2 + \beta_1)\hat{h}_{t+s-1|t}, \quad (4.124)$$

or directly from

$$\hat{h}_{t+s|t} = \omega \sum_{i=0}^{s-1}((\alpha_1 + \gamma_1)/2 + \beta_1)^i + ((\alpha_1 + \gamma_1)/2 + \beta_1)^{s-1}h_{t+1},$$
$$(4.125)$$

compare the analogous expressions for the GARCH(1,1) model, as given in (4.115) and (4.116).

For the LSTGARCH model given in (4.55) the same formulae apply. This follows because ε_{t+i}^2 and the logistic function $F(\varepsilon_{t+i}) = [1+\exp(-\theta\varepsilon_{t+i})]^{-1}$ are uncorrelated, combined with the fact that $F(\varepsilon_{t+i})$ is anti-symmetric around the expected value of ε_{t+i} $(= 0)$ and, thus, $\mathrm{E}[F(\varepsilon_{t+i})] = F(\mathrm{E}[\varepsilon_{t+i}]) = 0.5$. In general, a function $G(x)$ is said to be anti-symmetric around a if $G(x + a) - G(a) = -(G(-x + a) - G(a))$ for all x. If furthermore x is symmetrically distributed with mean a it holds that $\mathrm{E}[G(x)] = G(\mathrm{E}[x]) = G(a)$.

Using the properties of the indicator function $I[\varepsilon_t > 0]$ and the logistic function $F(\varepsilon_t)$ noted above, it is straightforward to show that s-step-ahead forecasts for the conditional variance from the VS-GARCH model in (4.59) and the ANST-GARCH model in (4.61) can be computed either recursively from

$$\hat{h}_{t+s|t} = \omega + ((\alpha_1 + \gamma_1)/2 + (\beta_1 + \delta_1)/2)\hat{h}_{t+s-1|t}, \tag{4.126}$$

or directly from

$$\hat{h}_{t+s|t} = \omega \sum_{i=0}^{s-1} ((\alpha_1 + \gamma_1)/2 + (\beta_1 + \delta_1)/2)^i$$
$$+ ((\alpha_1 + \gamma_1)/2 + (\beta_1 + \delta_1)/2)^{s-1} h_{t+1}. \tag{4.127}$$

For the QGARCH(1,1) model given in (4.63), the asymmetry term $\gamma_1\varepsilon_{t-1}$ does not affect the forecasts for the conditional variance, as the conditional expectation of ε_{t+i} with $i > 0$ is 0 by assumption. Hence, point forecasts for the conditional variance can be obtained using the expressions given in (4.115) and (4.116) for the GARCH(1,1) model. Note, however, that $\gamma_1\varepsilon_{t-1}$ does alter the forecast error $v_{t+s|t}$, which now becomes

$$\begin{aligned}
v_{t+s|t} &\equiv h_{t+s} - \hat{h}_{t+s|t} \\
&= \gamma_1\varepsilon_{t+s-1} + \alpha_1(\varepsilon_{t+s-1}^2 - \hat{\varepsilon}_{t+s-1|t}^2) \\
&\quad + \beta_1(h_{t+s-1} - \hat{h}_{t+s-1|t}) \\
&= \gamma_1\varepsilon_{t+s-1} + \alpha_1 v_{t+s-1} + (\alpha_1 + \beta_1)v_{t+s-1|t} \\
&= \alpha_1 \sum_{i=1}^{s-1} (\alpha_1 + \beta_1)^{i-1} v_{t+s-i} + \gamma_1 \sum_{i=1}^{s-1} (\alpha_1 + \beta_1)^{i-1} \varepsilon_{t+s-i}.
\end{aligned} \tag{4.128}$$

As $\mathrm{E}[v_{t+s-i}|\Omega_t] = \mathrm{E}[\varepsilon_{t+s-i}|\Omega_t] = 0$ for all $i = 1, \ldots, s-1$, the forecasts are unbiased, in the sense that $\mathrm{E}[v_{t+s|t}|\Omega_t] = 0$. However, the conditional variance of $v_{t+s|t}$ and, hence, the uncertainty in the forecast of h_{t+s} will be larger than in the GARCH(1,1) case.

Of the nonlinear GARCH models discussed in subsection 4.1.2, the only model for which analytic expressions for multiple-step-ahead forecasts of the conditional variance cannot be obtained is the ESTGARCH model given in (4.55) with (4.58). The exponential function $F(\varepsilon_{t+1}) = 1 - \exp(-\theta\varepsilon_{t+1}^2)$ is correlated with ε_{t+1}^2, and it also is not the case that $E[F(\varepsilon_{t+1})] = F(E[\varepsilon_{t+1}])$. Therefore, it is not possible to derive a recursive or direct formula for the s-step-ahead forecast $\hat{h}_{t+s|t}$ in this case. Instead, forecasts for future conditional variances have to be obtained by means of simulation.

Finally, analytic expressions for multiple-step-ahead forecasts of the conditional variance for the Markov-Switching GARCH model given in (4.67) can be obtained by exploiting the properties of the Markov-process (see Hamilton and Lin, 1996; Dueker, 1997; Klaassen, 1999).

Evaluating forecasts of conditional volatility

As just discussed, it is quite difficult to select a suitable nonlinear GARCH model on the basis of specification tests only. The out-of-sample forecasting ability of various GARCH models is an alternative approach to judge the adequacy of different models. Obviously, if a volatility model is to be of any use to practitioners in financial markets, it should be capable of generating accurate predictions of future volatility.

Whereas forecasting the future conditional volatility from (nonlinear) GARCH models is fairly straightforward, evaluating the forecasts is a more challenging task. In the following we assume that a GARCH model has been estimated using a sample of n observations, whereas observations at $t = n + 1, \ldots n + m + s - 1$ are held back for evaluation of s-step-ahead forecasts for the conditional variance.

Most studies use statistical criteria such as the mean squared prediction error (MSPE), which for a set of m s-step-ahead forecasts is computed as

$$\text{MSPE} = \frac{1}{m} \sum_{j=0}^{m-1} (\hat{h}_{n+s+j|n+j} - h_{n+s+j})^2 \tag{4.129}$$

(see Akgiray, 1989; West and Cho, 1995; Brailsford and Faff, 1996; Franses and van Dijk, 1996, among many others), or the regression

$$h_{n+s+j} = a + b\hat{h}_{n+s+j|n+j} + e_{n+s+j}, \quad j = 0, \ldots, m-1 \tag{4.130}$$

(see Pagan and Schwert, 1990; Day and Lewis, 1992; Cumby, Figlewski and Hasbrouck, 1993; Lamoureux and Lastrapes, 1993; Jorion, 1995). In this case $\hat{h}_{n+s+j|n+j}$ is an unbiased forecast of h_{n+s+j}, $a = 0$, $b = 1$ and

$E(e_{n+s+j}) = 0$ in (4.130). The MSPE as defined in (4.129) cannot be computed as the true volatility h_{n+s+j} is unobserved, whereas for the same reason the parameters in (4.130) cannot be estimated. To make these forecast evaluation criteria operational, h_t is usually replaced by the squared shock $\varepsilon_{n+s+j}^2 = z_{n+s+j}^2 h_{n+s+j}$. As $E[z_{n+s+j}^2] = 1$, ε_{n+s+j}^2 is an unbiased estimate of h_{n+s+j}.

A common finding from forecast competitions is that all GARCH models provide seemingly poor volatility forecasts and explain only very little of the variability of asset returns, in the sense that the MSPE (or any other measure of forecast accuracy) is very large while the R^2 from the regression (4.130) is very small, typically below 0.10. In addition, the forecasts from GARCH appear to be biased, as it commonly found that $\hat{a} \neq 0$ in (4.130). Andersen and Bollerslev (1998) and Christodoulakis and Satchell (1998) demonstrated that this poor forecasting performance is caused by the fact that the unobserved true volatility h_{n+s+j} is approximated with the squared shock ε_{n+s+j}^2. As shown by Andersen and Bollerslev (1998), for a GARCH(1,1) model with a finite unconditional fourth moment the population R^2 from the regression (4.130) for $s = 1$ and h_{n+s+j} replaced by ε_{n+s+j}^2 is equal to

$$R^2 = \frac{\alpha_1^2}{1 - \beta_1^2 - 2\alpha_1\beta_1}. \tag{4.131}$$

As the condition for a finite unconditional fourth moment in the GARCH(1,1) model is given by $\kappa\alpha_1^2 + \beta_1^2 + 2\alpha_1\beta_1 < 1$, it follows that the population R^2 is bounded from above by $1/\kappa$. Where z_t is normally distributed, the R^2 cannot be larger than 1/3, while the upper bound is even smaller if, for example, z_t is assumed to be Student-t-distributed.

Christodoulakis and Satchell (1998) explain the occurrence of apparent bias in GARCH volatility forecasts by noting that

$$\ln(\varepsilon_{n+s+j}^2) = \ln(h_{n+s+j}) + \ln(z_{n+s+j}^2), \tag{4.132}$$

or

$$\ln(\varepsilon_{n+s+j}^2) - \ln(\hat{h}_{n+s+j|n+j}) = \left(\ln(h_{n+s+j}) - \ln(\hat{h}_{n+s+j|n+j})\right)$$
$$+ \ln(z_{n+s+j}^2). \tag{4.133}$$

As $\ln(x) \approx -(1-x)$ for small x, the left-hand-side of (4.133) is approximately equal to the observed bias $\varepsilon_{n+s+j}^2 - \hat{h}_{n+s+j|n+j}$. If the GARCH forecasts are unbiased, the first term on the right-hand-side of (4.133) is equal to zero. Hence, the expected observed bias is equal to $E[\ln(z_{n+s+j}^2)]$, which in the case of normally distributed z_t is equal to -1.27.

Andersen and Bollerslev (1998) suggest that a (partial) solution to the above-mentioned problems might be to estimate the unobserved volatility with data which is sampled more frequently than the time series of interest. For example, if y_t is a time series of weekly returns, the corresponding daily returns – if available – might be used to obtain a more accurate measure of the weekly volatility.

Other criteria have also been considered to evaluate the forecasts from GARCH models. Examples are the profitability of trading or investment strategies which make use of GARCH models to forecast conditional variance (see Engle *et al.*, 1993), or utility-based measures (see West, Edison and Cho, 1993).

Example 4.10: Forecasting the volatility of the Tokyo stock index   As an alternative way to evaluate the nonlinear GARCH models estimated previously for weekly returns on the Tokyo stock index we compare their out-of-sample forecasting performance. To obtain forecasts of the conditional volatility we follow the methodology used in Franses and van Dijk (1996) (see also Donaldson and Kamstra, 1997). GARCH, GJR-GARCH, QGARCH and VS-GARCH models are estimated using a moving window of 5 years of data (260 observations). We start with the sample ranging from the first week of January 1986 until the last week of December 1990. The fitted models then are used to obtain 1- to 5-steps-ahead forecasts of h_t – that is, the conditional variance during the first 5 weeks of 1991. Next, the window is moved 1 week into the future, by deleting the observation from the first week of January 1986 and adding the observation for the first week of January 1991. The various GARCH models are re-estimated on this sample, and are used to obtain forecasts for h_t during the second until the sixth week of 1991. This procedure is repeated until the final estimation sample consists of observations from the first week of 1991 until the last week of 1995. In this way, we obtain 260 1- to 5-steps-ahead forecasts of the conditional variance. To evaluate and compare the forecasts from the different models, several forecast evaluation criteria are computed, with true volatility measured by the squared realized return. Table 4.14 reports the ratio of the forecast error criteria of the nonlinear GARCH models to those of the GARCH(1,1) model. For example, the figure 0.94 in the row $h = 1$ and column MSPE for the GJR-GARCH model means that the MSPE for 1-step-ahead forecasts from this model is 6 per cent smaller than the corresponding criterion for forecasts from the linear GARCH model. It is seen that the GJR-GARCH and QGARCH model perform better on all four criteria across all forecast horizons considered. Also reported are p-values for the predictive accuracy test of Diebold and Mariano (1995) as given in (2.75), based on both absolute and squared prediction errors. These p-values suggest that, even though the difference in the forecast error criteria is substantial, the forecasts from the linear and nonlinear GARCH models need not be significantly different from each other.

Table 4.14 *Forecast evaluation of nonlinear GARCH models for weekly returns on the Tokyo stock index, as compared to the GARCH (1,1) model*

Model	h	MSPE	MedSPE	DM(S)	MAPE	MedAPE	DM(A)
GJR-GARCH	1	0.94	0.74	0.05	0.95	0.86	0.05
	2	0.93	0.77	0.15	0.93	0.88	0.06
	3	0.92	0.75	0.27	0.91	0.87	0.07
	4	0.89	0.80	0.26	0.92	0.90	0.12
	5	0.89	0.75	0.35	0.90	0.87	0.12
QGARCH	1	0.95	0.83	0.19	0.93	0.91	0.01
	2	0.94	0.87	0.32	0.91	0.93	0.01
	3	0.92	0.92	0.25	0.90	0.96	0.02
	4	0.94	0.88	0.48	0.91	0.94	0.05
	5	0.89	0.86	0.37	0.89	0.93	0.06
VS-GARCH	1	1.01	0.54	0.87	0.86	0.74	0.00
	2	1.03	0.36	0.77	0.82	0.60	0.00
	3	1.04	0.37	0.84	0.80	0.61	0.00
	4	1.02	0.32	0.96	0.79	0.56	0.00
	5	1.05	0.27	0.83	0.77	0.52	0.01

Notes: Forecast evaluation criteria for nonlinear GARCH models for weekly returns on the Tokyo stock index.

Out-of-sample forecasts are constructed for the period January 1991–December 1995, with models estimated on a rolling window of 5 years.

The columns labelled DM(S) and DM(A) contain p-values for the prediction accuracy test given in (2.75), based on squared and absolute prediction errors, respectively.

Finally, table 4.15 contains parameter estimates, with standard errors in parentheses, and R^2 measures from the regression of (demeaned) returns on the forecasts of conditional variance. Only for the linear GARCH model are the estimate of the intercept $\hat{a}$ and the slope $\hat{b}$ significantly different from 0 and 1, respectively. Hence it appears that forecasts from the GARCH model are not unbiased, whereas for the nonlinear GARCH models they generally are. The low values of the R^2 suggest that the models explain only a small fraction of the variability in the conditional variance of the returns, which confirms previous findings as discussed above.

4.6 Impulse response functions

Of particular interest in the context of GARCH models is the influence of shocks on future conditional volatility, or the persistence of shocks. A natural measure of this influence is the expectation of the conditional volatility s-periods

Table 4.15   *Forecast evaluation of nonlinear GARCH models for weekly returns on the Tokyo stock index*

Model	h	1	2	3	4	5
GARCH	$\hat{a}$	3.58	2.93	3.68	4.80	4.13
		(1.71)	(1.72)	(1.76)	(1.80)	(1.80)
	$\hat{b}$	0.56	0.61	0.53	0.42	0.47
		(0.12)	(0.12)	(0.12)	(0.12)	(0.12)
	R^2	0.07	0.09	0.07	0.04	0.05
GJR-GARCH	$\hat{a}$	2.21	1.04	1.70	2.07	1.42
		(1.77)	(1.78)	(1.84)	(1.90)	(1.93)
	$\hat{b}$	0.75	0.88	0.81	0.78	0.86
		(0.14)	(0.15)	(0.15)	(0.16)	(0.17)
	R^2	0.10	0.12	0.10	0.08	0.09
QGARCH	$\hat{a}$	1.99	0.39	0.51	3.45	0.34
		(1.93)	(1.96)	(2.05)	(2.19)	(2.18)
	$\hat{b}$	0.82	0.98	0.98	0.66	0.99
		(0.17)	(0.18)	(0.19)	(0.20)	(0.20)
	R^2	0.08	0.11	0.05	0.04	0.08
VS-GARCH	$\hat{a}$	2.56	-1.00	0.55	1.68	2.10
		(2.08)	(2.19)	(2.39)	(2.54)	(2.62)
	$\hat{b}$	1.13	1.93	1.87	1.82	1.89
		(0.28)	(0.35)	(0.44)	(0.52)	(0.60)
	R^2	0.06	0.11	0.07	0.04	0.04

Notes: Summary statistics for regressions of observed (demeaned) squared return on forecast of conditional variance from nonlinear GARCH models for weekly returns on the Tokyo stock index.
Out-of-sample forecasts are constructed for the period January 1991–December 1995, with models estimated on a rolling window of 5 years.

ahead, conditional on a particular current shock and current conditional volatility, that is

$$E[h_{t+s}|\varepsilon_t = \delta, h_t = h]. \qquad (4.134)$$

Notice that for $s = 1$, (4.134) is in fact the definition of the news impact curve (NIC) discussed in subsection 4.1.2. The NIC measures the direct impact of a shock on the conditional variance. By examining how the conditional expectation (4.134) changes as s increases, one can obtain an impression of the dynamic effect of a particular shock or, more generally, about the propagation of shocks. It turns out that for most (nonlinear) GARCH models a simple recursive relationship between the conditional expectations at different horizons can be derived. For example, for the GARCH(1,1) model it is straightforward to show that

$$E[h_{t+s}|\varepsilon_t = \delta, h_t = h] = (\alpha_1 + \beta_1)E[h_{t+s-1}|\varepsilon_t = \delta, h_t = h],$$

(4.135)

for all $s \geq 2$. Hence, the effect of the shock ε_t on h_{t+s} decays exponentially with rate $\alpha_1 + \beta_1$. Similarly, for the GJR-GARCH model given in (4.53),

$$E[h_{t+s}|\varepsilon_t = \delta, h_t = h]$$
$$= ((\alpha_1 + \gamma_1)/2 + \beta_1)E[h_{t+s-1}|\varepsilon_t = \delta, h_t = h].$$

(4.136)

The so-called *conditional volatility profile* (4.134) is discussed in detail in Gallant, Rossi and Tauchen (1993) for univariate volatility models. Hafner and Herwartz (1998a, 1998b) provide a generalization to multivariate GARCH models.

The conditional expectation (4.134) is closely related to impulse response functions. For example, Lin (1997) defines the impulse response function for (multivariate) linear GARCH models as

$$TIRF_h(s, \delta) = E[h_{t+s}|\varepsilon_t = \delta, h_t = h] - E[h_{t+s}|\varepsilon_t = 0, h_t = h].$$

(4.137)

Notice that this definition is similar to the traditional impulse response function for the conditional mean of a time series as given in (3.95), in the sense that the conditional expectation (4.134) is compared with the conditional expectation given that the current shock is equal to zero. Given that the conditional variance essentially measures the expected value of ε_t^2, this might not be the most appropriate benchmark profile for comparison. It appears more natural to set ε_t to its expected value h_t in the second term on the right-hand-side of (4.137).

Alternatively, one can compare $E[h_{t+s}|\varepsilon_t = \delta, h_t = h]$ with the expectation of h_{t+s} conditional only on the current conditional variance as in the generalized impulse response functions (GIRF) discussed in section 3.6. That is, a GIRF for the conditional variance may be defined as

$$GIRF_h(s, \delta, h) = E[h_{t+s}|\varepsilon_t = \delta, h_t = h] - E[h_{t+s}|h_t = h].$$

(4.138)

The second conditional expectation can also be computed analytically for most nonlinear GARCH models, although the algebra can become quite tedious. An alternative is to resort to simulation techniques, as discussed in section 3.6.

4.7   On multivariate GARCH models

The GARCH models discussed so far all are univariate. Given the interpretation of shocks as news and the fact that at least certain news items affect various assets simultaneously, it might be suggested that the volatility of different assets moves together over time. Consequently, it is of interest to consider multivariate models to describe the volatility of several time series jointly, to exploit possible linkages which exist. An alternative motivation for multivariate models is that an important subject of financial economics is the construction of portfolios from various assets. The covariances among the assets play a crucial role in this decision problem, as in the CAPM, for example. Multivariate GARCH models can be used to model the time-varying behaviour of these conditional covariances.

A general multivariate GARCH model for the k-dimensional process $\boldsymbol{\varepsilon}_t = (\varepsilon_{1t}, \ldots, \varepsilon_{kt})'$ is given by

$$\boldsymbol{\varepsilon}_t = \mathbf{z}_t \mathbf{H}_t^{1/2}, \tag{4.139}$$

where $\mathbf{z}_t$ is a k-dimensional i.i.d. process with mean zero and covariance matrix equal to the identity matrix I_k. From these properties of $\mathbf{z}_t$ and (4.139), it follows that $E[\boldsymbol{\varepsilon}_t|\Omega_{t-1}] = \mathbf{0}$ and $E[\boldsymbol{\varepsilon}_t \boldsymbol{\varepsilon}_t'|\Omega_{t-1}] = \mathbf{H}_t$. To complete the model, a parameterization for the conditional covariance matrix $\mathbf{H}_t$ needs to be specified. This turns out to be a nontrivial task. As in the univariate GARCH models, one may want to allow $\mathbf{H}_t$ to depend on lagged shocks $\boldsymbol{\varepsilon}_{t-i}$, $i = 1, \ldots, q$, and on lagged conditional covariance matrices $\mathbf{H}_{t-i}$, $i = 1, \ldots, p$. Several parameterizations have been proposed, some of which are discussed below. To simplify the exposition, we discuss only the case $p = q = 1$.

The vec model

Let vech($\cdot$) denote the operator which stacks the lower portion of a matrix in a vector. As the conditional covariance matrix is symmetric, vech($\mathbf{H}_t$) contains all unique elements of $\mathbf{H}_t$. A general representation for the multivariate analogue of the GARCH(1,1) model in (4.13) is given by

$$\text{vech}(\mathbf{H}_t) = W^* + A_1^* \text{vech}(\boldsymbol{\varepsilon}_{t-1} \boldsymbol{\varepsilon}_{t-1}') + B_1^* \text{vech}(\mathbf{H}_{t-1}), \tag{4.140}$$

where W^* is a $k(k+1)/2 \times 1$ vector and A_1^* and B_1^* are $(k(k+1)/2 \times k(k+1)/2)$ matrices. This general model, which is called the vec representation by Engle and Kroner (1995), is very flexible as it allows all elements of $\mathbf{H}_t$ to depend on all elements of the cross-products of $\boldsymbol{\varepsilon}_{t-1}$ and all elements of the lagged conditional covariance matrix $\mathbf{H}_t$.

The vec model has two important drawbacks. First, the number of parameters in (4.140) equals $(k(k+1)/2)(1 + 2(k(k+1)/2))$, which becomes excessively large as k increases. For example, in the bivariate case, (4.140) takes the form,

$$
\begin{pmatrix} h_{11,t} \\ h_{12,t} \\ h_{22,t} \end{pmatrix} = \begin{pmatrix} \omega_{11}^* \\ \omega_{12}^* \\ \omega_{22}^* \end{pmatrix} + \begin{pmatrix} \alpha_{11}^* & \alpha_{12}^* & \alpha_{13}^* \\ \alpha_{21}^* & \alpha_{22}^* & \alpha_{23}^* \\ \alpha_{31}^* & \alpha_{32}^* & \alpha_{33}^* \end{pmatrix} \begin{pmatrix} \varepsilon_{1,t-1}^2 \\ \varepsilon_{1,t-1}\varepsilon_{2,t-1} \\ \varepsilon_{2,t-1}^2 \end{pmatrix}
$$

$$
+ \begin{pmatrix} \beta_{11}^* & \beta_{12}^* & \beta_{13}^* \\ \beta_{21}^* & \beta_{22}^* & \beta_{23}^* \\ \beta_{31}^* & \beta_{32}^* & \beta_{33}^* \end{pmatrix} \begin{pmatrix} h_{11,t-1} \\ h_{12,t-1} \\ h_{22,t-1} \end{pmatrix}. \tag{4.141}
$$

For this simplest possible case, the model already contains 21 parameters which have to be estimated. Estimation of this general model may therefore be quite problematic. The second shortcoming of the vec model is that conditions on the matrices A_1^* and B_1^* which guarantee positive semi-definiteness of the conditional covariance matrix $\mathbf{H}_t$ are not easy to impose.

The diagonal model

   Bollerslev, Engle and Wooldridge (1988) suggest reducing the number of parameters in the multivariate GARCH model by constraining the matrices A_1^* and B_1^* in (4.140) to be diagonal. In this case, the conditional covariance between $\varepsilon_{i,t}$ and $\varepsilon_{j,t}$, $h_{ij,t}$, depends only on lagged cross-products of the two shocks involved and lagged values of the covariance itself,

$$
h_{ij,t} = \omega_{ij} + \alpha_{ij}\varepsilon_{i,t-1}\varepsilon_{j,t-1} + \beta_{ij}h_{ij,t-1}, \tag{4.142}
$$

where α_{ij} and β_{ij} are the (i, j)th element of the $(k \times k)$ matrices A_1 and B_1, respectively, which are implicitly defined by $A_1^* = \mathrm{diag}(\mathrm{vech}(A_1))$ and $B_1^* = \mathrm{diag}(\mathrm{vech}(B_1))$. These definitions allow the complete model to be written as

$$
\mathbf{H}_t = W + A_1 \odot (\boldsymbol{\varepsilon}_{t-1}\boldsymbol{\varepsilon}_{t-1}') + B_1 \odot \mathbf{H}_{t-1}, \tag{4.143}
$$

where $\odot$ again denotes the Hadamard or element-by-element product.

   The number of parameters in the diagonal GARCH(1,1) model equals $3(k(k+1)/2)$. For the bivariate case, setting all off-diagonal elements α_{ij}^* and β_{ij}^*, $i \neq j$, in (4.141) equal to zero, it is seen that 9 parameters remain to be estimated. An additional advantage of the diagonal model is that conditions which ensure that the conditional covariance matrix is positive definite are quite easy to check. In particular, $\mathbf{H}_t$ is positive definite if W is positive definite and A_1 and B_1 are positive semi-definite, see Attanasio (1991).

   On the other hand, the diagonal model may be considered too restrictive, as it does not allow the conditional variance of one series to depend on the history of other variables in the system.

The BEKK model

An alternative representation of the multivariate GARCH(1,1) model is given by

$$\mathbf{H}_t = \mathbf{W} + \mathbf{A}_1' \boldsymbol{\varepsilon}_{t-1} \boldsymbol{\varepsilon}_{t-1}' \mathbf{A}_1 + \mathbf{B}_1' \mathbf{H}_{t-1} \mathbf{B}_1, \tag{4.144}$$

where $\mathbf{W}$, $\mathbf{A}_1$ and $\mathbf{B}_1$ are $(k \times k)$ matrices, with $\mathbf{W}$ symmetric and positive definite. Engle and Kroner (1995) discuss this formulation, which they dub the BEKK representation after Baba *et al.* (1991). As the second and third terms on the right-hand-side of (4.144) are expressed as quadratic forms, $\mathbf{H}_t$ is guaranteed to be positive definite without the need for imposing constraints on the parameter matrices $\mathbf{A}_i$ and $\mathbf{B}_i$. This is the main advantage of the BEKK representation. On the other hand, the number of parameters in (4.144) equals $2k^2 + k/2$, which still becomes very large as k increases. In the bivariate case, the BEKK model is given by

$$\begin{pmatrix} h_{11,t} & h_{12,t} \\ h_{12,t} & h_{22,t} \end{pmatrix} = \begin{pmatrix} w_{11} & w_{12} \\ w_{12} & w_{22} \end{pmatrix}$$

$$+ \begin{pmatrix} \alpha_{11} & \alpha_{12} \\ \alpha_{21} & \alpha_{22} \end{pmatrix}' \begin{pmatrix} \varepsilon_{1,t-1}^2 & \varepsilon_{1,t-1}\varepsilon_{2,t-1} \\ \varepsilon_{1,t-1}\varepsilon_{2,t-1} & \varepsilon_{2,t-1}^2 \end{pmatrix} \begin{pmatrix} \alpha_{11} & \alpha_{12} \\ \alpha_{21} & \alpha_{22} \end{pmatrix}$$

$$+ \begin{pmatrix} \beta_{11} & \beta_{12} \\ \beta_{21} & \beta_{22} \end{pmatrix}' \begin{pmatrix} h_{11,t-1} & h_{12,t-1} \\ h_{12,t-1} & h_{22,t-1} \end{pmatrix} \begin{pmatrix} \beta_{11} & \beta_{12} \\ \beta_{21} & \beta_{22} \end{pmatrix}, \tag{4.145}$$

which is seen to contain 12 parameters, compared with 21 for the vec model in (4.141). By applying the vech operator to (4.144), the model can be expressed in the vec representation (4.140). As shown by Engle and Kroner (1995), this vec representation is unique. Conversely, every vec model which can be rewritten as a BEKK representation renders positive definite covariance matrices $\mathbf{H}_t$.

The constant correlation model

Bollerslev (1990) put forward an alternative way to simplify the general model (4.140), by assuming that the conditional correlations between the elements of $\boldsymbol{\varepsilon}_t$ are time-invariant. This implies that the conditional covariance $h_{ij,t}$ between ε_{it} and ε_{jt} is proportional to the product of their conditional standard deviations. The individual conditional variances are assumed to follow univariate GARCH(1,1) models. The diagonal model is given by

$$h_{ii,t} = \omega_{ii} + \alpha_{ii}\varepsilon_{i,t-1}^2 + \beta_{ii}h_{ii,t-1} \quad \text{for } i = 1, \dots, k, \tag{4.146}$$

$$h_{ij,t} = \rho_{ij}\sqrt{h_{ii,t}}\sqrt{h_{jj,t}} \qquad \qquad \text{for all } i \neq j, \tag{4.147}$$

or alternatively,

$$\mathbf{H}_t = \boldsymbol{D}_t^{1/2} \boldsymbol{R} \boldsymbol{D}_t^{1/2}, \tag{4.148}$$

where $\mathbf{D}_t$ is a $(k \times k)$ matrix with the conditional variances $h_{ii,t}$ on the diagonal, and $\boldsymbol{R}$ is a $(k \times k)$ matrix containing the correlations ρ_{ij}. For example, in the bivariate case

$$\mathbf{H}_t = \begin{pmatrix} \sqrt{h_{11,t}} & 0 \\ 0 & \sqrt{h_{22,t}} \end{pmatrix} \begin{pmatrix} 1 & \rho_{12} \\ \rho_{12} & 1 \end{pmatrix} \begin{pmatrix} \sqrt{h_{11,t}} & 0 \\ 0 & \sqrt{h_{22,t}} \end{pmatrix}. \tag{4.149}$$

It is seen from (4.149) that the dynamic properties of the covariance matrix $\mathbf{H}_t$ are determined entirely by the conditional variances in $\mathbf{D}_t$. All that is required for the conditional covariance matrix implied by the constant correlation model to be positive definite is that the univariate GARCH models for $h_{ii,t}$ render positive conditional variances and that the correlation matrix $\boldsymbol{R}$ is positive definite.

The factor model

One of the main motivations for considering multivariate GARCH models is that the volatility of different assets is driven or affected by the same sources of news. This can be made more explicit in the model by assuming the presence of so-called common factors, as suggested in Diebold and Nerlove (1989). An r-factor multivariate GARCH model can be represented as

$$\boldsymbol{\varepsilon}_t = \boldsymbol{B} \boldsymbol{f}_t + \boldsymbol{v}_t, \tag{4.150}$$

where $\boldsymbol{B}$ is a $(k \times r)$ matrix of full-column rank of so-called factor loadings, $\boldsymbol{f}_t$ is a $r \times 1$ vector containing the common factors and $\boldsymbol{v}_t$ is a $k \times 1$ vector of idiosyncratic noise. It is assumed that $\boldsymbol{f}_t$ and $\boldsymbol{v}_t$ have conditional mean zero and conditional variance matrices given by $\boldsymbol{\Lambda}_t$ and $\boldsymbol{\Sigma}_t$, respectively. Both $\boldsymbol{\Lambda}_t$ and $\boldsymbol{\Sigma}_t$ are diagonal, while it is also common to assume that $\boldsymbol{\Sigma}_t$ is constant over time. Finally, $\boldsymbol{f}_t$ and $\boldsymbol{v}_t$ are assumed to be uncorrelated. The preceding assumptions imply that the conditional covariance matrix of $\boldsymbol{\varepsilon}_t$ is given by

$$\mathbf{H}_t = \boldsymbol{B} \boldsymbol{\Lambda}_t \boldsymbol{B}' + \boldsymbol{\Sigma}. \tag{4.151}$$

For example, in the bivariate case, where we can have only one common factor, this amounts to

$$\begin{pmatrix} h_{11,t} & h_{12,t} \\ h_{12,t} & h_{22,t} \end{pmatrix} = \begin{pmatrix} \beta_1^2 & \beta_1\beta_2 \\ \beta_1\beta_2 & \beta_2^2 \end{pmatrix} \lambda_t + \begin{pmatrix} \sigma_1^2 & 0 \\ 0 & \sigma_2^2 \end{pmatrix}. \tag{4.152}$$

The conditional variance of ε_{it}, $i = 1, 2$, is composed of the variance of the news which is specific to the ith asset, σ_i^2 and the conditional variance of the common news factor f_t. A nonzero conditional covariance between ε_{1t} and ε_{2t} is caused solely by this common factor. For the common factor(s) a standard GARCH model can be postulated. Estimation of factor GARCH models is considered in Lin (1992). Applications to financial time series can be found in Engle, Ng and Rothschild (1990) and Ng, Engle and Rothschild (1992).

Common heteroscedasticity

An important consequence of the presence of common factors is that there are linear combinations of the elements of $\boldsymbol{\varepsilon}_t$ which have constant conditional variance. For example, in the bivariate factor GARCH model the conditional variance of the linear combination $\beta_2\varepsilon_{1,t} - \beta_1\varepsilon_{2,t}$ is given by $(\beta_2, -\beta_1)\mathbf{H}_t(\beta_2, -\beta_1)'$. Substituting $\mathbf{H}_t$ from (4.153), it follows that this conditional variance is constant and equal to $\beta_2^2\sigma_1^2 + \beta_1^2\sigma_2^2$. Engle and Susmel (1993) suggest a test for such common heteroscedasticity which avoids actually estimating a factor GARCH model. The test is based upon the intuitive idea that, for fixed τ, a test for ARCH in the linear combination $\varepsilon_{1,t} - \tau\varepsilon_{2,t}$ can be obtained as nR^2 where R^2 is the coefficient of determination of the regression of $\varepsilon_{1,t} - \tau\varepsilon_{2,t}$ on lagged squares and cross-products of $\varepsilon_{1,t}$ and $\varepsilon_{2,t}$ – that is, $\varepsilon_{j,t-i}^2$, $j = 1, 2, i = 1, \ldots, p$ and $\varepsilon_{1,t-i}\varepsilon_{2,t-i}$, $i = 1, \ldots, p$, similar to the univariate LM test for ARCH discussed in section 4.2. As τ is unknown, the test-statistic is obtained as the minimum of the point-wise statistic, where a grid search over τ is performed. As shown by Engle and Kozicki (1993), the resulting test-statistic follows a chi-squared distribution with $3p - 1$ degrees of freedom asymptotically.

Example 4.11: Testing for common ARCH in stock index and exchange rate returns   The test for common ARCH is computed for the indexes of the four 'big' stock markets – Frankfurt, London, New York and Tokyo – for the sample January 1986–December 1990, and for four European exchange rates British pound, Dutch guilder, French franc and German Dmark for the sample January 1991–December 1995. Table 4.16 shows p-values of the LM test for $q = 1, 5$ and 10, as well as the estimates of the parameter τ for which the $TR^2(\tau)$ function is minimized.

For the stock indexes, the null hypothesis of common ARCH can be rejected for most combinations of stock markets. An exception are the stock markets in Frankfurt and London. For the European exchange rates there appears to be more evidence for common ARCH. In particular, the conditional heteroscedasticity in the Dutch guilder, French franc and German Dmark appears to have a common source, whereas the conditional volatility of the British pound seems to behave independently from these currencies from the European continent.

Table 4.16 *Testing for common ARCH effects in weekly stock index and exchange rate returns*

	q	p-value			$\hat{\tau}$		
		1	5	10	1	5	10
Stock indexes							
Frankfurt/London		0.911	0.908	0.982	1.346	2.860	3.197
Frankfurt/New York		0.028	0.434	0.771	2.300	2.610	2.596
Frankfurt/Tokyo		0.018	0.000	0.010	3.077	2.016	1.877
London/New York		0.128	0.008	0.039	0.889	0.579	0.586
London/Tokyo		0.088	0.016	0.201	0.913	0.208	−0.353
New York/Tokyo		0.045	0.039	0.286	1.005	1.408	1.536
Exchange rates							
British pound/Dutch guilder		0.002	0.003	0.159	−0.521	−2.586	−2.307
British pound/French franc		0.000	0.000	0.032	−0.310	−0.829	−0.832
British pound/German Dmark		0.002	0.002	0.131	−0.508	−2.377	−2.220
Dutch guilder/French franc		0.993	0.841	0.938	−0.549	0.609	0.435
Dutch guilder/German Dmark		0.680	0.175	0.453	1.228	1.024	1.019
French franc/German Dmark		0.990	0.889	0.983	1.761	1.567	1.813

Notes: p-values of the LM test for common ARCH of order q for weekly stock index and exchange rate returns.

The sample runs from January 1986 until December 1990 for the stock indexes, and from January 1991 until December 1995 for the exchange rates.

The tests are applied to residuals from an AR(k) model, with k determined by the AIC. The final three columns report the value of the parameter τ for which the TR^2 function is minimized.

Finally, multivariate nonlinear GARCH models have only recently been considered, see Hafner and Herwartz (1998a, 1998b) and Kroner and Ng (1998). Kroner and Ng (1998) also discuss multivariate analogues of the Sign and Sign-Bias tests discussed in section 4.4, which can be used to test for the presence of asymmetric effects of positive and negative or large and small shocks. It seems that much further research is needed on issues as representation, specification, estimation, inference and forecasting for these models.

5 Artificial neural networks for returns

Artificial neural network models (ANNs) are nowadays used in a large variety of modelling and forecasting problems. In recent years neural networks have found their way into financial analysis as well, as evidenced by conferences such as 'Neural Networks in the Capital Markets', and a large number of books (Trippi and Turban, 1993; Azoff, 1994; Refenes, 1995; Gately, 1996) and articles in scientific journals dealing with financial applications of neural networks. A casual literature search suggests that each year about 20–30 of such articles are published, dealing with modelling and forecasting stock prices (Gençay, 1996; Haefke and Helmenstein, 1996a, 1996b; Gençay and Stengos, 1998; Qi and Maddala, 1999), exchange rates (Kuan and Liu, 1995; Franses and van Griensven, 1998; Franses and van Homelen, 1998; Gençay, 1999), interest rates (Swanson and White, 1995) and option pricing (Hutchinson, Lo and Poggio, 1994; Qi and Maddala, 1995), among others. See also Qi (1996) for a survey.

The main reason for this increased popularity of ANNs is that these models have been shown to be able to approximate almost any nonlinear function arbitrarily close. Hence, when applied to a time series which is characterized by truly nonlinear dynamic relationships, the ANN will detect these and provide a superior fit compared to linear time series models, without the need to construct a specific parametric nonlinear time series model. An often-quoted drawback of ANNs is that the parameters in the model are difficult, if not impossible, to interpret. An estimated ANN does not (necessarily) provide information on which type of parametric time series models might be suitable to describe the nonlinear patterns which are detected. For this reason, and also because it usually is difficult to assign meaning to the parameter values, ANNs often are considered as 'black box' models and constructed mainly for the purpose of pattern recognition and forecasting. However, the superior in-sample fit that can be achieved is no guarantee that an ANN performs well in out-of-sample forecasting. In fact, another drawback of ANNs is the danger of overfitting. By increasing the flexibility of the model, it is possible to obtain an almost perfect in-sample fit, with R^2-type measures attaining values close to unity. As part of the ANN may fit irregular (and unpredictable) noise in this case, the model may be less useful for out-of-sample forecasting. The topics mentioned above will be made more explicit and discussed in more detail later in this chapter.

The outline of this chapter is as follows. In section 5.1, we introduce a specific ANN, the so-called 'single hidden layer feedforward model', which is by far the most popular type of ANN among practitioners. Because ANNs are used in many different fields of scientific research and areas of application, a specific ANN nomenclature has developed. We briefly summarize this and relate this to common econometric terminology. We also demonstrate that an ANN can capture aberrant events, such as additive and innovative outliers and level shifts. In section 5.2, we describe several ways of estimating the parameters in an ANN. In section 5.3 we reflect upon issues related to model selection and evaluation. Forecasting and impulse response analysis are briefly discussed in section 5.4. In section 5.5, we discuss links with the regime-switching time series models discussed in chapter 3 and explore the ability of ANNs to capture nonlinearity as implied by S(E)TAR, Markov-Switching and GARCH models. In section 5.6, we discuss a general test for nonlinearity based on ANNs. In this chapter we consider only ANNs for (absolute) returns. An extension to a GARCH-type model is discussed in Donaldson and Kamstra (1997).

The aim of this chapter is not to provide a complete coverage of neural networks. In fact, we intend to give only a 'glimpse into the black box' by discussing the basic structure of ANNs, pointing out connections with models discussed in previous chapters, and addressing those topics which are most relevant for practitioners. Introductory texts on neural networks are available in abundance and for different audiences. Reviews of ANNs from statistical and econometric perspectives can be found in Cheng and Titterington (1994) and Kuan and White (1994), respectively.

5.1 Representation

Consider the following STAR model for a univariate time series y_t, which may be the (absolute) return on a financial asset,

$$y_t = \phi_0 + \beta_1 G(\gamma[y_{t-1} - c]) + \varepsilon_t, \tag{5.1}$$

where $G(\cdot)$ is the logistic function

$$G(z) = \frac{1}{1 + \exp(-z)}. \tag{5.2}$$

The model in (5.1) describes the situation where the conditional mean of y_t depends on the value of y_{t-1} relative to the threshold c. For $y_{t-1} \ll c$, the conditional mean of y_t is equal to ϕ_0, while it changes gradually to $\phi_0 + \beta_1$ as

y_{t-1} increases. An artificial neural network can now be obtained by assuming that the conditional mean of y_t depends on the value of a linear combination of p lagged values $y_{t-1}, \ldots, y_{t-p}$ relative to the threshold c. The model in (5.1) then becomes $y_t = \phi_0 + \beta_1 G(\gamma[\tilde{x}_t'\delta - c]) + \varepsilon_t$, where $\tilde{x}_t = (y_{t-1}, \ldots, y_{t-p})'$, or after some manipulation,

$$y_t = \phi_0 + \beta_1 G(x_t'\gamma_1) + \varepsilon_t, \tag{5.3}$$

where $x_t = (1, \tilde{x}_t')'$ and the individual elements of the parameter vector $\gamma_1 = (\gamma_{0,1}, \gamma_{1,1}, \ldots, \gamma_{p,1})'$, are easily obtained from γ, δ and c.

This ANN can be interpreted as a switching-regression model, where the switching is determined by a particular linear combination of the p lagged variables in the vector x_t. In applications of neural networks one does not usually focus on such a regime interpretation. Instead, the aim is to model the, possibly nonlinear, relationship between y_t and x_t. One way to achieve this is to include additional logistic components in the model, which gives

$$y_t = \phi_0 + \sum_{j=1}^{q} \beta_j G(x_t'\gamma_j) + \varepsilon_t. \tag{5.4}$$

Suppose that an appropriate relationship between y_t and x_t is given by

$$y_t = g(x_t; \xi) + \eta_t,$$

where $g(x_t; \xi)$ is a continuous function. It can be shown that ANNs of the form (5.4) can approximate any such function $g(x_t; \xi)$ to any desired degree of accuracy, provided that the number of nonlinear components q is sufficiently large. Technically, writing (5.4) as

$$y_t = F(x_t; \theta) + \varepsilon_t,$$

with

$$F(x_t; \theta) = \phi_0 + \sum_{j=1}^{q} \beta_j G(x_t'\gamma_j),$$

it can be shown that for any continuous function $g(x_t; \xi)$, every compact subset K of $\mathbf{R}^k$, and every $\delta > 0$, there exists an ANN $F(x_t; \theta)$ such that

$$\sup_{x \in K} |F(x; \theta) - g(x; \xi)| < \delta$$

(see Cybenko, 1989; Carroll and Dickinson, 1989; Funabashi, 1989; Hornik, Stinchcombe and White, 1989, 1990, for details).

Intuitively this result can be understood as follows. Consider the network (5.4) and assume that only y_{t-1} acts as an input – that is, $x_t = (1, y_{t-1})'$. Figure 5.1 shows the skeleton $F(x_t; \theta)$ of such a network with $\phi_0 = 2$, $q = 3$ and $\beta_1 = 8$, $\beta_2 = -12$, $\beta_3 = 6$, $G(x_t'\gamma_1) = 1/(1 + \exp[-40 - 10y_{t-1}])$, $G(x_t'\gamma_2) = 1/(1 + \exp[-y_{t-1}])$ and $G(x_t'\gamma_3) = 1/(1 + \exp[20 - 20y_{t-1}])$. The values of the logistic functions $G(x_t'\gamma_j)$, $j = 1, 2, 3$, are displayed on the horizontal axis. For large negative values of y_{t-1}, all three functions are equal to zero, and $F(x_t; \theta) = \phi_0$. Around the point $y_{t-1} = -4$, the function $G(x_t'\gamma_1)$ changes from 0 to 1 fairly rapidly, and the value of the skeleton increases accordingly. At the same time, the function $G(x_t'\gamma_2)$ becomes activated and slowly starts increasing. The skeleton declines smoothly until the point $y_{t-1} = 1$. Here $G(x_t'\gamma_3)$ goes from 0 to 1 almost instantaneously, causing a sharp increase in the value of $F(x_t; \theta)$. After this point the skeleton resumes its gradual decline owing to the continued increase in $G(x_t'\gamma_2)$. Summarizing, the value of the network skeleton changes as a function of the input y_{t-1} as the functions $G(x_t; \gamma_j)$, $j = 1, 2, 3$ change value. It will be clear that, by increasing the number of logistic components in (5.4), the resulting function $F(x_t; \theta)$ becomes very flexible, and should be able to approximate almost any type of nonlinear relationship that might exist between y_t and y_{t-1}. See Donaldson and Kamstra (1996) for a similar example.

To see how this generalizes to more complicated networks involving multiple inputs, consider a network in which $\tilde{x}_t$ contains the first two lags of y_t – that

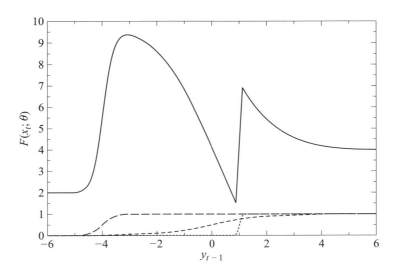

Figure 5.1   Skeleton $F(x_t; \theta)$ of an ANN (5.4) with a single input and $q = 3$ (solid line); the values of the activation functions $G(x_t'\gamma_j)$, $j = 1, 2, 3$, are shown on the horizontal axis

is, $\tilde{x}_t = (y_{t-1}, y_{t-2})'$. Then, the linear combination $x_t'\gamma_1$ divides the space of values that $\tilde{x}_t$ can take in two regimes, one regime for which $\gamma_{1,1}y_{t-1} + \gamma_{2,1}y_{t-2} < \gamma_{0,1}$ and another for which $\gamma_{1,1}y_{t-1} + \gamma_{2,1}y_{t-2} > \gamma_{0,1}$. In the one regime, the conditional mean of y_t is equal to ϕ_0, whereas in the other regime it is equal to $\phi_0 + \beta_1$ (assuming the transition of the logistic function $G(x_t'\gamma_1)$ from 0 to 1 is instantaneous). By increasing the number of logistic components, as in (5.4), the number of partitions of the space of (y_{t-1}, y_{t-2}) is increased, effectively increasing the number of regimes (each of which is characterized by a particular combination of 0-1 values of the $G(x_t'\gamma_j)$) and the number of different values that the conditional mean of y_t can take. Figure 5.2 shows an example of a partitioning resulting from four linear combinations $x_t'\gamma_1, \ldots, x_t'\gamma_4$. We also indicate the values of the associated logistic functions $G(x_t'\gamma_1), \ldots, G(x_t'\gamma_4)$ in each of the implied regimes. As the number of logistic components in (5.4) increases without bound, the partitioning of the (y_{t-1}, y_{t-2}) space becomes so dense that the conditional mean of y_t can more or less take on a distinct value for each value of (y_{t-1}, y_{t-2}). Hence, any type of nonlinear relationship that might exist between y_t and y_{t-1} and y_{t-2} can be approximated in this way.

The above makes clear that ANNs are closely related to *nonparametric methods*, which is the collective noun for a large set of techniques that, for example, can be applied to estimate the relationship between y_t and y_{t-1} without specifying a particular parametric form. To illustrate this, consider the general first-order nonlinear autoregressive model

$$y_t = g(y_{t-1}) + \varepsilon_t, \tag{5.5}$$

and suppose the interest lies in estimating the value of $g(\cdot)$ in a particular point $y_{t-1} = y^*$, using the observed time series $y_0, y_1, \ldots, y_n$. Most nonparametric estimation methods make use of what might be called 'local averaging'. For example, the local conditional mean estimator is given by the average of all observations y_t for which the corresponding y_{t-1} is inside the interval $(y^* - h, y^* + h)$ for certain $h > 0$, that is,

$$\hat{g}(y^*) = \frac{\sum_{t=1}^{n} I[|y^* - y_{t-1}| < h]y_t}{\sum_{t=1}^{n} I[|y^* - y_{t-1}| < h]}, \tag{5.6}$$

where $I[\cdot]$ is the indicator function as usual. More sophisticated methods make use of a weighted average of the observed y_ts, where the weights typically depend on the distance between y_{t-1} and y^*. For example, the Nadaraya–Watson kernel estimator is given by

$$\hat{g}(y^*) = \frac{\sum_{t=1}^{n} K((y^* - y_{t-1})/h)y_t}{\sum_{t=1}^{n} K((y^* - y_{t-1})/h)}, \tag{5.7}$$

where $K(z)$ is a kernel function which satisfies $\int K(z)\,dz = 1$. Usually $K(z)$

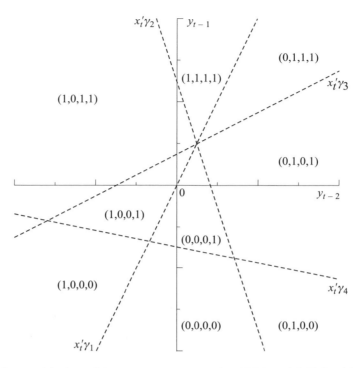

Figure 5.2   Partitioning of the (y_{t-1}, y_{t-2}) space by ANN model (5.4) with $q = 4$

is taken to be a unimodal probability density function such as the Gaussian kernel

$$K(z) = \frac{1}{\sqrt{2\pi}} \exp\left(-\frac{1}{2}z^2\right).$$

Another method for estimating $g(y^*)$ is local weighted regression. These estimators stem from the fact that the function $g(\cdot)$ can be approximated by a linear function in a neighborhood around y^*, that is

$$g(y) \approx \beta_0 + \beta_1(y^* - y) \quad \text{for } y \text{ close to } y^*.$$

The value of $g(y^*)$ then is estimated as $\hat{\beta}_0$, where $\hat{\beta}_0$ is obtained from minimizing the weighted sum of squared residuals

$$Q_n = \frac{1}{n} \sum_{t=1}^{n} (y_t - \beta_0 - \beta_1(y^* - y_{t-1}))^2 K((y^* - y_{t-1})/h). \quad (5.8)$$

Nonparametric methods constitute a large and rapidly developing field of research, which we cannot possibly cover here. The survey article by Härdle,

Lütkepohl and Chen (1997) gives an overview of the available techniques. More in-depth treatments can be found in Härdle (1990); Wand and Jones (1995); and Fan and Gijbels (1996), among others.

In econometric applications of ANNs, it is customary to incorporate the p lagged variables in $\tilde{x}_t$ directly as linear regressors – that is, to extend (5.4) to the augmented ANN

$$
\begin{aligned}
y_t &= \phi_0 + \tilde{x}_t' \phi + \sum_{j=1}^{q} \beta_j G(x_t' \gamma_j) + \varepsilon_t \\
&= \phi_0 + \phi_1 y_{t-1} + \phi_2 y_{t-2} + \cdots + \phi_p y_{t-p} \\
&\quad + \sum_{j=1}^{q} \beta_j G(\gamma_{0,j} + \gamma_{1,j} y_{t-1} + \gamma_{2,j} y_{t-2} + \cdots + \gamma_{p,j} y_{t-p}) + \varepsilon_t.
\end{aligned}
$$

(5.9)

Even though including these direct links from the explanatory variables to the endogenous variable is not necessary from an approximation point of view, it facilitates interpretation of the model. The term $\tilde{x}_t' \phi$ can be thought of as representing the linear part of the relationship between y_t and $\tilde{x}_t$, while the logistic components measure the amount of nonlinearity that is present.

The ANN in (5.9) can be generalized by including exogenous variables $z_{1,t}, \ldots, z_{m,t}$ in the vector of inputs $\tilde{x}_t$. In section 5.3 we discuss some possible choices for z_t in the context of financial applications. Below we refer to elements of $\tilde{x}_t$ as $x_{1,t}, \ldots, x_{k,t}$, $k = p + m$, such that $x_{i,t}$, $i = 1, \ldots, k$, can be a lagged endogenous variable y_{t-j}, $j = 1, \ldots, p$, or an exogenous variable $z_{j,t}$, $j = 1, \ldots, m$. We refer to the ANN (5.9) as ANN($k,q,1$), to identify that the network has k input variables $y_{t-1}, \ldots, y_{t-p}, z_{1,t}, \ldots, z_{m,t}$, q logistic components $G(x_t' \gamma_j)$, and one output variable y_t. Because we consider only the case with a single output, we often abbreviate this to ANN(k,q).

Network nomenclature

The terminology which is commonly used in discussions of neural networks is rather different from the usual econometric practice. Here we briefly summarize the meaning of the most important concepts (see Kuan and White, 1994; Warner and Misra, 1996, for more extensive discussions). Consider the graphical representation of the ANN(k,q) model with $k = 4$ and $q = 2$ in figure 5.3. The network is seen to consist of three different *layers*. At the basis is the *input layer*, consisting of the explanatory variables in x_t, which usually are called *inputs*. These inputs are multiplied by so-called *connection strengths* $\gamma_{i,j}$ as they enter the *hidden layer*, which consists of q *hidden units* – that is, the logistic functions $G(\cdot)$. The name 'hidden layer' arises from the fact that it

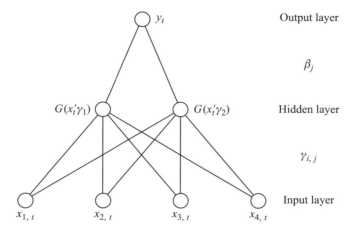

Figure 5.3   Graphical representation of the single hidden layer feedforward neural network ANN(k,q) with $k = 4$ and $q = 2$

is not directly observed. In the hidden layer, the linear combinations $x_t'\gamma_j$ are formed and transformed into a value between 0 and 1 by the *activation functions* $G(\cdot)$. Finally, these are multiplied by weights β_j to produce the *output* y_t. This type of ANN is usually referred to as *single hidden layer feedforward network model*, because it contains only one hidden layer and information flows only in one direction, from inputs to outputs. Extensions of the model to allow for multiple hidden layers or some form of feedback are possible. However, the single hidden layer feedforward model by far has been the most popular in (time series) econometrics, and in this chapter we therefore restrict attention to this particular ANN.

Parameter interpretation and pattern recognition

Given that the fit from an ANN can approximate unity, and given that sets of hidden layer units can fit random noise, it is clear that the individual parameters cannot be interpreted. It therefore is not possible to infer the type of nonlinearity that is captured by the ANN from (estimates of) the individual parameters. To gain some insight in the properties of the nonlinear part of the model, it is more appropriate to inspect the joint contribution of the nonlinear components, that is,

$$\sum_{j=1}^{q} \beta_j G(x_t'\gamma_j), \tag{5.10}$$

or the individual contributions of each hidden layer unit,

$$\beta_1 G(x_t'\gamma_1), \quad \beta_2 G(x_t'\gamma_2), \quad \ldots, \quad \beta_q G(x_t'\gamma_q). \tag{5.11}$$

Below we will show that this can be quite insightful. See also Franses and Draisma (1997), where the fitted hidden layer components are used to see if the data (in that case quarterly industrial production series) experience possible structural breaks.

To conclude this section, we illustrate the flexibility of ANNs by demonstrating that they are capable of capturing anomalous events, such as outliers of different sorts and level shifts.

Experiment 5.1: Capturing outliers and structural breaks with ANNs
We perform some simulation experiments to examine the behaviour of ANNs in the presence of outliers or level shifts. We generate time series x_t from the AR(2) model

$$x_t = \phi_1 x_{t-1} + \phi_2 x_{t-2} + \varepsilon_t \quad t = 1, \ldots, n, \tag{5.12}$$

with $\phi_1 = 0.7$, $\phi_2 = -0.2$. The shocks ε_t are drawn from a standard normal distribution and the sample size is set equal to $n = 500$. The series x_t is contaminated with an additive outlier (AO), innovative outlier (IO) or level shift (LS), each occurring at time $t = \tau$. That is, the observed series y_t is obtained as

$$(AO): \quad y_t = x_t + \omega I[t = \tau], \tag{5.13}$$

$$(IO): \quad y_t = x_t + \omega I[t = \tau]/\phi(L), \tag{5.14}$$

$$(LS): \quad y_t = x_t + \omega I[t = \tau]/(1 - L), \tag{5.15}$$

where $I[A]$ is the familiar indicator function for the event A and $\phi(L)$ is the lag polynomial, which in this case is equal to $\phi(L) = 1 - \phi_1 L - \phi_2 L^2$. In the AO and IO cases a single outlier of magnitude $\omega = 5$ occurs at $\tau = n/4$, whereas in the LS case, a level shift of the same magnitude occurs at $\tau = \lfloor n/6 \rfloor$. We fit ANN time series models as given in (5.9) with $p = 0, 1, 2$ and 3, and $q = 0, 1, 2$ and 3, using the first half of the sample. Thus, the AO and IO occur at the middle of the estimation sample, whereas the LS occurs at 1/3 of the estimation sample. The estimation method is outlined in section 5.2 below. In figures 5.4, 5.5, and 5.6 we give the output of the hidden layer $\sum_{j=1}^{q} \hat{\beta}_j G(x_t' \hat{\gamma}_j)$ for ANNs with $p = 2$ averaged over 100 replications for the AO, IO and LS cases, respectively. It is clearly seen that for both the AO and IO series, the output of the hidden layer is markedly different at the time the outlier occurs. In the LS experiments, the output of the hidden layer exhibits a level shift as well, thus absorbing (part of) the change in the level of the observed time series. Thus we are tempted to conclude that the ANN is capable of recognizing and 'modelling' the atypical events. In the third to sixth columns of tables 5.1 and 5.2 the average R^2 and in-sample success ratio are shown for the AO and IO

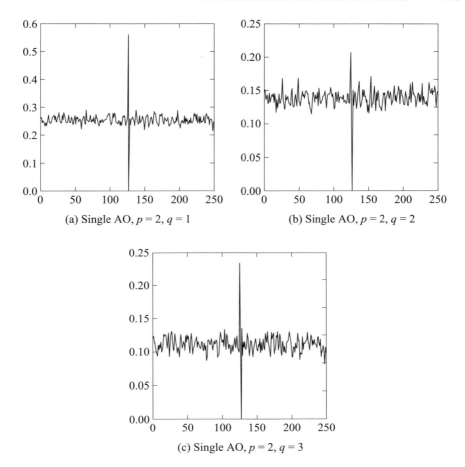

Figure 5.4   Average output of hidden layer in ANN(p,q) model (5.9), estimated on series of 250 observations generated according to the additive outlier model (5.12) with (5.13); a single AO of magnitude $\omega = 5$ occurs half-way through the sample

cases, respectively, together with the number of replications for which each of the models is preferred by the AIC and BIC. Except for BIC, these in-sample diagnostics confirm the conclusion that ANNs seem suitable to take care of anomalous events such as outliers and level shifts.

5.2 Estimation

The parameters in the ANN(k,q) model

$$y_t = x'_t \phi + \sum_{j=1}^{q} \beta_j G(x'_t \gamma_j) + \varepsilon_t,\tag{5.16}$$

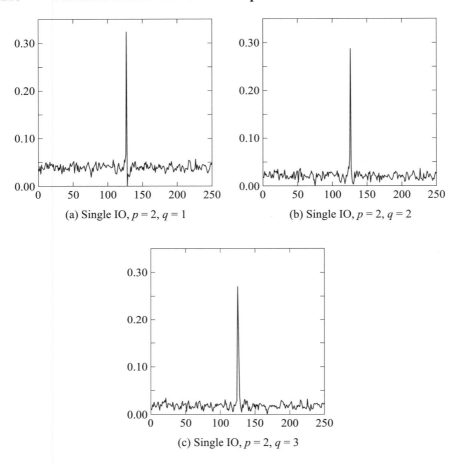

Figure 5.5   Average output of hidden layer in ANN(p,q) model (5.9), estimated on series of 250 observations generated according to the innovative outlier model (5.12) with (5.14); a single IO of magnitude $\omega = 5$ occurs half-way through the sample

can be estimated by minimizing the residual sum of squares function

$$Q_n(\theta) = \sum_{t=1}^{n} [y_t - F(x_t; \theta)]^2, \tag{5.17}$$

where

$$F(x_t; \theta) = x_t'\phi + \sum_{j=1}^{q} \beta_j G(x_t'\gamma_j),$$

with θ the vector consisting of the $k + 1 + q(k + 2)$ parameters in $\phi, \beta_1, \ldots, \beta_q, \gamma_1, \ldots, \gamma_q$. Because the ANN model usually is thought of as an approximating model rather than an underlying process that generates the data,

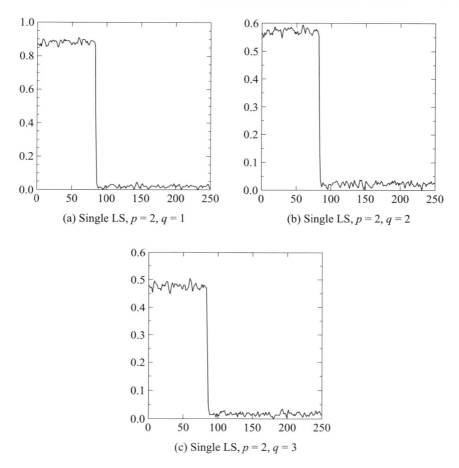

(a) Single LS, $p = 2$, $q = 1$

(b) Single LS, $p = 2$, $q = 2$

(c) Single LS, $p = 2$, $q = 3$

Figure 5.6   Average output of hidden layer in ANN(p,q) model (5.9), estimated on series of 250 observations generated according to the level shift model (5.12) with (5.15); a permanent level shift of magnitude $\omega = 5$ occurs at one-third of the sample

the model is inherently misspecified. The theory of least squares estimation in misspecified models is by now well developed (see Pötscher and Prucha, 1997, for a recent overview) and can be applied to obtain the properties of the nonlinear least squares estimator of θ in (5.17), denoted $\hat{\theta}_n$. Under general conditions, $\hat{\theta}_n$ converges to θ^*, defined as

$$\theta^* = \operatorname*{argmin}_{\theta}\ \mathrm{E}([y_t - F(x_t; \theta)]^2),$$

as the sample size n increases without bound. Furthermore, the normalized estimator $\sqrt{n}(\hat{\theta}_n - \theta^*)$ converges to a multivariate normal distribution with mean zero and a covariance matrix that can be estimated consistently.

Table 5.1 *Performance of ANNs when series are generated from an AR(2) model contaminated with AOs*

		In-sample				Out-of-sample				
p	*q*	R^2	*SR*	*AIC*	*BIC*	*SR*	*DA*	Rank	*MSPE*	*DM*
0	0	—	0.65	0	0	0.65	—	12.93	1.62	—
1	0	0.30	0.66	2	37	0.65	100–0	6.51	1.06	—
1	1	0.31	0.65	2	2	0.65	100–0	7.73	1.01	1–15
1	2	0.32	0.66	2	0	0.65	100–0	7.67	1.03	1–14
1	3	0.32	0.66	0	0	0.65	100–0	8.23	1.05	0–15
2	0	0.32	0.67	22	54	0.66	100–0	2.48	1.03	—
2	1	0.34	0.67	17	4	0.66	100–0	3.74	1.01	2–12
2	2	0.36	0.67	12	0	0.65	99–0	5.97	1.06	0–29
2	3	0.37	0.67	3	0	0.65	99–0	7.87	1.09	0–41
3	0	0.32	0.67	5	2	0.66	100–0	3.39	1.03	—
3	1	0.35	0.67	10	0	0.66	100–0	5.72	1.03	1–23
3	2	0.38	0.68	13	1	0.65	99–0	8.65	1.07	0–48
3	3	0.39	0.68	12	0	0.64	100–0	10.11	1.13	0–61

Notes: Performance of ANN(p,q) models (5.9) when estimated on time series generated from the AR(2) model with AO contamination (5.12) and (5.13).
Columns headed R^2 and SR contain the average R^2 and success ratio, *AIC* and *BIC* the number of replications for which the model is the preferred one according to the AIC and BIC, respectively, *DA* the number of replications for which the directional accuracy test as given in (2.81) is significantly positive–negative at the 5 per cent significance level.
Rank gives the average rank of the respective models according to MSPE.
MSPE contains the average MSPE for AR(p) models ($q = 0$), while for ANNs ($q = 1, 2, 3$), the average ratio of the MSPE of the model to the MSPE of the corresponding AR(p) model is given.
DM is the number of replications for which the Diebold–Mariano test-statistic as given in (2.75) based on squared forecast errors indicates that the ANN(p,q) model performs better–worse than the corresponding AR(p) model at the 5 per cent significance level.
All statistics are based upon 1-step-ahead forecasts for 100 replications of length $n = 500$, of which the first 250 observations are used for estimating the ANN.

Any conventional nonlinear least squares algorithm can be applied to obtain the estimate $\hat{\theta}_n$. Given estimates at the rth iteration, $\hat{\theta}_n^{(r)}$, one computes the sum of squared residuals $Q_n(\hat{\theta}_n^{(r)})$ and the gradient

$$\nabla Q_n(\hat{\theta}_n^{(r)}) = \frac{\partial Q_n(\hat{\theta}_n^{(r)})}{\partial \theta} \qquad (5.18)$$

Table 5.2   *Performance of ANNs when series are generated from an AR(2) model contaminated with IOs*

		In-sample				Out-of-sample				
p	q	R^2	SR	AIC	BIC	SR	DA	Rank	MSPE	DM
0	0	—	0.53	0	0	0.49	—	12.89	1.61	—
1	0	0.28	0.70	13	52	0.70	100–0	7.81	1.06	—
1	1	0.30	0.70	5	0	0.70	100–0	7.68	1.00	12–5
1	2	0.30	0.70	0	0	0.70	100–0	7.86	1.00	11–6
1	3	0.30	0.70	0	0	0.70	100–0	8.03	1.00	11–7
2	0	0.30	0.71	17	40	0.70	100–0	3.70	1.03	—
2	1	0.32	0.71	28	4	0.70	100–0	3.39	1.00	13–9
2	2	0.34	0.71	3	2	0.70	100–0	5.45	1.16	6–17
2	3	0.34	0.72	5	2	0.70	100–0	7.03	1.13	2–24
3	0	0.30	0.71	8	0	0.70	100–0	4.45	1.04	—
3	1	0.33	0.72	9	0	0.70	100–0	4.82	1.00	12–9
3	2	0.35	0.72	5	0	0.70	100–0	8.11	1.11	0–31
3	3	0.36	0.72	7	0	0.70	100–0	9.78	1.14	0–43

Notes: Performance of ANN(p,q) models (5.9) when estimated on time series generated from the AR(2) model with IO contamination (5.12) and (5.14).
All statistics are based upon 1-step-ahead forecasts for 100 replications of length $n = 500$, of which the first 250 observations are used for estimating the ANN.
See table 5.1 for explanation of the various entries.

to obtain a new estimate $\hat{\theta}_n^{(r+1)}$ as

$$\hat{\theta}_n^{(r+1)} = \hat{\theta}_n^{(r)} - \lambda A(\hat{\theta}_n^{(r)})^{-1} \nabla Q_n(\hat{\theta}_n^{(r)}), \qquad (5.19)$$

where λ is a step length and $A(\hat{\theta}_n^{(r)})$ is a matrix that possibly is a function of the parameters θ. For example, in the Newton–Raphson algorithm, $A(\hat{\theta}_n^{(r)})$ is taken to be the Hessian matrix. One method that has been particularly popular in the ANN literature is *steepest descent*, which amounts to setting $A(\hat{\theta}_n^{(r)})$ equal to the identity matrix. This usually is referred to as the method of *backpropagation*, which arises from the fact that the different elements in the gradient vector $\nabla Q_n(\hat{\theta}_n^{(r)})$ can be computed recursively. For example, the partial derivative of $Q_n(\theta)$ with respect to β_j is given by

$$\frac{\partial Q_n(\theta)}{\partial \beta_j} = -2 \sum_{t=1}^{n} [y_t - F(x_t; \theta)] G(x_t' \gamma_j), \qquad (5.20)$$

whereas the partial derivative of $Q_n(\theta)$ with respect to $\gamma_{i,j}$ is equal to

$$\frac{\partial Q_n(\theta)}{\partial \gamma_{i,j}} = -2 \sum_{t=1}^{n} [y_t - F(x_t; \theta)] \beta_j G(x_t' \gamma_j)[1 - G(x_t' \gamma_j)] x_{i,t}$$

$$= -2 \sum_{t=1}^{n} \frac{\partial q_t(\theta)}{\partial \beta_j} \beta_j [1 - G(x_t' \gamma_j)] x_{i,t}, \qquad (5.21)$$

where $q_t(\theta) = [y_t - F(x_t; \theta)]^2$ denotes the squared residual for the tth observation. The process of estimation then is considered to proceed as follows. Given estimates $\hat{\theta}_n^{(r)}$, one computes the value of the hidden units $\hat{\beta}_j^{(r)} G(x_t' \hat{\gamma}_j^{(r)})$, the fitted value $F(x_t; \hat{\theta}_n^{(r)})$ and the residual $\hat{\varepsilon}_t^{(r)} = y_t - F(x_t; \hat{\theta}_n^{(r)})$. Next, the residuals $\hat{\varepsilon}_t^{(r)}$ are used to evaluate the partial derivatives (5.20) at $\hat{\theta}_n^{(r)}$, which in turn are used to obtain the partial derivatives (5.21). Finally, the estimates are updated as $\hat{\theta}_n^{(r+1)} = \hat{\theta}_n^{(r)} - \lambda \nabla \theta_n(\hat{\theta}_n^{(r)})$. Hence, every iteration in the steepest descent algorithm consists of a loop, first going forward through the network and then back(propagating) again.

In the discussion above, the parameter estimates are updated using the information from all n observations in the sample (see (5.19)). An alternative that is very popular in applications of ANNs is to base the updating on a single observation only – that is, to use *recursive estimation*. Given starting values $\hat{\theta}_0$, the value of the gradient for the first observation, $\nabla q_1(\hat{\theta}_0)$, is computed and used to obtain a new set of estimates $\hat{\theta}_1$, which are used to obtain the gradient for the second observation, $\nabla q_2(\hat{\theta}_1)$, and so forth. This process is repeated until the parameter estimates have converged. If convergence has not been achieved when all observations have been processed, it is possible to continue by starting with the first observation again. As $\nabla q_t(\theta) = -2\nabla F(x_t; \theta)[y_t - F(x_t; \theta)]$, the updating formula for the parameter estimates now takes the form

$$\hat{\theta}_{t+1} = \hat{\theta}_t + \lambda \nabla F(x_{t+1}; \hat{\theta}_t)[y_{t+1} - F(x_{t+1}; \hat{\theta}_t)],$$

where $\hat{\theta}_t$ denotes the parameter estimates based on the first t observations. This method of estimating the parameters recursively is usually referred to as *learning* and was popularized by Rumelhart, Hinton and Williams (1986). Its asymptotic properties are analysed in detail in White (1989b) and Kuan and White (1994). Learning by means of steepest descent is shown to be inefficient compared to ordinary nonlinear least squares methods. In all examples and experiments in this chapter, we apply the Broyden–Fletcher–Goldfarb–Shanno algorithm (see Press *et al.*, 1986, pp. 346–50).

Local minima

The sum of squares function $Q_n(\theta)$ in (5.17) is known to possess many local minima. Hence, if the estimation algorithm converges, it cannot be guaranteed that one has obtained the *global* minimum. A commonly applied method of improving the chances of finding this global minimum is to estimate the ANN several times, using different starting values $\hat{\theta}_n^{(0)}$ and choose the estimates which achieve the smallest value of $Q_n(\theta)$. In all examples and experiments in this chapter, the ANNs are estimated 5 times. Starting values are obtained from the simplex algorithm of Nelder and Mead (1965), which is a fast method to search large parts of the parameter space (see Press *et al.*, 1986, pp. 326–330 for a description).

Data transformations

Another method to improve the properties of numerical nonlinear least squares methods is to transform the variables y_t and $x_{i,t}$, $i = 1, \ldots, k$, such that they are on a comparable scale. It is common to either transform the variables to the [0, 1] interval by applying

$$z_t^* = \frac{z_t - \min(z_t)}{\max(z_t) - \min(z_t)}, \tag{5.22}$$

or to rescale the variables such that they have zero mean and standard deviation equal to 1 by applying

$$z_t^* = \frac{z_t - \bar{z}_t}{\sigma(z_t)}, \tag{5.23}$$

where $\bar{z}_t$ and $\sigma(z_t)$ denote the mean and standard deviation of z_t, respectively, and z_t is either the output y_t or one of the inputs $x_{i,t}$. In all examples and experiments in this chapter, we transform the variables involved to the [0, 1] interval according to (5.22).

Weight decay

Finally, estimation of the parameters in ANNs may benefit by preventing individual parameter estimates from becoming unduly large. This can effectively be achieved by augmenting the sum of squares function in (5.17) with a penalty term, which is commonly referred to as *weight decay*. That is, the objective function which is to be minimized is taken to be

$$Q_n(\theta) = \sum_{t=1}^{n} [y_t - F(x_t; \theta)]^2 + r_\phi \sum_{i=0}^{k} \phi_i^2 + r_\beta \sum_{j=1}^{q} \beta_j^2 + r_\gamma \sum_{j=1}^{q} \sum_{i=0}^{k} \gamma_{ij}^2, \tag{5.24}$$

where r_ϕ, r_β and r_γ should be specified in advance. In all examples and experiments in this chapter, the weight decay parameters are set equal to $r_\phi = 0.01$, and $r_\beta = r_\gamma = 0.0001$. Notice that it is necessary to transform the input variables such that they are of comparable magnitude for weight decay to be meaningful.

Example 5.1: ANNs for weekly returns on the Japanese yen/US dollar exchange rate We illustrate the estimation method discussed above by applying ANN(p,q) models (5.9) to weekly returns on the Japanese yen/US dollar exchange rate. We use the period from January 1986 until December 1992 (364 observations) for estimation, and reserve the period from January 1993 until December 1995 for out-of-sample forecasting. We consider ANN(p,q) models with $p = 0, 1, \ldots, 4$ lagged returns as inputs and $q = 0, 1, \ldots, 4$ hidden units. The estimation results are summarized in table 5.3, which shows R^2, the in-sample success ratio, defined as the fraction of observations for which the sign of $\hat{y}_t$ corresponds with the sign of y_t, and the values of the AIC and BIC. It is seen that models with $p = 2$ attain a reasonable improvement in the in-sample success ratio. The ANN(2,3) is also preferred by AIC. Graphs of the contribution of the individual units in models with $p = 2$ are shown in figure 5.7. Figure 5.8 shows the skeleton $F(x_t; \theta)$, of the ANN(2,3) model on the entire space of possible input values $[0, 1] \times [0, 1]$. This clearly demonstrates that the relationship between y_t and its first two lags is nonlinear.

Example 5.2: ANNs for weekly absolute returns on the Frankfurt stock index Another illustration is provided by estimating ANN(p,q) models (5.9) for weekly absolute returns on the Frankfurt stock index. The 10-year sample is split 7–3 as in the example above. Other specifications for the estimation (transformation of variables, weight decay parameters, number of trials) also are taken the same. The estimation results are shown in table 5.4. Notice that in this case, the success ratio is defined as the fraction of observations for which the sign of $\hat{y}_t - y_{t-1}$ corresponds with the sign of $y_t - y_{t-1}$ as we are dealing with absolute returns. The increase of the R^2 measure as either the number of hidden units q or the number of inputs p increases clearly illustrates the approximating possibilities of ANNs. In figure 5.9 we show the output of the individual hidden units $\hat{\beta}_j G(x'_t \hat{\gamma}_j)$, $j = 1, \ldots, q$ for $q = 1, 2$ and 3 and $p = 2$. Figure 5.10 shows the skeleton of the ANN(2,2) model. Again there appears considerable evidence for nonlinearity.

5.3   Model evaluation and model selection

Consider again the ANN(p,q) model for y_t

$$y_t = \phi_0 + \phi_1 y_{t-1} + \phi_2 y_{t-2} + \cdots + \phi_p y_{t-p}$$

$$+ \sum_{j=1}^{q} \beta_j G(\gamma_{0,j} + \gamma_{1,j} y_{t-1} + \gamma_{2,j} y_{t-2} + \cdots + \gamma_{p,j} y_{t-p}) + \varepsilon_t,$$

$$(5.25)$$

Table 5.3 *Performance of ANNs applied to weekly returns on the Japanese yen exchange rate*

		In-sample				Out-of-sample			
p	q	R^2	SR	AIC	BIC	SR	DA	MSPE	DM
0	0	0.00	0.52	289.78	<u>293.67</u>	0.54	—	2.48	—
1	0	0.00	0.52	291.58	299.36	0.54	−0.92	2.48	−0.45
1	1	0.03	0.53	287.06	306.52	0.54	0.71	2.51	−0.43
1	2	0.06	0.57	282.34	313.47	0.51	0.14	4.82	−1.03
1	3	0.06	0.56	288.66	331.47	0.49	−0.49	2.71	−1.50°
1	4	0.06	0.57	292.33	346.82	0.52	0.43	3.14	−1.23
2	0	0.01	0.53	289.88	301.56	0.54	0.24	2.39	1.56*
2	1	0.04	0.54	286.24	313.48	0.61	2.57**	2.44	0.49
2	2	0.06	0.56	288.45	331.26	0.56	1.51*	2.47	0.08
2	3	0.09	0.59	<u>280.04</u>	338.42	0.57	1.80**	2.60	−0.85
2	4	0.09	0.59	288.26	362.20	0.59	2.33**	3.39	−0.94
3	0	0.02	0.58	289.03	304.60	0.56	0.98	2.41	1.02
3	1	0.05	0.60	285.57	320.60	0.56	1.38*	2.45	0.28
3	2	0.08	0.61	283.36	337.85	0.53	0.43	2.51	−0.25
3	3	0.10	0.60	286.24	360.18	0.51	0.14	2.66	−1.01
3	4	0.13	0.60	283.15	376.55	0.49	−0.28	2.76	−1.50°
4	0	0.02	0.56	290.98	310.43	0.54	0.59	2.42	0.93
4	1	0.07	0.60	284.94	327.75	0.55	1.02	2.59	−1.07
4	2	0.11	0.61	280.78	346.94	0.57	1.51*	2.58	−0.85
4	3	0.14	0.61	280.20	369.71	0.55	1.09	2.78	−1.44°
4	4	0.16	0.62	282.20	395.05	0.56	1.40*	3.13	−1.97°°

Notes: Performance of ANN(p,q) models (5.9) for weekly returns on the Japanese yen/US dollar exchange rate.

The networks are estimated over the sample period January 1986–December 1992 (364 observations).

SR denotes the success ratio.

DA is the directional accuracy test given in (2.81), *DM* denotes the Diebold–Mariano test-statistic given in (2.75) based on squared forecast errors, relative to forecasts from the random walk model.

The preferred models by AIC and BIC are underlined.

*,** (o,oo) indicate that the ANN performs significantly better (worse) than the corresponding linear model at the 10 and 5 per cent significance level, respectively.

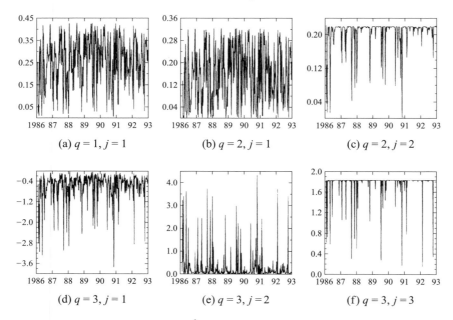

Figure 5.7   Output of hidden units $\hat{\beta}_j G(x_t'\hat{\gamma}_j)$ in ANN(2,q) models applied to weekly returns on the Japanese yen/US dollar exchange rate over the period January 1986–December 1992

which contains $p + 1 + q(p + 2)$ parameters to be estimated. Implementing an ANN(p,q) model requires several decisions to be made:

- choosing the activation function $G(\cdot)$
- choosing the number of hidden units q
- choosing the number of lags p to use as input variables.

Very often, the choice of the activation function is not considered to be a decision problem. The logistic function is used almost invariably, although other choices, such as the hyperbolic tangent function $G(z) = \tanh(z)$, are sometimes applied as well.

There are various different strategies one can follow to decide upon the appropriate values of q and p in (5.25). The first is to estimate all possible ANN models with $p \in \{1, 2, \ldots, p^*\}$ and $q \in \{0, 1, 2, \ldots, q^*\}$, for certain pre-set values of p^* and q^*, and to use a model selection criterion such as the AIC

$$AIC = n \ln(\hat{\sigma}^2) + 2k, \tag{5.26}$$

with $k = p + 1 + q(p + 2)$, or BIC

$$BIC = n \ln(\hat{\sigma}^2) + k \ln n, \tag{5.27}$$

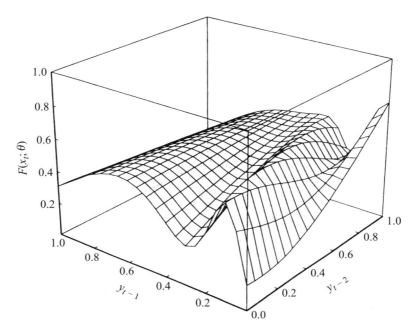

Figure 5.8 Skeleton $F(x_t; \theta)$ of the estimated ANN(2,3) model for weekly returns on the Japanese yen/US dollar exchange rate

where $\hat{\sigma}^2$ denotes the estimate of the residual variance. Notice that in this strategy the number of hidden units and the number of input lags are chosen simultaneously.

An alternative strategy is to decide upon the value of p first, by specifying a linear AR(p) model for y_t, using AIC, BIC or other criteria to select the appropriate order. In a second stage, one can add hidden units to the model, while keeping the value of p fixed. Again the AIC and BIC can be used to decide upon the appropriate value of q. This strategy is subject to the caveats as discussed in section 3.1, in the sense that the order p which is selected in the first stage can be far too small or far too large.

When implementing ANN models which may include exogenous variables among the k inputs, similar decisions have to be made to the ones discussed above. In fact, the situation is more complicated, because one not only has to decide upon k, the number of inputs to include, but also upon which variables to use as inputs. This can be thought of as choosing the k appropriate inputs from a set of m candidates $x_{1,t}, \ldots, x_{m,t}$. If the number of variables in this set m is large, the first strategy probably is too time-consuming. The number of models to be estimated if one wants to decide upon q, k and which of the m variables to include as inputs at the same time simply becomes too large. It seems necessary to use economic reasoning to decide

Table 5.4   *Performance of ANNs applied to absolute weekly returns on the Frankfurt stock index*

		In-sample				Out-of-sample			
p	q	R^2	SR	AIC	BIC	SR	DA	MSPE	DM
0	0	—	0.70	505.89	509.78	0.78	—	1.93	—
1	0	0.03	0.70	496.70	504.47	0.78	7.34**	1.97	—
1	1	0.04	0.70	499.74	519.17	0.80	7.67**	1.90	2.51**
1	2	0.05	0.70	501.51	532.59	0.78	7.20**	1.91	1.43**
1	3	0.06	0.70	503.61	546.36	0.78	7.20**	1.95	0.46
1	4	0.06	0.71	510.46	564.87	0.78	7.20**	1.95	0.41
2	0	0.06	0.70	487.61	<u>499.27</u>	0.77	6.90**	2.03	—
2	1	0.09	0.69	483.07	510.27	0.80	7.67**	1.96	1.85**
2	2	0.12	0.70	<u>477.55</u>	520.30	0.79	7.52**	1.88	3.01**
2	3	0.14	0.71	479.07	537.36	0.79	7.30**	1.91	3.14**
2	4	0.14	0.70	485.58	559.41	0.79	7.30**	1.91	3.66**
3	0	0.06	0.71	487.98	503.53	0.78	7.14**	1.99	—
3	1	0.09	0.71	485.23	520.21	0.79	7.52**	1.91	1.83**
3	2	0.13	0.72	481.90	536.30	0.78	7.28**	1.95	1.09
3	3	0.13	0.71	489.87	563.71	0.78	7.12**	1.94	0.95
3	4	0.25	0.72	436.75	530.01	0.80	7.67**	1.91	1.98**
4	0	0.06	0.71	489.98	509.41	0.78	7.14**	1.98	—
4	1	0.11	0.70	485.55	528.30	0.79	7.52**	1.88	2.23**
4	2	0.13	0.71	487.10	553.16	0.78	7.00**	1.96	0.34
4	3	0.24	0.71	430.82	520.20	0.78	7.20**	1.83	2.70**
4	4	0.30	0.71	420.54	533.24	0.79	7.24**	1.89	1.65**

Notes: Performance of ANN(p,q) models (5.9) for absolute weekly returns on the Frankfurt stock index.

The networks are estimated over the sample period January 1986–December 1992 (364 observations).

The *DM* statistic compares the forecasts from ANN(p,q) models with $q > 0$ with the forecasts from the ANN($p,0$) model.

See table 5.3 for explanation of the various entries.

upon the appropriate inputs, or to rely upon the second strategy and select the inputs by means of linear regressions of y_t on various selections of the m candidates.

Swanson and White (1995, 1997a, 1997b) adopt a similar step-wise strategy, by adding inputs and hidden units to the model until no more improvement in a model selection criterion, such as BIC, can be obtained. At each step, the input which is added is the one which gives the largest improvement in the selection criterion that is used.

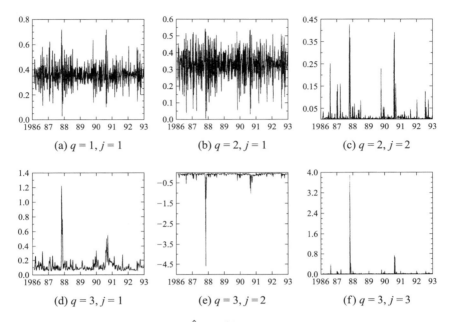

Figure 5.9 Output of hidden units $\hat{\beta}_j G(x_t'\hat{\gamma}_j)$ in ANN(2,q) models applied to weekly absolute returns on the Frankfurt stock index over the period January 1986–December 1992

Technical trading rules as input variables

In financial applications it might be worthwhile to include variables such as trading volume, returns on other assets, leading indicators, and macroeconomic data as inputs in an ANN model (see Hiemstra, 1996; Brooks, 1998; Qi and Maddala, 1999, for examples). Results in Gençay (1996, 1999), Gençay and Stengos (1998) and Franses and van Griensven (1998) show that it also may pay off to include functions of past y_t observations, where these functions correspond with technical trading rules.

Technical trading rules (TTR) are widely used among financial analysts in their decisions to buy or sell stocks, currencies or other assets. Roughly speaking, a TTR identifies moments at which to buy or sell an asset based on patterns in the recent development of its price. One of the most popular TTRs is based on moving averages, defined as

$$m_t(\tau) = \frac{1}{\tau} \sum_{i=0}^{\tau-1} p_{t-i}, \tag{5.28}$$

where p_t is the price of a stock or level of the exchange rate, for example. The *moving average trading rule* amounts to comparing a short-period and a

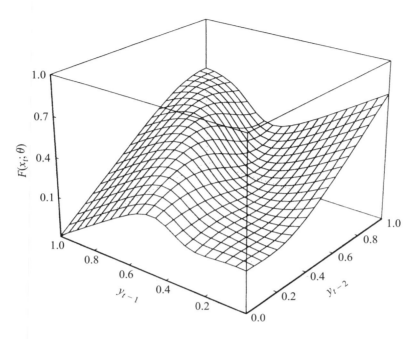

Figure 5.10   Skeleton $F(x_t; \theta)$ of the estimated ANN(2,2) model for weekly absolute returns on the Frankfurt stock index

long-period moving average. The simplest form of the strategy is to buy (sell) when the short-period average rises above (falls below) the long-period average. Put differently, one considers the signal

$$s_t(\tau_1, \tau_2) = m_t(\tau_1) - m_t(\tau_2),\qquad(5.29)$$

where $\tau_1 < \tau_2$. For daily data, typical choices of τ_1 are 1 and 5, while for τ_2 one tends to choose 50, 100, 150 or 200. Buy and sell signals are generated when $s_t(\tau_1, \tau_2)$ is positive and negative, respectively. It is common practice to incorporate a threshold above which the absolute value of $s_t(\tau_1, \tau_2)$ should rise before a buy or sell signal is given. This avoids spurious signals when the two moving averages are close. Figure 5.11 shows moving averages of the level of the Japanese yen/US dollar exchange rate comprising 10, 20, 30 and 40 weeks, together with the current level of the exchange rate. Also indicated are periods when the signal variable $s_t(\tau_1, \tau_2)$ based on these moving averages is positive. Obviously, longer moving averages generate fewer buy and sell signals.

Another popular TTR is the *trading range break-out rule* (see Brock, Lakonishok and LeBaron, 1992). This rule generates a buy signal when the price of an asset rises above the so-called *resistance level*, defined as the

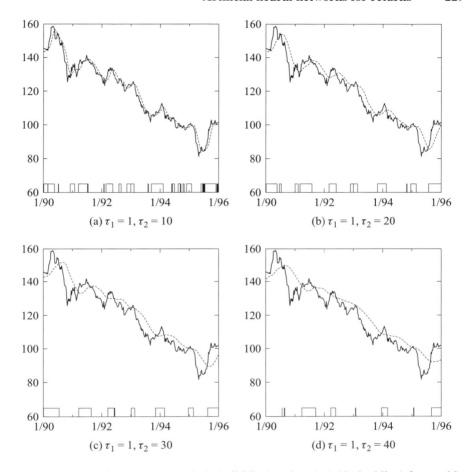

Figure 5.11   Moving averages $m_t(\tau_1)$ (solid line) and $m_t(\tau_2)$ (dashed line) for weekly observations on the Japanese yen/US dollar exchange rate; periods for which the signal $s_t(\tau_1, \tau_2)$ as given in (5.29) is positive are indicated on the horizontal axis

maximum price during the past τ periods. A sell signal is given when the price falls below the so-called support level, defined as the minimum price over the past τ periods. See Siddiqui (1998) for other examples of TTRs.

Historically, technical analysis has met much scepticism among academic researchers (see Malkiel, 1981). Because technical analysis lacks a sound scientific basis, it has long been avoided. In recent years, the interest in TTRs has increased considerably. Various studies have been performed to explore the potential usefulness of TTRs in predicting future prices or returns (see Brock, Lakonishok and LeBaron, 1992; Levich and Thomas, 1993, among others). Interestingly, Neftçi (1991) shows that TTRs can have predictive power over and above a linear time series model only if the underlying process is nonlinear.

This implies that a straightforward method to test the predictive value of technical analysis is to examine the significance of buy and sell signals in the augmented AR model

$$y_t = \phi_0 + \phi_1 y_{t-1} + \cdots + \phi_p y_{t-p} + \beta_1 s_{t-1}(\tau_1, \tau_2) + \varepsilon_t,$$

see Neftçi (1991) and Siddiqui (1998) for applications of this approach. Of course, obtaining a significant estimate of the parameter β_1 in this regression does not necessarily imply that $s_{t-1}(\tau_1, \tau_2)$ is helpful in predicting y_t out-of-sample.

An alternative aproach is taken in Gençay (1996, 1999), Gençay and Stengos (1998) and Franses and van Griensven (1998), who include signal variables such as the one given in (5.29) in an ANN, that is,

$$\begin{aligned} y_t = {} & \phi_0 + \phi_1 s_{t-1}(\tau_1, \tau_2) + \cdots + \phi_p s_{t-p}(\tau_1, \tau_2) \\ & + \sum_{j=1}^{q} \beta_j G(\gamma_{0,j} + \gamma_{1,j} s_{t-1}(\tau_1, \tau_2) \\ & + \cdots + \gamma_{p,j} s_{t-p}(\tau_1, \tau_2)) + \varepsilon_t. \end{aligned} \tag{5.30}$$

Example 5.3: Technical trading rules to forecast returns on the Japanese yen   We consider the usefulness of the moving average trading rule (5.29) as input in the ANN (5.30) to forecast weekly returns on the Japanese yen. We construct trading signals $s_t(\tau_1, \tau_2)$ with $\tau_1 = 1$ and $\tau_2 = 10, 20, 30$ and 40. We set the number of lagged trading signals p equal to 2, and vary the number of hidden units among $q = 0, 1, \ldots, 4$. As the longest moving average which is considered comprises 40 weeks, we use the period from November 1986 until December 1992 to estimate the parameters in the model and use the period from January 1993 until December 1995 for forecasting. In table 5.5 we document measures of within-sample model adequacy and the forecasting results. It is seen that linear models with lagged values of the signal variable as regressor do not result in improved fit or forecast performance. By contrast, including hidden units leads to a higher out-of-sample success ratio and lower MSPE.

Model evaluation
Consider again the ANN(k,q) model

$$y_t = x_t' \phi + \sum_{j=1}^{q} \beta_j G(x_t' \gamma_j) + \varepsilon_t, \tag{5.31}$$

with $x_t = (1, \tilde{x}_t)'$, $\tilde{x}_t = (x_{1,t}, x_{2,t}, \ldots, x_{k,t})'$. No formal guidelines exist on

Table 5.5   *Performance of ANNs with technical trading rule applied to weekly returns on Japanese yen*

p	q	In-sample				Out-of-sample			
		R^2	SR	AIC	BIC	SR	DA	MSPE	DM
0	0	0.00	0.50	251.54	<u>255.33</u>	0.54	—	2.48	—
$\tau_2 = 10$									
2	0	0.01	0.51	253.71	265.07	0.54	0.46	2.44	1.42*
2	1	0.02	0.56	254.28	280.78	0.57	1.59*	2.42	1.28
2	2	0.04	0.56	258.85	300.51	0.58	1.85**	2.42	0.93
2	3	0.05	0.56	261.57	318.37	0.56	1.44*	2.40	1.41*
2	4	0.06	0.54	267.69	339.64	0.59	1.95**	2.40	1.33*
$\tau_2 = 20$									
2	0	0.00	0.49	255.26	266.62	0.56	0.95	2.47	1.13
2	1	0.01	0.58	257.99	284.50	0.56	1.44*	2.50	−0.29
2	2	0.03	0.57	261.60	303.25	0.54	1.13	2.51	−0.63
2	3	0.08	0.53	<u>251.48</u>	308.28	0.46	−0.81	2.47	0.12
2	4	0.09	0.57	252.62	324.58	0.58	1.96**	2.42	0.62
$\tau_2 = 30$									
2	0	0.00	0.50	255.42	266.78	0.54	−0.92	2.48	−0.77
2	1	0.01	0.51	260.49	287.00	0.56	1.15	2.47	0.44
2	2	0.02	0.55	263.97	305.63	0.60	2.17**	2.46	0.58
2	3	0.06	0.54	257.47	314.27	0.57	1.36*	2.48	−0.06
2	4	0.06	0.56	263.26	335.21	0.58	1.77**	2.47	0.24
$\tau_2 = 40$									
2	0	0.00	0.52	255.06	266.42	0.54	0.14	2.49	−0.62
2	1	0.01	0.53	259.22	285.73	0.54	0.13	2.47	1.20
2	2	0.03	0.53	261.09	302.74	0.59	1.95**	2.45	1.08
2	3	0.03	0.54	267.68	324.48	0.58	1.77**	2.45	0.77
2	4	0.08	0.56	257.00	328.95	0.54	0.75	2.46	0.31

Notes: Performance of ANN(p,q) models as given in (5.30) for weekly returns on the Japanese yen/US dollar exchange rate.
The networks are estimated over the sample period November 1986–December 1992 (326 observations).
See table 5.3 for explanation of the various entries.

how to determine the significance of individual input variables $x_{i,t}$. As individual parameters in the ANN do not have a well defined meaning, t-statistics of, for example, the connection strengths $\gamma_{i,j}$ cannot be used for this purpose. White (1989b) and Kuan and White (1994) discuss a statistic to test the significance of all parameters related to $x_{i,t}$ jointly and argue that this might be useful to test the significance of the input variable. If S_i is the $(q+1) \times (k+1) + q(k+2)$ selection matrix that selects ϕ_i and $\gamma_{i,j}$, $j = 1, \ldots, p$, from the full parameter vector θ, the null hypothesis that $x_{i,t}$ is not relevant can be expressed as $H_0 : S_i\theta = 0$. Given an estimate $\hat{\theta}_n$ of θ, this hypothesis can be tested using the Wald-statistic

$$W = n\hat{\theta}_n' S_i' (S_i \widehat{C}_n S_i')^{-1} S_i \hat{\theta}_n, \tag{5.32}$$

where $\widehat{C}_n = \widehat{A}_n^{-1} \widehat{B}_n \widehat{A}_n^{-1}$ with

$$\widehat{A}_n = \frac{1}{n} \sum_{t=1}^{n} \frac{\partial^2 Q_n(\hat{\theta}_n)}{\partial\theta \partial\theta'},$$

with $Q_n(\theta)$ the sum of squares function given in (5.17), and

$$\widehat{B}_n = \frac{1}{n} \sum_{t=1}^{n} \frac{\partial Q_n(\hat{\theta}_n)}{\partial\theta} \frac{\partial Q_n(\hat{\theta}_n)}{\partial\theta'}.$$

Under the null hypothesis, the Wald-statistic W has an asymptotic χ^2 distribution with $q+1$ degrees of freedom.

Another method to evaluate the influence of the input $x_{i,t}$ on the output y_t is to perform a sensitivity analysis. In this approach, the other inputs $x_{1,t}, x_{2,t}, \ldots, x_{i-1,t}, x_{i+1,t}, \ldots, x_{k,t}$ are fixed at, for example, their mean values, while the input of interest $x_{i,t}$ is varied among a range of different values. The change in output owing to a change in $x_{i,t}$ gives an impression of the importance of this input variable.

A related diagnostic check is the derivative of y_t with respect to $x_{i,t}$. For the ANN(k,q) model in (5.31) this derivative is equal to

$$\frac{\partial y_t}{\partial x_{i,t}} = \phi_i - \sum_{j=1}^{q} \beta_j \gamma_{i,j} G(x_t'\gamma_j)[1 - G(x_t'\gamma_j)], \tag{5.33}$$

where we have used

$$\frac{\partial G(x_t'\gamma_j)}{\partial x_{i,t}} = -\gamma_{i,j} G(x_t'\gamma_j)[1 - G(x_t'\gamma_j)].$$

Examples 5.1/5.2: ANNs for weekly returns on Japanese yen/US dollar exchange rate and absolute returns on the Frankfurt stock index
Figures 5.12 and 5.13 show the partial derivatives $\partial y_t/\partial y_{t-1}$ and $\partial y_t/\partial y_{t-2}$

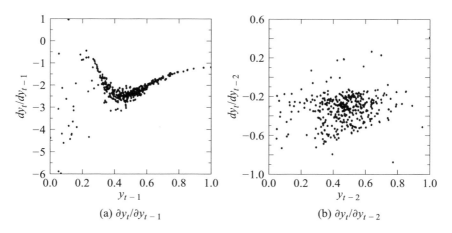

(a) $\partial y_t / \partial y_{t-1}$ (b) $\partial y_t / \partial y_{t-2}$

Figure 5.12   Partial derivatives of the output y_t with respect to the inputs y_{t-1} and y_{t-2} in ANN(2,3) model for weekly returns on the Japanese yen/US dollar exchange rate

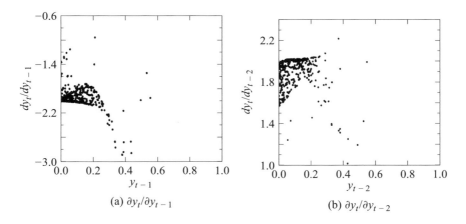

(a) $\partial y_t / \partial y_{t-1}$ (b) $\partial y_t / \partial y_{t-2}$

Figure 5.13   Partial derivatives of the output y_t with respect to the inputs y_{t-1} and y_{t-2} in ANN(2,2) model for weekly absolute returns on the Frankfurt stock index

based on the estimated ANN(2,3) model for weekly returns on the Japanese yen/US dollar exchange rate and the estimated ANN(2,2) model for absolute returns on the Frankfurt stock index. These graphs confirm figures 5.8 and 5.10 in that they show that the links between y_t and y_{t-1} and y_{t-2} are highly nonlinear.

5.4   Forecasting

As mentioned before, ANNs are frequently considered to be 'black box' models and constructed mainly for the purpose of forecasting. A survey of empirical applications of forecasting with ANNs can be found in Zhang, Patuwo and Hu (1998). Forecasting with neural networks is analogous to forecasting with other parametric nonlinear models, such as SETAR and STAR models. The main features can be summarized as follows. First, a 1-step-ahead forecast of y_{n+1} can be computed directly from an ANN(p,q) model as

$$\hat{y}_{t+1|t} = x_t'\phi + \sum_{j=1}^{q} \beta_j G(x_t'\gamma_j), \qquad (5.34)$$

where $x_t = (1, y_t, \ldots, y_{t-p+1})'$. Under the additional assumption that the shocks ε_t in (5.9) are normally distributed, the 1-step-ahead forecast error $e_{t+1|t} = y_{t+1} - y_{t+1|t}$ is normally distributed (since $e_{t+1|t} = \varepsilon_{t+1}$ by definition) and forecast confidence intervals can be constructed in the usual way. Second, for multiple-step-ahead forecasts things become much more complicated. No closed-form expressions exist for $\hat{y}_{t+h|t}$ where $h > 1$ and one has to rely on simulation techniques to obtain such forecasts. For construction of forecast confidence intervals for multiple-step-ahead forecasts and evaluation of forecasts from ANNs one can use the methods outlined in section 3.5.

Examples 5.1/5.2: ANNs for weekly returns on Japanese yen/US dollar exchange rate and absolute returns on the Frankfurt stock index
Tables 5.3 and 5.4 (pp. 223 and 226) show statistics related to the out-of-sample forecast performance of ANN(p,q) models for weekly returns on Japanese yen/US dollar exchange rate and absolute returns on the Frankfurt stock index. For the absolute returns on the DAX index, it seems that there is not much to be gained by using ANNs in terms of predicting the direction of change. The improvement in the out-of-sample success ratio is very small. By contrast, when the ANNs are compared with AR(p) models on the basis of MSPE it is clear that the nonlinear components have some predictive value. For the Japanese yen, the opposite appears to be true: the ANN(p,q) models perform worse in terms of MSPE than linear AR models, and only when $p = 2$ or 4 do they achieve a higher success ratio.

Here it is important to stress again the danger of overfitting with neural networks. By increasing the number of hidden units q, the ANN can be made very flexible, such that an almost perfect in-sample fit can be obtained. It is not to say that this automatically implies an improved out-of-sample forecast performance.

Rather, the opposite appears to be true. If the number of hidden units becomes large, some of these units are bound to be used to capture noise or one-time events such as outliers. It is not at all unlikely that such hidden units are activated during the forecast period and, hence, predict outliers that are not there.

Experiment 5.1: Capturing outliers with ANNs   To illustrate the dangers of using ANNs for forecasting in an automated fashion – that is, without a proper examination of its properties – we use the estimated ANNs in the AO and IO experiments to form 1-step-ahead forecasts for the second half of the time series (during which no outliers occur). The out-of-sample forecast performance is summarized in the right half of tables 5.1 and 5.2 (pp. 218 and 219) by means of various statistics. For both the AO and IO cases, the AR(2) model has the lowest average rank based on the MSPE criterion – hence, on average this model performs best in terms of mean squared prediction error. This is also illustrated by the average ratio of the MSPE of the ANN(p,q) model to the MSPE of the AR(p) model, which is always larger than 1. Finally, the forecasts from the ANNs quite often are significantly worse than the AR forecasts according to the DM statistic.

The balance between in-sample fit and out-of-sample forecast performance is also influenced by the amount of weight decay that is used. When the penalty term in the objective function is decreased, individual parameters are allowed to become larger, which again causes certain hidden units to be used for fitting outliers and the like. Thus, reducing the amount of weight decay leads to a better fit for the estimation sample, but to worse out-of-sample forecasts.

It is not obvious how one can achieve an optimal balance between in-sample fit and out-of-sample forecast performance. Obviously, the number of hidden units q and the values of the weight decay parameters are important. A method to limit the danger of overfitting that frequently is applied is so-called *cross-validation*. In this case, the available observations are divided into an estimation sample and a test sample. The parameters of the ANN are estimated using the observations in the estimation sample only, but during the iterative optimization the sum of squared errors for the observations in the test sample are recorded as well. Estimation is stopped when this sum of squared errors starts to increase, as it is believed that then the parameters are such that they can describe the general nonlinear patterns that are present in the data, while any further improvement of the fit in the estimation sample that can be attained would mean that the network starts describing outliers or other atypical events. See LeBaron and Weigend (1998) for a discussion of this approach and the effects of different splits of the data into estimation and test samples.

Another sensible possibility to safeguard against predicting nonexistent outliers or other one-time events is to examine the hidden units in the model to
check whether they are activated for only one or a few observations. If such
spurious hidden units are indeed present, it might be a good strategy to omit
them from the model at the forecasting stage. That is, suppose one estimates an
ANN(k,q) model

$$y_t = x_t'\phi + \beta_1 G(x_t'\gamma_1) + \cdots + \beta_q G(x_t'\gamma_q) + \varepsilon_t,$$

where $x_t = (1, y_{t-1}, \ldots, y_{t-p}, z_{1t}, \ldots, z_{mt})'$ and $k = p+m$ and upon inspection of the individual activation functions finds that only the first $q_1 < q$ help
in describing the nonlinear relationships in the time series while the remaining units are used to capture one-time events. One might then use the reduced
model

$$y_t = x_t'\phi + \beta_1 G(x_t'\gamma_1) + \cdots + \beta_{q_1} G(x_t'\gamma_{q_1}) + \sum_{j=q_1+1}^{q} \beta_j \overline{G(x_t'\gamma_j)} + \eta_t,$$

for out-of-sample forecasting, where $\overline{G(x_t'\gamma_j)}$ is the average value of the jth
activation function, excluding the observation(s) for which it is activated. Notice
that this procedure requires some subjective judgement to decide whether or
not certain hidden units contribute to explaining regular patterns in the data
or only one-time events. It is not immediately clear whether objective rules or
guidelines can be developed to formalize this procedure.

Forecast evaluation can proceed along the same lines as for other (nonlinear)
models. Criteria such as MSPE and MAPE and statistics such as the directional
accuracy test of Pesaran and Timmermann (1992) given in (2.80) or the forecast comparison statistic of Diebold and Mariano (1995) given in (2.74) can be
applied to assess the (relative) forecast performance of ANNs. In financial applications of ANNs, it is usual to consider other measures of forecast performance
as well. For example, the forecasts often are used in a trading strategy involving
active buying and selling stocks or currencies. A natural performance measure
is then to compare the profits from such an active strategy with the profits from
a buy-and-hold strategy; see Gençay (1998) for an example. The use of statistical or economic criteria can lead to radically different outcomes (see Leitch
and Tanner, 1991; Satchell and Timmermann, 1995). By means of an example
involving interest rate forecasting, Leitch and Tanner (1991) demonstrate that
the correlation between criteria such as MSPE and actual profits is not significant or even positive. By contrast, directional accuracy and profits appear to be
closely related. Satchell and Timmermann (1995) arrive at the same conclusion
by more formal arguments.

Impulse response analysis in neural networks

Similar to the regime-switching models in chapter 3, it is virtually impossible to examine the propagation of shocks in ANNs by using only the parameter estimates. Persistence of shocks is difficult to define in ANN(p,q) models. For specific models, one may derive parameter restrictions which ensure that the effect of shocks eventually dies out. In most cases, however, this cannot be done, and one has to rely on simulation techniques, such as the generalized impulse response functions discussed in chapter 3.

Example 5.2: ANNs for weekly absolute returns on the Frankfurt stock index Figure 5.14 shows GIRFs for the ANN(2,2) model estimated for weekly absolute returns on the DAX index, for different combinations of the values taken by the activation functions $G(x_t'\gamma_1)$ and $G(x_t'\gamma_2)$. The figures on the left-hand-side give GIRFs for shocks of magnitude $-4,-3,-2$ and -1 times the standard deviation of the in-sample residuals, whereas the figures on the right-hand-side give GIRFs for positive shocks of the same magnitudes. It is seen that the effects of shocks depend markedly on the values of the hidden units and on the sign of the shocks. When both activation functions are equal to zero, the impulse response declines fairly rapidly, in a monotonic and oscillatory fashion for negative and positive shocks, respectively. Where $G(x_t'\gamma_1) = 1$ and $G(x_t'\gamma_2) = 0$ negative shocks of moderate size again die out quickly. By contrast, large negative shocks are amplified as the horizon increases. Positive shocks are seen to have a negative impact, after which their effect decreases monotonically. Finally, where both hidden units are activated, the GIRFs are mirror images from the case where they both are not activated, in the sense that now the response to negative shocks declines in an oscillatory way, while the response to positive shocks declines monotonically.

5.5 ANNs and other regime-switching models

In this section we describe the relations between ANNs and the regime-switching models discussed in chapter 3, and explore whether ANNs are capable of capturing different types of regime-switching behaviour and other forms of nonlinearity.

Given that the ANN with one hidden unit in (5.3) was obtained from the STAR model in (5.1), it is not difficult to understand that these two models are closely related. In fact, the ANN($p,1$) model

$$y_t = \phi_0 + \phi_1 y_{t-1} + \phi_2 y_{t-2} + \cdots + \phi_p y_{t-p}$$
$$+ \beta_1 G(\gamma_{0,1} + \gamma_{1,1} y_{t-1} + \gamma_{2,1} y_{t-2} + \cdots + \gamma_{p,1} y_{t-p}) + \varepsilon_t,$$
$$(5.35)$$

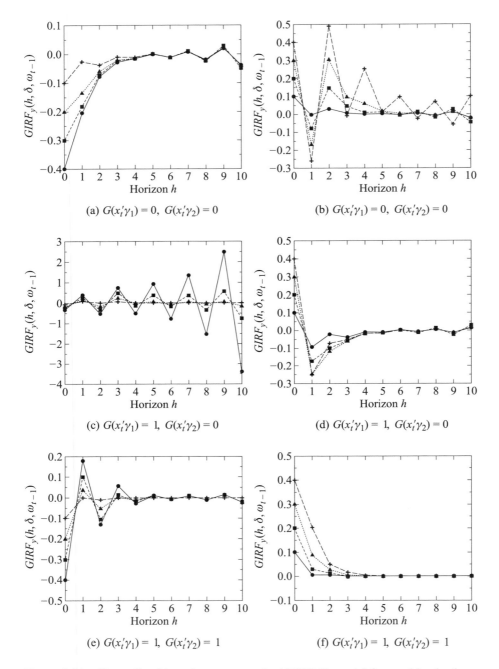

Figure 5.14 Generalized impulse responses in ANN(2,2) model for weekly absolute returns on the Frankfurt stock index, for different combinations of values of the activation functions in the hidden units

Panels (a), (c) and (e) give GIRFs for shocks of magnitude $-4, -3, -2$ and -1 times the standard deviation of the in-sample residuals, whereas panels (b), (d) and (f) give GIRFs for positive shocks of the same magnitudes can be regarded as both a generalization and a simplification of the STAR model as discussed in subsection 3.1.1,

$$
\begin{aligned}
y_t &= \phi_0 + \phi_1 y_{t-1} + \phi_2 y_{t-2} + \cdots + \phi_p y_{t-p} \\
&\quad + (\theta_0 + \theta_1 y_{t-1} + \theta_2 y_{t-2} + \cdots + \theta_p y_{t-p}) \\
&\quad \times G(\gamma_0 + \gamma_{1,1} y_{t-1}) + \eta_t.
\end{aligned} \tag{5.36}
$$

On the one hand, (5.35) generalizes (5.36) because the regime-switching is determined by p lagged values of y_t instead of only 1. On the other hand, (5.35) is simpler than (5.36) because only the intercept is allowed to switch, from ϕ_0 to $\phi_0 + \beta_1$, whereas in (5.36) all parameters (can) change, from ϕ_i to $\phi_i + \theta_i$, $i = 0, 1, \ldots, p$. A model which combines the added features of the ANN(p,1) and the STAR(p) model is given by

$$
y_t = x_t'\phi + x_t'\theta G(x_t'\gamma_1) + \varepsilon_t, \tag{5.37}
$$

where $x_t = (1, y_{t-1}, \ldots, y_{t-p})'$. So far, this extended ANN has not been used very often in practice.

Similarly, the ANN(p,q) model in (5.9) can be related to the Multiple Regime STAR (MRSTAR) model discussed in subsection 3.1.1. For example, consider the 4-regime MRSTAR model given in (3.14),

$$
\begin{aligned}
y_t &= [x_t'\phi_1(1 - G_1(y_{t-1})) + x_t'\phi_2 G_1(y_{t-1})][1 - G_2(y_{t-2})] \\
&\quad + [x_t'\phi_3(1 - G_1(y_{t-1})) + x_t'\phi_4 G_1(y_{t-1})]G_2(y_{t-2}) + \varepsilon_t,
\end{aligned} \tag{5.38}
$$

where both G_1 and G_2 are logistic functions $G_j(y_{t-j}) = (1+\exp\{-\gamma_j[y_{t-j} - c_j]\})^{-1}$, $j = 1, 2$. By imposing the restrictions $\phi_{i,j} = 0$, $i = 1, \ldots, p$, $j = 2, \ldots, 4$ and $\phi_{4,0} = \phi_{2,0} + \phi_{3,0} - \phi_{1,0}$, the model in (5.38) can be rewritten as

$$
y_t = x_t'\phi_1^* + \phi_{2,0}^* G_1(y_{t-1}) + \phi_{3,0}^* G_2(y_{t-2}) + \varepsilon_t, \tag{5.39}
$$

where $\phi_{1,j}^* = \phi_{1,j}$, $j = 1, \ldots, p$, $\phi_{2,0}^* = \phi_{2,0} - \phi_{1,0}$ and $\phi_{3,0}^* = \phi_{3,0} - \phi_{1,0}$. An ANN($p$,2) model is then obtained by replacing the arguments y_{t-1} and y_{t-2} in the logistic functions with general linear combinations $x_t'\gamma_1$ and $x_t'\gamma_2$.

Given that STAR models nest SETAR models as a special case, it is not surprising that ANNs also are closely related to SETAR models. In fact, ANNs with indicator functions instead of logistic functions in the hidden layer are among the first ones considered historically (see Warner and Misra, 1996, for an overview of the historical developments concerning ANNs). An ANN(p,q) with so-called threshold units is given by

$$
y_t = \beta_0 + \sum_{j=1}^{q} \beta_j I[x_t'\gamma_j] + \varepsilon_t, \tag{5.40}
$$

where $I[x_t'\gamma_j] = 1$ if $x_t'\gamma_j > 0$ and 0 otherwise. The ANN with logistic activation functions as given in (5.4) contains (5.40) as a special case. The logistic function $G(x_t'\gamma_j) = [1 + \exp(-x_t'\gamma_j)]^{-1}$ approaches the indicator function $I[x_t'\gamma_j]$ if one of the parameters $\gamma_{1,j}, \ldots, \gamma_{p,j}$ becomes very large. To see this, note that the logistic function can be rewritten in the format which should be familiar from the discussion on STAR models,

$$G(x_t'\gamma_j) = \frac{1}{1 + \exp(-\gamma_{h,j}[\tilde{x}_t'\tilde{\gamma}_j^* - \gamma_{0,j}^*])},$$

where $\tilde{\gamma}_j^* = (\gamma_{1,j}^*, \ldots, \gamma_{p,j}^*)'$, $\gamma_{i,j}^* = \gamma_{i,j}/\gamma_{h,j}$ for $i = 0, 1, \ldots, p$, and $1 \le h \le p$. If the parameter $\gamma_{h,j}$ becomes large, the transition of $G(x_t'\gamma_j)$ from 0 to 1 becomes almost instantaneous at $\tilde{x}_t'\tilde{\gamma}_j^* - \gamma_{0,j}^* = 0$. As this normalization of the activation function can be done with respect to any $\gamma_{h,j}$, $h = 1, \ldots, p$, it follows that only a single connection strength needs to become large for the logistic function to approximate an indicator function.

The relation between ANNs and Markov-Switching (MSW) models is less clear. In the MSW model, the regime-switching is governed by the unobserved Markov-process s_t, instead of lagged values of the time series itself or other observable variables, as in the SETAR and STAR models. Even though this implies nonlinear dynamic behaviour of the resultant time series y_t, it is not clear *a priori* whether or not this type of nonlinearity can be captured by ANNs. We will investigate this further in one of the simulation experiments below.

How do neural networks deal with different forms of nonlinearity?

In practice it sometimes may be difficult to select a specific parametric nonlinear time series model. As discussed in chapter 3, test-statistics do not always provide enough information on the particular type of nonlinearity that is present in a time series, while economic theory is not always helpful either. In such cases, one may maintain one or several ANN models. Because of their ability to approximate any nonlinear function, the output of the hidden layer(s) of the ANN may give some hint to the appropriate form of nonlinearity. Alternatively, one can just settle for ANNs from a forecasting perspective, and investigate whether any forecasting gains can be obtained by using these models. Our next set of experiments aims to investigate whether ANN models are useful when the data are indeed nonlinear. See Kuan and White (1994) for a similar exercise for chaotic time series.

In all experiments below, we generate 100 time series y_t of length $n = 1,000$. We estimate ANN(p,q) models as given in (5.9), with $p = 0, 1, 2, 3$ and $q = 0, 1, 2, 3$, using the first 750 observations by means of the estimation method as discussed in section 5.2. We compute the R^2, the in-sample success ratio SR, and the AIC and BIC to compare the in-sample fit of the various models. Using the estimated network, we compute 1-step-ahead forecasts for the final 250 observations of each series. To evaluate the models on their forecasting performance we compute the out-of-sample success ratio, the directional accuracy statistic of Pesaran and Timmermann (1992) as given in (2.81), MSPE and MAPE criteria and the test-statistic of Diebold and Mariano (1995) as given in (2.75). For time series generated from models which contain a linearly predictable component (experiments 5.2 and 5.3) we compare the forecast performance of the ANN(p,q) models with the forecast performance of the corresponding linear AR(p) model ($q = 0$), while we define the success ratio as the fraction of observations for which the predicted change $\hat{y}_{t|t-1} - y_t$ and the actual change $y_t - y_{t-1}$ have the same sign, where for the in-sample comparison $\hat{y}_{t|t-1}$ is the fitted value. For time series which cannot be forecast with linear models because they have zero autocorrelations at all lags (experiments 5.4 and 5.5), we compare the forecast performance of the neural networks with that of an AR(0) model, and compute the success ratio using the signs of $\hat{y}_{t|t-1}$ and y_t.

Experiment 5.2: SETAR model In the first experiment we generate data from the SETAR model

$$y_t = (\phi_{0,1} + \phi_{1,1}y_{t-1} + \phi_{2,1}y_{t-2})(1 - I[y_{t-1} > c])$$
$$+ (\phi_{0,2} + \phi_{1,2}y_{t-1} + \phi_{2,2}y_{t-2})I[y_{t-1} > c] + \varepsilon_t. \tag{5.41}$$

We set the autoregressive parameters equal to $\phi_{0,1} = 0$, $\phi_{1,1} = 1.4$, $\phi_{2,1} = -0.65$, $\phi_{0,2} = 0$, $\phi_{1,1} = 0.5$, $\phi_{2,1} = 0.14$, while the threshold c is set equal to 0. The residuals ε_t are drawn from a normal distribution with mean zero and variance 0.2^2. Table 5.6 shows the in- and out-of-sample summary statistics. Clearly, the ANN(p,q) model has no difficulty in detecting the SETAR-type nonlinearity and easily outperforms linear models, both in- and out-of-sample.

Experiment 5.3: Markov-Switching model To investigate whether ANNs can capture nonlinearity which is not driven by the time series itself but by another, unrelated process, we use the Markov-Switching model

$$y_t = \begin{cases} \phi_{0,1} + \phi_{1,1}y_{t-1} + \phi_{2,1}y_{t-2} + \varepsilon_t & \text{if } s_t = 1, \\ \phi_{0,2} + \phi_{1,2}y_{t-1} + \phi_{2,2}y_{t-2} + \varepsilon_t & \text{if } s_t = 2, \end{cases} \tag{5.42}$$

to generate artificial data. The autoregressive parameters in the two regimes are set to the same values as for the SETAR model considered above. The transition probabilities of the Markov chain s_t are specified as $p_{11} = 0.8$ and $p_{22} = 0.7$. The implied unconditional regime probabilities are equal to $P(s_t = 1) = 0.6$ and $P(s_t = 2) = 0.4$, see (3.17) and (3.18), which roughly correspond to the

Table 5.6 *Performance of ANNs when series are generated from a SETAR model*

p	q	In-sample				Out-of-sample				
		R^2	SR	AIC	BIC	SR	DA	Rank	MSPE	DM
0	0	—	0.61	0	0	0.61	—	13.00	0.14	—
1	0	0.59	0.61	0	0	0.61	100–0	11.51	0.06	—
1	1	0.60	0.61	0	0	0.61	100–0	10.03	0.99	11–0
1	2	0.60	0.61	0	0	0.61	99–0	10.11	0.99	11–0
1	3	0.60	0.61	0	0	0.61	99–0	10.32	0.99	11–0
2	0	0.65	0.66	0	0	0.66	100–0	7.56	0.05	—
2	1	0.68	0.68	0	35	0.68	100–0	4.93	0.90	80–0
2	2	0.70	0.69	23	57	0.69	100–0	2.60	0.87	91–0
2	3	0.70	0.70	57	6	0.69	100–0	2.21	0.86	88–0
3	0	0.65	0.66	0	0	0.66	100–0	7.34	0.05	—
3	1	0.68	0.68	0	1	0.68	100–0	4.92	0.90	77–0
3	2	0.70	0.70	5	1	0.69	100–0	3.13	0.87	85–0
3	3	0.70	0.70	15	0	0.69	100–0	3.34	0.87	83–0

Notes: Performance of ANN(p,q) models (5.9) when estimated on time series generated from the SETAR model (5.41).

Columns headed R^2 and SR contain the average R^2 and success ratio, AIC and BIC the number of replications for which the model is the preferred one according to the AIC and BIC, respectively, DA the number of replications for which the directional accuracy test as given in (2.81) is significantly positive–negative at the 5 per cent significance level. Rank is the average rank of the respective models according to MSPE.

MSPE contains the average MSPE for AR(p) models ($q = 0$), while for ANNs ($q = 1, 2, 3$), the average ratio of the MSPE of the model to the MSPE of the corresponding AR(p) model is given.

DM gives the number of replications for which the Diebold–Mariano test-statistic as given in (2.75) based on squared forecast errors indicates that the model performs better–worse than the AR(0) model at the 5 per cent significance level. All statistics are based upon 1-step-ahead forecasts for 100 replications of length $n = 1,000$, of which the first 750 observations are used for estimating the ANN.

probabilities that the series from the SETAR model (5.41) is in each of the two regimes.

The results set out in table 5.7 demonstrate that the ANN(p,q) model does not improve upon a linear AR(p) model, either in terms of in-sample fit or in terms of out-of-sample forecasting. Hence we conclude that neural networks cannot capture Markov-Switching-type nonlinearity.

Table 5.7   *Performance of ANNs when series are generated from a Markov-Switching model*

		In-sample				Out-of-sample				
p	q	R^2	*SR*	*AIC*	*BIC*	*SR*	*DA*	Rank	*MSPE*	*DM*
0	0	—	0.61	0	0	0.60	—	13.00	0.16	—
1	0	0.64	0.61	0	0	0.60	99–0	9.69	0.06	—
1	1	0.64	0.61	0	0	0.60	99–0	10.24	1.00	0–3
1	2	0.64	0.61	0	0	0.60	99–0	10.37	1.00	0–6
1	3	0.64	0.61	0	0	0.60	99–0	10.20	1.01	0–6
2	0	0.68	0.64	9	62	0.64	100–0	3.99	0.05	—
2	1	0.68	0.64	4	0	0.64	100–0	4.72	1.01	4–9
2	2	0.68	0.65	2	0	0.64	100–0	4.91	1.01	5–12
2	3	0.68	0.65	3	0	0.63	100–0	5.77	1.02	3–21
3	0	0.68	0.65	36	38	0.64	100–0	3.24	0.05	—
3	1	0.68	0.65	17	0	0.64	100–0	4.13	1.01	3–14
3	2	0.69	0.65	16	0	0.64	100–0	4.96	1.02	2–16
3	3	0.69	0.65	13	0	0.64	100–0	5.78	1.03	1–22

Notes: Performance of ANN(p,q) models (5.9) when estimated on time series generated from the Markov-Switching model (5.42).
See table 5.6 for explanation of the various entries.

Experiment 5.4: Bilinear model   As a third experiment, we generate time series from the bilinear model

$$y_t = \beta y_{t-2}\varepsilon_{t-1} + \varepsilon_t, \tag{5.43}$$

with $\beta = 0.6$. As shown by Granger and Andersen (1978), this model has zero autocorrelations at all lags and therefore cannot be forecast with linear models. The statistics shown in table 5.8 confirm that AR(p) models are not useful to describe or forecast these series. By contrast, the performance of ANN(p,q) models is quite encouraging. If the number of lags of y_t is taken at least equal to 2, which corresponds with the lag order of y_t in the bilinear term in (5.43), both the in-sample fit and the out-of-sample forecast performance improve considerably.

Experiment 5.5: GARCH(1,1) model   In the final experiment, we generate data from the GARCH(1,1) model

$$y_t = z_t \sqrt{h_t}, \tag{5.44}$$

$$h_t = \omega + \alpha_1 y_{t-1}^2 + \beta_1 h_{t-1}, \tag{5.45}$$

Table 5.8   *Performance of ANNs when series are generated from a bilinear model*

		In-sample				Out-of-sample				
p	q	R^2	SR	AIC	BIC	SR	DA	Rank	$MSPE$	DM
0	0	—	0.51	0	0	0.51	—	8.77	1.00	—
1	0	0.00	0.51	0	0	0.50	0–13	8.86	1.00	3–8
1	1	0.01	0.52	0	0	0.50	3–13	9.92	1.01	3–10
1	2	0.01	0.52	0	0	0.51	7–7	10.46	1.02	3–10
1	3	0.02	0.52	0	0	0.50	7–5	10.64	1.02	3–11
2	0	0.00	0.52	0	0	0.50	14–12	9.61	1.00	4–12
2	1	0.10	0.59	0	0	0.58	85–0	6.03	0.93	50–0
2	2	0.19	0.62	0	14	0.61	99–0	3.17	0.85	80–0
2	3	0.20	0.62	0	2	0.61	98–0	3.85	0.87	78–0
3	0	0.01	0.52	0	0	0.50	9–7	9.93	1.01	2–14
3	1	0.11	0.59	0	0	0.58	80–0	5.84	0.94	42–0
3	2	0.22	0.62	4	37	0.62	98–0	2.07	0.83	84–0
3	3	0.26	0.63	96	47	0.62	97–0	1.85	0.83	77–0

Notes: Performance of ANN(p,q) models (5.9) when estimated on time series generated from the bilinear model (5.43).

The forecast comparison of ANN(p,q) models in the columns headed *MSPE* and *DM* is relative to the random walk.

See table 5.6 for explanation of the various entries.

where we set $\alpha_1 = 0.2$, $\beta_1 = 0.6$ and $\omega = 1 - \alpha_1 - \beta_1$. The shocks z_t are drawn from a standard normal distribution.

At first sight it might seem rather strange to expect that an ANN can capture GARCH-type effects because the nonlinearity in GARCH models occurs in the (conditional) second moment of y_t, whereas ANNs are nonlinear models for the (conditional) first moment. However, the motivation for this experiment is (at least) twofold. First, GARCH and bilinear models have been shown to be closely related, in the sense that the resultant time series from these two models have similar properties and it might be quite difficult to distinguish between them (see Bera and Higgins, 1997). Given the successful modelling of bilinear time series in the previous experiment, one may wonder whether GARCH effects also can be captured with ANNs. Second, GARCH-type properties are one of the most prominent features of daily and weekly financial data, as we observed in chapter 4.

The results for this experiment are displayed in table 5.9, and clearly suggest that GARCH-type nonlinearity cannot be predicted with ANN models.

Table 5.9   *Performance of ANNs when series are generated from a GARCH(1,1) model*

		In-sample				Out-of-sample				
p	q	R^2	SR	AIC	BIC	SR	DA	Rank	MSPE	DM
0	0	—	0.51	10	93	0.50	—	4.27	1.00	—
1	0	0.00	0.51	0	1	0.50	3–20	4.56	1.00	4–6
1	1	0.01	0.52	2	1	0.51	8–11	5.69	1.05	3–7
1	2	0.02	0.52	2	1	0.50	5–8	6.92	1.06	1–12
1	3	0.02	0.52	2	0	0.50	5–5	6.98	1.06	2–10
2	0	0.00	0.51	1	1	0.50	5–7	4.75	1.00	1–6
2	1	0.02	0.52	4	1	0.51	10–2	6.55	1.03	4–3
2	2	0.03	0.53	5	1	0.50	6–2	8.33	1.05	2–21
2	3	0.04	0.53	13	0	0.50	5–4	9.19	1.05	1–25
3	0	0.01	0.52	1	1	0.50	5–8	5.29	1.01	1–12
3	1	0.03	0.53	4	0	0.50	8–6	7.87	1.04	0–18
3	2	0.05	0.53	13	0	0.50	9–2	9.73	1.12	0–27
3	3	0.06	0.54	43	0	0.50	5–3	10.87	1.17	0–41

Notes: Performance of ANN(p,q) models (5.9) when estimated on time series generated from the GARCH(1,1) model (5.44)–(5.45).
The forecast comparison of ANN(p,q) models in the columns headed *MSPE* and *DM* is relative to the random walk.
See table 5.6 for explanation of the various entries.

5.6   Testing for nonlinearity using ANNs

Even though an ANN is a parametric nonlinear model and we can give at least some interpretation to its structure, it is not common to think of an ANN as the actual data-generating process, but much more as an approximating model. For that reason, it does not make sense to test for neural network-type nonlinearity (in contrast to testing for SETAR, STAR and Markov-Switching-type nonlinearity, for example). However, precisely because of the approximation capabilities of ANNs, it is possible to use them to test for nonlinearity *in general*. White (1989a) and Lee, White and Granger (1993) develop such a portmanteau test for nonlinearity based on ANNs.

Consider again the ANN(p,q) model for y_t with q hidden units and p lags of the time series itself as inputs (extending the discussion below to ANNs with exogenous inputs is straightforward),

$$y_t = x_t'\phi + \sum_{j=1}^{q} \beta_j G(x_t'\gamma_j) + \varepsilon_t \quad t = 1, \ldots, n, \tag{5.46}$$

where $x_t = (1, y_{t-1}, \ldots, y_{t-p})'$. In case the dynamics in y_t are linear, the output of the hidden layer $\sum_{j=1}^{q} \beta_j G(x_t' \gamma_j)$ should be equal to zero (or at least constant). The null hypothesis of linearity in this model thus can be expressed as $H_0 : \beta_1 = \cdots = \beta_q = 0$. Notice that if this null hypothesis is true, the parameters γ_j are not identified, similar to the case of testing for STAR-type nonlinearity as discussed in subsection 3.3.2. White (1989a) suggests solving this identification problem by fixing these parameters *a priori*, by drawing them randomly from some distribution. The neural network test for neglected nonlinearity then is obtained in a number of steps. First, one estimates an AR(p) model for y_t, which renders residuals $\hat{u}_t$. Second, one draws random parameter values $\gamma_{i,j}^*$, $i = 0, \ldots, p$, $j = 1, 2, \ldots, q$, and computes the activation functions $G(x_t' \gamma_j^*)$, $j = 1, \ldots, q$. The test-statistic then can be computed as nR^2 from the auxiliary regression

$$\hat{u}_t = x_t' \alpha + \delta_1 G(x_t' \gamma_1^*) + \delta_2 G(x_t' \gamma_2^*) + \cdots + \delta_q G(x_t' \gamma_q^*) + \eta_t. \quad (5.47)$$

The resultant test has a χ^2 distribution with q degrees of freedom asymptotically.

Before the test can be implemented, two decisions have to be made. The most critical of these is the choice of the number of hidden units q in the alternative model (5.46). Lee, White and Granger (1993) suggest setting q fairly large – say, equal to 10 or 20 – in order to obtain a representative set of the possible patterns that the activation functions $G(\cdot)$ can take. A drawback of setting q large is that the resultant auxiliary regressors $G(x_t' \gamma_j^*)$ tend to be highly collinear. Lee, White and Granger (1993) therefore recommend including the first q^* principal components of $G(x_t' \gamma_j^*)$, $j = 1, \ldots, q$, in the auxiliary regression instead of the original activation functions. The number of principal components should be set fairly small – say, $q^* = 2$ or 3 – whereas they should also be orthogonal to the inputs x_t. This can be achieved by disregarding the largest principal component and using the second until $(q^* + 1)$st largest ones. The second decision to be made concerns the distribution from which to draw the parameters $\gamma_{i,j}$. Lee, White and Granger (1993) use a uniform distribution on the interval $[-2, 2]$. Notice that in the presence of exogenous inputs $z_{1t}, \ldots, z_{kt}$, it is crucial to rescale the variables such that they are of comparable magnitude.

The value of the neural network test obviously depends on the randomly drawn values for the unidentified parameters $\gamma_{i,j}$. Hence, the decision to reject or not reject the null hypothesis is to some extent due to chance. For one set of $\gamma_{i,j}^*$s one might reject linearity, while for another set one might not. An alternative method proposed by Lee, White and Granger (1993) is to compute the neural network test for several different draws of the $\gamma_{i,j}$ and use the Bonferroni inequality to obtain an upper bound on the p-value of the test.

Suppose the test is computed r times, with corresponding p-values $p_1, \ldots, p_r$ obtained from the asymptotic $\chi^2(q)$ distribution, and denote the ordered p-values as $p_{(1)}, \ldots, p_{(r)}$, with $p_{(1)}$ being the smallest. Intuitively, the Bonferroni inequality states that, if the null hypothesis is true, the probability of not rejecting on any of the r tests is at least $1 - r\alpha$, where α is the significance level used for the individual statistics. Put differently, the probability of at least one rejection is at most $r\alpha$. By reversing the argument, if the overall significance level of the r tests is to be α^*, the null hypothesis is rejected if $p_{(1)} \leq \alpha^*/r$. The classic Bonferroni bound thus is given by $rp_{(1)}$, which can be interpreted as the overall p-value of the r tests. Because this bound depends only on the smallest observed p-value, it might not be very accurate. Lee, White and Granger (1993) employ a modification due to Hochberg (1988). The decision rule in this case is to reject the null hypothesis at the α^* level if there exists a j such that $p_{(j)} \leq \alpha^*/(r - j + 1)$ for $j = 1, \ldots, r$. The improved Bonferroni bound of the p-value of the r tests jointly then becomes $\min_{j=1,\ldots,r}(r - j + 1)p_{(j)}$. Simulation evidence in Lee, White and Granger (1993) suggests that the neural network test indeed is a useful diagnostic check for neglected nonlinearity of various forms, and compares favourably with other portmanteau tests for nonlinearity such as the tests of Keenan (1985) and Tsay (1986), the RESET test of Ramsey (1969) and Thursby and Schmidt (1977), the information matrix test of White (1987, 1992), the bispectrum tests of Hinich (1982) and Ashley, Patterson and Hinich (1986). We refer to Granger and Teräsvirta (1993, chapter 6) for an overview of these test statistics.

In the neural network test above, the identification problem in the ANN (5.46) is handled by replacing the unidentified nuisance parameters $\gamma_{i,j}$ with random values. Teräsvirta, Lin and Granger (1993) tackle the problem in a different manner, analogous to the solution applied in testing for STAR-type nonlinearity. That is, the activation functions $G(x_t'\gamma_j)$ are replaced by third-order Taylor approximations around the null hypothesis, which alternatively can be expressed as $\gamma_j = 0$, $j = 1, \ldots, q$. This renders the reparameterized model

$$
y_t = x_t'\phi^* + \sum_{i=1}^{p}\sum_{j=i}^{p} \xi_{ij} y_{t-i} y_{t-j} + \sum_{i=1}^{p}\sum_{j=i}^{p}\sum_{k=j}^{p} \psi_{ijk} y_{t-i} y_{t-j} y_{t-k} + \eta_t,
$$

$$(5.48)$$

where ϕ^*, ξ_{ij} and ψ_{ijk} are functions of the parameters in the original model (5.46), such that the null hypothesis $\gamma_j = 0$, $j = 1, \ldots, q$, corresponds with $\xi_{ij} = 0$, $\psi_{ijk} = 0$, $i = 1, \ldots, p$, $j = i, \ldots, p$ and $k = j, \ldots, p$. This null hypothesis can be tested in a straightforward manner with a standard variable addition test. One drawback of this test is that the number of restrictions that is tested is equal to $p(p + 1)/2 + p(p + 1)(p + 2)/6$, which becomes large very quickly when p increases. Hence, to be able to apply the test, p needs to be set fairly small or the length of the time series has to be sufficiently large. Simulation results obtained by Teräsvirta, Lin and Granger (1993) suggest that this test performs better than the test based on (5.47).

Example 5.4: Testing for nonlinearity in weekly (absolute) stock index and exchange rate returns   We apply the two ANN-based tests for nonlinearity to weekly (absolute) stock index and exchange rate returns, over the sample from January 1986 until December 1992. Both tests are computed for $p = 1, 2, 3$ and 4 lagged returns as inputs. For the test of White (1989a), we follow the

Table 5.10   *Testing for nonlinearity in weekly stock index and exchange rate returns with ANN-based tests*

		ANN test				LM test			
	p	1	2	3	4	1	2	3	4
Stock market									
Amsterdam		0.000	0.020	0.001	0.398	0.000	0.000	0.000	0.000
Frankfurt		0.917	0.012	0.000	0.308	0.826	0.001	0.000	0.001
Hong Kong		0.015	0.077	0.003	0.073	0.013	0.011	0.000	0.000
London		0.000	0.000	0.011	0.194	0.000	0.000	0.002	0.037
New York		0.000	0.010	0.102	0.069	0.000	0.000	0.001	0.001
Paris		0.559	0.650	0.199	0.869	0.689	0.380	0.287	0.042
Singapore		0.000	0.001	0.001	0.066	0.000	0.000	0.000	0.000
Tokyo		0.139	0.475	0.351	0.092	0.058	0.017	0.000	0.000
Exchange rate									
Australian dollar		0.773	0.949	0.998	0.596	0.590	0.333	0.616	0.418
British pound		0.609	0.808	0.663	0.414	0.387	0.006	0.011	0.045
Canadian dollar		0.249	0.245	0.517	0.575	0.103	0.053	0.045	0.058
Dutch guilder		0.399	0.342	0.013	0.012	0.099	0.004	0.000	0.001
French franc		0.558	0.069	0.029	0.039	0.182	0.005	0.000	0.001
German Dmark		0.448	0.328	0.012	0.014	0.123	0.004	0.000	0.001
Japanese yen		0.110	0.055	0.126	0.310	0.033	0.087	0.024	0.051
Swiss franc		0.832	0.302	0.049	0.020	0.290	0.033	0.001	0.002

Notes: p-values of the ANN test for nonlinearity based on (5.47) [ANN test] and the test based on the reparameterized model (5.48) [LM test], applied to weekly stock and exchange rate returns.
The sample runs from January 1986 until December 1992. The p-value for the ANN test is the improved Bonferroni bound obtained from $r = 10$ replications of the statistic.

Table 5.11   *Testing for nonlinearity in weekly absolute stock index and exchange rate returns with ANN-based tests*

	p	ANN test				LM test			
		1	2	3	4	1	2	3	4
Stock market									
Amsterdam		0.000	0.001	0.262	0.036	0.000	0.000	0.000	0.000
Frankfurt		0.479	0.007	0.339	0.382	0.282	0.002	0.070	0.019
Hong Kong		0.000	0.011	0.000	0.117	0.000	0.000	0.000	0.000
London		0.000	0.000	0.000	0.000	0.000	0.000	0.000	0.000
New York		0.001	0.003	0.019	0.172	0.001	0.024	0.063	0.005
Paris		0.619	0.194	0.742	0.491	0.431	0.266	0.219	0.431
Singapore		0.000	0.001	0.011	0.168	0.000	0.000	0.000	0.000
Tokyo		0.588	0.001	0.067	0.670	0.212	0.004	0.019	0.016
Exchange rate									
Australian dollar		0.481	0.196	0.695	0.078	0.122	0.114	0.286	0.424
British pound		0.000	0.000	0.002	0.024	0.000	0.000	0.001	0.001
Canadian dollar		0.981	0.786	0.008	0.629	0.918	0.444	0.014	0.002
Dutch guilder		0.144	0.000	0.001	0.264	0.063	0.000	0.001	0.021
French franc		0.604	0.000	0.010	0.426	0.512	0.000	0.001	0.002
German Dmark		0.157	0.000	0.001	0.567	0.063	0.000	0.002	0.027
Japanese yen		0.366	0.357	0.444	0.003	0.190	0.154	0.182	0.118
Swiss franc		0.933	0.333	0.002	0.639	0.618	0.121	0.025	0.192

Notes: p-values of the ANN test for nonlinearity based on (5.47) [ANN test] and the test based on the reparameterized model (5.48) [LM test], applied to weekly absolute stock and exchange rate returns.

The sample runs from January 1986 until December 1992.

The p-value for the ANN test is the improved Bonferroni bound obtained from $r = 10$ replications of the statistic.

recommendations of Lee, White and Granger (1993). We start with an ANN with $q = 10$ hidden units, and sample the parameters $\gamma_{i,j}$ from a uniform distribution on $[-2, 2]$. Next, we compute the second and third largest principal components of $G(x_t' \gamma_1^*), \ldots, G(x_t' \gamma_{10}^*)$ and compute the test-statistic as n times the R^2 from a regression of the residuals from an AR(p) model on x_t and these principal components. This procedure is repeated $r = 10$ times, and the p-value is computed using the improved Bonferroni bound as discussed above.

Not unexpectedly, the test results in tables 5.10 and 5.11 show that there is ample evidence of nonlinearity in (absolute) returns.

Conclusion

In this chapter we reviewed several modelling and inference issues for artificial neural networks. We demonstrated that they can be useful for pattern recognition, forecasting and diagnostic checking. Finally, we illustrated that it pays off to open the 'black box', and spend some time analysing the properties of a neural network.

6 Conclusions

In this book we discussed nonlinear time series models for financial asset returns, which can be used for generating out-of-sample forecasts for returns and volatility. The reason for considering nonlinear models is the observation that many financial time series display typical nonlinear characteristics, as documented in chapters 1 and 2. Important examples of those features are the occasional presence of (sequences of) aberrant observations and the possible existence of regimes within which returns and volatility display different dynamic behaviour. Through an extensive forecasting experiment (for a wide range of daily data on stock markets and exchange rates), we also demonstrated that linear time series models do not yield reliable forecasts. Of course, this does not automatically imply that nonlinear time series models do but, as we argued in this book, it is worth a try. As there is a host of possible nonlinear time series models, we decided to review in chapters 3, 4 and 5, the (what we believe to be) currently most relevant ones and the ones that are most likely to persist as practical descriptive and forecasting devices.

In chapter 3, we discussed several regime-switching models such as the self-exciting threshold model, the smooth transition model and the Markov-Switching model. In this chapter we confined the analysis to the returns on financial assets, although they can also be considered for measures of risk (or volatility) like squared or absolute returns. We considered tools for specifying, estimating and evaluating these models and methods to generate out-of-sample forecasts. Illustrations for several empirical series showed that these models can be quite useful in practice.

In chapter 4, we considered similar kinds of regime-switching models for unobserved volatility, which in fact amounted to various extensions of the basic GARCH model. This well known and often-applied model exploits the empirical regularity that aberrant observations in financial time series appear in clusters (thereby indicating periods of high volatility), and hence that out-of-sample forecasts for volatility can be generated. The models in chapter 4 mainly challenge the assumption in the basic GARCH model that the model parameters are constant over time and/or that positive and negative news have the same impact on subsequent volatility. Indeed, the empirical analysis in this chapter shows that it seems worthwhile to consider a relaxation of these assumptions. Again, we discussed tools for specification, estimation and evaluation, and we outlined how out-of-sample forecasts can be generated and evaluated.

Finally, in chapter 5, we dealt with a currently fashionable class of models – that is, with artificial neural networks. In contrast to the prevalent strategy in the empirical finance literature (which may lead people to believe that these models are merely a passing fad), we decided to 'open up the black box', so to say, and to explicitly demonstrate how and why these models can be useful in practice. Indeed, the empirical applications in this chapter suggest that neural networks can be quite useful for out-of-sample forecasting and for recognizing a variety of patterns in the data.

Having reviewed these three areas in modelling empirical finance data, we are well aware of the fact that we have missed out (or at least, have not discussed in similar detail) several other potentially fruitful models. Examples of these are the stochastic volatility models and the models that address possible fractional integration properties of financial returns (and volatility). Also, to keep matters at a tractable level, we completely abstained from detailed discussions of seasonality. Indeed, there is a large body of literature documenting that financial returns display day-of-the-week or month-of-the-year effects. It seems to us, though, that extending the models presented in this book to incorporate seasonal features should not be too complicated. Additionally, we did not treat models for data that are measured at higher frequencies than a day. As intra-day data have become available, the time series analyst faces new opportunities, which may include (but probably will expand on) the models discussed in this book: for example, this abundance of data facilitates the use of nonparametric methods. Finally, we did not treat multivariate nonlinear models in substantial detail. Only for this last omission do we have a good excuse – that the analysis of multivariate nonlinear models has been taken up only very recently, and at the time of writing there are no generally accepted ideas on how to construct such multivariate models in the first place. It is our experience so far that these models contain a wealth of parameters and that they are not easy to analyse in practice. We do believe, though, that developing useful multivariate (linear and nonlinear) time series models is a very important area of further research.

Another area of future research, which we would like to address in a little more detail here, concerns the practical use of the models discussed in this book. One of the main conclusions from the material presented, at least as we see it, is that the informative content in financial data (that can be exploited for generating reliable forecasts) is not equally distributed over the observations. Put otherwise, some data points are more important than others in the sense that they can be predicted relatively easily or that they can serve a useful basis for generating forecasts. In practical terms this would imply that, even though the model is specified for all observations, it is used only infrequently: for example, an ARCH-type model would then be used only during volatile periods. One may even consider extending this notion of more and less relevant observations by modifying parameter estimation methods.

As the title already indicates, this book mainly deals with time series models. A natural question is now whether these models can be usefully implemented in day-to-day financial practice. Of course, having reliable forecasts at hand can be rather important, but still the question remains open whether one learns anything about the underlying economic process. We would not want to claim that the practical adequacy of a nonlinear time series model refutes, for example, the market efficiency hypothesis, but we do believe that the empirical evidence should be taken seriously when considering, for example, Value-at-Risk, option pricing and portfolio management. Much too often it is assumed that returns have a symmetric distribution (and often unconditional normal) around a constant mean and with common variance. The empirical finance literature provides ample evidence that this assumption is not even close to being valid. The inclusion of this empirical evidence into theoretical and empirical models in finance seems to us a genuine challenge for further research.

Bibliography

Abraham, A. and D.L. Ikenberry, 1994. The individual investor and the weekend effect, *Journal of Financial and Quantitative Analysis* 29, 263–78

Akaike, H., 1974. A new look at statistical model identification, *IEEE Transactions on Automatic Control* AC-19, 716–23

Akgiray, V., 1989. Conditional heteroskedasticity in time series of stock returns: evidence and forecasts, *Journal of Business* 62, 55–80

Al-Qassam, M.S. and J.A. Lane, 1989. Forecasting exponential autoregressive models of order 1, *Journal of Time Series Analysis* 10, 95–113

Anděl, J., 1989. Stationary distribution of some nonlinear AR(1) processes, *Kybernetika* 25, 453–60

Andersen, T. and T. Bollerslev, 1998. Answering the skeptics: yes, standard volatility models do provide accurate forecasts, *International Economic Review* 39, 885–906

Anderson, H.M., 1997. Transaction costs and nonlinear adjustment towards equilibrium in the US Treasury Bill market, *Oxford Bulletin of Economics and Statistics* 59, 465–84

Anderson, H.M. and F. Vahid, 1998. Testing multiple equation systems for common nonlinear components, *Journal of Econometrics* 84, 1–36

Anderson, H.M., K. Nam and F. Vahid, 1999. Asymmetric nonlinear smooth transition GARCH models, in P. Rothman (ed.), *Nonlinear Time Series Analysis of Economic and Financial Data*, Boston: Kluwer, 191–207

Anderson, T.W., 1971. *The Statistical Analysis of Time Series*, New York: John Wiley

Ashley, R., D.M. Patterson and M.J. Hinich, 1986. A diagnostic test for nonlinear serial dependence in time series fitting errors, *Journal of Time Series Analysis* 7, 165–78

Astatkie, T., D.G. Watts and W.E. Watt, 1997. Nested threshold autoregressive (NeTAR) models, *International Journal of Forecasting* 13, 105–16

Attanasio, O.P., 1991. Risk, time varying second moments and market efficiency, *Review of Economic Studies* 58, 479–94

Azoff, E.M., 1994. *Neural Network Time Series Forecasting of Financial Markets*, Chichester: Wiley

Baba, Y., R.F. Engle, D.F. Kraft and K.F. Kroner, 1991. Multivariate simultaneous generalized ARCH, Department of Economics, University of California, San Diego, unpublished manuscript

Bacon, D.W. and D.G. Watts, 1971. Estimating the transition between two intersecting straight lines, *Biometrika* 58, 525–34

Bai, J., 1997. Estimating multiple breaks one at a time, *Econometric Theory* 13, 315–52

Bai, J. and P. Perron, 1998. Estimating and testing linear models with multiple structural changes, *Econometrica* 66, 47–78

Baillie, R.T. and T. Bollerslev, 1991. Intra-day and inter-market volatility in foreign exchange rates, *Review of Economic Studies* 58, 565–85

1992. Prediction in dynamic models with time-dependent conditional variances, *Journal of Econometrics* 52, 91–113

Baillie, R.T., T. Bollerslev and H.-O. Mikkelsen, 1996. Fractionally integrated generalized autoregressive conditional heteroskedasticity, *Journal of Econometrics* 74, 3–30

Balke, N.S. and T.B. Fomby, 1997. Threshold cointegration, *International Economic Review* 38, 627–46

Banerjee, A., J.J. Dolado, J.W. Galbraith and D.F. Hendry, 1993. *Co-integration, Error-correction, and the Econometric Analysis of Nonstationary Data*, Oxford: Oxford University Press

Bates, D.M. and D.G. Watts, 1988. *Nonlinear Regression and its Applications*, New York: John Wiley

Bera, A.K. and M.L. Higgins, 1993. A survey of ARCH models: properties, estimation and testing, *Journal of Economic Surveys* 7, 305–66

1997. ARCH and bilinearity as competing models for nonlinear dependence, *Journal of Business & Economic Statistics* 15, 43–50

Bera, A.K., M.L. Higgins and S. Lee, 1992. Interaction between autocorrelation and conditional heteroskedasticity: a random coefficients approach, *Journal of Business & Economic Statistics* 10, 133–42

Beran, J., 1995. Maximum likelihood estimation of the differencing parameter for invertible short and long memory autoregressive integrated moving average models, *Journal of the Royal Statistical Society* B 57, 654–72

Berben, R.-P. and D. van Dijk, 1999. Unit root tests and asymmetric adjustment – a reassessment, *Econometric Institute Report* 9902, Erasmus University Rotterdam

Berndt, E.R., B.H. Hall, R.E. Hall and J.A. Hausman, 1974. Estimation and inference in nonlinear statistical models, *Annals of Economic and Social Measurement* 3, 653–65

Bessembinder, H. and M.G. Hertzel, 1993. Return autocorrelations around nontrading days, *Review of Financial Studies* 6, 155–89

Black, F., 1976. The pricing of commodity contracts, *Journal of Financial Economics* 3, 167–79

Boldin, M.D., 1996. A check on the robustness of Hamilton's Markov Switching model approach to the economic analysis of the business cycle, *Studies in Nonlinear Dynamics and Econometrics* 1, 35–46

Bollerslev, T., 1986. Generalized autoregressive conditional heteroscedasticity, *Journal of Econometrics* 31, 307–27

1987. A conditionally heteroskedastic time series model for speculative prices and rates of return, *Review of Economics and Statistics* 69, 542–7

1988. On the correlation structure for the generalized autoregressive conditional heteroskedastic process, *Journal of Time Series Analysis* 9, 121–31

1990. Modelling the coherence in short-run nominal exchange rates: A multivariate generalized ARCH approach, *Review of Economics and Statistics* 72, 498–505

Bollerslev, T. and E. Ghysels, 1996. Periodic autoregressive conditional heteroskedasticity, *Journal of Business & Economic Statistics* 14, 139–51

Bollerslev, T. and H.-O. Mikkelsen, 1996. Modeling and pricing long memory in stock
market volatility, *Journal of Econometrics* 73, 151–84

Bollerslev, T. and J.M. Wooldridge, 1992. Quasi-maximum likelihood estimation and
inference in dynamic models with time-varying covariances, *Econometric Reviews*
11, 143–72

Bollerslev, T., R.Y. Chou and K.F. Kroner, 1992. ARCH modeling in finance: a review
of the theory and empirical evidence, *Journal of Econometrics* 52, 5–59

Bollerslev, T., R.F. Engle and D.B. Nelson, 1994. ARCH models, in R.F. Engle and D.L.
McFadden (eds.), *Handbook of Econometrics IV*, Amsterdam: Elsevier Science,
2961–3038

Bollerslev, T., R.F. Engle and J.M. Wooldridge, 1988. A capital asset pricing model
with time varying covariances, *Journal of Political Economy* 96, 116–31

Bos, C., P.H. Franses and M. Ooms, 1999. Re-analyzing inflation rates: evidence of
long memory and level shifts, *Empirical Economics* 24, 427–49

Boswijk, H.P., 2001. *Asymptotic Theory for Integrated Processes*, Oxford: Oxford
University Press

Boudoukh, J., M.P. Richardson and R.F. Whitelaw, 1994. A tale of three schools: insights
on autocorrelations of short-horizon stock returns, *Review of Financial Studies*
7, 539–73

Box, G.E.P. and G.M. Jenkins, 1970. *Time Series Analysis; Forecasting and Control*,
San Francisco: Holden-Day

Box, G.E.P., G.M. Jenkins and G.C. Reinsel, 1994. *Time Series Analysis; Forecasting
and Control*, 3rd edn., Englewood Cliffs: Prentice-Hall

Brailsford, T.J. and R.W. Faff, 1996. An evaluation of volatility forecasting techniques,
Journal of Banking and Finance 20, 419–38

Breusch, T.S. and A.R. Pagan, 1979. A simple test for heteroscedasticity and random
coefficient variation, *Econometrica* 47, 1287–94

Brock, W.A. and C. Hommes, 1998. Heterogeneous beliefs and routes to chaos in a simple asset pricing model, *Journal of Economic Dynamics and Control* 22, 1235–74

Brock, W.A., D.A. Hsieh and B. LeBaron, 1991. *A Test of Nonlinear Dynamics, Chaos
and Instability: Theory and Evidence*, Cambridge, MA: MIT Press

Brock, W.A., J. Lakonishok and B. LeBaron, 1992. Simple technical trading rules and
the stochastic properties of stock returns, *Journal of Finance* 47, 1731–65

Brock, W.A., W. Dechert, J.A. Scheinkman and B. LeBaron, 1996. A test for independence based on the correlation dimension, *Econometric Reviews* 15, 197–235

Brockwell, P. and J. Davis, 1997. *Time Series Analysis*, Berlin: Springer Verlag

Brooks, C., 1996. Testing for nonlinearity in daily sterling exchange rates, *Applied
Financial Economics* 6, 307–17

1997. Linear and nonlinear (non-)forecastibility of high-frequency exchange rates,
Journal of Forecasting 16, 125–45

1998. Predicting stock index volatility: can market volume help?, *Journal of Forecasting* 17, 57–80

Brooks, C. and S.P. Burke, 1997. Large and small sample information criteria for
GARCH models based on estimation of Kullback–Leibler, *Discussion Papers in
Quantitative Economics and Computing* 53, University of Reading

1998. Forecasting exchange rate volatility using conditional variance models selected by information criteria, *Economics Letters* 61, 273–8

Brown, B.Y. and R.S. Mariano, 1989. Predictors in dynamic nonlinear models: large sample behaviour, *Econometric Theory* 5, 430–52

Bustos, O.H. and V.J. Yohai, 1986. Robust estimates for ARMA models, *Journal of the American Statistical Association* 81, 155–68

Cai, J., 1994. A Markov model of switching-regime ARCH, *Journal of Business & Economic Statistics* 12, 309–16

Campbell, J.Y., A.W. Lo and A.C. MacKinlay, 1997. *The Econometrics of Financial Markets*, Princeton: Princeton University Press

Caner, M. and B.E. Hansen, 1997. Threshold autoregressions with a unit root, *Working Papers in Economics* 381, Boston College

Cao, C.Q. and R.S. Tsay, 1992. Nonlinear time series analysis of stock volatilities, *Journal of Applied Econometrics* 7, S165–S185

Carroll, S.M. and B.W. Dickinson, 1989. Construction of neural nets using the radon transform, *Proceedings of the IEEE Conference on Neural Networks* (Washington DC), New York: IEEE Press, 607–11

Chan, K.S., 1990. Testing for threshold autoregression, *Annals of Statistics* 18, 1886–94

1991. Percentage points for likelihood ratio tests for threshold autoregression, *Journal of the Royal Statistical Society* B 53, 691–6

1993. Consistency and limiting distribution of the least squares estimator of a threshold autoregressive model, *Annals of Statistics* 21, 520–33

Chan, K.S. and H. Tong, 1985. On the use of the deterministic Lyapunov function for the ergodicity of stochastic difference equations, *Advances in Applied Probability* 17, 666–78

1986. On estimating thresholds in autoregressive models, *Journal of Time Series Analysis* 7, 179–90

1990. On likelihood ratio tests for threshold autoregression, *Journal of the Royal Statistical Society* B 52, 469–76

Chan, K.S., J.D. Petrucelli, H. Tong and S.W. Woolford, 1985. A multiple threshold AR(1) model, *Journal of Applied Probability* 22, 267–79

Chan, W.S. and S.H. Cheung, 1994. On robust estimation of threshold autoregressions, *Journal of Forecasting* 13, 37–49

Chappell, D., J. Padmore, P. Mistry and C. Ellis, 1996. A threshold model for the French franc/Deutschmark exchange rate, *Journal of Forecasting* 15, 155–64

Chen, C. and L.-M. Liu, 1993. Joint estimation of model parameters and outlier effects in time series, *Journal of the American Statistical Association* 88, 284–97

Chen, R., 1995. Threshold variable selection in open-loop threshold autoregressive models, *Journal of Time Series Analysis* 16, 461–81

Cheng, B. and D.M. Titterington, 1994. Neural networks: a review from a statistical perspective, *Statistical Science* 9, 2–54

Cheung, Y.-W., 1993. Long memory in foreign-exchange rates, *Journal of Business & Economic Statistics* 11, 93–101

Christodoulakis, G.A. and S.E. Satchell, 1998. Hashing GARCH: a re-assessment of volatility forecasting performance, in J. Knight and S.E. Satchell (eds.), *Forecasting Volatility in the Financial Market*, New York: Butterworth-Heinemann

Christoffersen, P.F., 1998. Evaluating interval forecasts, *International Economic Review* 39, 841–62

Chu, C.-S.J., 1995. Detecting parameter shifts in GARCH models, *Econometric Reviews* 14, 241–66

Clare, A.D., Z. Psaradakis and S.H. Thomas, 1995. An analysis of seasonality in the UK equity market, *Economic Journal* 105, 398–409

Clements, M.P. and D.F. Hendry, 1998. *Forecasting Economic Time Series*, Cambridge: Cambridge University Press

Clements, M.P. and J. Smith, 1997. The performance of alternative forecasting methods for SETAR models, *International Journal of Forecasting* 13, 463–75

   1998. Nonlinearities in exchange rates, University of Warwick, unpublished manuscript

   1999. A Monte Carlo study of the forecasting performance of empirical SETAR models, *Journal of Applied Econometrics* 14, 123–42

Crato, N. and P.J.F. de Lima, 1994. Long-memory and nonlinearity: a time series analysis of stock returns and volatilities, *Managerial Finance* 20, 49–67

Creedy, J. and V.L. Martin, 1994. *Chaos and Non-linear Models in Economics: Theory and Applications*, Brookfield, VT: Edward Elgar

Cumby, R., S. Figlewski and J. Hasbrouck, 1993. Forecasting volatility and correlations with EGARCH models, *Journal of Derivatives* Winter, 51–63

Cybenko, G., 1989. Approximation by superpositions of a sigmoid function, *Mathematics of Control Signals and Systems* 2, 303–14

Dacco, R. and S.E. Satchell, 1999. Why do regime-switching models forecast so badly?, *Journal of Forecasting* 18, 1–16

Danielsson, J., 1994. Stochastic volatility in asset prices: estimation with simulated maximum likelihood, *Journal of Econometrics* 61, 375–400

Danielsson, J. and J.-F. Richard, 1993. Accelerated Gaussian importance sampler with application to dynamic latent variable models, *Journal of Applied Econometrics* 8, S153–S174

Davidson, R. and J.G. MacKinnon, 1985. Heteroskedasticity-robust tests in regression directions, *Annales de l'INSEE* 59/60, 183–218

Davies, R.B., 1977. Hypothesis testing when a nuisance parameter is present only under the alternative, *Biometrika* 64, 247–54

   1987. Hypothesis testing when a nuisance parameter is present only under the alternative, *Biometrika* 74, 33–43

Day, T.E. and C.M. Lewis, 1992. Stock market volatility and the information content of stock index options, *Journal of Econometrics* 52, 267–87

de Gooijer, J.G., 1998. On threshold moving-average models, *Journal of Time Series Analysis* 19, 1–18

de Gooijer, J.G. and P. de Bruin, 1998. On forecasting SETAR processes, *Statistics and Probability Letters* 37, 7–14

de Gooijer, J.G. and K. Kumar, 1992. Some recent developments in non-linear time series modelling, testing and forecasting, *International Journal of Forecasting* 8, 135–56

Dempster, A.P., N.M. Laird and D.B. Rubin, 1977. Maximum likelihood from incomplete data using the EM algorithm, *Journal of the Royal Statistical Society* B39, 1–38

Denby, L. and R.D. Martin, 1979. Robust estimation of the first-order autoregressive parameter, *Journal of the American Statistical Association* 74, 140–6

Dickey, D.A. and W.A. Fuller, 1979. Distribution of the estimators for autoregressive time series with a unit root, *Journal of the American Statistical Association* 74, 427–31

1981. Likelihood ratio statistics for autoregressive time series with a unit root, *Econometrica* 49, 1057–72

Dickey, D.A. and S.G. Pantula, 1987. Determining the order of differencing in autoregressive processes, *Journal of Business & Economic Statistics* 5, 455–61

Diebold, F.X. and J.A. Lopez, 1995. Modelling volatility dynamics, in K. Hoover (ed.), *Macroeconometrics – Developments, Tensions and Prospects*, Boston: Kluwer, 427–72

Diebold, F.X. and R.S. Mariano, 1995. Comparing predictive accuracy, *Journal of Business & Economic Statistics* 13, 253–63

Diebold, F.X. and J.A. Nason, 1990. Nonparametric exchange rate prediction, *Journal of International Economics* 28, 315–32

Diebold, F.X. and M. Nerlove, 1989. The dynamics of exchange rate volatility: a multivariate latent factor GARCH model, *Journal of Applied Econometrics* 4, 1–21

Ding, Z. and C.W.J. Granger, 1996. Modeling volatility persistence of speculative returns: a new approach, *Journal of Econometrics* 73, 185–215

Ding, Z., C.W.J. Granger and R.F. Engle, 1993. A long memory property of stock market returns and a new model, *Journal of Empirical Finance* 1, 83–106

Donaldson, R.G. and M. Kamstra, 1996. Forecast combining with neural networks, *Journal of Forecasting* 15, 49–61

1997. An artificial neural network-GARCH model for international stock return volatility, *Journal of Empirical Finance* 4, 17–46

Dueker, M.J., 1997. Markov Switching in GARCH processes and mean-reverting stock-market volatility, *Journal of Business & Economic Statistics* 15, 26–34

Duffie, D. and K.J. Singleton, 1993. Simulated moments estimation of Markov models of asset prices, *Econometrica* 61, 929–52

Dwyer, G.P., P. Locke and W. Yu, 1996. Index arbitrage and nonlinear dynamics between the S&P 500 futures and cash, *Review of Financial Studies* 9, 301–32

Eitrheim, Ø. and T. Teräsvirta, 1996. Testing the adequacy of smooth transition autoregressive models, *Journal of Econometrics* 74, 59–76

Enders, W. and C.W.J. Granger, 1998. Unit-root tests and asymmetric adjustment with an example using the term structure of interest rates, *Journal of Business & Economic Statistics* 16, 304–11

Engle, R.F., 1982. Autoregressive conditional heteroscedasticity with estimates of the variance of United Kingdom inflation, *Econometrica* 50, 987–1007

1983. Estimates of the variance of US inflation based upon the ARCH model, *Journal of Money, Credit, and Banking* 15, 286–301

Engle, R.F. and T. Bollerslev, 1986. Modelling the persistence of conditional variances, *Econometric Reviews* 5, 1–50 (with discussion)

Engle, R.F. and G. González-Rivera, 1991. Semiparametric ARCH models, *Journal of Business & Economic Statistics* 9, 345–60

Engle, R.F. and S. Kozicki, 1993. Testing for common features, *Journal of Business & Economic Statistics* 11, 369–95 (with discussion)

Engle, R.F. and K.F. Kroner, 1995. Multivariate simultaneous generalized ARCH, *Econometric Theory* 11, 122–50

Engle, R.F. and V.K. Ng, 1993. Measuring and testing the impact of news on volatility, *Journal of Finance* 48, 1749–78

Engle, R.F. and R. Susmel, 1993. Common volatility in international equity markets, *Journal of Business & Economic Statistics* 11, 167–76

Engle, R.F., D.F. Hendry and D. Trumble, 1985. Small-sample properties of ARCH estimators and tests, *Canadian Journal of Economics* 18, 66–93

Engle, R.F., T. Ito and W.-L. Lin, 1990. Meteor showers or heat waves? Heteroskedastic intra-daily volatility in the foreign exchange market, *Econometrica* 58, 525–42

Engle, R.F., D.M. Lilien and R.P. Robins, 1987. Estimating time varying risk premia in the term structure: the ARCH-M model, *Econometrica* 55, 391–407

Engle, R.F., V.K. Ng and M. Rothschild, 1990. Asset pricing with a factor ARCH covariance structure: empirical estimates for Treasury Bills, *Journal of Econometrics* 45, 213–38

Engle, R.F., C.-H. Hong, A. Kane and J. Noh, 1993. Arbitrage valuation of variance forecasts with simulated options, in D.M. Chance and R.R. Trippi (eds.), *Advances in Futures and Options Research*, Greenwich, CN: JAI Press

Fama, E.F., 1965. The behavior of stock market prices, *Journal of Business* 38, 34–105

Fan, J. and I. Gijbels, 1996. *Local Polynomial Modeling and its Applications*, London: Chapman & Hall

Fiorentini, G., G. Calzolari and L. Panatoni, 1996. Analytic derivatives and the computation of GARCH estimates, *Journal of Applied Econometrics* 11, 399–417

Fornari, F. and A. Mele, 1996. Modeling the changing asymmetry of conditional variances, *Economics Letters* 50, 197–203

1997. Sign- and volatility-switching ARCH models: theory and applications to international stock markets, *Journal of Applied Econometrics* 12, 49–65

Franses, P.H., 1995. IGARCH and variance changes in the long run US interest rate, *Applied Economics Letters* 2, 113–14

1996. *Periodicity and Stochastic Trends in Economic Time Series*, Oxford: Oxford University Press

1998. *Time Series Models for Business and Economic Forecasting*, Cambridge: Cambridge University Press

Franses, P.H. and G. Draisma, 1997. Recognizing changing seasonal patterns using artificial neural networks, *Journal of Econometrics* 81, 273–80

Franses, P.H. and H. Ghijsels, 1999. Additive outliers, GARCH and forecasting volatility, *International Journal of Forecasting* 15, 1–9

Franses, P.H. and R. Paap, 2000. Modeling day-of-the-week seasonality in the S&P 500 index, *Applied Financial Economics*

Franses, P.H. and D. van Dijk, 1996. Forecasting stock market volatility using nonlinear GARCH models, *Journal of Forecasting* 15, 229–35

Franses, P.H. and K. van Griensven, 1998. Forecasting exchange rates using neural networks for technical trading rules, *Studies in Nonlinear Dynamics and Econometrics* 2, 109–16

Franses, P.H. and P. van Homelen, 1998. On forecasting exchange rates using neural networks, *Applied Financial Economics* 8, 589–96

Franses, P.H., D. van Dijk and A. Lucas, 1998. Short patches of outliers, ARCH, and volatility modeling, Tinbergen Institute Discussion Paper 98-057/4

French, K.R., 1980. Stock returns and the weekend effect, *Journal of Financial Economics* 8, 55–69

Friedman, B.M. and D.I. Laibson, 1989. Economic implications of extraordinary movements in stock prices, *Brookings Papers on Economic Activity* 20, 137–89 (with comments and discussion)

Fuller, W.A., 1996. *Introduction to Statistical Time Series*, 3rd edn. New York: John Wiley (1st edn. 1976)

Funabashi, K., 1989. On the approximate realization of continuous mappings by neural networks, *Neural Networks* 2, 183–92

Gallant, A.R., 1987. *Nonlinear Statistical Models*, New York: John Wiley

Gallant, A.R., P.E. Rossi and G. Tauchen, 1992. Stock prices and volume, *Review of Financial Studies* 5, 199–242

1993. Nonlinear dynamic structures, *Econometrica* 61, 871–908

Gately, E., 1996. *Neural Networks for Financial Forecasting*, New York: John Wiley

Gençay, R., 1996. Non-linear prediction of security returns with moving average rules, *Journal of Forecasting* 15, 165–74

1998. Optimization of technical trading rules and the profitability in security markets, *Economics Letters* 59, 249–54

1999. Linear, non-linear and essential foreign exchange rate prediction with simple technical trading rules, *Journal of International Economics* 47, 91–107

Gençay, R. and T. Stengos, 1998. Moving average rules, volume and the predictability of security returns with feedforward networks, *Journal of Forecasting* 17, 401–14

Ghysels, E., A.C. Harvey and E. Renault, 1996. Stochastic volatility, in G.S. Maddala and C.R. Rao (eds.), *Handbook of Statistics, 14*, Amsterdam: Elsevier Science, 119–91

Giles, D.E.A., J.A. Giles and J.K. Wong, 1993. Testing for ARCH-GARCH errors in a misspecified regression, *Computational Statistics* 8, 109–26

Glosten, L.R., R. Jagannathan and D.E. Runkle, 1993. On the relation between the expected value and the volatility of the nominal excess return on stocks, *Journal of Finance* 48, 1779–801

Godfrey, L.G., 1979. Testing the adequacy of a time series model, *Biometrika* 66, 67–72

González-Rivera, G., 1998. Smooth transition GARCH models, *Studies in Nonlinear Dynamics and Econometrics* 3, 61–78

Gourieroux, C., 1997. *ARCH Models and Financial Applications*, Berlin: Springer-Verlag

Gourieroux, C., A. Monfort and E. Renault, 1993. Indirect inference, *Journal of Applied Econometrics* 8, S85–S118

Granger, C.W.J., 1992. Forecasting stock market prices: lessons for forecasters, *International Journal of Forecasting* 8, 3–13

1993. Strategies for modelling nonlinear time-series relationships, *The Economic Record* 69, 233–8

Granger, C.W.J. and A. Andersen, 1978. *An Introduction to Bilinear Time Series Models*, Göttingen: Vandenhoeck & Ruprecht

Granger, C.W.J. and R. Joyeux, 1980. An introduction to long-memory time series models and fractional differencing, *Journal of Time Series Analysis* 1, 15–39

Granger, C.W.J. and P. Newbold, 1986. *Forecasting Economic Time Series*, 2nd edn., London: Academic Press

Granger, C.W.J. and T. Teräsvirta, 1993. *Modelling Nonlinear Economic Relationships*, Oxford: Oxford University Press

1999. A simple nonlinear time series model with misleading linear properties, *Economics Letters* 62, 161–5

Granger, C.W.J., H. White and M. Kamstra, 1989. Interval forecasting – an analysis based upon ARCH-quantile estimators, *Journal of Econometrics* 40, 87–96

Haefke, C. and C. Helmenstein, 1996a. Forecasting Austrian IPOs: an application of linear and neural network error-correction models, *Journal of Forecasting* 15, 237–51

1996b. Neural networks in the capital markets: an application to index forecasting, *Computational Economics* 9, 37–50

Hafner, C. and H. Herwartz, 1998a. Structural analysis of multivariate GARCH models using impulse response functions, *CORE Discussion Paper* 9847

1998b. Structural analysis of portfolio risk using beta impulse response functions, *Statistica Neerlandica* 52, 336–55

Hagerud, G.E., 1997. A new non-linear GARCH model, PhD thesis, IFE, Stockholm School of Economics

Haldrup, N., 1998. An econometric analysis of $I(2)$ variables, *Journal of Economic Surveys* 12, 595–650

Hall, A., 1994. Testing for a unit root in time series with pretest data-based model selection, *Journal of Business & Economic Statistics* 12, 461–70

Hall, A.D. and M. McAleer, 1989. A Monte Carlo study of some tests of model adequacy in time series analysis, *Journal of Business & Economic Statistics* 7, 95–106

Hall, A.D., H.M. Anderson and C.W.J. Granger, 1992. A cointegration analysis of Treasury Bill yields, *Review of Economics and Statistics* 74, 116–26

Hamilton, J.D., 1989. A new approach to the economic analysis of nonstationary time series subject to changes in regime, *Econometrica* 57, 357–84

1990. Analysis of time series subject to changes in regime, *Journal of Econometrics* 45, 39–70

1993. Estimation, inference and forecasting of time series subject to changes in regime, in G.S. Maddala, C.R. Rao and H.D. Vinod (eds.), *Handbook of Statistics, 11*, Amsterdam, North-Holland, 231–60

1994. *Time Series Analysis*, Princeton: Princeton University Press

1996. Specification testing in Markov-switching time series models, *Journal of Econometrics* 70, 127–57

Hamilton, J.D. and G. Lin, 1996. Stock market volatility and the business cycle, *Journal of Applied Econometrics* 11, 573–93

Hamilton, J.D. and R. Susmel, 1994. Autoregressive conditional heteroskedasticity and changes in regime, *Journal of Econometrics* 64, 307–33

Hampel, H.R., E.M. Ronchetti, P.J. Rousseeuw and W.A. Stahel, 1986. *Robust Statistics – The Approach based on Influence Functions*, New York: John Wiley

Hansen, B.E., 1992. The likelihood ratio test under nonstandard assumptions: testing the Markov Switching model of GNP, *Journal of Applied Econometrics* 7, S61–S82; erratum (1996) 11, 195–8

1996. Inference when a nuisance parameter is not identified under the null hypothesis, *Econometrica* 64, 413–30

1997. Inference in TAR models, *Studies in Nonlinear Dynamics and Econometrics* 2, 1–14

2000. Sample splitting and threshold estimation, *Econometrica*

Härdle, W., 1990. *Applied Nonparametric Regression*, Cambridge: Cambridge University Press

Härdle, W., H. Lütkepohl and R. Chen, 1997. A review of nonparametric time series analysis, *International Statistical Review* 65, 49–72

Harvey, A.C., 1989. *Forecasting, Structural Time Series Models and the Kalman Filter*, Cambridge: Cambridge University Press

Harvey, A.C., E. Ruiz and N. Shephard, 1994. Multivariate stochastic variance models, *Review of Economic Studies* 61, 247–64

Hassler, U. and J. Wolters, 1995. Long memory in inflation rates: international evidence, *Journal of Business & Economic Statistics* 13, 37–46

Hatanaka, M., 1996. *Time-Series-Based Econometrics, Unit Roots and Cointegration*, Oxford: Oxford University Press

He, C. and T. Teräsvirta, 1999a. Fourth moment structure of the GARCH(p,q) process, *Econometric Theory* 15, 824–46

1999b. Properties of moments of a family of GARCH processes, *Journal of Econometrics* 92, 173–92

Hendry, D.F., 1995. *Dynamic Econometrics*, Oxford: Oxford University Press

Hentschel, L.F., 1995. All in the family: nesting linear and nonlinear GARCH models, *Journal of Financial Economics* 39, 139–64

Hiemstra, C. and J.D. Jones, 1994. Testing for linear and nonlinear Granger causality in the stock price-volume relation, *Journal of Finance* 49, 1639–64

Hiemstra, Y., 1996. Linear regression versus backpropagation networks to predict quarterly stock market excess returns, *Computational Economics* 9, 67–76

Hinich, M.J., 1982. Testing for gaussianity and linearity of a stationary time series, *Journal of Time Series Analysis* 3, 169–76

Hinich, M.J. and D.M. Patterson, 1985. Evidence of nonlinearity in daily stock returns, *Journal of Business & Economic Statistics* 3, 69–77

Hochberg, Y., 1988. A sharper Bonferroni procedure for multiple tests of significance, *Biometrika* 75, 800–2

Holst, U., G. Lindgren, J. Holst and M. Thuvesholmen, 1994. Recursive estimation in switching autoregressions with a Markov regime, *Journal of Time Series Analysis* 15, 489–506

Hong, P.Y., 1991. The autocorrelation structure for the GARCH-M process, *Economics Letters* 37, 129–32

Hornik, K., M. Stinchcombe and H. White, 1989. Multilayer feedforward networks are universal approximators, *Neural Networks* 2, 359–66

1990. Universal approximation of an unknown mapping and its derivatives using multilayer feedforward networks, *Neural Networks* 3, 551–60

Hosking, J.R.M., 1981. Fractional differencing, *Biometrika* 68, 165–76

Hotta, L.K. and R.S. Tsay, 1998. Outliers in GARCH processes, Graduate School of Business, University of Chicago, unpublished manuscript

Hsieh, D.A., 1983. A heteroscedasticity-consistent covariance matrix estimator for time series regressions, *Journal of Econometrics* 22, 281–90

1989. Testing for nonlinear dependence in daily foreign exchange rates, *Journal of Business* 62, 339–69

1991. Chaos and nonlinear dynamics: application to financial markets, *Journal of Finance* 46, 1839–77

Huber, P.J., 1981. *Robust Statistics*, New York: John Wiley

Hutchinson, J.M., A.W. Lo and T. Poggio, 1994. A nonparametric approach to pricing and hedging derivative securities via learning networks, *Journal of Finance* 49, 851–89

Hylleberg, S., R.F. Engle, C.W.J. Granger and B.S. Yoo, 1990. Seasonal integration and cointegration, *Journal of Econometrics* 44, 215–38

Hyndman, R.J., 1995. Highest-density forecast regions for nonlinear and nonnormal time series, *Journal of Forecasting* 14, 431–41

1996. Computing and graphing highest-density regions, *American Statistican* 50, 120–6

Jacquier, E., N.G. Polson and P.E. Rossi, 1994. Bayesian analysis of stochastic volatility models, *Journal of Business & Economic Statistics* 12, 371–417 (with discussion)

Jones, C.M., O. Lamont and R.L. Lumsdaine, 1998. Macroeconomic news and bond market volatility, *Journal of Financial Economics* 47, 315–37

Jorion, P., 1995. Predicting volatility in the foreign exchange market, *Journal of Finance* 50, 507–28

Kaul, G., 1996. Predictable components in stock returns, in G.S. Maddala and C.R. Rao (eds.), *Handbook of Statistics, 14*, Amsterdam: Elsevier Science, 269–96

Keenan, D.M., 1985. A Tukey nonadditivity-type test for time series nonlinearity, *Biometrika* 72, 39–44

Kim, C.-J., 1993. Unobserved-components time series models with Markov-Switching heteroskedasticity: changes in regime and the link between inflation rates and inflation uncertainty, *Journal of Business & Economic Statistics* 11, 341–9

Klaassen, F., 1999. Improving GARCH volatility forecasts, Tilburg University, unpublished manuscript

Koop, G., M.H. Pesaran and S.M. Potter, 1996. Impulse response analysis in nonlinear multivariate models, *Journal of Econometrics* 74, 119–47

Kräger, H. and P. Kugler, 1993. Nonlinearities in foreign exchange markets: a different perspective, *Journal of International Money and Finance* 12, 195–208

Krolzig, H.-M., 1997. *Markov-Switching Vector Autoregressions – Modelling, Statistical Inference and Applications to Business Cycle Analysis*, Lecture Notes in Economics and Mathematics 454, Berlin: Springer-Verlag

Kroner, K.F. and V.K. Ng, 1998. Modelling asymmetric comovements of asset returns, *Review of Financial Studies* 11, 817–44

Kuan, C.-M. and T. Liu, 1995. Forecasting exchange rates using feedforward and recurrent neural networks, *Journal of Applied Econometrics* 10, 347–64

Kuan, C.-M. and H. White, 1994. Artificial neural networks: an econometric perspective, *Econometric Reviews* 13, 1–143 (with discussion)

Kwiatkowski, D., P.C.B. Phillips, P. Schmidt and Y. Shin, 1992. Testing the null hypothesis of stationarity against the alternative of a unit root, *Journal of Econometrics* 54, 159–78

Lamoureux, C.G. and W.D. Lastrapes, 1990. Persistence in variance, structural change, and the GARCH model, *Journal of Business & Economic Statistics* 8, 225–34

1993. Forecasting stock return variances: towards understanding stochastic implied volatility, *Review of Financial Studies* 6, 293–326

LeBaron, B., 1992. Some relationships between volatility and serial correlations in stock market returns, *Journal of Business* 65, 199–219

LeBaron, B. and A.S. Weigend, 1998. A bootstrap evaluation of the effect of data splitting on financial time series, *IEEE Transactions on Neural Networks* 9, 213–20

Lee, J.H.H., 1991. A Lagrange multiplier test for GARCH models, *Economics Letters* 37, 265–71

Lee, S.-W. and B.E. Hansen, 1994. Asymptotic theory for the GARCH(1,1) quasi-maximum likelihood estimator, *Econometric Theory* 10, 29–52

Lee, T.-H., H. White and C.W.J. Granger, 1993. Testing for neglected nonlinearity in time series models, *Journal of Econometrics* 56, 269–90

Leitch, G. and J.E. Tanner, 1991. Economic forecast evaluation: profits versus the conventional error measures, *American Economic Review* 81, 580–90

Levich, R.M. and L.R. Thomas, 1993. The significance of technical trading-rule profits in the foreign exchange market: a bootstrap approach, *Journal of International Money and Finance* 12, 451–74

Leybourne, S., P. Newbold and D. Vougas, 1998. Unit roots and smooth transitions, *Journal of Time Series Analysis* 19, 83–97

Li, C.W. and W.K. Li, 1996. On a double-threshold autoregressive heteroscedastic time series model, *Journal of Applied Econometrics* 11, 253–74

Li, W.K., 1984. On the autocorrelation structure and identification of some bilinear time series models, *Journal of Time Series Analysis* 5, 172–81

Li, W.K. and T.K. Mak, 1994. On the squared residual autocorrelations in nonlinear time series analysis with conditional heteroskedasticity, *Journal of Time Series Analysis* 15, 627–36

Lin, J.-L. and C.W.J. Granger, 1994. Forecasting from nonlinear models in practice, *Journal of Forecasting* 13, 1–9

Lin, W.-L., 1992. Alternative estimators for factor GARCH models – a Monte Carlo comparison, *Journal of Applied Econometrics* 7, 259–79

1997. Impulse response functions for conditional volatility in GARCH models, *Journal of Business & Economic Statistics* 15, 1–14

Lintner, J., 1965. Security prices, risk, and maximal gains from diversification, *Journal of Finance* 20, 587–615

Liu, J., W.K. Li and C.W. Li, 1997. On a threshold autoregression with conditional heteroscedastic variances, *Journal of Statistical Planning and Inference* 62, 279–300

Ljung, G.M. and G.E.P. Box, 1978. On a measure of lack of fit in time series models, *Biometrika* 65, 297–303

Lomnicki, Z.A., 1961. Tests for departure from normality in the case of linear stochastic processes, *Metrika* 4, 27–62

Lucas, A., 1996. *Outlier Robust Unit Root Analysis*, PhD thesis, Rotterdam: Tinbergen Institute

Lucas, A., R. van Dijk and T. Kloek, 1996. Outlier robust GMM estimation of leverage determinants in linear dynamic panel data models, *Tinbergen Institute Discussion Paper* 94-132

Lumsdaine, R.L., 1995. Finite-sample properties of the maximum likelihood estimator in GARCH(1,1) and IGARCH(1,1) models: a Monte Carlo investigation, *Journal of Business & Economic Statistics* 13, 1–10

   1996. Consistency and asymptotic normality of the quasi-maximum likelihood estimator in IGARCH(1,1) and covariance stationary GARCH(1,1) models, *Econometrica* 64, 575–96

Lumsdaine, R.L. and S. Ng, 1999. Testing for ARCH in the presence of a possibly misspecified conditional mean, *Journal of Econometrics* 93, 257–79

Lundbergh, S. and T. Teräsvirta, 1998a. Modelling economic high-frequency time series with STAR-GARCH models, *Working Papers in Economics and Finance* 291, Stockholm School of Economics

   1998b. Evaluating GARCH models, *Working Papers in Economics and Finance* 292, Stockholm School of Economics

Lundbergh, S., T. Teräsvirta and D. van Dijk, 1999. Time-varying smooth transition autoregressive models, Stockholm School of Economics, unpublished manuscript

Luukkonen, R., P. Saikkonen and T. Teräsvirta, 1988. Testing linearity against smooth transition autoregressive models, *Biometrika* 75, 491–9

Malkiel, B., 1981. *A Random Walk Down Wall Street*, New York: Norton

Mandelbrot, B., 1963a. New methods in statistical economics, *Journal of Political Economy* 71, 421–40

   1963b. The variation of certain speculative prices, *Journal of Business* 36, 394–419

   1967. The variation of some other speculative prices, *Journal of Business* 40, 393–413

Martens, M., P. Kofman and A.C.F. Vorst, 1998. A threshold error correction for intraday futures and index returns, *Journal of Applied Econometrics* 13, 245–63

McLeod, A.I. and W.K. Li, 1983. Diagnostic checking ARMA time series models using squared-residual autocorrelations, *Journal of Time Series Analysis* 4, 269–73

Melino, A. and S.M. Turnbull, 1990. Pricing foreign currency options with stochastic volatility, *Journal of Econometrics* 45, 239–65

Merton, R.C., 1973. An intertemporal capital asset pricing model, *Econometrica* 41, 867–87

Milhøj, A., 1985. The moment structure of ARCH models, *Scandinavian Journal of Statistics* 12, 281–92

Mills, T.C., 1990. *Time Series Techniques for Economists*, Cambridge: Cambridge University Press

   1999. *The Econometric Modelling of Financial Time Series*, 2nd edn., Cambridge: Cambridge University Press

Moeanaddin, R. and H. Tong, 1990. Numerical evaluation of distributions in nonlinear autoregression, *Journal of Time Series Analysis* 11, 33–48

Mossin, J., 1966. Equilibrium in a capital asset market, *Econometrica* 34, 768–83

Neftçi, S.N., 1991. Naïve trading rules in financial markets and Wiener-Kolmogorov prediction theory: a study of 'technical analysis', *Journal of Business* 64, 549–71

Nelder, J.A. and R. Mead, 1965. A simplex method for function minimization, *The Computer Journal* 7, 308

Nelson, C.R., 1976. The interpretation of R^2 in autoregressive moving average time series models, *American Statistican* 30, 175–80

Nelson, D.B., 1990. Stationarity and persistence in the GARCH(1,1) model, *Econometric Theory* 6, 318–34

Nelson, D.B., 1991. Conditional heteroskedasticity in asset returns: a new approach, *Econometrica* 59, 347–70

Nelson, D.B and C.Q. Cao, 1992. Inequality constraints in the univariate GARCH model, *Journal of Business & Economic Statistics* 10, 229–35

Newey, W.K. and K.D. West, 1987. A simple, positive semi-definite, heteroskedasticity and autocorrelation consistent covariance matrix, *Econometrica* 55, 703–8

1994. Automatic lag selection in covariance matrix estimation, *Review of Economic Studies* 61, 631–53

Ng, S. and P. Perron, 1995. Unit root tests in ARMA models with data-dependent methods for the selection of the truncation lag, *Journal of the American Statistical Association* 90, 268–81

Ng, V.K., R.F. Engle and M. Rothschild, 1992. A multi-dynamic factor model for stock returns, *Journal of Econometrics* 52, 245–65

Osborn, D.R., 1990. A survey of seasonality in UK macroeconomic variables, *International Journal of Forecasting* 6, 327–36

Pagan, A.R., 1996. The econometrics of financial markets, *Journal of Empirical Finance* 3, 15–102

Pagan, A.R. and G.W. Schwert, 1990. Alternative models for conditional stock volatility, *Journal of Econometrics* 45, 267–90

Palm, F.C., 1996. GARCH models of volatility, in G.S. Maddala and C.R. Rao (eds.), *Handbook of Statistics, 14*, Amsterdam: Elsevier Science, 209–40

Peel, D.A. and A.E.H. Speight, 1996. Is the US business cycle asymmetric? Some further evidence, *Applied Economics* 28, 405–15

Pemberton, J., 1987. Exact least squares multi-step prediction from nonlinear autoregressive models, *Journal of Time Series Analysis* 8, 443–8

Pesaran, M.H. and A. Timmermann, 1992. A simple nonparametric test of predictive performance, *Journal of Business & Economic Statistics* 10, 461–5

Phillips, P.C.B., 1987. Time series regression with a unit root, *Econometrica* 55, 277–301

Phillips, P.C.B. and P. Perron, 1988. Testing for a unit root in time series regression, *Biometrika* 75, 335–46

Phillips, P.C.B. and Z. Xiao, 1998. A primer on unit root testing, *Journal of Economic Surveys* 12, 423–69

Pötscher, B.M. and I.V. Prucha, 1997. *Dynamic Nonlinear Econometric Models – Asymptotic Theory*, Berlin: Springer-Verlag

Potter, S.M., 1994. Asymmetric economic propagation mechanisms, in W. Semmler (ed.), *Business Cycles: Theory and Empirical Methods*, Boston: Kluwer, 313–30

1995. Nonlinear models of economic fluctuations, in K. Hoover (ed.), *Macroeconometrics – Developments, Tensions and Prospects*, Boston: Kluwer, 517–60

Press, W.H., B.P. Flannery, S.A. Teukolsky and W.T. Vetterling, 1986. *Numerical Recipes – The Art of Scientific Computing*, Cambridge: Cambridge University Press

Priestley, M.B., 1980. State-dependent models: a general approach to non-linear time series analysis, *Journal of Time Series Analysis* 1, 47–71

1988. *Nonlinear and Nonstationary Time Series Analysis*, London: Academic Press

Qi, M., 1996. Financial applications of artifical neural networks, in G.S. Maddala and C.R. Rao (eds.), *Handbook of Statistics, 14*, Amsterdam: Elsevier Science, 529–52

Qi, M. and G.S. Maddala, 1995. Option pricing using ANN: the case of S&P 500 index call options, *Neural Networks in Financial Engineering: Proceedings of the 3rd International Conference on Neural Networks in the Capital Markets*, London, 78–91

   1999. Economic factors and the stock market: a new perspective, *Journal of Forecasting* 18, 151–66

Quandt, R., 1983. Computational problems and methods, in Z. Griliches and M.D. Intriligator (eds.), *Handbook of Econometrics, I*, Amsterdam: Elsevier Science, 699–746

Rabemananjara, R. and J.M. Zakoïan, 1993. Threshold ARCH models and asymmetries in volatility, *Journal of Applied Econometrics* 8, 31–49

Ramsey, J.B., 1969. Tests for specification errors in classical linear least-squares regression analysis, *Journal of the Royal Statistical Society* B 31, 350–71

Refenes, A.N. (ed.), 1995. *Neural Networks in the Capital Markets*, Chichester: John Wiley

Rissanen, J., 1978. Modeling by shortest data description, *Automatica* 14, 465–71

Rumelhart, D.E., G.E. Hinton and R.J. Williams, 1986. Learning internal representations by error propagation, in D.E. Rumelhart and J.L. McLelland (eds.), *Parallel Distributed Processing: Explorations in the Microstructures of Cognition*, Cambridge, MA: MIT Press, 318–62

Said, S.E. and D.A. Dickey, 1984. Testing for unit roots in autoregressive-moving average models of unknown order, *Biometrika* 71, 599–607

Sakata, S. and H. White, 1998. High breakdown point conditional dispersion estimation with application to S&P 500 daily returns volatility, *Econometrica* 66, 529–67

Satchell, S.E. and A. Timmermann, 1995. An assessment of the economic value of non-linear foreign exchange rate forecasts, *Journal of Forecasting* 14, 477–97

Scheinkmann, J.A. and B. LeBaron, 1989. Nonlinear dynamics and stock returns, *Journal of Business* 62, 311–37

Schwarz, G., 1978. Estimating the dimension of a model, *Annals of Statistics* 6, 461–4

Schwert, G.W., 1989. Tests for unit roots: a Monte Carlo investigation, *Journal of Business & Economic Statistics* 7, 147–60

Sentana, E., 1995. Quadratic ARCH models, *Review of Economic Studies* 62, 639–61

Sharpe, W.F., 1964. Capital asset prices: a theory of market equilibrium under conditions of risk, *Journal of Finance* 19, 425–42

Shephard, N., 1996. Statistical aspects of ARCH and stochastic volatility, in O.E. Barndorff-Nielsen, D.R. Cox and D.V. Hinkley (eds.), *Statistical Models in Econometrics, Finance and other Fields*, London: Chapman & Hall, 1–67

Siddiqui, S., 1998. A qualitative threshold model of daily exchange rate movements, *Economics Letters* 59, 243–8

Silverman, B.W., 1986. *Density Estimation for Statistics and Data Analysis*, New York: Chapman & Hall

Simpson, D.G., D. Ruppert and R.J. Carroll, 1992. On one-step GM estimates and stability of inferences in linear regression, *Journal of the American Statistical Association* 87, 439–50

Sims, C., 1980. Macroeconomics and reality, *Econometrica* 48, 1–48

Sin, C.-Y. and H. White, 1996. Information criteria for selecting possibly misspecified parametric models, *Journal of Econometrics* 71, 207–25

Sowell, F., 1992. Maximum likelihood estimation of stationary univariate fractionally integrated time series models, *Journal of Econometrics* 53, 165–88

Sullivan, M.J. and D.E.A. Giles, 1995. The robustness of ARCH/GARCH tests to first-order autocorrelation, *Journal of Quantitative Economics* 11, 35–61

Swanson, N.R. and H. White, 1995. A model selection approach to assessing the information in the term structure using linear models and artificial neural networks, *Journal of Business & Economic Statistics* 13, 265–75

1997a. Forecasting economic time series using flexible versus fixed specification and linear versus nonlinear econometric models, *International Journal of Forecasting* 13, 439–61

1997b. A model selection approach to real-time macroeconomic forecasting using linear models and artificial neural networks, *Review of Economics and Statistics* 79, 540–50

Taylor, J.W., 1999. Evaluating volatility and interval forecasts, *Journal of Forecasting* 18, 111–28

Taylor, N., D. van Dijk, P.H. Franses and A. Lucas, 2000. SETS, arbitrage activity, and stock price dynamics, *Journal of Banking and Finance*

Taylor, S.J., 1986. *Modelling Financial Time Series*, New York: John Wiley

Teräsvirta, T., 1994. Specification, estimation, and evaluation of smooth transition autoregressive models, *Journal of the American Statistical Association* 89, 208–18

1996. Two stylized facts and the GARCH(1,1) model, *Working Paper Series in Economics and Finance* 96, Stockholm School of Economics

1998. Modelling economic relationships with smooth transition regressions, in A. Ullah and D.E.A. Giles (eds.), *Handbook of Applied Economic Statistics*, New York: Marcel Dekker, 507–52

Teräsvirta, T. and H.M. Anderson, 1992. Characterizing nonlinearities in business cycles using smooth transition autoregressive models, *Journal of Applied Econometrics* 7, S119–S136

Teräsvirta, T., C-F.J. Lin and C.W.J. Granger, 1993. Power of the neural network linearity test, *Journal of Time Series Analysis* 14, 209–20

Thursby, J.G. and P. Schmidt, 1977. Some properties of tests for specification error in a linear regression model, *Journal of the American Statistical Association* 72, 634–41

Tiao, G.C. and R.S. Tsay, 1994. Some advances in non-linear and adaptive modelling in time-series , *Journal of Forecasting* 13, 109–40 (with discussion)

Tjøstheim, D., 1986. Some doubly stochastic time series models, *Journal of Time Series Analysis* 7, 51–72

Tong, H., 1978. On a threshold model, in C.H. Chen (ed.), *Pattern Recognition and Signal Processing*, Amsterdam: Sijthoff & Noordhoff, 101–41

1990. *Non-Linear Time Series: A Dynamical Systems Approach*, Oxford: Oxford University Press

1995. A personal overview of non-linear time series analysis from a chaos perspective, *Scandinavian Journal of Statistics* 22, 399–445

Tong, H. and K.S. Lim, 1980. Threshold autoregressions, limit cycles, and data, *Journal of the Royal Statistical Society* B 42, 245–92 (with discussion)

Trippi, R. and E. Turban (eds.), 1993. *Neural Networks in Finance and Investing: Using Artificial Intelligence to Improve Real-World Performance*, Chicago: Probus

Tsay, R.S., 1986. Nonlinearity tests for time series, *Biometrika* 73, 461–6

1988. Outliers, level shifts, and variance changes in time series, *Journal of Forecasting* 7, 1–20

1989. Testing and modeling threshold autoregressive processes, *Journal of the American Statistical Association* 84, 231–40

1998. Testing and modeling multivariate threshold models, *Journal of the American Statistical Association* 93, 1188–1202

van Dijk, D., 1999. *Smooth Transition Models: Extensions and Outlier Robust Inference*, PhD thesis, Rotterdam: Tinbergen Institute

van Dijk, D. and P.H. Franses, 2000. Nonlinear error-correction models for interest rates in the Netherlands, in W.A. Barnett, D.F. Hendry, S. Hylleberg, T. Teräsvirta, D. Tjøstheim and A.H. Würtz (eds.), *Nonlinear Econometric Modeling*, Cambridge: Cambridge University Press

1999. Modeling multiple regimes in the business cycle, *Macroeconomic Dynamics* 3, 311–40

van Dijk, D., P.H. Franses and A. Lucas, 1999a. Testing for smooth transition nonlinearity in the presence of additive outliers, *Journal of Business & Economic Statistics* 17, 217–35

1999b. Testing for ARCH in the presence of additive outliers, *Journal of Applied Econometrics* 14, 539–62

Wand, M.P. and M.C. Jones, 1995. *Kernel Smoothing*, London: Chapman & Hall

Warner, B. and M. Misra, 1996. Understanding neural networks as statistical tools, *American Statistican* 50, 284–93

Wecker, W.E., 1981. Asymmetric time series, *Journal of the American Statistical Association* 76, 16–21

Weise, C.L., 1999. The asymmetric effects of monetary policy, *Journal of Money, Credit and Banking* 31, 85–108

Weiss, A.A., 1984. ARMA models with ARCH errors, *Journal of Time Series Analysis* 5, 129–43

1986. Asymptotic theory for ARCH models: estimation and testing, *Econometric Theory* 2, 107–31

West, K.D. and D. Cho, 1995. The predictive ability of several models of exchange rate volatility, *Journal of Econometrics* 69, 367–91

West, K.D., H.J. Edison and D. Cho, 1993. A utility based comparison of some models of exchange rate volatility, *Journal of International Economics* 35, 23–45

White, H., 1980. A heteroskedasticity-consistent covariance matrix estimator and a direct test for heteroskedasticity, *Econometrica* 48, 817–38

1987. Specification testing in dynamic models, in T.F. Bewley (ed.), *Advances in Econometrics Fifth World Congress – I*, Cambridge: Cambridge University Press, 1–58

1989a. An additional hidden unit test for neglected nonlinearity in multilayer feed-forward networks, *Proceedings of the International Joint Conference on Neural Networks* (Washington, DC), New York: IEEE Press, 451–5

1989b. Some asymptotic results for learning in single hidden-layer feedforward network models, *Journal of the American Statistical Association* 84, 1003–13

1992. *Estimation, Inference and Specification Analysis*, New York: Cambridge University Press

White, H. and I. Domowitz, 1984. Nonlinear regression with dependent observations, *Econometrica* 52, 143–61

Wong, C.S. and W.K. Li, 1997. Testing for threshold autoregression with conditional heteroskedasticity, *Biometrika* 84, 407–18

Wooldridge, J.M., 1990. A unified approach to robust, regression-based specification tests, *Econometric Theory* 6, 17–43

    1991. On the application of robust, regression-based diagnostics to models of conditional means and conditional variances, *Journal of Econometrics* 47, 5–46

Zhang, G., B.E. Patuwo and M.Y. Hu, 1998. Forecasting with artificial neural networks: the state of the art, *International Journal of Forecasting* 14, 35–62

Author index

Abraham, A., 60
Akaike, H., 38
Akgiray, V., 142, 194
Al-Qassam, M.S., 120
Anděl, J., 80
Andersen, A., 30, 243
Andersen, T., 195, 196
Anderson, H.M., 77, 132–4, 153, 154
Anderson, T.W., 20
Ashley, R., 83, 247
Astatkie, T., 81
Attanasio, O.P., 201
Azoff, E.M., 206

Baba, Y., 202
Bacon, D.W., 73
Bai, J., 113
Baillie, R.T., 58, 132, 144, 188, 192
Balke, N.S., 133
Banerjee, A., 53
Bates, D.M., 91
Bera, A.K., 136, 163, 244
Beran, J., 58
Berben, R.-P., 80
Berndt, E.R., 173
Bessembinder, H., 60
Black, F., 135, 148
Boldin, M.D., 83
Bollerslev, T., 58, 60, 132, 135, 136, 139, 141,
    142, 144, 146, 156, 172, 173, 184, 188,
    192, 195, 196, 201, 202
Bos, C., 58
Boswijk, H.P., 53
Boudoukh, J., 60
Box, G.E.P., 20, 22, 27, 32–4, 39
Brailsford, T.J., 194
Breusch, T.S., 110
Brock, W.A., 76, 83, 228, 229, 247
Brockwell, P., 3, 20, 32
Brooks, C., 69, 124, 142, 227

Brown, B.Y., 119
Burke, S.P., 142
Bustos, O.H., 64

Cai, J., 156
Calzolari, G., 173
Campbell, J.Y., 6, 25
Caner, M., 80
Cao, C.Q., 142
Carroll, R.J., 67
Carroll, S.M., 208
Chan, K.S., 73, 74, 79, 85, 100
Chan, W.S., 96
Chappell, D., 70
Chen, C., 64, 178, 180
Chen, R., 87, 212
Cheng, B., 207
Cheung, S.H., 96
Cheung, Y.-W., 58
Cho, D., 194, 196
Chou, R.Y., 136, 142, 146
Christodoulakis, G.A., 195
Christoffersen, P.F., 42
Chu, C.-S.J., 186
Clare, A.D., 60
Clements, M.P., 40, 121, 124, 125
Crato, N., 69
Creedy, J., 76
Cumby, R., 194
Cybenko, G., 208

Dacco, R., 125
Danielsson, J., 147
Davidson, R., 35, 105
Davies, R.B., 100
Davis, J., 3, 20, 32
Day, T.E., 194
de Bruin, P., 120
de Gooijer, J.G., 70, 120, 124
de Lima, P.J.F., 69

Dechert, W., 83, 247
Dempster, A.P., 95
Denby, L., 64
Dickey, D.A., 55
Dickinson, B.W., 208
Diebold, F.X., 42, 43, 124, 136, 203, 236, 241
Ding, Z., 141, 143, 144, 186
Dolado, J.J., 53
Domowitz, I., 90
Donaldson, R.G., 196, 207, 209
Draisma, G., 214
Dueker, M.J., 156, 174, 194
Duffie, D., 147
Dwyer, G.P., 133

Edison, H.J., 196
Eitrheim, Ø., 108, 111, 113
Ellis, C., 70
Enders, W., 80
Engle, R.F., 5, 60, 132, 135–9, 142, 143, 145,
    148, 155, 157, 160, 161, 163, 173, 176,
    183, 185, 186, 188, 196, 200–2, 204

Faff, R.W., 194
Fama, E.F., 135
Fan, J., 212
Figlewski, S., 194
Fiorentini, G., 173
Flannery, B.P., 220, 221
Fomby, T.B., 133
Fornari, F., 152, 153
Franses, P.H., 3, 20, 58, 60, 81, 105, 114, 133,
    165, 166, 178, 180, 182, 186, 194, 196,
    206, 214, 227, 230
French, K.R., 45
Friedman, B.M., 178
Fuller, W.A., 3, 20, 26, 55
Funabashi, K., 208

Galbraith, J.W., 53
Gallant, A.R., 90, 132, 199
Gately, E., 206
Gençay, R., 206, 227, 230, 236
Ghijsels, H., 178, 180, 182
Ghysels, E., 60, 148
Gijbels, I., 212
Giles, D.E.A., 163
Giles, J.A., 163
Glosten, L.R., 150
Godfrey, L.G., 34
González-Rivera, G., 151, 173
Gourieroux, C., 136, 147
Granger, C.W.J., 4, 20, 30, 58, 60, 69, 73, 78,
    80, 83, 103, 105, 121, 132, 141, 143, 144,
    157, 186, 190, 243, 245–9

Haefke, C., 206
Hafner, C., 199, 205
Hagerud, G.E., 151, 162, 185, 186
Haldrup, N., 54
Hall, A., 55
Hall, A.D., 34, 132
Hall, B.H., 173
Hall, R.E., 173
Hamilton, J.D., 3, 20, 82, 83, 90, 94, 115–17,
    121, 156, 174, 194
Hampel, H.R., 64
Hansen, B.E., 80, 83, 85, 86, 100, 101, 104–6,
    172
Härdle, W., 211, 212
Harvey, A.C., 38, 147, 148
Hasbrouck, J., 194
Hassler, U., 58
Hatanaka, M., 53
Hausman, J.A., 173
He, C., 156
Helmenstein, C., 206
Hentschel, L.T., 148
Hendry, D.F., 40, 53, 90, 124, 163
Hertzel, M.G., 60
Herwartz, H., 199, 205
Hiemstra, C., 132
Hiemstra, Y., 227
Higgins, M.L., 136, 163, 244
Hinich, M.J., 69, 83, 247
Hinton, G.E., 220
Hochberg, Y., 247
Holst, J., 82
Holst, U., 82
Hommes, C., 76
Hong, C.-H., 196
Hong, P.Y., 145
Hornik, K., 208
Hosking, J.R.M., 58
Hotta, L.K., 178
Hsieh, D.A., 36, 69, 76
Hu, M.Y., 234
Huber, P.J., 64
Hutchinson, J.M., 206
Hylleberg, S., 60
Hyndman, R.J., 122, 123

Ikenberry, D.L., 60
Ito, T., 132

Jacquier, E., 147
Jagannathan, R., 150
Jenkins, G.M., 20, 22, 27, 32, 33, 39
Jones, C.M., 144
Jones, J.D., 132

Jones, M.C., 13, 212
Jorion, P., 194
Joyeux, R., 58

Kamstra, M., 190, 196, 207, 209
Kane, A., 196
Kaul, G., 2
Keenan, D.M., 247
Kim, C.-J., 94, 156
Klaassen, F., 156, 194
Kloek, T., 66
Kofman, P., 133
Koop, G., 129, 130
Kozicki, S., 204
Kraft, D.F., 202
Kräger, H., 70, 80, 89
Krolzig, H.-M., 133
Kroner, K.F., 136, 142, 146, 200, 202, 205
Kuan, C.-M., 206, 207, 212, 220, 231, 240
Kugler, P., 70, 80, 89
Kumar, K., 124
Kwiatkowski, D., 56

Laibson, D.I., 178
Laird, N.M., 95
Lakonishok, J., 228, 229
Lamont, O., 144
Lamoureux, C.G., 186, 194
Lane, J.A., 120
Lastrapes, W.D., 186, 194
LeBaron, B., 69, 76, 83, 88, 228, 229, 235, 247
Lee, J.H.H., 157
Lee, S., 163
Lee, S.-W., 172
Lee, T.-H., 245–7, 249
Leitch, G., 236
Levich, R.M., 229
Lewis, C.M., 194
Leybourne, S., 91
Li, C.W., 174
Li, W.K., 30, 35, 106, 157, 174, 183
Lilien, D.M., 145
Lim, K.S., 71
Lin, C.-F.J., 247, 248
Lin, G., 194
Lin, J.-L., 121
Lin, W.-L., 132, 199, 204
Lindgren, G., 82
Lintner, J., 135
Liu, J., 174
Liu, L.-M., 64, 178, 180
Liu, T., 206
Ljung, G.M., 34
Lo, A.W., 6, 25, 206

Locke, P., 133
Lomnicki, Z.A., 38
Lopez, J.A., 136
Lucas, A., 62, 64, 66, 105, 133, 165, 166
Lumsdaine, R.L., 144, 164, 172, 173
Lundbergh, S., 114, 174, 183, 184, 186
Lütkepohl, H., 212
Luukkonen, R., 102, 103

MacKinlay, A.C., 6, 25
MacKinnon, J.G., 35, 105
Maddala, G.S., 206, 227
Mak, T.K., 183
Malkiel, B., 229
Mandelbrot, B., 135
Mariano, R.S., 42, 43, 119, 236, 241
Martens, M., 133
Martin, R.D., 64
Martin, V.L., 76
McAleer, M., 34
McLeod, A.I., 35, 157, 183
Mead, R., 221
Mele, A., 152, 153
Melino, A., 147
Merton, R.C., 135
Mikkelsen, H.-O., 58, 144
Milhøj, A., 139
Mills, T.C., 1, 20
Misra, M., 212, 239
Mistry, P., 70
Moeanaddin, R., 80
Monfort, A., 147
Mossin, J., 135

Nam, K., 153, 154
Nason, J.A., 124
Neftçi, S.N., 229, 230
Nelder, J.A., 221
Nelson, C.R., 38
Nelson, D.B., 136, 142, 143, 149
Nerlove, M., 203
Newbold, P., 20, 91
Newey, W.K., 56
Ng, S., 55, 164
Ng, V.K., 148, 155, 160, 161, 185, 204, 205
Noh, J., 196

Ooms, M., 58
Osborn, D.R., 60

Paap, R., 60
Padmore, J., 70
Pagan, A.R., 110, 136, 148, 194
Palm, F.C., 136
Panatoni, L., 173

Pantula, S.G., 55
Patterson, D.M., 69, 83, 247
Patuwo, B.E., 234
Peel, D.A., 77
Pemberton, J., 120
Perron, P., 55, 56, 113
Pesaran, M.H., 43, 44, 129, 130, 236, 241
Petrucelli, J.D., 79
Phillips, P.C.B., 55, 56
Poggio, T., 206
Polson, N.G., 147
Potter, S.M., 129, 130
Pötscher, B.M., 90, 217
Press, W.H., 220, 221
Priestley, M.B., 69, 129
Prucha, I.V., 90, 217
Psaradakis, Z., 60

Qi, M., 206, 227
Quandt, R., 90

Rabemananjara, R., 152
Ramsey, J.B., 247
Refenes, A.N., 206
Reinsel, G.C., 32
Renault, E., 147, 148
Richard, J.-F., 147
Richardson, M.P., 60
Rissanen, J., 38
Robins, R.P., 145
Ronchetti, E.M., 64
Rossi, P.E., 132, 147, 199
Rothschild, M., 204
Rousseeuw, P.J., 64
Rubin, D.B., 95
Ruiz, E., 147
Rumelhart, D.E., 220
Runkle, D.E., 150
Ruppert, D., 67

Said, S.E., 55
Saikkonen, P., 102, 103
Sakata, S., 178
Satchell, S.E., 125, 195, 236
Scheinkman, J.A., 69, 83, 247
Schmidt, P., 56, 247
Schwarz, G., 38
Schwert, G.W., 55, 148, 194
Sentana, E., 154, 155, 161
Sharpe, W.F., 135
Shephard, N., 136, 147, 148
Shin, Y., 56
Siddiqui, S., 229, 230
Silverman, B.W., 13
Simpson, D.G., 67

Sims, C., 57
Sin, C.-Y., 78
Singleton, K.J., 147
Smith, J., 121, 124, 125
Sowell, F., 58
Speight, A.E.H., 77
Stahel, W.A., 64
Stengos, T., 206, 227, 230
Stinchcombe, M., 208
Sullivan, M.J., 163
Susmel, R., 132, 156, 174, 204
Swanson, N.R., 206, 226

Tanner, J.E., 236
Tauchen, G., 132, 199
Taylor, J.W., 190
Taylor, N., 133
Taylor, S.J., 30, 146, 147
Teräsvirta, T., 69, 72, 73, 77, 78, 83, 102–5, 108, 111, 113, 114, 156, 157, 174, 183, 184, 186, 247, 248
Teukolsky, S.A., 220, 221
Thomas, L.R., 229
Thomas, S.H., 60
Thursby, J.G., 247
Thuvesholmen, M., 82
Tiao, G.C., 125
Timmermann, A., 43, 44, 236, 241
Titterington, D.M., 207
Tjøstheim, D., 121
Tong, H., 69, 71, 73, 74, 76, 79, 80, 83, 88, 100, 109, 125
Trippi, R., 206
Trumble, D., 163
Tsay, R.S., 64, 125, 133, 142, 178, 247
Turban, E., 206
Turnbull, S.M., 147

Vahid, F., 133, 134, 153, 154
van Dijk, D., 80, 81, 98, 105, 114, 133, 165, 166, 194, 196
van Dijk, R., 66
van Griensven, K., 206, 227, 230
van Homelen, P., 206
Vetterling, W.T., 220, 221
Vorst, A.C.F., 133
Vougas, D., 91

Wand, M.P., 13, 212
Warner, B., 212, 239
Watt, W.E., 81
Watts, D.G., 73, 81, 91
Wecker, W.E., 70
Weigend, A.S., 235

Weise, C.L., 133
Weiss, A.A., 172
West, K.D., 56, 194, 196
White, H., 36, 78, 90, 178, 190, 206–8, 212,
    220, 226, 231, 240, 245–9
Whitelaw, R.F., 60
Williams, R.J., 220
Wolters, J., 58
Wong, C.S., 106
Wong, J.K., 163

Wooldridge, J.M., 35, 105, 172, 173, 201
Woolford, S.W., 79

Xiao, Z., 55
Yohai, V.J., 64
Yoo, B.S., 60
Yu, W., 133

Zakoïan, J.M., 152
Zhang, G., 234

Subject index

Akaike Information Criterion (AIC), 38, 224
artificial neural network (ANN)
  activation function, 213
  and outliers, 214
  compared with bilinear model, 243
  compared with GARCH model, 243
  compared with MSW model, 240, 241
  compared with multiple regime STAR
    model, 239
  compared with SETAR model, 239, 241
  compared with STAR model, 237
  connection strengths, 212
  hidden layer, 212, 240
  hidden units, 212
  input layer, 212
  input variables, 212
  logistic components, 208
  number of regimes, 210
  output variable, 212
  single hidden layer feedforward, 213
asymmetric behaviour, 2
asymmetric impact
  of large and small shocks, 152
  of positive and negative shocks, 148, 152
atypical events, 3
autocorrelation function, 27
  of AR model, 28
  of MA model, 29
  of squares of ARCH(1) process, 139
  of squares of GARCH(1,1) process, 141
  of squares of IGARCH process, 143
  of squares of SV process, 147
autoregression, *see* autoregressive model
autoregressive conditional heteroscedasticity
  (ARCH)
  asymmetric nonlinear smooth transition
    GARCH (ANST-GARCH), 153
  common ARCH, 204

component GARCH, 144
exponential GARCH (EGARCH), 149
fractionally integrated GARCH
  (FIGARCH), 143
GARCH in mean (GARCH-M), 145
GARCH-t, 156
generalized ARCH (GARCH), 140
GJR-GARCH, 150
integrated GARCH (IGARCH), 142
Markov-Switching GARCH
  (MSW-GARCH), 155
multivariate GARCH models, 200–205:
  BEKK model, 202; constant
  correlation model, 202; diagonal
  model, 201; factor model, 203; vec
  model, 200
quadratic GARCH (QGARCH), 154
smooth transition GARCH (STGARCH),
  151
volatility switching GARCH (VS-GARCH),
  152
autoregressive integrated moving average
  model, 25
autoregressive model, 21
  autocovariance of AR(1) model, 24
  characteristic equation, 25
  variance of AR(1) model, 24
autoregressive moving average model, 22

bilinear time series model, 30

common nonlinearity, 133
conditional volatility profile, 199
covariance stationarity, 22
  of AR(p) model, 25
  of ARCH(q) model, 139
  of ARCH(1) model, 138
  of ARMA model, 23
  of GARCH(p,q) model, 142

277

covariance stationarity (*cont.*)
 of GARCH(1,1) model, 140
 of GJR-GARCH model, 151
 of QGARCH model, 155
 of STGARCH model, 152
 testing for, 56

diagnostic testing (of residuals)
 for homoscedasticity, 35: McLeod-Li test,
  35
 for normality, 37
 for residual autocorrelation, 33: Lagrange
  Multiplier test, 34; Ljung–Box (LB)
  test, 34
 of GARCH models: for higher order
  GARCH, 184; for parameter constancy,
  186; for QGARCH nonlinearity, 185;
  for remaining GARCH, 183; for
  STGARCH nonlinearity, 185; Negative
  Size Bias test, 185; Positive Size Bias
  test, 185; Sign Bias test, 185
 of MSW models, 115
 of SETAR and STAR models: for parameter
  non-constancy, 114; for remaining
  nonlinearity, 112; for residual
  autocorrelation, 109
difference-stationary, 54
differenced series, 25

estimation
 of ANNs, 215–22: backpropagation, 219;
  cross-validation, 235; data
  transformation, 221; learning, 220;
  recursive estimation, 220; steepest
  descent, 219; weight decay, 221
 of GARCH models, 170–8: maximum
  likelihood (ML), 171; quasi MLE
  (QMLE), 172
 of linear ARMA models, 31–3
 of MSW models, 92–6
 of SETAR models, 84–9
 of STAR models, 90–2
 of SV models, 147–8

forecast evaluation criteria, 41–4
 directional accuracy test, 44
 loss differential test, 43
 mean absolute prediction error, 42
 mean squared prediction error, 42
 median absolute prediction error, 42
 median squared prediction error, 42
 success ratio, 43
forecasts
 from ANNs, 234–6

from GARCH models: conditional squared
  prediction error, 189; evaluation of
  volatility, 194–6; interval forecasts,
  190; point forecasts of conditional
  mean, 188; point forecasts of volatility,
  190–4; uncertainty of volatility
  forecasts, 191
 from linear models, 39–41: interval
  forecasts, 40; point forecast, 39;
  squared prediction error, 40, 41
 from nonlinear models, 117–25: evaluation
  of, 124; highest density region, 122;
  interval forecasts, 121; point forecasts,
  118–21
fractional integration, 58

heteroscedasticity-consistent standard errors,
 36

impulse response function (IRF)
 benchmark profile, 126
 conditional GIRF, 129
 for ANNs, 237
 for GARCH models, 197–9
 for linear models, 56–7
 for nonlinear models, 125–32
 generalized IRF (GIRF), 129, 199
 traditional IRF (TIRF), 126, 199
information set, 21
integrated of order d, 25

kurtosis
 of ARCH(1) process, 138
 of GARCH process, 156
 of GARCH(1,1) process, 141
 of QGARCH process, 155
 of residuals, 38
 of SV process, 146
 of time series, 10

lag operator, 21
lag order selection
 in GARCH models, 142
 in linear models, 27
 in SETAR models, 77
long-run variance, 56

Markov-Switching (MSW) model, 81–3
 multiple regime, 82
 regime probabilities: forecast of, 93;
  inference of, 93; smoothed inference
  of, 93
mean-reverting behaviour, 53
median absolute deviation, 66

model selection
  by comparing forecasts, 41
  by evaluating in-sample fit, 38
moving average model, 22
  invertibility, 26

news impact curve (NIC), 148
  of ANST-GARCH model, 153
  of EGARCH model, 149
  of GARCH model, 148
  of GJR-GARCH model, 151
  of STGARCH model, 152
  of VS-GARCH model, 153
nonlinear time series models, 3
  attractor, 75
  deterministic simulation, 77
  domain of attraction, 75
  endogenous dynamics, 76
  equilibrium, 74
  limit cycle, 76
  multivariate, 132–4
  skeleton, 74, 77: fixed point, 74; of ANN,
    209; of STAR model, 90
  stable equilibrium, 74
  Volterra expansion, 128
nonparametric methods
  kernel density estimator, 12
  local weighted regression, 211
  Nadaraya–Watson estimator, 210

outliers, 61–8
  additive, 62
  and tests for ARCH, 165
  and tests for nonlinearity, 105
  innovative, 62
  level shift, 64
  robust estimation methods: for GARCH
    models, 178–82; for linear models,
    64–7, 166; for SETAR models, 96–9

partial autocorrelation function, 28
  of AR model, 29
  of MA model, 29

regime-switching
  stochastic, 69
regime-switching behaviour, 69

Schwarz Information Criterion (BIC), 39, 224
seasonality, 58–61
  periodic autoregressive models, 60
shocks
  permanent, 25
  transitory, 25

skewness
  of residuals, 38
  of time series, 13
smooth transition autoregressive (STAR)
    model, 72
  choosing the transition variable, 104
  logistic, 72
  multiple regime, 80–1
  smoothness parameter, 72
  stationarity, 79
  stationary distribution, 80
  threshold, 72
  transition function, 72
specification strategy
  for linear models, 27
  for nonlinear models, 83
state-dependent behaviour, 69
stochastic volatility (SV) model, 146

technical trading rules, 227–30
  moving average rule, 227
  resistance level, 228
  trading range break-out rule, 228
testing
  for MSW nonlinearity, 104–5
  for nonlinearity based on ANNs, 245–9
  for SETAR nonlinearity, 100–1
  for STAR nonlinearity, 101–4
  unidentified nuisance parameters, 100
testing for (nonlinear) GARCH
  and misspecification, 163
  Negative Size Bias test, 160
  outlier robust, 166
  Positive Size Bias test, 160
  Sign bias test, 160
  test for common ARCH, 204
  test for linear GARCH, 157–9
  test for QGARCH, 161
  test for STGARCH, 162
threshold autoregressive (TAR) model, 71
  choosing the threshold variable, 87
  multiple regime, 80–1
  nested, 81
  self-exciting TAR (SETAR), 71
  stationarity, 79
  stationary distribution, 80
  threshold value, 71
  threshold variable, 71
trend-stationary, 53

unconditional variance, 137
  of ARCH(q) process, 139
  of ARCH(1) process, 138
  of GARCH(1,1) process, 140
  of GARCH-M process, 145
  of GJR-GARCH process, 151

unconditional variance (*cont.*)
   of QGARCH process, 155
   of VS-GARCH process, 153
unit roots, 51–6
   Augmented Dickey–Fuller (ADF) test, 55
   I(1), 54
   I(2), 54

seasonal, 60
stochastic trend, 53

volatility, 2
volatility clustering, 135

white noise, 21